SYRIA

OIL AND GAS EXPLORATION LAWS, REGULATIONS HANDBOOK

VOLUME 1
STRATEGIC INFORMATION AND REGULATIONS

International Business Publications, USA
Washington DC, USA - Syria

SYRIA

OIL AND GAS EXPLORATION LAWS, REGULATIONS HANDBOOK
VOLUME 1 STRATEGIC INFORMATION AND REGULATIONS

UPDATED ANNUALLY

We express our sincere appreciation to all government agencies and international organizations which provided information and other materials for this handbook

Cover Design: **International Business Publications, USA**

2018 Updated Reprint International Business Publications, USA
ISBN 1-4330-7899-6

For additional analytical, business and investment opportunities information,
please contact Global Investment & Business Center, USA
at (703) 370-8082. Fax: (703) 370-8083. E-mail: ibpusa3@gmail.com
Global Business and Investment Info Databank - www.ibpus.com

SYRIA

OIL, GAS EXPLORATION LAWS AND REGULATIONS HANDBOOK

VOLUME 1
STRATEGIC INFORMATION AND REGULATIONS

TABLE OF CONTENTS

STRATEGIC AND DEVELOPMENT PROFILES

STRATEGIC AND BUSINESS PROFILE

Capital	Damascus 33°30′N 36°18′E33.500°N 36.300°E
Largest city	Aleppo
Official languages	Arabic
Government	Dominant-party unitary semi-presidential state
- President	Bashar al-Assad
- Prime Minister	Wael Nader al-Halqi
- Speaker of the People's Council	Mohammad Jihad al-Laham
Legislature	People's Council
Establishment	
- Independence from Ottoman Empire	1 September 1918
- Independence from France	17 April 1946
- Secession from the United Arab Republic	28 September 1961
Area	
- Total	186,475 km^2 (89th) 71,479 sq mi
- Water (%)	1.1
Population	
- estimate	22,530,746 (53rd)
- Density	118.3/km^2 (101st) 306.5/sq mi
GDP (PPP)	estimate
- Total	$107.831 billion
- Per capita	$5,100
GDP (nominal)	2010 estimate
- Total	$59.957 billion
- Per capita	$2,802
Gini	35.8 medium
HDI	▼0.632 medium · 119th
Currency	Syrian pound (SYP)
Time zone	EET (UTC+2)
- Summer (DST)	EEST (UTC+3)
Drives on the	right
Calling code	+963
ISO 3166 code	SY
Internet TLD	‏.sy, .سوريا‎

Syria officially the **Syrian Arab Republic**, is a country in Western Asia, bordering Lebanon and the Mediterranean Sea to the west, Turkey to the north, Iraq to the east, Jordan to the south, and Israel to the southwest. Its capital Damascus is among the oldest continuously-inhabited cities in the world. A country of fertile plains, high mountains, and deserts, it is home to diverse ethnic and religious groups, including Arabs, Greeks, Armenians, Assyrians, Kurds, Circassians, Mhallami, Mandeans and Turks. Religious groups include Sunni, Christians, Alawite, Druze religion, Mandeanism and Yezidi. Sunni Arabs make up the largest population group in Syria.

In English, the name "Syria" was formerly synonymous with the Levant (known in Arabic as *al-Sham*) while the modern state encompasses the sites of several ancient kingdoms and empires, including the Eblan civilization of the 3rd millennium BC. In the Islamic era, Damascus was the seat of the Umayyad Caliphate and a provincial capital of the Mamluk Sultanate in Egypt.

The modern Syrian state was established after World War I as a French mandate, and represented the largest Arab state to emerge from the formerly Ottoman-ruled Arab Levant. It gained independence in April 1946, as a parliamentary republic. The post-independence period was tumultuous, and a large number of military coups and coup attempts shook the country in the period 1949–1971. Between 1958-61, Syria entered a brief union with Egypt, which was terminated by a military coup. The Arab Republic of Syria came into being in 1963, transforming from the Republic of Syria in the Ba'athist coup d'état. Syria was under Emergency Law from 1963 to 2011, effectively suspending most constitutional protections for citizens, and its system of government is considered to be non-democratic. Bashar al-Assad has been president since 2000 and was preceded by his father Hafez al-Assad, who was in office from 1970 to 2000.

Syria is a member of one international organization other than the United Nations, the Non-Aligned Movement; it is currently suspended from the Arab League and the Organisation of Islamic Cooperation, and self-suspended from the Union for the Mediterranean. Since March 2011, Syria has been embroiled in an uprising against Assad and the Ba'athist government as part of the Arab Spring, a crackdown which contributed to the Syrian Civil War and Syria becoming among the least peaceful countries in the world. The Syrian Interim Government was formed by the opposition umbrella group, the Syrian National Coalition, in March 2013. Representatives of this government were subsequently invited to take up Syria's seat at the Arab League

GEOGRAPHY

Location: Middle East, bordering the Mediterranean Sea, between Lebanon and Turkey
Geographic coordinates: 35 00 N, 38 00 E
Map references: Middle East

Area:
total: 185,180 sq km
land: 184,050 sq km
water: 1,130 sq km
note: includes 1,295 sq km of Israeli-occupied territory

Area—comparative: slightly larger than North Dakota

Land boundaries:
total: 2,253 km
border countries: Iraq 605 km, Israel 76 km, Jordan 375 km, Lebanon 375 km, Turkey 822 km

Coastline: 193 km

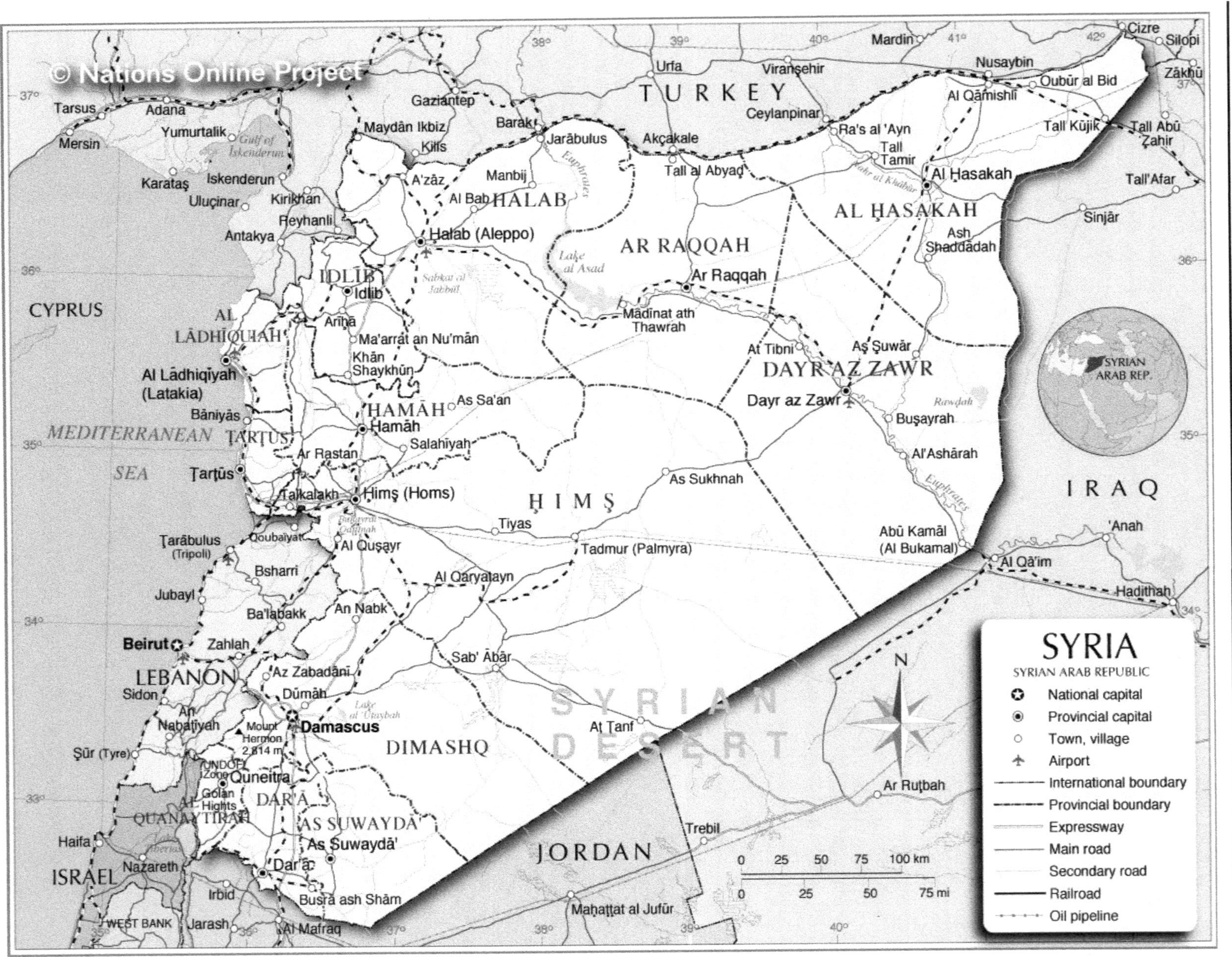
© Nations Online Project
TURKEY
Mardin
Urfa
Viranşehir
Nusaybin
Cizre
Silopi
Zakhu
Tarsus
Adana
Yumurtalik
Mersin
Karataş
Uluçinar
Iskenderun
Kirikhan
Reyhanli
Antakya
Gulf of Iskenderun
Gaziantep
Maydan Ikbiz
Kilis
Barak
Jarabulus
A'zaz
Manbij
Al Bab
HALAB
Halab (Aleppo)
Akçakale
Tall al Abyad
Ceylanpinar
Ra's al 'Ayn
Tall Tamir
Al Qamishli
Al Hasakah
Oubur al Bid
Tall Kujik
Tall Abu Zahir
Tall'Afar
Sinjar
AL HASAKAH
Ash Shaddadah
Euphrates
Nahr al Khabur
AR RAQQAH
Lake al Asad
Sabkat al Jabbul
Ar Raqqah
Madinat ath Thawrah
At Tibni
Aş Şuwar
DAYR AZ ZAWR
Dayr az Zawr
Busayrah
Al'Asharah
Rawdah
Euphrates
SYRIAN ARAB REP.
IRAQ
'Anah
Abu Kamal
(Al Bukamal)
Al Qa'im
Hadithah
IDLIB
Idlib
Ariha
CYPRUS
AL LADHIQIYAH
Al Ladhiqiyah
(Latakia)
Baniyas
MEDITERRANEAN
SEA
TARTUS
Tartus
Talkalakh
Ar Rastan
Ma'arrat an Nu'man
Khan Shaykhun
As Sa'an
HAMAH
Hamah
Salahiyah
Qoubaiyat
Tarabulus
(Tripoli)
Bsharri
Jubayl
Ba'labakk
Al Qusayr
Hims (Homs)
HIMS
Tiyas
As Sukhnah
Tadmur (Palmyra)
Al Qaryatayn
An Nabk
Beirut
Zahlah
Az Zabadani
LEBANON
Sidon
An Nabatiyah
Şur (Tyre)
Dumah
Mount Hermon
2,814 m
UNDOF Zone
Golan Hights
Quneitra
QUANAYTIRAH
Damascus
DIMASHQ
Sab' Abar
At Tanf
SYRIAN DESERT
Trebil
Ar Rutbah
JORDAN
Mahattat al Jufur
DARA
AS SUWAYDA
As Suwayda'
Dar'a
Busra ash Sham
Haifa
Nazareth
ISRAEL
WEST BANK
Jarash
Irbid
Al Mafraq
SYRIA
SYRIAN ARAB REPUBLIC
National capital
Provincial capital
Town, village
Airport
International boundary
Provincial boundary
Expressway
Main road
Secondary road
Railroad
Oil pipeline
N
0 25 50 75 100 km
0 25 50 75 mi
42° 41° 40° 39° 38° 37° 36° 35° 34° 33°

Maritime claims:
contiguous zone: 41 nm
territorial sea: 35 nm

Climate: mostly desert; hot, dry, sunny summers (June to August) and mild, rainy winters (December to February) along coast; cold weather with snow or sleet periodically hitting Damascus

Terrain: primarily semiarid and desert plateau; narrow coastal plain; mountains in west

Elevation extremes:
lowest point: unnamed location near Lake Tiberias -200 m
highest point: Mount Hermon 2,814 m

Natural resources: petroleum, phosphates, chrome and manganese ores, asphalt, iron ore, rock salt, marble, gypsum

Land use:
arable land: 28%
permanent crops: 4%
permanent pastures: 43%
forests and woodland: 3%
other: 22%

Irrigated land: 9,060 sq km

Natural hazards: dust storms, sandstorms

Environment—current issues: deforestation; overgrazing; soil erosion; desertification; water pollution from dumping of raw sewage and wastes from petroleum refining; inadequate supplies of potable water

Environment—international agreements:
party to: Biodiversity, Climate Change, Desertification, Hazardous Wastes, Nuclear Test Ban, Ozone Layer Protection, Ship Pollution
signed, but not ratified: Environmental Modification

Geography—note: there are 42 Israeli settlements and civilian land use sites in the Israeli-occupied Golan Heights (August 1997 est.)

PEOPLE

Population: 16,673,282
note: in addition, there are 35,150 people living in the Israeli-occupied Golan Heights—18,150 Arabs (16,500 Druze and 1,650 Alawites) and 17,000 Israeli settlers

Age structure:
0-14 years: 46% (male 3,937,575; female 3,748,881)
15-64 years: 51% (male 4,342,022; female 4,157,268)
65 years and over: 3% (male 240,603; female 246,933) (July 1998 est.)

Population growth rate: 3.23%
Birth rate: 37.83 births/1,000 population
Death rate: 5.55 deaths/1,000 population
Net migration rate: 0 migrant(s)/1,000 population

Sex ratio:
at birth: 1.05 male(s)/female
under 15 years: 1.05 male(s)/female
15-64 years: 1.04 male(s)/female
65 years and over: 0.97 male(s)/female

Infant mortality rate: 37.6 deaths/1,000 live births

Life expectancy at birth:
total population: 67.76 years
male: 66.48 years
female: 69.11 years

Total fertility rate: 5.55 children born/woman

Nationality:
noun: Syrian(s)
adjective: Syrian

Ethnic groups: Arab 90.3%, Kurds, Armenians, and other 9.7%

Religions: Sunni Muslim 74%, Alawite, Druze, and other Muslim sects 16%, Christian (various sects) 10%, Jewish (tiny communities in Damascus, Al Qamishli, and Aleppo)

Languages: Arabic (official); Kurdish, Armenian, Aramaic, Circassian widely understood; French, English somewhat understood

Literacy:
definition: age 15 and over can read and write
total population: 70.8%
male: 85.7%
female: 55.8%

GOVERNORATES OF SYRIA

Syria has fourteen governorates, or *muhafazat* (singular: *muhafazah*). The governorates are divided into sixty districts, or *manatiq* (sing. *mintaqah*), which are further divided into subdistricts, or *nawahi* (sing. *nahia*). The *nawahi* contain villages, which are the smallest administrative units.

A governor, whose appointment is proposed by the minister of the interior, approved by the cabinet, and announced by executive decree, heads each governorate. The governor is responsible for administration, health, social services, education, tourism, public works, transportation, domestic trade, agriculture, industry, civil defense, and maintenance of law and order in the province. The minister of local administration works closely with each governor to coordinate and supervise local development projects. The governor is assisted by a provincial council, three-quarters of whose members are popularly elected for a term of four years, the remainder being appointed by the minister of the interior and the governor. In addition, each council has an executive arm consisting of six to ten officers appointed by the central government from among the council's elected members. Each executive officer is charged with specific functions.

Districts and subdistricts are administered by officials appointed by the governor, subject to the approval of the minister of the interior. These officials work with elected district councils to attend to assorted local needs and serve as intermediaries between central government authority and traditional local leaders, such as village chiefs, clan leaders, and councils of elders.

Syria is divided into 14 governorates, which are sub-divided into 61 districts, which are further divided into sub-districts.

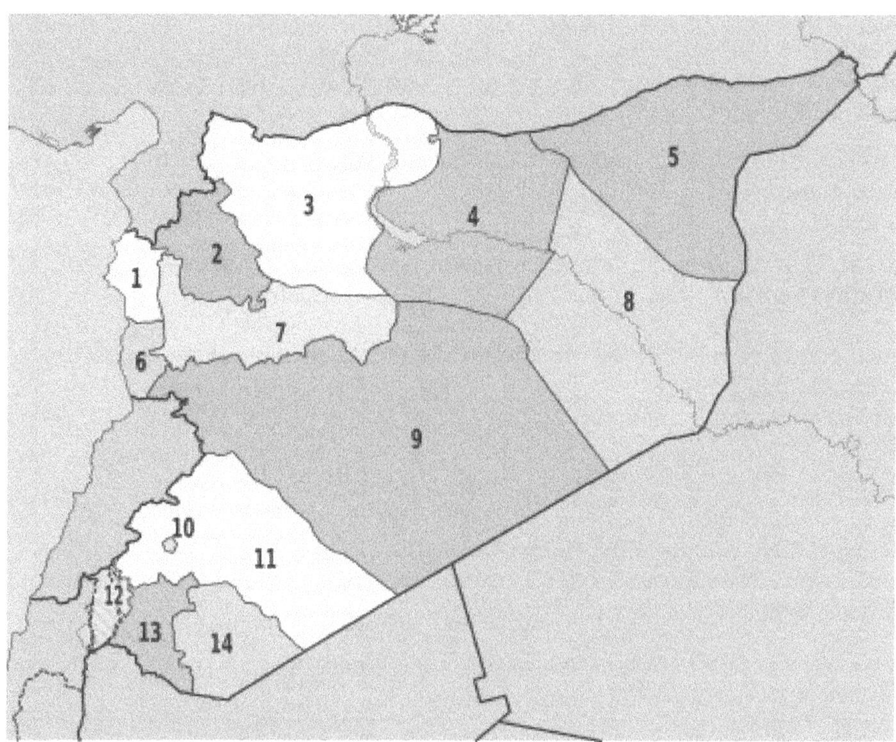

No.	Governorate	Capital
1	Latakia	Latakia
2	Idlib	Idlib
3	Aleppo	Aleppo
4	Al-Raqqah	Al-Raqqah
5	Al-Hasakah	Al-Hasakah
6	Tartus	Tartus
7	Hama	Hama
8	Deir ez-Zor	Deir ez-Zor
9	Homs	Homs
10	Damascus	–
11	Rif Dimashq	–
12	Quneitra	Quneitra
13	Daraa	Daraa
14	Al-Suwayda	Al-Suwayda

GOVERNMENT

Country name:
conventional long form: Syrian Arab Republic
conventional short form: Syria

local long form: Al Jumhuriyah al Arabiyah as Suriyah
local short form: Suriyah
former: United Arab Republic (with Egypt)
Data code: SY
Government type: republic under military regime since March 1963
National capital: Damascus

Administrative divisions: 14 provinces (muhafazat, singular—muhafazah); Al Hasakah, Al Ladhiqiyah, Al Qunaytirah, Ar Raqqah, As Suwayda', Dar'a, Dayr az Zawr, Dimashq, Halab, Hamah, Hims, Idlib, Rif Dimashq, Tartus

Independence: 17 April 1946 (from League of Nations mandate under French administration)
National holiday: National Day, 17 April (1946)
Constitution: 13 March 1973
Legal system: based on Islamic law and civil law system; special religious courts; has not accepted compulsory ICJ jurisdiction
Suffrage: 18 years of age; universal

Executive branch:

chief of state: President Bashar al-ASAD (since 17 July 2000); Vice President Farouk al-SHARA (since 21 February 2006) oversees foreign policy; Vice President Najah al-ATTAR (since 23 March 2006) oversees cultural policy

head of government: Prime Minister Wael al-HALQI (since 9 August)

cabinet: Council of Ministers appointed by the president; note - new Council appointed on 14 April 2011

elections: president approved by popular referendum for a second seven-year term (no term limits); referendum last held on 27 May 2007 (next to be held in May 2014); the president appoints the vice presidents, prime minister, and deputy prime ministers

election results: Bashar al-ASAD approved as president; percent of vote - Bashar al-ASAD 97.6%, other 2.4%

Legislative branch:

unicameral People's Assembly or Majlis al-Shaab (250 seats; members elected by popular vote to serve four-year terms)

elections: last held on 7 May (next to be held in 2016)

election results: percent of vote by party - NA; seats by party - NA

Judicial branch: Supreme Constitutional Court, justices are appointed for four-year terms by the president; High Judicial Council; Court of Cassation; State Security Courts

Political parties and leaders:
National Progressive Front includes: the ruling Arab Socialist Renaissance (Ba'th) Party, Hafiz al-ASAD, president of the republic, secretary general of the party, and chairman of the National Progressive Front; Syrian Arab Socialist Party (ASP), Ghassan 'Abd-al-Aziz UTHMAN; Arab Socialist Union (ASU), Fayiz ISMAIL; Syrian Communist Party (SCP), Yusuf FAYSAL; Arab Socialist Unionist Party, Safwan QUDSI; Socialist Union Democratic Party, Ahmad al-ASAD

Political pressure groups and leaders: non-Ba'th parties have little effective political influence; Communist party ineffective; conservative religious leaders; Muslim Brotherhood

International organization participation: ABEDA, AFESD, AL, AMF, CAEU, CCC, ESCWA, FAO, G-24, G-77, IAEA, IBRD, ICAO, ICC, ICRM, IDA, IDB, IFAD, IFC, IFRCS, IHO, ILO, IMF, IMO, Intelsat, Interpol, IOC, ISO, ITU, NAM, OAPEC, OIC, UN, UNCTAD, UNESCO, UNIDO, UNRWA, UPU, WFTU, WHO, WMO, WToO

Diplomatic representation in the US:
chief of mission: Ambassador Walid MUALEM
chancery: 2215 Wyoming Avenue NW, Washington, DC 20008
telephone: (202) 232-6313
FAX: (202) 234-9548

Diplomatic representation from the US:
chief of mission: Ambassador-designate Ryan CROCKER
embassy: Abou Roumaneh, Al-Mansur Street, No. 2, Damascus
mailing address: P. O. Box 29, Damascus
telephone: [963] (11) 333-2814, 333-0788, 332-0783
FAX: [963] (11) 224-7938

Flag description: three equal horizontal bands of red (top), white, and black with two small green five-pointed stars in a horizontal line centered in the white band; similar to the flag of Yemen, which has a plain white band and of Iraq, which has three green stars (plus an Arabic inscription) in a horizontal line centered in the white band; also similar to the flag of Egypt, which has a symbolic eagle centered in the white band

ECONOMY

Despite modest economic growth and reform prior to the outbreak of unrest, Syria's economy continues to deteriorate amid the ongoing conflict that began in 2011. The economy further contracted in 2013 because of international sanctions, widespread infrastructure damage, reduced domestic consumption and production, and sharply rising inflation. The government has struggled to address the effects of economic decline, which include dwindling foreign exchange reserves, rising budget and trade deficits, and the decreasing value of the Syrian pound.

The ongoing conflict and economic decline have created a humanitarian crisis, prompting widespread need for international aid. Prior to the unrest, Damascus began liberalizing economic policies, including cutting lending interest rates, opening private banks, consolidating multiple exchange rates, raising prices on some subsidized items, and establishing the Damascus Stock Exchange.

The economy remains highly regulated by the government. Long-run economic constraints include foreign trade barriers, declining oil production, high unemployment, rising budget deficits, increasing pressure on water supplies caused by heavy use in agriculture, rapid population growth, industrial expansion, and water pollution.

GDP (purchasing power parity):

$107.6 billion
country comparison to the world: 73
$110.1 billion (2010 est.)
$106.5 billion (2009 est.)
note: data are in 2011 US dollars
the war driven deterioration of the economy resulted in a disappearance of quality national level statistics in -13

GDP (official exchange rate):

$64.7 billion

GDP - real growth rate:

-2.3%
country comparison to the world: 213
3.4% (2010 est.)

GDP - per capita (PPP):

$5,100
country comparison to the world: 159
$5,100 (2010 est.)
$5,200 (2010 est.)
note: data are in 2011 US dollars

Gross national saving:

5.4% of GDP (2013 est.)
country comparison to the world: 146
12.8% of GDP (est.)
15% of GDP

GDP - composition, by end use:

household consumption: 68.3%
government consumption: 19.7%
investment in fixed capital: 20.1%
investment in inventories: 9.3%
exports of goods and services: 11.3%
imports of goods and services: -28.6%
(2013 est.)

GDP - composition, by sector of origin:

agriculture: 17.6%
industry: 22.2%
services: 60.2% (2013 est.)

Agriculture - products:

wheat, barley, cotton, lentils, chickpeas, olives, sugar beets; beef, mutton, eggs, poultry, milk

Industries:

petroleum, textiles, food processing, beverages, tobacco, phosphate rock mining, cement, oil seeds crushing, automobile assembly

Industrial production growth rate:

-20.6% (2013 est.)
country comparison to the world: 194

Labor force:

5.014 million (2013 est.)
country comparison to the world: 75

Labor force - by occupation:

agriculture: 17%
industry: 16%
services: 67% (2008 est.)

Unemployment rate:

17.8% (2013 est.)
country comparison to the world: 155
18% (est.)

Population below poverty line:

11.9% (2006 est.)

Household income or consumption by percentage share:

lowest 10%: NA%
highest 10%: NA%

Budget:

revenues: $2.38 billion
expenditures: $7.56 billion (2013 est.)

Taxes and other revenues:

3.7% of GDP (2013 est.)
country comparison to the world: 214

Budget surplus (+) or deficit (-):

-8% of GDP (2013 est.)
country comparison to the world: 194

Public debt:

58.9% of GDP (2013 est.)

country comparison to the world: 51
52.4% of GDP (est.)

Fiscal year:

calendar year

Inflation rate (consumer prices):

59.1% (2013 est.)
country comparison to the world: 223
36.9% (est.)

Central bank discount rate:

0.75% (31 December 2013 est.)
country comparison to the world: 71
5% (31 December est.)

Commercial bank prime lending rate:

10.5% (31 December 2013 est.)
country comparison to the world: 69
11.7% (31 December est.)

Stock of narrow money:

$8.097 billion (31 December 2013 est.)
country comparison to the world: 87
$16.78 billion (31 December est.)

Stock of broad money:

$12.77 billion (31 December 2013 est.)
country comparison to the world: 96
$27.11 billion (31 December est.)

Stock of domestic credit:

$7.777 billion (31 December 2013 est.)
country comparison to the world: 102
$17.41 billion (31 December est.)

Market value of publicly traded shares:

$NA

Current account balance:

-$5.879 billion (2013 est.)

country comparison to the world: 170
-$6.706 billion (est.)

Exports:

$2.675 billion (2013 est.)
country comparison to the world: 133
$3.876 billion (est.)

Exports - commodities:

crude oil, minerals, petroleum products, fruits and vegetables, cotton fiber, textiles, clothing, meat and live animals, wheat

Exports - partners:

Iraq 58.4%, Saudi Arabia 9.7%, Kuwait 6.4%, UAE 5.5%, Libya 4.1% ()

Imports:

$8.917 billion (2013 est.)
country comparison to the world: 107
$10.78 billion (est.)

Imports - commodities:

machinery and transport equipment, electric power machinery, food and livestock, metal and metal products, chemicals and chemical products, plastics, yarn, paper

Imports - partners:

Saudi Arabia 22.8%, UAE 11.2%, Iran 8.3%, China 7.3%, Iraq 6.8% ()

Reserves of foreign exchange and gold:

$1.895 billion (31 December 2013 est.)
country comparison to the world: 124
$4.793 billion (31 December est.)

Debt - external:

$9.796 billion (31 December 2013 est.)
country comparison to the world: 100
$8.394 billion (31 December est.)

Exchange rates:

Syrian pounds (SYP) per US dollar -
105.3 (2013 est.)
64.392 (est.)

11.225 (2010 est.)
46.708 (2009)
46.5281 (2008)

ENERGY

Electricity - production:

43.76 billion kWh
country comparison to the world: 55

Electricity - consumption:

35.61 billion kWh
country comparison to the world: 57

Electricity - exports:

1.043 billion kWh
country comparison to the world: 57

Electricity - imports:

0 kWh
country comparison to the world: 203

Electricity - installed generating capacity:

8.323 million kW
country comparison to the world: 63

Electricity - from fossil fuels:

89.2% of total installed capacity
country comparison to the world: 78

Electricity - from nuclear fuels:

0% of total installed capacity
country comparison to the world: 182

Electricity - from hydroelectric plants:

10.8% of total installed capacity
country comparison to the world: 111

Electricity - from other renewable sources:

0% of total installed capacity
country comparison to the world: 125

Crude oil - production:

182,500 bbl/day
country comparison to the world: 40

Crude oil - exports:

152,400 bbl/day
country comparison to the world: 34

Crude oil - imports:

0 bbl/day
country comparison to the world: 124

Crude oil - proved reserves:

2.5 billion bbl
country comparison to the world: 33

Refined petroleum products - production:

253,600 bbl/day
country comparison to the world: 48

Refined petroleum products - consumption:

258,800 bbl/day
country comparison to the world: 49

Refined petroleum products - exports:

36,210 bbl/day
country comparison to the world: 65

Refined petroleum products - imports:

104,800 bbl/day
country comparison to the world: 50

Natural gas - production:

7.87 billion cu m
country comparison to the world: 45

Natural gas - consumption:

9.63 billion cu m
country comparison to the world: 48

Natural gas - exports:

0 cu m
country comparison to the world: 187

Natural gas - imports:

250 million cu m
country comparison to the world: 69

Natural gas - proved reserves:

240.7 billion cu m
country comparison to the world: 45

Carbon dioxide emissions from consumption of energy:

63.14 million Mt

COMMUNICATIONS

Telephones - main lines in use:

4.425 million
country comparison to the world: 36

Telephones - mobile cellular:

12.928 million
country comparison to the world: 66

Telephone system:

general assessment: fair system currently undergoing significant improvement and digital upgrades, including fiber-optic technology and expansion of the network to rural areas; the armed insurgency that began in 2011 has led to major disruptions to the network and has caused telephone and Internet outages throughout the country
domestic: the number of fixed-line connections has increased markedly since 2000; mobile-cellular service growing with telephone subscribership nearly 60 per 100 persons in 2011
international: country code - 963; submarine cable connection to Egypt, Lebanon, and Cyprus; satellite earth stations - 1 Intelsat (Indian Ocean) and 1 Intersputnik (Atlantic Ocean region); coaxial cable and microwave radio relay to Iraq, Jordan, Lebanon, and Turkey; participant in Medarabtel

Broadcast media:

state-run TV and radio broadcast networks; state operates 2 TV networks and a satellite channel; roughly two-thirds of Syrian homes have a satellite dish providing access to foreign TV broadcasts; 3 state-run radio channels; first private radio station launched in

2005; private radio broadcasters prohibited from transmitting news or political content

Internet country code:

.sy

Internet hosts:

416
country comparison to the world: 187

Internet users:

4.469 million
country comparison to the world: 52

TRANSPORTATION

Airports:

90
country comparison to the world: 62

Airports - with paved runways:

total: 29
over 3,047 m: 5
2,438 to 3,047 m: 16
914 to 1,523 m: 3
under 914 m: 5

Airports - with unpaved runways:

total: 61
1,524 to 2,437 m: 1
914 to 1,523 m: 12
under 914 m:
48

Heliports:

6

Pipelines:

gas 3,170 km; oil 2,029 km

Railways:

total: 2,052 km
country comparison to the world: 72

standard gauge: 1,801 km 1.435-m gauge
narrow gauge: 251 km 1.050-m gauge

Roadways:

total: 69,873 km
country comparison to the world: 67
paved: 63,060 km
unpaved: 6,813 km

Waterways:

900 km (navigable but not economically significant) (2011)
country comparison to the world: 69

Merchant marine:

total: 19
country comparison to the world: 95
by type: bulk carrier 4, cargo 14, carrier 1
registered in other countries: 166 (Barbados 1, Belize 4, Bolivia 4, Cambodia 22, Comoros 5, Dominica 4, Georgia 24, Lebanon 2, Liberia 1, Malta 4, Moldova 5, North Korea 4, Panama 34, Saint Vincent and the Grenadines 9, Sierra Leone 13, Tanzania 23, Togo 6, unknown 1)

Ports and terminals:

major seaport(s): Baniyas, Latakia, Tartus

MILITARY

Military branches:

Syrian Armed Forces: Land Forces, Naval Forces, Air Forces (includes Air Defense Forces)

Military service age and obligation:

18 years of age for compulsory and voluntary military service; conscript service obligation is 18 months; women are not conscripted but may volunteer to serve; re-enlistment obligation 5 years, with retirement after 15 years or age 40 (enlisted) or 20 years or age 45 (NCOs)

Manpower available for military service:

males age 16-49: 5,889,837
females age 16-49: 5,660,751

Manpower fit for military service:

males age 16-49: 5,055,510
females age 16-49: 4,884,151

Manpower reaching militarily significant age annually:

male: 256,698
female: 244,712

TRANSNATIONAL ISSUES

Disputes - international:

Golan Heights is Israeli-occupied with the almost 1,000-strong UN Disengagement Observer Force patrolling a buffer zone since 1964; lacking a treaty or other documentation describing the boundary, portions of the Lebanon-Syria boundary are unclear with several sections in dispute; since 2000, Lebanon has claimed Shab'a Farms in the Golan Heights; 2004 Agreement and pending demarcation settles border dispute with Jordan

Refugees and internally displaced persons:

refugees (country of origin): 146,200 (Iraq) (2013); 517,255 (Palestinian Refugees (UNRWA)) (2014)
note: the ongoing civil war had created more than 2.8 million Syrian refugees - dispersed in Egypt, Iraq, Jordan, Lebanon, and Turkey - as of February 2014
IDPs: 6.5 million (ongoing civil war since 2011) (2014)
stateless persons: 221,000 (); note - Syria's stateless population is composed of Kurds and Palestinians; stateless persons are prevented from voting, owning land, holding certain jobs, receiving food subsidies or public healthcare, enrolling in public schools, or being legally married to Syrian citizens; in 1962, some 120,000 Syrian Kurds were stripped of their Syrian citizenship, rendering them and their descendants stateless; in 2011, the Syrian Government granted citizenship to thousands of Syrian Kurds as a means of appeasement; however, resolving the question of statelessness is not a priority given Syria's ongoing civil war

Trafficking in persons:

current situation: due to Syria's political uprising and violent unrest, hundreds of thousands of Syrians, foreign migrant workers, and refugees have fled the country and are vulnerable to human trafficking; the lack of security and inaccessibility of the majority of the country makes it impossible to conduct a thorough analysis of the ongoing conflict and the scope and magnitude of Syria's human trafficking situation; prior to the uprising, Syria was principally a destination country for women and children subjected to forced labor or sex trafficking; thousands of women - the majority from Indonesia, the Philippines, Somalia, and Ethiopia - were recruited to work as domestic servants but were subsequently subjected to forced labor; Filipina domestic workers continue to be sent to Syria and are vulnerable to forced labor; the Syrian armed forces and opposition forces are using Syrian children in combat and support roles and as human shields; Iraqi women and girls continue to be sexually exploited, and Syrian children still face conditions of forced labor
tier rating: Tier 3 - the government does not fully comply with the minimum standards for the elimination of trafficking and is not making significant efforts to do so; the government does not demonstrate evidence of increasing efforts to investigate and punish trafficking offenses, provide protective services to victims, inform the public about human trafficking, or provide much-needed anti-trafficking training to law enforcement and social welfare officials; the government does not refer any victims to NGO-operated shelters and has failed to institute procedures for the identification, interview, and referral of trafficking

victims; the status of the national plan of action against trafficking is unknown (2013)

Illicit drugs:

a transit point for opiates, hashish, and cocaine bound for regional and Western markets; weak anti-money-laundering controls and bank privatization may leave it vulnerable to money laundering

IMPORTANT INFORMATION FOR UNDERSTANDING SYRIA

BASIC INFORMATION

Geography
Area: 185,170 sq. km. (71,504 sq. mi.), including 1,295 sq. km. of Israeli-occupied territory; about the size of North Dakota.
Cities: *Capital*--Damascus (1.7 million). *Other cities*--Metropolitan Damascus (excluding city) (2.7 million), Aleppo (4.6 million), Homs (1.7 million), Hama (1.5 million), Idleb (1.4 million), al-Hasakeh (1.4 million), Dayr al-Zur (1.1 million), Latakia (1 million), Dar'a (1 million), al-Raqqa (900,000), and Tartus (800,000).
Terrain: Narrow coastal plain with a double mountain belt in the west; large, semiarid and desert plateau to the east.
Climate: Mostly desert; hot, dry, sunny summers (June to August) and mild, rainy winters (December to February) along coast.

People
Nationality: *Noun and adjective*--Syrian(s).
Population (2009 est.)*: 21 million.
Population growth rate (2009 est.): 2.37%.
Major ethnic groups: Arabs (90%), Kurds (9%), Armenians, Circassians, Turkomans.
Religions: Sunni Muslims (74%), Alawis (12%), Christians (10%), Druze (3%), and small numbers of other Muslim sects, Jews, and Yazidis.
Languages: Arabic (official), Kurdish, Armenian, Aramaic, Circassian widely understood, French, English somewhat understood, principally in major cities.
Education (2008 est.): *Years compulsory*--primary, 6 yrs. *Attendance*--97.9%. *Literacy*--90.8%, *illiteracy*--9.2%.
Health (2009 est.): *Infant mortality rate*--17/1,000. *Life expectancy*--69.8 yrs. male, 72.68 yrs. female.
Work force (5.5 million, 2008 est.): Services (including government) 26%, agriculture 19%, industry 14%, commerce 16%, construction 15%, transportation 7%, and finance 3%.
Unemployment (2008 est.): 9.8%.

Government
Type: Republic, under authoritarian military-dominated Arab Socialist Ba'ath Party regimes since March 1963.
Independence: April 17, 1946.
Constitution: March 13, 1973. Since 1963, Syria has been under Emergency Law, which effectively suspends most constitutional protections.
Branches: *Executive*--president, two vice presidents, prime minister, Council of Ministers (cabinet). *Legislative*--unicameral People's Council. *Judicial*--Supreme Judicial Council, Supreme Constitutional Court, Court of Cassation, Appeals Courts, Economic Security Courts, Supreme State Security Court, Personal Status and local levels courts.
Administrative subdivisions: 14 provinces
Political parties: The National Progressive Front, an umbrella organization for several parties permitted by the government including the Arab Socialist Renaissance (Ba'ath) Party; Socialist Unionist Democratic Party; Syrian Arab Socialist Union or ASU, Syrian Communist Party (two branches); Syrian Social Nationalist Party; Unionist Socialist Party; and other parties not legally recognized but quasi-tolerated, generally considered opposition-oriented but enfeebled and reluctant to challenge the government. There are also several illegal Kurdish parties.
Suffrage: Universal at 18.

PEOPLE

Ethnic Syrians are of Semitic stock. Syria's population is 90% Muslim--74% Sunni, and 16% other Muslim groups, including the Alawi, Shi'a, and Druze--and 10% Christian. There also is a tiny Syrian Jewish community.

Arabic is the official, and most widely spoken, language. Arabs, including some 500,000 Palestinian and up to 1 million Iraqi refugees, make up 90% of the population. Many educated Syrians also speak English or French, but English is the more widely understood. The Kurds, many of whom speak the banned Kurdish language, make up 9% of the population and live mostly in the northeast corner of Syria, though sizable Kurdish communities live in most major Syrian cities as well. Armenian and Turkic are spoken among the small Armenian and Turkoman populations.

Most people live in the Euphrates River valley and along the coastal plain, a fertile strip between the coastal mountains and the desert. Education is free and compulsory from ages 6 to 12. Schooling consists of 6 years of primary education followed by a 3-year preparatory or vocational training period and a 3-year secondary or vocational program. The second 3-year period of secondary schooling is required for university admission. Total enrollment at post-secondary schools is over 150,000. The illiteracy rate of Syrians aged 15 and older is 9.3% for males and 17.8% for females.

Ancient Syria's cultural and artistic achievements and contributions are many. Archaeologists have discovered extensive writings and evidence of a brilliant culture rivaling those of Mesopotamia and Egypt in and around the ancient city of Ebla. Later Syrian scholars and artists contributed to Hellenistic and Roman thought and culture. Zeno of Sidon founded the Epicurean school; Cicero was a pupil of Antiochus of Ascalon at Athens; and the writings of Posidonius of Apamea influenced Livy and Plutarch. Syrians have contributed to Arabic literature and music and have a proud tradition of oral and written poetry. Although declining, the world-famous handicraft industry still employs thousands.

HISTORY

Archaeologists have demonstrated that Syria was the center of one of the most ancient civilizations on earth. Around the excavated city of Ebla in northern Syria, discovered in 1975, a great Semitic empire spread from the Red Sea north to Turkey and east to Mesopotamia from 2500 to 2400 B.C. The city of Ebla alone during that time had a population estimated at 260,000. Scholars believe the language of Ebla to be the oldest Semitic language.

Syria was occupied successively by Canaanites, Phoenicians, Hebrews, Arameans, Assyrians, Babylonians, Persians, Greeks, Romans, Nabataeans, Byzantines, and, in part, Crusaders before finally coming under the control of the Ottoman Turks. Syria is significant in the history of Christianity; Paul was converted on the road to Damascus and established the first organized Christian Church at Antioch in ancient Syria, from which he left on many of his missionary journeys.

Damascus, settled about 2500 B.C., is one of the oldest continuously inhabited cities in the world. It came under Muslim rule in A.D. 636. Immediately thereafter, the city's power and prestige reached its peak, and it became the capital of the Omayyad Empire, which extended from Spain to India from A.D. 661 to A.D. 750, when the Abbasid caliphate was established at Baghdad, Iraq.

Damascus became a provincial capital of the Mameluke Empire around 1260. It was largely destroyed in 1400 by Tamerlane, the Mongol conqueror, who removed many of its craftsmen to Samarkand. Rebuilt, it continued to serve as a capital until 1516. In 1517, it fell under Ottoman rule. The Ottomans remained for the next 400 years, except for a brief occupation by Ibrahim Pasha of Egypt from 1832 to 1840.

French Occupation

In 1920, an independent Arab Kingdom of Syria was established under King Faysal of the Hashemite family, who later became King of Iraq. However, his rule over Syria ended after only a few months, following the clash between his Syrian Arab forces and regular French forces at the battle of Maysalun. French troops occupied Syria later that year after the League of Nations put Syria under French mandate. With the fall of France in 1940, Syria came under the control of the Vichy Government until the British and Free French occupied the country in July 1941. Continuing pressure from Syrian nationalist groups forced the French to evacuate their troops in April 1946, leaving the country in the hands of a republican government that had been formed during the mandate.

Independence to 1970

Although rapid economic development followed the declaration of independence of April 17, 1946, Syrian politics from independence through the late 1960s were marked by upheaval. A series of military coups, begun in 1949, undermined civilian rule and led to army colonel Adib Shishakli's seizure of power in 1951. After the overthrow of President Shishakli in a 1954 coup, continued political maneuvering supported by competing factions in the military eventually brought Arab nationalist and socialist elements to power.

Syria's political instability during the years after the 1954 coup, the parallelism of Syrian and Egyptian policies, and the appeal of Egyptian President Gamal Abdel Nasser's leadership in the wake of the 1956 Suez crisis created support in Syria for union with Egypt. On February 1, 1958, the two countries merged to create the United Arab Republic, and all Syrian political parties ceased overt activities.

The union was not a success, however. Following a military coup on September 28, 1961, Syria seceded, reestablishing itself as the Syrian Arab Republic. Instability characterized the next 18 months, with various coups culminating on March 8, 1963, in the installation by leftist Syrian Army officers of the National Council of the Revolutionary Command (NCRC), a group of military and civilian officials who assumed control of all executive and legislative authority. The takeover was engineered by members of the Arab Socialist Resurrection Party (Ba'ath Party), which had been active in Syria and other Arab countries since the late 1940s. The new cabinet was dominated by Ba'ath members.

The Ba'ath takeover in Syria followed a Ba'ath coup in Iraq the previous month. The new Syrian Government explored the possibility of federation with Egypt and Ba'ath-controlled Iraq. An agreement was concluded in Cairo on April 17, 1963, for a referendum on unity to be held in September 1963. However, serious disagreements among the parties soon developed, and the tripartite federation failed to materialize. Thereafter, the Ba'ath regimes in Syria and Iraq began to work for bilateral unity. These plans foundered in November 1963, when the Ba'ath regime in Iraq was overthrown. In May 1964, President Amin Hafiz of the NCRC promulgated a provisional constitution providing for a National Council of the Revolution (NCR), an appointed legislature composed of representatives of mass organizations--labor, peasant, and professional unions--a presidential council, in which executive power was vested, and a cabinet. On February 23, 1966, a group of army officers carried out a successful, intra-party coup, imprisoned President Hafiz, dissolved the cabinet and the NCR, abrogated the provisional constitution, and designated a regionalist, civilian Ba'ath government. The coup leaders described it as a "rectification" of Ba'ath Party principles. The defeat of the Syrians and Egyptians in the June 1967 war with Israel weakened the radical socialist regime established by the 1966 coup. Conflict developed between a moderate military wing and a more extremist civilian wing of the Ba'ath Party. The 1970 retreat of Syrian forces sent to aid the PLO during the "Black September" hostilities with Jordan reflected this political disagreement within the ruling Ba'ath leadership. On November 13, 1970, Minister of Defense Hafiz al-Asad affected a bloodless military coup, ousting the civilian party leadership and assuming the role of prime minister.

1970 to 2000

Upon assuming power, Hafiz al-Asad moved quickly to create an organizational infrastructure for his government and to consolidate control. The Provisional Regional Command of Asad's Arab Socialist Ba'ath Party nominated a 173-member legislature, the People's Council, in which the Ba'ath Party took 87 seats. The remaining seats were divided among "popular organizations" and other minor parties. In March 1971, the party held its regional congress and elected a new 21-member Regional Command headed by Asad. In the same month, a national referendum was held to confirm Asad as President for a 7-year term. In March 1972, to broaden the base of his government, Asad formed the National Progressive Front, a coalition of parties led by the Ba'ath Party, and elections were held to establish local councils in each of Syria's 14 governorates. In March 1973, a new Syrian constitution went into effect followed shortly thereafter by parliamentary elections for the People's Council, the first such elections since 1962.

The authoritarian regime was not without its critics, though most were quickly dealt with. A serious challenge arose in the late 1970s, however, from fundamentalist Sunni Muslims, who reject the basic values of the secular Ba'ath program and object to rule by the Alawis, whom they consider heretical. From 1976 until its suppression in 1982, the archconservative Muslim Brotherhood led an armed insurgency against the regime. In response to an attempted uprising by the brotherhood in February 1982, the government crushed the fundamentalist opposition centered in the city of Hama, leveling parts of the city with artillery fire and causing many thousands of dead and wounded. Since then, public manifestations of anti-regime activity have been very limited.

Syria's 1990 participation in the U.S.-led multinational coalition aligned against Saddam Hussein marked a dramatic watershed in Syria's relations both with other Arab states and with the West. Syria participated in the multilateral Middle East Peace Conference in Madrid in October 1991. During the 1990s, Syria engaged in direct, face-to-face negotiations with Israel; these negotiations failed.

Hafiz Al-Asad died on June 10, 2000, after 30 years in power. Immediately following Al-Asad's death, the parliament amended the constitution, reducing the mandatory minimum age of the president from 40 to 34 years old, which allowed his son, Bashar Al-Asad legally to be eligible for nomination by the ruling Ba'ath Party. On July 10, 2000, Bashar Al-Asad was elected President by referendum in which he ran unopposed, garnering 97.29% of the vote, according to Syrian Government statistics. He was inaugurated into office on July 17, 2000 for a 7-year term.

2000 to 2011

In the aftermath of the September 11, 2001 terrorist attacks in the United States, the Syrian Government began limited cooperation with U.S. counterterrorism efforts. However, Syria opposed the Iraq war in March 2003, and bilateral relations with the United States swiftly deteriorated. In December 2003, President George W. Bush signed into law the Syria Accountability and Lebanese Sovereignty Restoration Act of 2003, which provided for the imposition of a series of sanctions against Syria if Syria did not end its support for Palestinian terrorist groups, curtail its military and security interference in Lebanon, cease its pursuit of weapons of mass destruction, and meet its obligations under United Nations Security Council resolutions regarding the stabilization and reconstruction of Iraq. In May 2004, the President determined that Syria had not met these conditions and implemented sanctions that prohibit the export to Syria of U.S. products except for food and medicine, and the taking off from or landing in the United States of Syrian Government-owned aircraft. At the same time, the U.S. Department of the Treasury announced its intention to order U.S. financial institutions to sever correspondent accounts with the Commercial Bank of Syria based on money-laundering concerns, pursuant to Section 311 of the USA PATRIOT Act. Acting under the International Emergency Economic Powers Act (IEEPA), the President also authorized the Secretary of the Treasury, in consultation with the Secretary of State, to freeze assets belonging to certain Syrian individuals and entities.

Tensions between Syria and the United States intensified from mid-2004 to early 2009, primarily over issues relating to Iraq and Lebanon. The U.S. Government recalled its ambassador to Syria in February 2005, after the assassination of former Lebanese Prime Minister Rafiq Hariri. Prior to the assassination, France and the U.S. in 2004 had co-authored UN Security Council Resolution (UNSCR) 1559 calling for "all remaining foreign forces to withdraw from Lebanon." Under pressure following the assassination, Syrian troops stationed in Lebanon since 1976 were withdrawn by April 2005. Sensing its international isolation, the Syrians strengthened their relations with Iran and radical Palestinians groups based in Damascus, and cracked down on any signs of internal dissent. However, during the July-August 2006 conflict between Israel and Hizballah, Syria placed its military forces on alert but did not intervene directly on behalf of its ally Hizballah.

On May 27, 2007, President Al-Asad was reaffirmed by referendum for a second 7-year term with 97.6% of the vote. During 2008, though Syria's relations with the U.S. remained strained, Syria's international isolation was slowly being overcome as indirect talks between Israel and Syria, mediated by Turkey, were announced and a Qatar-brokered deal in Lebanon was reached. Shortly thereafter, French president Nicolas Sarkozy invited President Asad to participate in the Euro-Mediterranean summit in Paris, spurring a growing stream of diplomatic visits to Damascus. Since January 2009, President Barack Obama's administration has continued to review Syria policy, and there have been a succession of congressional and U.S. administration officials who have visited Syria while in the region.

Despite high hopes when President Al-Asad first took power in 2000, there has been little movement on political reform, with more public focus on limited economic liberalizations. The Syrian Government provided some cooperation to the UN Independent International Investigation Commission, which investigated the killing of Hariri until superseded by the Special Tribunal for Lebanon. Since the 34-day conflict in Lebanon in July and August 2006, evidence of Syrian compliance with its obligations under UN Security Council Resolution 1701 not to rearm the Lebanese group Hizballah is unpersuasive. On April 17, 2007, the United Nations Security Council welcomed the Secretary General's intention to evaluate the situation along the entire Syria-Lebanon border and invited the Secretary General to dispatch an independent mission to fully assess the monitoring of the border, and to report back on its findings and recommendations. As of March 2011, the border had yet to be demarcated.

Since 2009, the U.S. has attempted to engage with Syria to find areas of mutual interest, reduce regional tensions, and promote Middle East peace. These efforts have included congressional and executive meetings with senior Syrian officials, including President Asad, and the return of a U.S. Ambassador to Damascus.

GOVERNMENT

The Syrian constitution vests the Arab Socialist Ba'ath Party with leadership functions in the state and society and provides broad powers to the president. The president, approved by referendum for a 7-year term, is also Secretary General of the Ba'ath Party and leader of the National Progressive Front, which is a coalition of 10 political parties authorized by the regime. The president has the right to appoint ministers, to declare war and states of emergency, to issue laws (which, except in the case of emergency, require ratification by the People's Council), to declare amnesty, to amend the constitution, and to appoint civil servants and military personnel. The Emergency Law, which effectively suspends most constitutional protections for Syrians, has been in effect since 1963.

The National Progressive Front also acts as a forum in which economic policies are debated and the country's political orientation is determined. However, because of Ba'ath Party dominance, the National Progressive Front has traditionally exercised little independent power.

The Syrian constitution of 1973 requires that the president be Muslim but does not make Islam the state religion. Islamic jurisprudence, however, is required to be a main source of legislation. The judicial system in Syria is an amalgam of Ottoman, French, and Islamic laws, with three levels of courts: courts of first instance, courts of appeals, and the constitutional court, the highest tribunal. In addition, religious courts handle questions of personal and family law.

The Ba'ath Party emphasizes socialism and secular Arabism. Although Ba'ath Party doctrine seeks to build pan-Arab rather than ethnic identity, ethnic, religious, and regional allegiances remain important in Syria.

Members of President Asad's own minority sect, the Alawis, hold most of the important military and security positions, while Sunnis (in 2006) controlled ten of 14 positions on the powerful Ba'ath Party Regional Command. In recent years there has been a gradual decline in the party's preeminence. The party also is heavily influenced by the security services and the military, the latter of which consumes a large share of Syria's economic resources.

Syria is divided administratively into 14 provinces, one of which is Damascus. A governor for each province is appointed by the president. The governor is assisted by an elected provincial council.

Principal Government Officials

Pres., **Bashar al-ASAD**
Vice Pres., **Farouk al-SHARA**
Vice Pres., **Najah al-ATTAR**
Prime Min., **Wael al-HALQI**
Dep. Prime Min., **Fahd Jasim al-FURAYJ,** *Lt. Gen.*
Dep. Prime Min., **Walid al-MUALEM**
Dep. Prime Min. for Economic Affairs, **Qadri JAMIL**
Dep. Prime Min. for Services Affairs, **Umar Ibrahim GHALAWANJI**
Min. of Agriculture, **Subhi Ahmad al-ABDALLAH**
Min. of Culture, **Lubanah MUSHAWEH**
Min. of Defense, **Fahd Jasim al-FURAYJ,** *Lt. Gen.*
Min. of Domestic Trade & Consumer Protection, **Qadri JAMIL**
Min. of Economy & Foreign Trade, **Muhammad Zafir MAHABIK**
Min. of Education, **Hazwan al-WAZZ**
Min. of Electricity, **Imad Muhammad Deeb KHAMIS**
Min. of Finance, **Muhammad al-JULAYLATI**
Min. of Foreign & Expatriate Affairs, **Walid al-MUALEM**
Min. of Health, **Wael Nader al-HALAQI**
Min. of Higher Education, **Muhammad Yahya MU'ALLA**
Min. of Housing & Urban Development, **Safwan al-ASSAF**
Min. of Industry, **Fuad Shukri KURDI**
Min. of Information, **Umran Ahid al-ZA'BI**
Min. of the Interior, **Muhammad Ibrahim al-SHA'AR**
Min. of Justice, **Radwan HABIB**
Min. of Local Admin., **Umar Ibrahim GHALAWANJI**
Min. of Petroleum & Mineral Wealth, **Said Ma'za HANIDI**
Min. of Presidential Affairs, **Mansur Fadlallah AZZAM**

Min. of Public Works, **Yasser al-SIBA'I**
Min. of Religious Endowments, **Muhammad Abd al-Sattar al-SAYYID**
Min. of Social Affairs & Labor, **Jasim Muhammad ZAKARIYA**
Min. of Telecommunication & Technology, **Imad SABBUNI**
Min. of Tourism, **Hala Muhammad al-NASER**
Min. of Transport, **Mahmoud Ibrahim SAID**
Min. of Water Resources, **Bassam HANNA**
Min. of State, **Husayn Mahmoud FARZAT**
Min. of State, **Abdallah Khalil HUSAYN**
Min. of State, **Najm al-Din KHRIIT**
Min. of State, **Muhammad Turki al-SAYYID**
Min. of State, **Jamal Shaaban SHAHEEN**
Min. of State, **Joseph SUWAYD**
Min. of State for Environmental Affairs, **Nazira Farah SARKIS**
Min. of State for National Reconciliation Affairs, **Ali HAYDAR**
Governor, Central Bank, **Adib MAYALA**
Ambassador to the US,
Permanent Representative to the UN, New York, **Bashar al-JAFARI**

Syria maintains an **embassy** in the United States at 2215 Wyoming Avenue, NW, Washington, DC 20008 (tel. 202-232-6313; fax 202-234-9548). Consular section hours are 9:15 a.m.-3:15 p.m., Monday-Friday. Syria also has three honorary consuls: 1022 Wirt Rd., Suite 300, Houston, TX 77055 (tel. 713-622-8860; fax 713-622-8872); 3 San Joaquin Plaza, #190, Newport Beach, CA 92660 (tel. 949-640-9888; fax 949-640-9292); and P.O. Box 2392, Birmingham, MI 48012-2392 (tel. 248-519-2496; fax 248-519-2399).

POLITICAL CONDITIONS

Officially, Syria is a republic. In reality, however, it is an authoritarian regime that exhibits only the forms of a democratic system. Although citizens ostensibly vote for the president and members of parliament, they do not have the right to change their government. The late President Hafiz Al-Asad was confirmed by unopposed referenda five times. His son, Bashar Al-Asad, also was confirmed by an unopposed referendum in July 2000 and May 2007. The President and his senior aides, particularly those in the military and security services, ultimately make most basic decisions in political and economic life, with a very limited degree of public accountability. Political opposition to the President is not tolerated. Syria has been under a state of emergency since 1963. Syrian governments have justified martial law by the state of war that continues to exist with Israel and by continuing threats posed by terrorist groups.

The Asad regime (little has changed since Bashar Al-Asad succeeded his father) has held power longer than any other Syrian government since independence; its survival is due partly to a strong desire for stability and the regime's success in giving groups such as religious minorities and peasant farmers a stake in society. The expansion of the government bureaucracy has also created a large class loyal to the regime. The President's continuing strength is due also to the army's continued loyalty and the effectiveness of Syria's large internal security apparatus. The leadership of both is comprised largely of members of Asad's own Alawi sect. The several main branches of the security services operate independently of each other and outside of the legal system. Each continues to be responsible for human rights violations.

All three branches of government are guided by the views of the Ba'ath Party, whose primacy in state institutions is assured by the constitution. The Ba'ath platform is proclaimed succinctly in the party's slogan: "Unity, freedom, and socialism." The party has traditionally been considered both socialist, advocating state ownership of the means of industrial production and the redistribution of agricultural land, and revolutionary, dedicated to carrying a socialist revolution to every part of the Arab world. Founded by Michel 'Aflaq, a Syrian Christian and Salah al-Din Al-Bitar, a Syrian

Sunni, the Ba'ath Party embraces secularism and has attracted supporters of all faiths in many Arab countries, especially Iraq, Jordan, and Lebanon. Since August 1990, however, the party has tended to de-emphasize socialism and to stress both pan-Arab unity and the need for gradual reform of the Syrian economy.

Nine smaller political parties are permitted to exist and, along with the Ba'ath Party, make up the National Progressive Front (NPF), a grouping of parties that represents the sole framework of legal political party participation for citizens. Created to give the appearance of a multi-party system, the NPF is dominated by the Ba'ath Party and does not change the essentially one-party character of the political system. Non-Ba'ath parties included in the NPF represent small political groupings of a few hundred members each and conform strictly to Ba'ath Party and government policies. There were reports in 2005, in the wake of the June Ba'ath Party Congress, that the government was considering legislation to permit the formation of new political parties and the legalization of parties previously banned. These changes have not taken place. In addition, some 15 small independent parties outside the NPF operate without government sanction.

The Ba'ath Party dominates the parliament, which is known as the People's Council. With members elected every 4 years, the Council has no independent authority. The executive branch retains ultimate control over the legislative process, although parliamentarians may criticize policies and modify draft laws; according to the constitution and its bylaws, a group of 10 parliamentarians can propose legislation. During 2001, two independent members of parliament, Ma'mun al-Humsy and Riad Seif, who had advocated political reforms, were stripped of their parliamentary immunity and tried and convicted of charges of "attempting to illegally change the constitution." Seif was released from prison in early 2006, but was detained and sentenced to prison again in January 2008.

The government has allowed independent non-NPF candidates to run for a limited allotment of seats in the 250-member People's Council. Following the April 22-23, 2007 parliamentary elections, the NPF strengthened its hold on parliament, with the number of non-NPF deputies shrinking from 83 to 80, ensuring a permanent absolute majority for the Ba'ath Party-dominated NPF.

There was a surge of interest in political reform after Bashar al-Asad assumed power in 2000. Human rights activists and other civil society advocates, as well as some parliamentarians, became more outspoken during a period referred to as "Damascus Spring" (July 2000-February 2001). Asad also made a series of appointments of reform-minded advisors to formal and less formal positions, and included a number of similarly oriented individuals in his cabinet. The 2001 arrest and long-term detention of the two reformist parliamentarians and the apparent marginalizing of some of the reformist advisors in the past 10 years, indicate that the pace of any political reform in Syria is likely to be much slower than the short-lived Damascus Spring promised. A crackdown on civil society in 2005, in the wake of Syria's withdrawal from Lebanon, and again in the late winter and spring of 2006, coupled with the early-2011 mobilization of security forces to prevent protests and demonstrations have reinforced the perception that any steps toward political reform were likely to be halting and piecemeal at best.

In October 2008, 12 members of the Damascus Declaration National Council were sentenced to 2-1/2 years in prison. The Damascus Declaration is a civil society reform document written in 2005 and signed by a confederation of opposition parties and individual activists who seek to work with the government to ensure greater civil liberties and democratic political reform. The government has shown no hesitation in suppressing those who advocate for human, legal, or minority rights.

Although Internet access is increasing and non-political private media is slowly being introduced, the government continues to ban numerous newspaper and news journal publications from circulating in the country, including Al-Hayat and Al-Sharq Al-Auwsat (both Saudi owned). It has recently allowed access to previously blocked websites, including YouTube.com, Amazon.com, and Facebook.com, but since many computer users in Syria had already learned to circumvent these restrictions, the move is largely cosmetic.

ECONOMY

The **economy of Syria** is based on agriculture, oil, industry and services. Its GDP per capita expanded 80% in the 1960s reaching a peak of 336% of total growth during the 1970s. This proved unsustainable for Syria and the economy shrank by 33% during the 1980s. However the GDP per capita registered a very modest total growth of 12% (1.1% per year on average) during the 1990s due to successful diversification. More recently, the International Monetary Fund (IMF) projected real GDP growth at 3.9% in 2009 from close to 6% in 2008. The two main pillars of the Syrian economy used to be agriculture and oil, which together accounted for about one-half of GDP. Agriculture, for instance, accounted for about 25% of GDP and employed 25% of the total labor force. However, poor climatic conditions and severe drought badly affected the agricultural sector, thus reducing its share in the economy to about 17% of 2008 GDP, down from 20.4% in 2007, according to preliminary data from the Central Bureau of Statistics. On the other hand, higher crude oil prices countered declining oil production and led to higher budgetary and export receipts.

Since the out break of the Syrian civil war, the Syrian economy has been hit by massive economic sanctions restricting trade with the Arab League, Australia, Canada, the European Union, (as well as the European countries of Albania, Iceland, Liechtenstein, Macedonia, Moldova, Montenegro, Norway, Serbia, and Switzerland) Georgia, Japan, Turkey, and the United States. These sanctions and the instability associated with the civil war have reversed previous growth in the Syrian economy to a state of decline for the years 2011 and . According to the UN, total economic damages of the Syrian civil war are estimated at $143 billion as of late 2013

Syria is a middle-income, developing country with an economy based on agriculture, oil, industry, and tourism. However, Syria's economy faces serious challenges and impediments to growth, including: a large and poorly performing public sector; declining rates of oil production; widening non-oil deficit; widescale corruption; weak financial and capital markets; and high rates of unemployment tied to a high population growth rate. In addition, Syria currently is subject to U.S. economic sanctions under the Syria Accountability Act, which prohibits or restricts the export and re-export of most U.S. products to Syria.

As a result of an inefficient and corrupt centrally planned economy, Syria has low rates of investment, and low levels of industrial and agricultural productivity. The IMF projected real GDP growth at 3.9% in 2009 from close to 6% in 2008. The two main pillars of the Syrian economy used to be agriculture and oil, which together accounted for about one-half of GDP. Agriculture, for instance, accounted for about 25% of GDP and employed 25% of the total labor force. However, poor climatic conditions and severe drought badly affected the agricultural sector, thus reducing its share in the economy to about 17% of 2008 GDP, down from 20.4% in 2007, according to preliminary data from the Central Bureau of Statistics. On the other hand, higher crude oil prices countered declining oil production and led to higher budgetary and export receipts.

Water and energy are among the most pervasive issues facing the agriculture sector. Another difficulty the agricultural sector suffered from is the government's decision to liberalize the prices of fertilizers, which have increased between 100% and 400%. Drought was an alarming problem in 2008; however, the drought situation slightly improved in 2009. Wheat and barley production about doubled in 2009 compared to 2008. In spite of that, the livelihoods of up to 1 million agricultural workers have been threatened. In response, the UN launched an emergency appeal for $20.2 million. Wheat has been one of the crops most affected, and for the first time in 2 decades Syria has moved from being a net exporter of wheat to a net importer.

Damascus has implemented modest economic reforms in the past few years, including cutting lending interest rates; opening private banks; consolidating all of the multiple exchange rates; raising prices on some subsidized items, most notably diesel, other oil derivatives, and fertilizers; and establishing the Damascus Stock Exchange, which began operations in 2009. In May 2008, Damascus raised the price of subsidized diesel by 357%, and in January 2009 the price of fuel oil was raised by 50%. In addition, President Asad signed legislative decrees to encourage corporate ownership reform and allowed the Central Bank to issue Treasury bills and bonds for government debt. Despite these reforms, the economy remains highly controlled by the government. Long-run economic constraints include declining oil production, high unemployment and inflation rates, rising budget deficits, increasing pressure on water supplies caused by heavy use in agriculture, increasing demand for electricity, rapid population growth, industrial expansion, and water pollution.

The government hopes to attract new investment in the tourism, natural gas, and service sectors to diversify its economy and reduce its dependence on oil and agriculture. The government has begun to institute economic reforms aimed at liberalizing most markets, but reform thus far has been slow and ad hoc. For ideological reasons, privatization of government enterprises is still not widespread, but is in its initial stage for port operations, power generation, and air transport. Most sectors are open for private investment except for cotton mills, land telecommunications, and bottled water.

The Bashar al-Asad government started its reform efforts by changing the regulatory environment in the financial sector, including the introduction of private banks and the opening of a stock exchange in March 2009. In 2001, Syria legalized private banking and the sector, while still nascent, has been growing. As of January 2010, 13 private banks had opened, including two Islamic banks. Syria has taken gradual steps to loosen controls over foreign exchange. In 2003, the government canceled a law that criminalized private sector use of foreign currencies, and in 2005 it issued legislation that allowed licensed private banks to sell specific amounts of foreign currency to Syrian citizens under certain circumstances and to the private sector to finance imports. In October 2009, the Syrian Government further loosened its restrictions on foreign currency transfers by allowing Syrians travelling abroad to withdraw the equivalent of up to U.S. $10,000 from their Syrian Pound accounts. In practice, the decision allows local banks to open accounts of a maximum of U.S. $10,000 that their clients can use for their international payment cards. The holders of these accounts will be able to withdraw up to U.S. $10,000 per month while travelling abroad.

To attract investment and to ease access to credit, the government allowed investors in 2007 to receive loans and other credit instruments from foreign banks, and to repay the loans and any accrued interest through local banks using project proceeds. In February 2008, the government permitted investors to receive loans in foreign currencies from local private banks to finance capital investment. Syria's exchange rate is fixed, and the government maintains two official rates--one rate on which the budget and the value of imports, customs, and other official transactions are based, and a second set by the Central Bank on a daily basis that covers all other financial transactions. The government passed a law in 2006 which permits the operation of private money exchange companies. However, a small black market for foreign currency is still active.

Given the policies adopted from the 1960s through the late 1980s, which included nationalization of companies and private assets, Syria failed to join an increasingly interconnected global economy. Syria withdrew from the General Agreement on Tariffs and Trade (GATT) in 1951 because of Israel's accession. It is not a member of the World Trade Organization (WTO), although it submitted a request to begin the accession process in 2001 and again in 2004. Syria is developing regional free trade agreements. As of January 1, 2005, the Greater Arab Free Trade Agreement (GAFTA) came into effect and customs duties were eliminated between Syria and all other members of GAFTA. Syria's free trade agreement with Turkey came into force in January 2007. Syria is a signatory to free trade agreements with Jordan, India, Belarus, and Slovakia. In 2004 Syria and the European Union initialed an Association Agreement; the ratification process had not been finalized as of March 2011. Although Syria claims a recent boom in non-oil exports, its trade numbers are notoriously inaccurate and out-of-date. Syria's main exports include crude oil, refined products, rock phosphate, raw cotton, clothing, fruits and vegetables, and spices. The bulk of Syrian imports are raw materials essential for industry, petroleum products, vehicles, agricultural equipment, and heavy machinery. Earnings from oil exports as well as remittances from Syrian workers are the government's most important sources of foreign exchange.

Syria has produced heavy-grade oil from fields located in the northeast since the late 1960s. In the early 1980s, light-grade, low-sulphur oil was discovered near Dayr al-Zur in eastern Syria. Syria's rate of oil production has been decreasing steadily, from a peak close to 610,000 barrels per day (bpd) in 1995 down to approximately 379,000 bpd in 2008. In parallel, Syria's oil reserves are being gradually depleted and reached 2.5 billion barrels in January 2009. Recent developments have helped revitalize the energy sector, including new discoveries and the successful development of its hydrocarbon reserves. According to the 2009 Syria Report of the Oxford Business Group, the oil sector accounted for 23% of government revenues, 20% of exports, and 22% of GDP in 2008. Experts generally agree that Syria will become a net importer of petroleum by the end of the next decade. Syria exported roughly 150,000 bpd in 2008, and oil still accounts for a majority of the country's export income. Syria also produces about 22 million cubic meters of gas per day, with estimated reserves around 240 billion cubic meters or 8.5 trillion cubic feet. While the government has begun to work with international energy companies in the hopes of eventually becoming a gas exporter, all gas currently produced is consumed domestically. Demand for electricity is growing at a rate of about 10% per year and is barely met by current generation capacity, and ongoing and planned projects are not expected to be sufficient to meet future demand.

Some basic commodities, such as bread, continue to be heavily subsidized, and social services are provided for nominal charges. The subsidies are becoming harder to sustain as the gap between consumption and production continues to increase. Syria has a population of approximately 21 million people, and Syrian Government figures place the population growth rate at 2.37%, with 65% of the population under the age of 35 and more than 40% under the age of 15. Approximately 200,000 people enter the labor market every year. According to Syrian Government statistics, the unemployment rate in 2009 was 12.6%; however, more accurate independent sources placed it closer to 20%. Government and public sector employees constitute about 30% of the total labor force and are paid very low salaries and wages. Government officials acknowledge that the economy is not growing at a pace sufficient to create enough new jobs annually to match population growth. The UN Development Program announced in 2005 that 30% of the Syrian population lives in poverty and 11.4% live below the subsistence level.

Syria has made progress in easing its heavy foreign debt burden through bilateral rescheduling deals with its key creditors in Europe, most importantly Russia, Germany, and France. Syria has also settled its debt with Iran and the World Bank. In December 2004, Syria and Poland reached an agreement by which Syria would pay $27 million out of the total $261.7 million debt. In January 2005, Russia forgave 73% of Syria's $14.5 billion long-outstanding debt and in June 2008, Russia's parliament ratified the agreement. In 2007, Syria and Romania reached an agreement by which Syria will pay 35% of the $118.1 million debt. In May 2008, Syria settled all the debt it owed to the Czech Republic and Slovakia.

NATIONAL SECURITY

President Bashar Al-Asad is commander in chief of the Syrian armed forces, comprised of some 400,000 troops upon mobilization. The military is a conscripted force; males serve 18 months in the military upon reaching the age of 18, though exemptions do exist. Some 17,000 Syrian soldiers formerly deployed in Lebanon were withdrawn to Syria in 2005 in accordance with UNSCR 1559.

Syria's military remains one of the largest in the region, although the breakup of the Soviet Union--long the principal source of training, material, and credit for the Syrian forces--slowed Syria's ability to acquire modern military equipment. Syria received significant financial aid from Gulf Arab states in the 1990s as a result of its participation in the first Gulf War, with a sizable portion of these funds earmarked for military spending. Besides sustaining its conventional forces, Syria seeks to develop its weapons of mass destruction (WMD) capability, including chemical munitions and delivery systems.

In September 2007 Israeli warplanes attacked a purported nuclear facility in Syria. Investigation by the International Atomic Energy Agency (IAEA) discovered particles of enriched uranium at the site, with a low probability they were introduced by the missiles used to attack the facility. As of March 2011, the IAEA continued to investigate the issue with only limited cooperation from the Syrian Government.

FOREIGN RELATIONS

Ensuring regime survival, increasing influence among its Arab neighbors, and achieving a comprehensive Arab-Israeli peace settlement, which includes the return of the Golan Heights, are the primary goals of President Asad's foreign policy.

Relations with Other Arab Countries

Syria reestablished full diplomatic relations with Egypt in 1989. In the 1990-91 Gulf War, Syria joined other Arab states in the U.S.-led multinational coalition against Iraq. In 1998, Syria began a slow rapprochement with Iraq, driven primarily by economic needs. Syria continues to play an active pan-Arab role and has emerged from its relative isolation following the Hariri assassination, to assert its influence regionally and expand diplomatic relations with Europe, Latin America, and China.

Though it voted in favor of UNSCR 1441 in 2002, Syria was against coalition military action in Iraq in 2003. However, the Syrian Government accepted UNSCR 1483 (after being absent for the actual vote), which lifted sanctions on Iraq and established a framework to assist the Iraqi people in determining their political future and rebuilding their economy. Syria also voted for UNSCR 1511, which called for greater international involvement in Iraq and addressed the transfer of sovereignty from the U.S.-led coalition. Since the transfer of sovereignty in Iraq on June 28, 2004, Syria extended qualified support to the Iraqi Government and pledged to cooperate in the areas of border security, repatriation of Iraqi assets, and eventual restoration of formal diplomatic relations.

While Syria has taken some steps to tighten controls along the Syria-Iraq border, Syria remains one of the primary transit points for foreign fighters entering Iraq. Consequently, relations between Syria and the Iraqi Government remained strained. Following a series of visits between high-level officials from both governments--including Foreign Minister Mu'allim's November 2006 visit to Baghdad and Iraqi President Talabani's subsequent visit to Damascus--formal diplomatic relations were established in December 2006. That same month, the Ministers of Interior from both countries signed a Memorandum of Security Understanding aimed at improving border security and combating terrorism and crime. However, both nations withdrew their ambassadors following August 2009 bombings in Baghdad. While Iraq continues to call for more action on the part of Syria to control its border and to prevent Iraqi and Arab elements residing in--or transiting--Syria from contributing financially, politically, or militarily to the insurgency in Iraq, relations have improved. Both countries returned their ambassadors in 2010.

Up to an estimated 1 million Iraqi refugees live in Syria since the 2003 U.S.-led intervention in Iraq, of which more than 224,000 have officially registered with the UN High Commissioner for Refugees. The U.S. remains the largest single contributor to UN and non-governmental organization (NGO) efforts to assist Iraqi refugees in the region. Total U.S. support region-wide in 2008 approached $400 million--up from $171 million in 2007. By the end of September 2008, 13,823 Iraqi refugees had arrived for resettlement in the United States, surpassing the target of 12,000. This figure represents a more than eightfold increase over the 1,608 Iraqis admitted in the previous year. Most of the Iraqis who arrived in the U.S.--over 9,000--came from Jordan and Syria, the two countries hosting the most Iraqi refugees. Smaller groups came from Turkey, Lebanon, and Egypt. The U.S. remains committed to assisting Iraqi refugees and plans to continue to help meet the needs of Iraq's displaced population. Between October 2008 and September 2009 the U.S. pledged to admit a minimum of 17,000 of the most vulnerable Iraqis for resettlement in the U.S. through the U.S. Refugee Admissions Program.

Involvement in Lebanon

Syria has played an important role in Lebanon by virtue of its history, size, power, and economy. Lebanon was part of post-Ottoman Syria until 1926. The presence of Syrian troops in Lebanon dated to 1976, when President Hafiz al-Asad intervened in the Lebanese civil war on behalf of Maronite Christians. Following the 1982 Israeli invasion of Lebanon, Syrian and Israeli forces clashed in eastern Lebanon. However, Syrian opposition blocked implementation of the May 17, 1983, Lebanese-Israeli accord on the withdrawal of Israeli forces from Lebanon.

In 1989, Syria endorsed the Charter of National Reconciliation, or "Taif Accord," a comprehensive plan for ending the Lebanese conflict negotiated under the auspices of Saudi Arabia, Algeria, and Morocco. In May 1991, Lebanon and Syria signed the treaty of brotherhood, cooperation, and coordination called for in the Taif Accord.

According to the U.S. interpretation of the Taif Accord, Syria and Lebanon were to have decided on the redeployment of Syrian forces from Beirut and other coastal areas of Lebanon by September 1992. Israeli occupation of Lebanon until May 2000, the breakdown of peace negotiations between Syria and Israel that same year, and intensifying Arab/Israeli tensions since the start of the second Palestinian uprising in September 2000 helped delay full implementation of the Taif Accords.

The United Nations declared that Israel's May 2000 withdrawal from southern Lebanon fulfilled the requirements of UN Security Council Resolution 425. However, Syria and Lebanon claimed that UNSCR 425 had not been fully implemented because Israel did not withdraw from an area of the Golan Heights called Sheba Farms, which had been occupied by Israel in 1967, and which Syria now claimed was part of Lebanon. The United Nations does not recognize this claim. However, Hizballah uses it to justify attacks against Israeli forces in that region. The danger of Hizballah's tactics was highlighted when Hizballah's abduction of two Israeli soldiers on July 12, 2006 sparked a 34-day conflict in Lebanon. After the conflict, the passing of UNSCR 1701 authorized the enhancement of the UN Interim Force in Lebanon (UNIFIL). Before the conflict, UNIFIL authorized a presence of 2,000 troops in southern Lebanon; post-conflict, this ceiling was raised to 15,000. UNIFIL is tasked with ensuring peace and security along the frontier and overseeing the return of effective Lebanese government and military authority throughout the border region.

Until its withdrawal in April 2005, Syria maintained approximately 17,000 troops in Lebanon. A September 2004 vote by Lebanon's Chamber of Deputies to amend the constitution to extend

Lebanese President Lahoud's term in office by 3 years amplified the question of Lebanese sovereignty and the continuing Syrian presence. The vote was clearly taken under Syrian pressure, exercised in part through Syria's military intelligence service, whose chief in Lebanon had acted as a virtual proconsul for many years. The UN Security Council expressed its concern over the situation by passing Resolution 1559, which called for the withdrawal of all remaining foreign forces from Lebanon, disbanding and disarmament of all Lebanese and non-Lebanese militias in accordance with the Taif Accord, the deployment of the Lebanese Armed Forces throughout the country, and a free and fair electoral process in the presidential election.

Former Prime Minister Rafiq Hariri and 19 others were assassinated in Beirut by a car bomb on February 14, 2005. The assassination spurred massive protests in Beirut and international pressure that led to the withdrawal of the remaining Syrian military troops from Lebanon on April 26, 2005. Rafiq Hariri's assassination was just one of a number of attacks that targeted high-profile Lebanese critics of Syria. The UN International Independent Investigative Commission (UNIIIC) investigated Hariri's assassination until the Special Tribunal for Lebanon (STL) was established by the UN Security Council. The STL began operating in March 2009, continuing UNIIIC's work with an aim toward prosecuting the individuals suspected of being behind the attacks.

Syrian-Lebanese relations have improved since 2008 when, in response to French and Saudi engagement with Syria, Damascus recognized Lebanon's sovereignty and the two countries agreed to exchange ambassadors. Syria sent Ali Abdul Karim Ali to Beirut as its ambassador to Lebanon in May 2009. Following his election in November 2009, Prime Minister Saad Hariri, son of the slain leader, traveled to Damascus for discussions with President Asad. During the visit, the two countries agreed to demarcate their border for the first time. As of March 2011, the border had yet to be demarcated.

Syrian relations with Prime Minister Saad Hariri became strained due to his support for the STL and Syria's continued support of Hizballah. Hizballah and its parliamentary allies engineered the fall of the Hariri government on January 12, 2011 when they resigned from the cabinet en masse, triggering a constitutional crisis. The new Prime Minister-designate, Najib Mikati, has strong connections to the Syrian regime.

The United States supports a sovereign, independent Lebanon, free of all foreign forces, and believes that the best interests of both Lebanon and Syria are served by a positive and constructive relationship based upon principles of mutual respect and non-intervention between two neighboring sovereign and independent states. The United States calls for Syrian non-interference in Lebanon, consistent with UNSCR 1559 and 1701.

Arab-Israeli Relations

Syria was an active belligerent in the 1967 Arab-Israeli War, which resulted in Israel's occupation of the Golan Heights and the city of Quneitra. Following the October 1973 Arab-Israeli War, which left Israel in occupation of additional Syrian territory, Syria accepted UN Security Council Resolution 338, which signaled an implicit acceptance of Resolution 242. Resolution 242, which became the basis for the peace process negotiations begun in Madrid in 1981, calls for a just and lasting Middle East peace to include withdrawal of Israeli armed forces from territories occupied in 1967; termination of the state of belligerency; and acknowledgment of the sovereignty, territorial integrity, and political independence of all regional states and of their right to live in peace within secure and recognized boundaries.

As a result of the mediation efforts of then U.S. Secretary of State Henry Kissinger, Syria and Israel concluded a disengagement agreement in May 1974, enabling Syria to recover territory lost in the October war and part of the Golan Heights occupied by Israel since 1967, including Quneitra. The two sides have effectively implemented the agreement, which is monitored by UN forces.

In December 1981, the Israeli Knesset voted to extend Israeli law to the part of the Golan Heights over which Israel retained control. The UN Security Council subsequently passed a resolution calling on Israel to rescind this measure. Syria participated in the Middle East Peace Conference in Madrid in October 1991. Negotiations were conducted intermittently through the 1990s, and came very close to succeeding. However, the parties were unable to come to an agreement over Syria's nonnegotiable demand that Israel withdraw to the positions it held on June 4, 1967. The peace process collapsed following the outbreak of the second Palestinian (Intifada) uprising in September 2000, though Syria continues to call for a comprehensive settlement based on UN Security Council Resolutions 242 and 338, and the land-for-peace formula adopted at the 1991 Madrid conference.

Tensions between Israel and Syria increased as the second Intifada dragged on, primarily as a result of Syria's unwillingness to stop giving sanctuary to Palestinian terrorist groups conducting operations against Israel. In October 2003, following a suicide bombing carried out by a member of Palestinian Islamic Jihad in Haifa that killed 20 Israeli citizens, Israeli Defense Forces attacked a suspected Palestinian terrorist training camp 15 kilometers north of Damascus. This was the first such Israeli attack deep inside Syrian territory since the 1973 war.

During the summer of 2006 tensions again heightened due to Israeli fighter jets buzzing President Asad's summer castle in response to Syria's support for the Palestinian group Hamas, Syria's support of Hizballah during the July-August 2006 conflict in Lebanon, and the rearming of Hizballah in violation of UN Resolution 1701. Rumors of negotiations between the Israeli and Syrian Governments were initially discounted by both Israel and Syria, with spokespersons for both countries indicating that any such talks were not officially sanctioned. However, the rumors were confirmed in early 2008 when it was announced that indirect talks facilitated by Turkey were taking place. The talks continued until December 2008 when Syria withdrew in response to Israel's shelling of the Gaza Strip.

Membership in International Organizations
Syria is a member of the Arab Bank for Economic Development in Africa, Arab Fund for Economic and Social Development, Arab Common Market, Arab League, Arab Monetary Fund, Council of Arab Economic Unity, Customs Cooperation Council, Economic and Social Commission for Western Asia, Food and Agricultural Organization, Group of 24, Group of 77, International Atomic Energy Agency, International Bank for Reconstruction and Development, International Civil Aviation Organization, International Chamber of Commerce, International Development Association, Islamic Development Bank, International Fund for Agricultural Development, International Finance Corporation, International Labor Organization, International Monetary Fund, International Maritime Organization, INTERPOL, International Olympic Committee, International Organization for Standardization, International Telecommunication Union, International Federation of Red Cross and Red Crescent Societies, Non-Aligned Movement, Organization of Arab Petroleum Exporting Countries, Organization of the Islamic Conference, United Nations, UN Conference on Trade and Development, UN Industrial Development Organization, UN Relief and Works Agency for Palestine Refugees in the Near East, Universal Postal Union, World Federation of Trade Unions, World Health Organization, World Meteorological Organization, and World Tourism Organization.

Syria's 2-year term as a nonpermanent member of the UN Security Council ended in December 2003.

U.S.-SYRIAN RELATIONS

U.S.-Syrian relations, severed in 1967, were resumed in June 1974, following the achievement of the Syrian-Israeli disengagement agreement. In 1990-91, Syria cooperated with the United States as a member of the multinational coalition of forces in the Gulf War.

The U.S. and Syria also consulted closely on the Taif Accord ending the civil war in Lebanon. In 1991, President Asad made a historic decision to accept President George H.W. Bush's invitation to attend a Middle East peace conference and to engage in subsequent bilateral negotiations with Israel. Syria's efforts to secure the release of Western hostages held in Lebanon and its lifting of restrictions on travel by Syrian Jews helped to further improve relations between Syria and the United States. There were several presidential summits; the last one occurred when President Bill Clinton met the late President Hafiz al-Asad in Geneva in March 2000. In the aftermath of the September 11, 2001 terrorist attacks in the United States, the Syrian Government began limited cooperation with U.S. counterterrorism efforts.

Syria has been on the U.S. list of state sponsors of terrorism since the list's inception in 1979. Because of its continuing support and safe haven for terrorist organizations, Syria is subject to legislatively mandated penalties, including export sanctions and ineligibility to receive most forms of U.S. aid or to purchase U.S. military equipment. In 1986, the U.S. withdrew its ambassador and imposed additional administrative sanctions on Syria in response to evidence of direct Syrian involvement in an attempt to blow up an Israeli airplane. A U.S. ambassador returned to Damascus in 1987, partially in response to positive Syrian actions against terrorism such as expelling the Abu Nidal Organization from Syria and helping free an American hostage earlier that year.

Relations cooled as a consequence of U.S. intervention in Iraq in 2003, declined following the imposition of U.S. economic sanctions in May 2004, and worsened further in February 2005 after the assassination of former Lebanese Prime Minister Hariri. Issues of U.S. concern include the Syrian Government's failure to prevent Syria from becoming a major transit point for foreign fighters entering Iraq, its refusal to deport from Syria former Saddam regime elements who are supporting the insurgency in Iraq, its ongoing interference in Lebanese affairs, its protection of the leadership of Palestinian rejectionist groups in Damascus, its deplorable human rights record, and its pursuit of weapons of mass destruction. In May 2004, the U.S. Government, pursuant to the provisions of the Syrian Accountability and Lebanese Sovereignty Restoration Act, imposed sanctions on Syria which banned nearly all exports to Syria except food and medicine. In February 2005, in the wake of the Hariri assassination, the U.S. recalled its ambassador to Washington.

On September 12, 2006 the U.S. Embassy was attacked by four armed assailants with guns, grenades, and a car bomb (which failed to detonate). Syrian security forces successfully countered the attack, killing all four attackers. Two other Syrians killed during the attack were a government security guard and a passerby. The Syrian Government publicly stated that terrorists had carried out the attack. The U.S. Government has not received an official Syrian Government assessment of the motives or organization behind the attack, but security was upgraded at U.S. facilities. Both the Syrian ambassador to the U.S., Imad Mushtapha, and President Bashar Asad, however, blamed U.S. foreign policy in the region for contributing to the incident.

After a military action occurred at the Iraq-Syria border in October 2008, in which purportedly there were several Syrian casualties, the Syrian Government ordered the closure of Damascus Community, the American Language Center (ALC), and the American Cultural Center (ACC).

Since 2009, the U.S. has attempted to engage with Syria to find areas of mutual interest, reduce regional tensions, and promote Middle East peace. These efforts have included congressional and executive meetings with senior Syrian officials, including President Asad, and the return of a U.S. Ambassador to Damascus.

Principal U.S. Officials

U.S. Special Envoy for Syria-- Daniel Rubinstein

Term of Appointment: 03/17/14 to present

In March 2014, Daniel Rubinstein was appointed as the U.S. Special Envoy for Syria.

Deputy Chief of Mission--Charles Hunter
Head of the Political Section--Amy Tachco
Head of the Economic Section--Joanne Cummings
Consul General--Andre Goodfriend
Management Counselor--Natalie Cropper
Public Affairs Officer--Angela Williams
Defense Attache--Robert Friedenberg

The U.S. Embassy is located at Abu Roumaneh, Al-Mansur St. No. 2; P.O. Box 29; tel. (963)(11) 3391-4444, 3391-3333 (after hours); Public Affairs Section tel: 3391-4162; fax (963)(11) 3391-3999. More information about embassy hours of operation, and consular and American citizen services can be obtained at the embassy's website: **http://damascus.usembassy.gov/**

TRAVEL AND BUSINESS INFORMATION

The U.S. Department of State's Consular Information Program advises Americans traveling and residing abroad through Country Specific Information, Travel Alerts, and Travel Warnings. **Country Specific Information** exists for all countries and includes information on entry and exit requirements, currency regulations, health conditions, safety and security, crime, political disturbances, and the addresses of the U.S. embassies and consulates abroad. **Travel Alerts** are issued to disseminate information quickly about terrorist threats and other relatively short-term conditions overseas that pose significant risks to the security of American travelers. **Travel Warnings** are issued when the State Department recommends that Americans avoid travel to a certain country because the situation is dangerous or unstable.

For the latest security information, Americans living and traveling abroad should regularly monitor the Department's Bureau of Consular Affairs Internet web site at http://www.travel.state.gov, where the current Worldwide Caution, Travel Alerts, and Travel Warnings can be found. Consular Affairs Publications, which contain information on obtaining passports and planning a safe trip abroad, are also available at http://www.travel.state.gov. For additional information on international travel, see http://www.usa.gov/Citizen/Topics/Travel/International.shtml.

The Department of State encourages all U.S. citizens traveling or residing abroad to register via the State Department's travel registration website or at the nearest U.S. embassy or consulate abroad. Registration will make your presence and whereabouts known in case it is necessary to contact you in an emergency and will enable you to receive up-to-date information on security conditions.

Emergency information concerning Americans traveling abroad may be obtained by calling 1-888-407-4747 toll free in the U.S. and Canada or the regular toll line 1-202-501-4444 for callers outside the U.S. and Canada.The National Passport Information Center (NPIC) is the U.S. Department of State's single, centralized public contact center for U.S. passport information. Telephone: 1-877-4-USA-PPT (1-877-487-2778); TDD/TTY: 1-888-874-7793. Passport information is available 24 hours, 7 days a week. You may speak with a representative Monday-Friday, 8 a.m. to 10 p.m., Eastern Time, excluding federal holidays.

SYRIA, MINERALS, OIL AND GAS SECTOR: STRATEGIC INFORMATION AND DEVELOPMENTS

THE MINERAL INDUSTRY OF SYRIA

In May 2010, Syria was granted observer status at the World Trade Organization (WTO) after the United States lifted its opposition to Syria's application to join the WTO. The Government announced that it expects to sign a partnership agreement with the European Union by the end of 2010. The Government, based on the assumption that the country's crude oil reserves are sufficient to supply 300,000 bbl/d for the next 40 years, was focusing on developing other sources of energy, such as natural gas and shale oil and promoting private sector involvement in power generation activity in the country through financing and operating the first independent powerplant company.

Private investment in the cement and steel sectors is expected to address the chronic shortages of cement and rebar commodities in the local markets. Phosphate rock and phosphate fertilizer production is likely to increase significantly following the entry of Indian fertilizer production companies to the phosphate production market of Syria (Alexander's Gas & Oil Connections, 2009; Ministry of Petroleum and Mineral Resources, 2010a, b).

Crude oil and phosphate rock were Syria's main contributions to the world supply of minerals in 2009. Syria produced about 1.9% of the world's phosphate rock output and was the world's ninth ranked producer of phosphate rock. Other raw and processed mineral commodities produced in Syria included cement, gypsum, industrial sand (silica), marble, natural crude asphalt, nitrogen fertilizer, phosphate fertilizer, salt, steel, and volcanic tuff (Jasinski, 2010).

MINERALS IN THE NATIONAL ECONOMY

The global economic downturn of 2009 had affected the Syrian economy and caused a 28% decrease in the value of exports because of the decrease of the volume of international trade and a 2.7% decrease in remittances of Syrian expatriates because of the slowdown of the regional economies in 2009. Nevertheless, Syria's real gross domestic product (GDP) grew at a rate of 4.0% in 2009 compared with 5.2% in 2008. Crude oil production was decreased by about 3.6% to 376,000 barrels per day (bbl/d) from 390,000 bbl/d in 2008.

The volume of gross crude oil exports, however, which averaged 250,200 bbl/d in 2009, was a decrease of 16% compared with the export volume in 2005. Net petroleum exports averaged 148,000 bbl/d and were marketed exclusively by the state-owned marketing company Sytrol mainly to European countries, including France, Germany, and Italy. Revenue from the hydrocarbon sector accounted for 4.6% of the GDP compared with 5.2% of the GDP in 2008. The value of crude oil exports decreased by 36% to about $3.5 billion from $5.5 billion in 2008. The value of crude oil and refined oil products decreased by 43% to $3.2 billion from about $5.6 billion in 2008. The decrease in the value and volume of crude oil exports was attributable to increased local consumption of petroleum products and to a decrease in international oil prices (Bank Audi S.A.L., 2010, p. 1, 12; International Monetary Fund, 2010, p. 17-18; Organization of Arab Petroleum Exporting Countries, 2010, p. 19, 57; U.S. Energy Information Administration, 2010).

GOVERNMENT POLICIES AND PROGRAMS

On February 14, 2009, the Government passed law Nos. 14 and 15, which reorganized the state-owned petroleum companies. Law No. 14 created the General Corporation for Refining and Distribution of Petroleum Products. The new agency included Banias Refinery Co., Homs

Refinery Co., Syrian Company for Distribution and Storage of Petroleum Products, and Syrian Company for Gas Distribution. Law No. 15 created the General Petroleum Corp. (GPC), which included Syrian Gas Co., Syrian Petroleum Co. (SPC), and Syrian Petroleum Transportation Co. The mission of the GPC was to establish policies related to the development, exploration, and investment in the hydrocarbon sector and to monitor international oil companies' projects in the country (Ministry of Petroleum and Mineral Resources, 2009a, b).

In 2009, the General Establishment of Geology and Mineral Resources (GEGMR) mapped an area of 3,410 square kilometers, drilled 12,718 meters, and analyzed 6,611 samples. The GEGMR had been promoting the development of the country's mining sector by focusing on upgrading rock phosphate production at the As-Sharqiyah and the Khunayfis Mines; building phosphate-based fertilizer plants and phosphate washing and drying units; developing natural crude asphalt mining at the Al-Bishri and the Kafrayya Mines; rehabilitating the marble plants in Damascus and Latakia; increasing the production of volcanic tuff; and starting a bentonite and zeolite mining industry (General Establishment of Geology and Mineral Resources, 2010, p. 11).

In 2009, GEGMR issued 944 licenses for quarrying for building material throughout the country; 17 of these licenses were for cement production. GEGMR invited international companies to invest in the mining of natural crude asphalt from the Al-Bishri deposit to produce petroleum products, generate electricity, and make asphalt mixes for road pavement. The General Company for Phosphate and Mines (GCPM) called on consulting companies to provide technical, feasibility, and environmental studies for the treatment and beneficiation of phosphate rock tailings at the Khunayifis and the As-Sharquiah Mines. In 2010, GPC invited bids for crude oil and natural gas exploration on eight onshore blocks and eight offshore blocks as well as a bid round to develop seven oilfields in the country.

Damascus Securities Exchange (DSE) was reopened in 2009 after 40 years of closure, which was the period when the country was experimenting with a socialist economy. As of yearend 2009, the majority of companies listed on the DSE were financial institutions (Roscoe, 2010, p. 39).

PRODUCTION

In 2009, production of asphalt increased by 57% and gross natural gas output increased by 5% compared with that of 2008. Notable decreases in the output of minerals in 2009 compared with 2008 included gypsum output, which decreased by 30%; rock phosphate, by 23%; marble slabs, by 25%; industrial sand (silica), by 15%; and salt, by 12% (table 1).

STRUCTURE OF THE MINERAL INDUSTRY

State-owned companies that were administrated by the Ministry of Industry or the Ministry of Petroleum and Mineral Resources (MoPMR) carried out the majority of mining activity in Syria. These companies included the General Company for Marble and Asphalt (GEMA), the General Company for Phosphate and Mines, the GPC, the General Organization for Cement and Building Materials (GOCBM), General Fertilizers Co., and the General Company for Iron and Steel Products (Hadeed Hama). Several private local and international investors were involved in the process of building new greenfield cement plants, including Al-Badia Cement Co. J.S.C., Al Rajhi Cement, and Lafarge Cement Syria S.A. Private finished steel producers included Al Wahib Group, Arabian Steel Co. (ASCO), Hmisho International Steel S.A., International Company for Steel Rolling (ICSR), Joudco Steel Ltd., and Syria Steel and Iron Co. (SALB) (table 2).

COMMODITY REVIEW

METALS

Iron and Steel.—Syria's imports of steel products, which included crude, semifinished, and finished steel, had been increasing in recent years because of the inability of the existing plants to meet the increased demand of the construction sector for reinforcement bar (rebar). The country imported 2.2 million metric tons per year (Mt/yr) of steel products in 2009 compared with 2.0 Mt/yr in 2008 and 2.8 Mt/yr in 2007. Steel products were mainly imported from Ukraine, which accounted for 44% of Syria's steel imports, by volume, followed by Russia, which accounted for 13% of the total steel imports, by volume (Arab Steel, 2010).

Apollo Metalex Pvt. Ltd. of India moved forward with upgrading Hadeed Hamas's scrap melting plant. The $34 million project was expected to increase the plant's capacity to 288,000 metric tons per year (t/yr) of billet from 70,000 t/yr by 2010 (Arab Steel, 2009).

Joudco Steel produced 132,000 metric tons (t) of rebar at its plant in Latakia compared with 133,000 t in 2008. All but 575 t of the company's output was sold on the local market. The company was building a new 75,000-t/yr-capacity plant in Adra Industrial City northeast of Damascus for the production of hot-rolled billets. The new billet plant, which was a joint venture with an unnamed foreign investor, was expected to be completed by yearend 2010 (Arab Steel, 2010).

In 2009, Hmisho Steel, produced low-and medium-carbon-content rebar from its newly built mill in Latakia. The company built a new billet plant with an electric arc furnace (EAF), a ladle furnace, and a four-strand billet continuous-casting machine at Adra Industrial City. The capacity to produce 500,000 t/yr of steel was supplied by Daniel Centro Metal Co. of Italy. In October, International Company for Steel Rolling commissioned production of its rolling mill plant, which is located in Hisyah Industrial Zone near Homs. The plant had the capacity to produce 300,000 t/yr of rebar (Hmisho Steel S.A., 2010; International Company for Steel Rolling, 2010).

INDUSTRIAL MINERALS

Cement.—Cement production in Syria, which totaled about 5.5 million metric tons (Mt) in 2009, was expected to double following the completion of projects currently under construction. The country's cement consumption in 2010 was expected to exceed 8 Mt. Lafarge Cement Syria, which was owned by Lafarge S.A. of France (85%) and Mas Economic Group (15%), continued building a new greenfield plant at Manbej, which is located 160 kilometers (km) northeast of Aleppo and 25 km south of the border with Turkey. The 3-Mt/yr-capacity plant was expected to be completed by June 2010. Lafarge had a plan to build a second cement plant near Damascus (Lafarge Cement Syria S.A., 2010).

Al-Badia Cement Co. JSC, which was a joint venture of Muhaidib & Sons Group of Saudi Arabia, Ciment Francais (a subsidiary of Italcementi Group of Italy), and other investors, moved forward with the construction of a new 3.2-Mt/yr-capacity plant at Abu Ash-Shamat, which is located 80 km northeast of Damascus. The plant was being built by CBMI Construction Co. Ltd. of China and was expected to commence first-phase production of 1.6 Mt/yr in late 2010.

Rajhi Cement (a subsidiary of Al Rajhi Group of Saudi Arabia) signed a contract with Chengdu Design and Research Institute of Building Materials Industry Co. Ltd. of China to build a 1-Mt/yr cement plant in Syria (AME Info, 2008; China Cement Net, 2009).

In 2009, GOCBM, which operated eight state-owned cement plants in Syria, produced more than 5 Mt of clinker, which was 125,000 t more than output of 4.9 Mt in 2008, or an increase of 3%. Tartus Cement and Building Material Co. produced about 1.4 Mt of clinker; the Syrian Cement Manufacturing and Building Material Co. in Hama, 1.3 Mt; Arabian Cement Co., 824,000 t; Al Shahaba Cement and Building Material Co., 685,000 t; Adra Cement and Building Material Co.,

657,000 t; and Rastan Cement and Building Material Co., 114,000 t. A cement plant that was operated by the Military Housing Establishment of the Ministry of Defense produced 293,000 t of cement. GOCBM was in the process of upgrading and expanding the capacity of the Tartus plant to 1.85 Mt/yr from 1.23 Mt. Pharon Commercial Investment Group of Saudi Arabia financed the $50 million expansion plan in return for 400,000 t/yr of the plant's future production. Pharon Group was expected to upgrade the Adra cement plant to increase its capacity to about 1.5 Mt/yr from 845,000 t/yr in return for 461,000 t/yr of post-expansion production. Ehdas Sanat Co. of Iran completed building a new cement plant in Hama for GOCBM; the plant, which was initially scheduled for completion in 2007, had a capacity of 1.1 Mt/yr of cement (Syrian Arab News Agency, 2010).

In 2009, Guris Raqqa Cement Co., which was a subsidiary of Guris Construction and Engineering Co. Inc. of Turkey, completed the construction of a 1.5-Mt/yr-capacity clinker mill in Raqqa in northeastern Syria at a cost of $50 million. Guris also owned Al- Hasakeh Cement L.L.C. in the Yurubbiya Free Zone in northeastern Syria. Al-Hasakeh Cement was established in 2007 as a clinker production and milling plant as well as a cement sales outlet (Guris Construction and Engineering Co. Inc., 2010).

Phosphate Rock.—About 2.4 Mt of washed and unwashed phosphate rock was sold mainly to foreign fertilizer manufacturers in 2009. Phosphate rock production in the country decreased significantly for the second year in a row by 0.76 Mt in 2009 compared with that of 2008, which in turn was a decrease of about 0.5 Mt compared with that of 2007. Phosphate rock production was 35% less than the GCPM's production target for 2009. The company attributed the the significant decrease in production to reduced demand by international markets, insufficient mining equipment, and technical difficulties (General Establishment of Geology and Mineral Resources, 2010, p. 17).

In May 2010, the Governments of India and Syria signed a memorandum of understanding to establish a joint-venture company to develop phosphate rock production facilities in Syria, which would increase production to 10 Mt/yr from the current production of 2.2 Mt/yr. The new company would upgrade the phosphate rock mines in Alsharqiya and Kunayfis, transportation equipment, and the phosphate rock export terminal at Tartus Port. The joint venture would also build a phosphoric acid plant at a phosphate rock mine site. India was expected to import most of the phosphate rock, phosphoric acid, and phosphate fertilizer produced by the new company (Ministry of Petroleum and Mineral Resources, 2010a).

Stone, Dimension.—The General Institute for Geology of the MoPMR estimated that the country's dimension stones reserves were more than 50 Mt. In 2009, there were 32 active dimension stone quarries in the country. The GEMA operated 5 quarries directly and contracted 11 quarries; the remaining quarries were operated by private companies. A sector study conducted by the Syrian Enterprise Business Center and funded by the European Union identified 25 types of dimension stones in Syria, 5 of which were chosen for promotion at international markets. These designated types were the Bedrousi, the Rhaibani Light Biege, the Mussyaf, the Palmyra White, and the Palmyra Yellow (Damiani and Giovannangeli, 2008, p. 8).

MINERAL FUELS

Natural Gas.—Syria's natural gas reserves were estimated to be about 280 billion cubic meters. The country's gas production totaled 6.0 billion cubic meters, which was unchanged from the production level in 2008. The Government imported 728 million cubic meters of natural gas from Egypt by way of the Arab Gas Co. in 2009 (BP p.l.c., 2010, p. 24; Ministry of Petroleum and Mineral Resources, 2010b).

In November, the Syrian Gas Co. commenced production at the South Central Area gas treatment plant. The plant processed natural gas produced at the Abu Rabah, the Al Fayed, and the Qumqum gasfields. The plant, which was built by Stroytransgaz of Russia, was expected to produce about 2.5 billion cubic meters per year. Natural gas from the South Central Area plant would be used by the Adra cement plant, power stations, and fertilizer plant. Petrofac Ltd. of the United Kingdom moved forward with the construction of 1.4-billion-cubic-meter-per-year natural gas processing plant in central Syria. The plant would begin processing natural gas from the Hayan gasfield in the fourth quarter of 2010. In August, the Governments of Syria and Turkey signed a memorandum of understanding to connect the gas networks of both countries, which would enable Syria to buy between 0.5 billion cubic meter and 1.0 billion cubic meters of natural gas per year from Turkey for 5 years beginning in 2011. In July, the GPC signed an agreement with Total S.A. of France to develop the Al-Tabia gasfield, which was located in the Dayr az Zawr Province in northeastern Syria (U.S. Energy Information Administration, 2010).

Petroleum.—In 2009, production of crude oil and condensates in Syria averaged about 376,000 barrels per day (bbl/d), which was about the same level of output achieved in the previous 3 years. Syria's proved petroleum reserves as of yearend 2009 were estimated to be 2.5 billion barrels. State-owned SPC produced more than 191,000 bbl/d of crude oil and condensates, and the international companies working in Syria, including Al-Furat Petroleum Co., Dier Ezour Petroleum Co., Dijla Petroleum Co., Hayan Petroleum Co., Oudeh Oil Co., and Sino Syrian Al Kawkab Oil Co., produced about 180,000 bb/d combined. The country's two petroleum refineries had the capacity to refine 240,000 bbl/d of crude oil. The Banias refinery had the capacity to refine 133,000 bbl/d of petroleum products. and the Homs refinery had the capacity to refine 107,000 bbl/d (Ministry of Petroleum and Mineral Resources, 2010b; U.S. Energy Information Administration, 2010).

The GPC was working with a number of international companies on crude oil and natural gas exploration to halt the downward trend in the country's crude oil production. These companies included Gulfsands Petroleum p.l.c. of the United Kingdom (Block 26), HBS International Egypt Ltd. (Block 22), INA Industrija Nafte of Croatia (Block 10), IPR Mediterranean Exploration Ltd. of the United States (Block 24), Loon Energy Corp. of Canada (Block 9), Morrell Broom Co. (Block 11), Royal Dutch Shell plc of the Netherlands (Blocks 57 and 58), Sayuz Co. of Ukraine (Block 12), Stratic Energy Corp. of Canada (Block 17), and Suncor Energy Inc. of Canada (Al Shaer and Al Sharefea gasfields, and Block 2) (General Petroleum Corp., 2010; Gulfsands Petroleum p.l.c., 2010).

The Government planned to upgrade the country's two refineries at Banias and Homs and to build two new greenfield refineries (one at Al-Furqlus east of Homs and another at Abu Khashab in Dayr az Zawr Province) to satisfy the increase in local demand for refined petroleum products, which was projected to increase by 5% annually for the next 20 years. The Al-Furqlus refinery project was a joint venture of the Governments of Iran, Syria, and Venezuela, and Al-Bukhari Group of Malaysia. It would have the capacity to refine 140,000 bbl/d of petroleum products and would cost about $3 billion to build. A second new greenfield petroleum refinery was planned at Dayr az Zawr in northeastern Syria. It would be built and financed by China National Petroleum Co. (CNPC) and would have a 100,000 bbl/d refining capacity and cost $2 billion to build. An economic feasibility study for the Dayr az Zawr refinery was expected to be completed in 2010.

OIL AND GAS SECTOR: BASIC INFORMATION

ENERGY OVERVIEW

Proven Oil Reserves (January 1, 2010E)	2.5 billion barrels
Total Oil Production	400 thousand barrels per day
Crude Oil Production	368 thousand barrels per day
Oil Consumption	252 thousand barrels per day

Net Petroleum Exports	192 thousand barrels per day
Crude Oil Distillation Capacity	240 thousand barrels per day
Proven Natural Gas Reserves	8.5 trillion cubic feet
Natural Gas Production	208 billion cubic feet
Natural Gas Consumption	213 billion cubic feet
Natural Gas Imports	5 billion cubic feet
Total Energy Consumption	0.8 quadrillion Btu*, of which Oil (69%), Natural Gas (27%), Hydroelectricity (4%)
Total Per Capita Energy Consumption	38.8 million Btu
Energy Intensity	9,388 Btu per $2000-PPP**

OIL AND GAS INDUSTRY

Organization	Upstream and downstream oil and gas sectors controlled by the state-owned Syrian Petroleum Company (SPC) and the Syrian Gas Company (SGC), both part of the Ministry of Petroleum and Mineral Resources. Since 2001, Syria has re-opened upstream oil and gas exploration to international oil companies through production sharing agreements. Investments in downstream infrastructure are also increasingly open to foreign investment.
Major Oil/Gas Ports	Baniyas, Tartous and Latakia
Foreign Company Involvement	Shell Oil, Total, Stroytransgaz, Gulfsands, Soyuzneftegaz, ONGC, CNPC, Petro-Canada, Petrofac, Sinochem, Sinopec, Tatneft.
Major Oil and Natural Gas Basins	Palmyra, Suweidiya, Deir Ez-Zour, Jbessa
Major Pipelines (capacity)	Arab Gas Pipeline (970 MMcf/d when completed to Turkey)
Major Refineries (capacity, bbl/d)	Baniyas (132,725), Homs (107,140)

Syria produces relatively modest quantities of oil and gas but the country's location is strategic in terms of energy transit.

Syria is the only significant crude oil producing country in the Eastern Mediterranean region, which includes Jordan, Lebanon, Israel, the West Bank, and Gaza. In 2009, Syria produced about 400,000 barrels per day (bbl/d) of crude and other petroleum liquids. Oil production has stabilized after falling for a number of years, and is poised to turn around as new fields come on line. In 2008, Syria produced 213 billion cubic feet (Bcf) of natural gas, and is expected to double its gas production by the end of 2010. While much of its oil is exported to Europe, Syria's natural gas is used in reinjection for enhanced oil recovery (EOR) and for domestic electricity generation.

Although Syria produces relatively modest quantities of oil and gas, its location is strategic in terms of regional security and prospective energy transit routes. Regional integration in the energy sector is expected to increase as a result of the 2008 opening of the Syrian link of the Arab Gas Pipeline and ongoing plans for the expansion of the pipeline network to include neighboring countries Turkey, Iraq, and Iran.

OIL

Syrian crude oil production has been in decline since the mid-1990s, but efforts are underway to turn it around in 2010.

According to *The Oil and Gas Journal*, Syria had 2.5 billion barrels of petroleum reserves as of January 1, 2010. Syria's known oil reserves are mainly in the eastern part of the country near its border with Iraq and along the Euphrates River; a number of smaller fields are located in the center of the country.

Organization

Syria's upstream oil production and development has traditionally been the mandate of the Syrian Petroleum Company (SPC), an arm of the Ministry of Petroleum and Mineral Resources. The SPC has undertaken efforts to reverse the trend toward declining oil production and exports by increasing oil exploration and production in partnership with foreign oil companies. The SPC directly controls about half of the country's oil production and takes a 50 percent stake in development work with foreign partners.

Foreign investment is vital for improving production levels. The main foreign producing consortium is the Al-Furat Petroleum Company, a joint venture established in 1985, which currently includes the SPC at 50 percent ownership, Shell Oil at 32 percent, and others, including China's CNPC. Asian national oil companies and smaller independents have been the most active in recent exploration tenders, including Gulfsands, led by Sinochem.

Production

Since peaking at 583,000 barrels per day (bbl/d) in 1996, Syrian crude oil production declined to an estimated 368,000 bbl/d in 2009, down from 390,000 bbl/d in 2008. Total oil liquids production, which includes crude and natural gas liquids (NGL), is estimated at about 400,000 bbl/d in 2009. Syrian oil minister Suffian Alao announced in April 2010 that the government expects oil production to increase in 2010 following 13 years of steady decline. Syria consumed 252,000 bbl/d of petroleum liquids in 2009.

The largest and most mature fields are Al-Furat's Omar and SPC's Jbessa fields, which reportedly had production capacity of 100,000 and 200,000 barrels per day, respectively, at the start of 2010. Other smaller mature fields, such as Oudeh, Gbeibe, and Tishrine, are under field rehabilitation contracts to CNPC and Sinopec, and their production capacity is on the rise. Contracts have been awarded to Shell and Total in 2008 and 2010 for exploration at greater depths in existing mature fields in the Euphrates and central areas. Gulfsands' Khurbet East field came onstream in 2008 with initial production of 10,000 bbl/d rising to 18,000 by the end of 2009.

Khurbet East capacity is currently expected to increase due to recent drilling successes along with development work. Gulfsands is also involved in developing the nearby Yousefieh field, which is currently producing about 1,200 bbl/d and is expected to produce 6,000 bbl/d by 2012. All of these activities have reportedly added more than 50,000 bbl/d of production over the past 2 years, and a further 15,000-20,000 bbl/d is set to come on stream in 2010 from fields discovered by India's ONGC and Russia's Tatneft.

Attempts to explore the offshore Mediterranean were unsuccessful in 2007, as no offers were confirmed for the four blocks tendered, reportedly because terms were deemed unfavorable and the blocks too small. However, in April 2010, it was announced that eight new blocks, located onshore mainly in the north and east of the country, are open for bidding before a September 15 deadline. And the SPC plans to reissue tenders for the offshore blocks in the near future.

Syria's Total Petroleum* Balance, 1990-2009

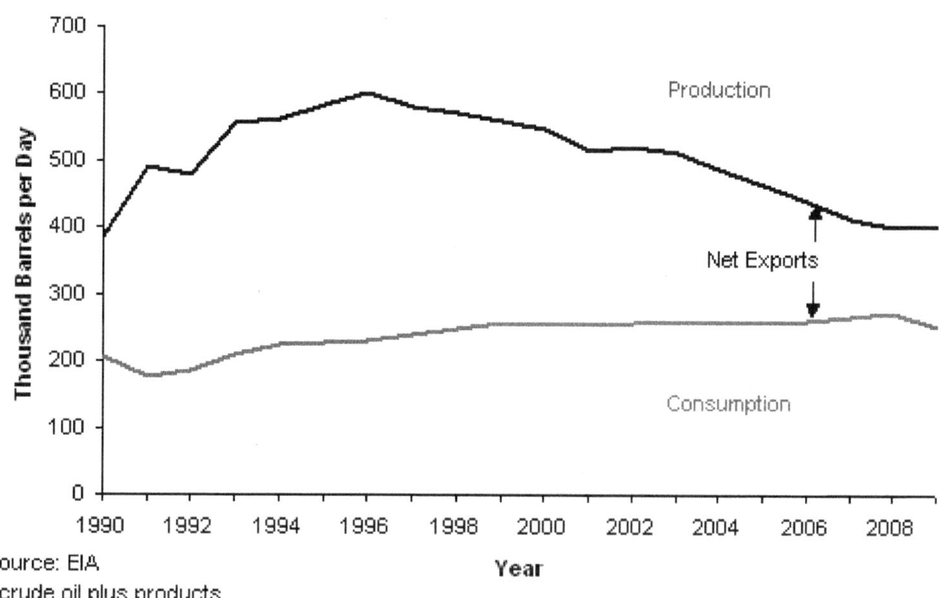

Exports

In 2009, Syria's net petroleum exports were estimated to be 148,000 bbl/d. All oil exports are marketed by Sytrol, Syria's state oil marketing firm, which sells most of its volumes under 12-month contracts. Syrian crude oil exports go mostly to OECD European countries, in particular Germany, Italy, and France, totaling an estimated 143,000 bbl/d in 2009, according to International Energy Agency (IEA) data.

Pipelines

Syria has a developed domestic pipeline system for transporting crude and petroleum products managed by the Syrian Company for Oil Transportation (SCOT). Pipelines include the 250,000-bbl/d, 347-mileTel Adas-Tartous crude line linking SPC and other fields to the port at Tartous with a connection to the refinery at Homs, and oil products pipelines linking the Homs refinery to Syria's major cities.

Syria has three Mediterranean oil export/import terminals, all managed by SCOT. Baniyas (7 berths) and Tartous (2 berths) are larger ports; Latakia handles smaller cargoes. The terminals are connected to refineries through the domestic pipeline network.

In 2009, it was reported that an initial agreement took place between Syria and Iraq to repair and reopen the Kirkuk-Banias oil pipeline, which extends 500 miles from oil fields in northern Iraq to the Syrian port of Banias on the Mediterranean. This pipeline, which could be used to export production from Iraq's northern fields, has been closed since 2003. However, to date no contract has been awarded.

Refining

According to *The Oil and Gas Journal*, Syria's total refining capacity was approximately 240,000 bbl/d as of January 2010. Syria's two state-owned refineries are located at Baniyas and Homs, which have 133,000 bbl/d and 107,000 bbl/d, respectively, of refining capacity. Syria faces shortages of gas oil and diesel, which are imported. A proposed new 100,000 bbl/d capacity refinery project by CNPC at Abu Khashab is currently under contract following the completion of an economic feasibility study in early 2010.

NATURAL GAS

Syria will almost double its natural gas production in 2010 , all of it slated for domestic use .

According to *The Oil and Gas Journal*, as of January 1, 2010, Syria's proven natural gas reserves were estimated at 8.5 trillion cubic feet (Tcf), about half of which is associated gas. Non-associated gas reserves are mainly located in the east and center of the country. Roughly 35 percent of Syrian natural gas production was reinjected into oilfields in 2008, about 2 percent was vented or flared, and the rest distributed to power generators and other domestic users.

Syria plans to substitute natural gas for oil in all of its domestic power generation and industrialuse by 2014. Over half of Syria's power generating facilities are still fueled by refined oil products, much of which must be imported due to inadequate refining capacity.

Production

In 2008, Syria produced an estimated 208 billion cubic feet per year (Bcf/y) of natural gas, imported 5 Bcf, and consumed 213 Bcf. Syria's natural gas production was declining from 2004 to 2008, but it is now poised to increase rapidly as a series of new projects come on stream. By the end of 2010, Syria reportedlyexpects to double its 2008 production level. According to Syrian Minister of Petroleum and Mineral Resources SufianAllao, reported by the Syrian Arab News Agency on April 14, 2010, Syrian natural gas production had reached 361 Bcf/y at that time and was expected to reach 412 Bcf/y by the end of 2010.

In November 2009, the South Central Area gas plant came online. Built by Russia's Stroytransgaz, the project produces about 88 Bcf per year of treated gas, thereby increasing Syria's total natural gas production by about 40 percent. Also in November 2009, an early production facility in Al Hayan gas field came onstream with the capacity to produce 7.8 Bcf per year. The main treatment plant at Al Hayan is being built by Petrofac, and is scheduled to start up in late 2010 with a capacity of about 50 Bcf per year. Suncor Energy (Petro-Canada) started up its Ebla gas plant in April 2010, producing about 29 Bcf per year from the Ebla gas fields. As natural gas production rises, gas demand for electric power generation grows and power plants switch from fuel oil to gas.

Natural Gas Imports and Pipelines

Syria is a natural gas importer since mid-2008, when it began importing an estimated 5 Bcf/y of natural gas from Egypt by way of the Arab Gas Pipeline (AGP). Syria's long-term aim is to become a transit state for Egyptian, Iraqi, Iranian, and even potentially Azerbaijani gas, which would gain it valuable transit revenues as well as help increase the availability of natural gas imports to Syria. According to a 2009 agreement with Turkey, Syria will import up to 35 Bcf of gas from Turkey starting in 2011 with the opening of the Syria-Turkey section of the Arab Gas Pipeline.

Syria's Natural Gas Balance, 1988-2008

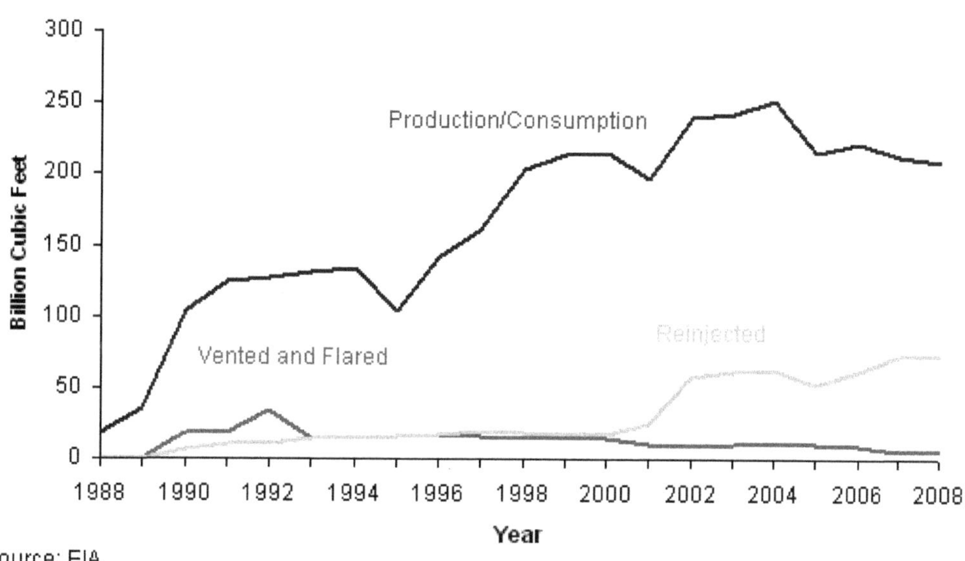

Source: EIA

Arab Gas Pipeline

The AGP currently links Egypt with Jordan, Syria, and Lebanon. Limited gas supplies to Lebanon from Egypt began at the end of 2009. Completion of the pipeline to Turkey is projected for 2011. A memorandum of understanding with Turkey was signed in 2009, under which Turkey will build a 56-mile pipeline on its side of the border to link into the line Syria is currently building from Aleppo to Kilis on the border. The Aleppo-Kilis line is to be completed by March 2011. According to the agreement, Syria will receive between 17.5 and 35 Bcf of Turkish gas annually for 5 years starting in 2011.

Syria-Iraq Gas Pipeline

Discussions are reportedly under way between Syria and Iraq to construct a new natural gas pipeline from the Akkas gas field in Iraq's western province of Al-Anbar, about 30 miles from the Syrian border. The main sticking points are terms for exports and Iraq's own domestic need for gas. Akkas has the potential to contribute to the supply of gas to Europe through tying into the Arab gas pipeline that will run to the Turkish border via Syria.

Persian Pipeline

Syria and Iran reportedly signed a cooperation agreement in April 2009 which includes plans for a natural gas pipeline between Iran and Syria via Iraq. The main sticking point is the security of the line through Iraq.

SUPERVISION AND CONTROL COMPANIES APPROVED BY S.P.C

Name	SOEX (SOYUZEXPERTIZA of the Russian Federation Chamber of Commerce and Industry)
Type	SERVICES

Product	INSPECTION and Supervision Company
Address	Russian Federation,125009,Moscow,13/17,M.Dmitrovka street
Box	
Telex	
Phon	+7(495)660-58-68
Fax	+7(495)621-56-75
Email	inbox@soex.ru
WebSite	WWW.soex.ru

Name	Baxcounsel LTD
Type	SERVICES
Product	INSPECTION and Supervision Company
Address	301, Trade Avenue Bldg, Suren Road , Andheri (East), Mumbai 400069
Box	
Telex	Tel2-3951 4271/4347/4346
Phon	2683 4158/4231/4652
Fax	0091-22-2683 9250
Email	baxin@giasbm01.vsnl.net.in
WebSite	www.baxcounsel.com

Name	TUV NORD GmbH
Type	SERVICES
Product	INSPECTION and Supervision Company
Address	Amtuv1 30519 Hannover
Box	
Telex	
Phon	00494085572348
Fax	00494085571015
Email	imulisch@tuev-nord.de
WebSite	www.tuev-nord.de

Name	RBGLTD
Type	SERVICES
Product	INSPECTION and Supervision Company
Address	Norfolk house pitmeden road dyce Aberdeen AB21 ODP-UK
Box	TELEX
Telex	
Phon	0044(0)1224722888 (CONTACT PERSON:-ADRIAN PAYNE)
Fax	0044(0)1224723406
Email	Adrian.payne@rbgltd.com

WebSite	www.rpgltd.com

Name	2R Engineering Ravenna
Type	SERVICES
Product	INSPECTION and Supervision Company
Address	Via Trieste '227.48100 (RAVENNA) ITALY
Box	
Telex	
Phon	00390544420025
Fax	00390544421540
Email	Info@dueerreravenna.com
WebSite	www.dueerreravenna.com

Name	MOODY INTERNATIONAL
Type	SERVICES
Product	INSPECTION and Supervision Company
Address	69,Road 161,intersection with Road 104, Ground Floor ,Maadi ,Cairo-Egypt
Box	
Telex	
Phon	+2025253841 /+2025244745 /+2025276026 /+20106849648
Fax	+2025275985
Email	e.sherif@moodyint.com
WebSite	www.moodyint.com

Name	SGS
Type	SERVICES
Product	INSPECTION and Supervision Company
Address	1 ,Place Des Alipes CH-1211 Geneval
Box	2152
Telex	422140 SGS
Phon	(41-22)739.91.11
Fax	(41-22)739.98.86
Email	enquiries@sgs.com
WebSite	www.sgs.com

Name	QUALITY SERVICES GROUP
Type	SERVICES
Product	INSPECTION and Supervision Company
Address	Head Office: 9,Gamal Eldin AbulMahasen St.,Garden City,Cairo
Box	
Telex	

Phon	(202)7923043 [3lines]
Fax	002034248838
Email	inspect@qsgegypt.com
WebSite	www.qsgegypt.com

Name	INNOSPECTION LIMITED
Type	SERVICES
Product	INSPECTION and Supervision Company
Address	Unit 1,Howemoss Avenue Kirkhill Industrial Estate,Dyce Aberdeen,AB21 0GP UK
Box	
Telex	
Phon	+44-1224-724-744
Fax	+44-1224-774-087
Email	s.mo@innospection.com
WebSite	www.innospection.com

Name	VELOSI
Type	SERVICES
Product	INSPECTION and Supervision Company
Address	Velosi Limited Unit 1,Woodside Business Park,Whitley Wood Lane,Reading,Berkshine,RG2 8LW,UK
Box	
Telex	
Phon	44(0)1189207030
Fax	+44(0)1189869749
Email	
WebSite	www.velosi.com

Name	Apave International
Type	SERVICES
Product	INSPECTION and Supervision Company
Address	Siège social:8rue Jean Jacques Vemazza -ZAC Saumaty-Séon -BP 193-13322 MARSEILLE Société par Actions Simplifiée au capital de 6 502500 €-No SIREN:775581812
Box	
Telex	
Phon	0496152260
Fax	0496152261
Email	
WebSite	www.apave.com

Name	Control Union
Type	SERVICES

Product	INSPECTION and Supervision Company
Address	GOLZHEIMER STR.120 Derendorf Deutschland
Box	40476 DUSSELDORF
Telex	
Phon	02115158590
Fax	0211483017
Email	info@controlunion.de
WebSite	www.controlunion.de

MINISTRY OF MINERAL RESOURCES CONTACTS

Name	mail-E	Website	Number Fax	Phone number	teSi
of Ministry and Petroleum Mineral Resources Central) (Administration	mopmr-cor@mail.sy	www.petroleum.gov.sy	0114463942	0114451624	Damascus
Syrian Petroleum Company	spccom1@scs-net.org spccom2@scs-net.org	www.spc-sy.com	0113137979 0113137977	0113137913 0113137935	Damascus
Gas Syrian Company	syrgasco@mail.sy	www.sgc.gov.sy	0312451932 0312451933	0312451925 To 0312451931	Homs
AFPC	sy.net.afpc@afpc	www.afpc-sy.com	0116184444	0116183333	Damascus
oil Zour-Al Deir					Damascus
Hayan Petroleum Company		www.hpc.com.sy	0113349821	0113349820 0113349822	Damascus
oil the of Planet company	com.sskoc@sskochq		0116122770	0116122772 0116122773 0116122774	Damascus
Syrian Oil for Company Transport	org.net-scs@50scot	www.scot-syria.com	043710418		Banias
General for Company Refinery Homs	sy.mail@homsrefinery	www.homsrefinery.com	0312516410 0312516411	0312470101 0312516401	Homs
Refinery Banias Company	sy.tarassul@3brc	www.brc-sy.comwww.brc-sy.net	043712325	043	Banias
Company Fuel					
Syrian for Company Distribution Gas	sy.gov.scdgaz@gaz_scd	www.scdgaz.gov.sy	0115812002	0115810939 0115811051	ascusDam
General Establishment	org.sy-geology@geo	www.geology-sy.org	0114465947	0114447755 0114450507	Damascus

and Geology of Mineral Resources				0114455426	
General for Company and Phosphate Mines					
General for ompanyC & Marble Asphalt	sy.mail@marble	www.marble.com.sy	041330102	041330106 To 041330109	Lattakia
Center National Earthquake for	sy.mail@snsn		0114429197	0114423578 0114420780	Damascus
Oil of Institute professional and in occupations Homs					

IMPORTANT DEVELOPMENTS

MINISTRY OF OIL AND MINERAL RESOURCES RESTRUCTURING

Decides as follows:

Article 1 - Amend label Directorate of planning and economic studies in the rules of procedure of the Ministry of Oil and Mineral Resources so that the "Directorate of Planning and International Cooperation."

Article 2 - Fold the International Cooperation Bureau of the organizational structure of the Ministry of Petroleum and Mineral Wealth. "

Article 3 - occur in the Directorate of Planning and International Cooperation Department called "Department of International Cooperation", assume the following tasks:

A - Preparation of correspondence with the countries and the Arab and foreign, institutions and international organizations.

B - Participation in the preparation of agreements and memorandums of understanding between the Ministry and the local, Arab and international, in the areas of the ministry's activities and its affiliates.

C - the follow-up implementation of agreements and memorandums of understanding signed between the Government of the Syrian Arab Republic and other countries, organizations and bodies, universities and institutes ..., in the work of the ministry and its affiliates.

D - participation in meetings of international cooperation, and preparation of correspondence relating thereto.

E - To undertake any other work assigned to them in the workplace.

And - the specific tasks book Presidency of the Council of Ministers No. 1997/15 date 08/02/2011.

Article 4 - A - Directorate of integrated services in the Directorate of Administrative Affairs.

Article 5 - In addition to the functions of the Directorate of Administration the following tasks:

A - Supervise the work of the reform of the electricity and plumbing, elevators and other services.

B - Supervision of the custodians and apportioned, cleaners and garden.

C - Directorate of Management consists of the following services:

1 - Service.

2 - Department of mechanisms: It consists of the Division and the Division of August Murr Register mechanisms.

3 - Department correspondence, consisting of Cabinet Division and the Division of Printing and Imaging Division archives.

D - circles and the people exercise their functions as specified in the rules of procedure.

Article 6 - A talk on behalf of the Directorate of the Directorate of Readiness Division of the tasks identified in the readiness and the presidency of the Council of Ministers Resolution No. 673 date 25.05.2009.

B - Readiness Directorate is composed of the following services:

1 - Department of Department of Readiness: The readiness of the Ministry and the headquarters and shelters, and related work queries.

2 - Department of Public Safety: and assume the functions of civil defense and fire services.

Article 7 - Works accompanying description card.

Article 8 - This resolution shall be and he is required to implement it.

OIL PRODUCTION

The total oil produced in Syria during the first quarter of 2011 amounted to 34.828 million barrels (of light and heavy oil and condensate) increased by the implementation of 100% or the rate of 387 thousand barrels per day, an increase of 4.7 thousand barrels per day for the first quarter of last year.

- The share of national companies (SPC - Syrian Gas) of the total production of oil 52% with the production of 18.341 million barrels, while the total production companies 16.487 million barrels, divided into companies (Euphrates, Deir Al-Zour, return, planet, Hayyan, the Tigris, Abu Kamal, Ebla)

- The total of the Muslim oil refineries 22.069 million barrels, of which 10.929 million barrels of light and 11.140 million barrels of heavy oil, while the total source of heavy oil and light 12.079 million barrels.

GAS PRODUCTION

- The total free gas and utilities product in the country during the first quarter of this year's 2.664 billion m 3 daily average of 29.6 million m 3, handed it to gas processing plants in Syria

2.497 billion m3 were produced 2.378 billion m 3 of clean gas were also imported 121 million m 3 of Egypt , The distribution of gas available to consumers of $ 2.008 billion m 3, as follows:

- Ministry of Electricity 1.789 billion m 3.

- Ministry of Industry 109 million m 3.

- Ministry of Oil and 116 million m 3.

Investment plan:

Report the total expenditure for the institution of public companies for oil for the same period 2.140 billion SP. O The distribution of expenditure in the following form:

- Syrian Petroleum Company: The total investment spending 1.168 billion SP. O.

- Syrian Company for Gas: 796 million for. O

- Syrian Company for Oil Transport: 176 million for. O.

Public Institution for refining

HRC:

Against the annual plan for HRC in 2011 to contribute to the realization of this plan economic and social development of Qatar by providing the local market's growing need of oil products and mineral oils.

Where the assumed production plan refining 1.296 million metric tons of crude oil during the first quarter of 2011 while the amounts of refined oil is actually 1.408 million metric tons by the implementation of 109% as the volume of oil produced is actually 11 799 metric tonnes compared to 15000 tons planned, an implementation rate of 79% .

With the volume of oil derivatives produced 1.351 million metric tons while the production quantities planned to 1.225 million metric tons by the implementation of 110% and total production of coke 42,000 tons while the total expenditure on the investment plan, the amount of $ 100 million for . o.

Banias Refinery:

Total crude oil refined in the Banias refinery for the first quarter of 2011, a total of 1.621 million metric tons compared to 1.620 million metric tons planned by the implementation of 100% while the total of derivatives processing 230,000 metric tons.

The total expenditure on the investment plan 55 million Syrian pounds by the implementation of 100% for the period included the replacement and renovation projects and the city center, unloading and project engineering solutions of the economics of refining

Fuel:

Total fuel sales for the first quarter of 2011, a total of 2.585 million tons of oil products, the following: (different kinds of gasoline, diesel, kerosene fuels), and total sales of (oil, grease, metal, asphalt fuel - gas, liquefied coke White Spirit and solvents) (1.771) million tons, bringing the total sales (3788) million tons (internally and externally), while the sales of bottled gas cylinders (20.070 million) and cylinder (25 416) a hollow cylinder.

Amounted to domestic purchases of the company (1178) million tons of (gasoline, diesel, kerosene fuels) and (1,400) million tons of (mineral oils, asphalt fuel - gas, liquefied coal and coke White Spirit solvent), bringing the total domestic purchases to (2578) million tons were imported in (1.168) million tons of "fuel oil - gasoline - fuel oil and liquid gas"

And has reached the value of total sales executed (84.411) billion Syrian pounds while the value of total purchases (133 479) billion Syrian pounds of them (45 837) billion Syrian pounds purchases of Foreign Affairs, ie that the value of purchases of the company's total increased value of sales for the first quarter of Alam current difference (49.068 billion) for. o to meet the needs of the local market of oil derivatives.

As for the investment plan amounted to actual expenditure (128 187) million Syrian pounds.

General Establishment of Geology and Mineral Resources

Raw materials and construction industry:

Produced the General Establishment of Geology and Mineral Resources, the amount of / 107 964 / tons of raw materials for marble / 140 230 / t the implementation of the scheme by 77%.

The company posted a rate of 161% for raw plaster with production of this article / 145 076 / tons, compared to / 90 000 / t while the total production of volcanic tuff / 254 171 / t, the planner / 232 000 / ton.

As has been the implementation of the insulation work for 75 282 m 2

As for the Quartz sand and rock salt has reached the amount of output generated from the rock salt / 16 386 / t, the planner / 17 500 / ton while the production quantity derived from the sand Quartz / 383 100 / t, the planner / 321 000 / ton.

The total sales of the corporation of building materials and raw materials industry (domestic + external) / 283 639 / l million. O.

Phosphate

Produced by the General Company for Phosphate and Mines during the first quarter of 2011 a total of 988,635 tons of phosphate compared to 809,800 tons by the implementation of planned and 122%, and the company's sales amounted to 882,724 tons of phosphate a value of 2.963 million for. O.

Investment plan:

Total actual expenditure of the Public Institution of Geology and Mineral Resources and the General Company for Phosphate for the same period to 121 million. O.

Said Sufian Al Alao Minister of Oil and Mineral Resources said that the technical committees completed the first phase of the international tender for oil exploration, development and production in eight blocks, covering about 40 percent of the area of Syria announced by the Oil Ministry and the General Organization of Petroleum last March.

The minister added in a statement to reporters on the sidelines of a workshop financing oil projects that Sunday, 13/3/2011 technical committees presented the results of studies on the High Commission was to identify companies that presented on appropriate terms, pointing out that the companies submitted their offers on four blocks, only block / 7 / and block / 3 / and block / 12 / and block / 5 / While not receive the remaining four blocks any view.

He pointed out that some of the presentations made by the companies were close to a large extent which made the request of these companies improve their offers are chosen to supply the most appropriate is supposed to be received replies companies and offers improved during the next few days as a prelude to announce the results of the tender before the end of this March .

On the subject of exploration in the sea, the minister explained that he was the processing and preparation of all necessary documentation for the Declaration and will write to companies qualified and receive the prequalification documents for companies wishing to participate in the announcement this month, pointing out that it has been divided into Syrian waters, which the ministry plans to ad to explore the three blocks .

He disclosed that the ministry plans to complete the procedures for Balsgel oil shale and blocks of advertising where to invest in the region has been divided into blocks in preparation for presentation to investors and qualified companies.

Referred to the results of prospecting and exploration for shale oil shale, which is an alternative source of energy in the long run showed the presence of more than 39 billion tons of raw shale oil shale in the area of Khanasser South honor of Aleppo on an area of 152 square kilometers and with a thickness ranging between 128-240 meters to the layers of raw The value of the thermal energy of the samples between 2466-5464 J / g has been divided to 14 blocks the site to be put on investment.

It is reported that 12 international companies from different nationalities made offers to tender blocks eight to explore for oil and gas and is the French company Total and Petro-Canada Canadian and Italy's Eni in partnership with Gulfsands British leading companies which submitted their offers for this tender as well as companies, CNPC of China and the color of Energy - Syria Branch Canadian and Dana UAE gas and HPC Tunisian and Egyptian and Pico Azvenska Swedish and American IPR and Sideragon French and Flournoy Energy Oil & Gas

/ Flournoy Oil & Gas /.

The General Organization of Petroleum indicated that the content of advertising aimed at the conclusion of a production-sharing for all the operations of prospecting and exploration for oil, develop and produce in the region, described the book of technical conditions and pursuant to the provisions, obligations and conditions contained in the draft contract attached to the book of the conditions prescribed for this purpose. The right of the viewer to bid separately for one block or more.

Eng Sufian Alao Minister of Oil and Mineral Resources, the workshop set up by the Arab Company for Petroleum Investments (APICORP) on the financing of oil projects and infrastructure projects for the oil industry in Syria and in the foundation building of the oil.

Participated in the workshop, specialists and technicians from the ministries of oil, finance and the economy and the State Planning Commission and the Central Bank of Syria and the Commercial Bank of Syria.

The Minister stressed that the company "APICORP" has considerable experience and wide in the area of project financing and how to obtain it and risks as well as ways and means of payment, insurance and all the related topics for pointing out that the exchange of experiences with "APICORP" in this area is very important particularly for large study for projects and securing funding.

He called on Minister of participants to take advantage of all the course topics and mainstream interest to the concerned departments in their organizations, pointing out that the Oil Ministry signed an agreement with APICORP to provide consultancy and expertise in the field of refineries or any other topics where you are sending experts and answer questions from the ministry in the areas agreed upon.

The aim of two-day workshop to give participants knowledge of application frameworks, structural study and analysis of major projects and to identify the key factors for the financing of mega projects and identify and assess key risks in project financing as well as the use and interpretation of the model of Mali is simple to evaluate the financing of projects.

The Chancellor spoke at the "APICORP" Richard Wilson on the basis of funding projects and frameworks, risk financing and study the structure of funding in addition to key aspects of the project agreements.

The «APICORP» Arab financial institution established in 1975 according to an international agreement between the Governments of Member States of the Organization of Arab Petroleum Exporting Countries, "OAPEC" including Syria, based in Saudi Arabia are classified Kmsrv multilateral development owned by the ten States members of the (OAPEC). The company contributed to the development and funding of Arab oil and energy sectors through funding, research and consultancy.

Oil Minister reviewed with the delegation of Polish economic aspects of cooperation in the field of oil, gas and mineral wealth

Engineer Sufian Alao Minister of Oil and Mineral Resources with the Polish economic delegation Monday, 21/02/2011 aspects of possible cooperation in oil and gas and refining industry and mineral wealth between the two countries.

And presentation of the Minister of events and activities the ministry and its institutions in the areas of prospecting and exploration for oil and gas and development of existing fields to increase the profitability of productivity and the transfer of crude oil in addition to oil refining and washing phosphate pointing to the importance of participation of companies of Poland in the tenders announced by the Ministry of Oil or one of its companies to supply equipment industry oil.

For his part, noted the potential of the Polish delegation, the Polish companies in the areas of extraction and production of oil and construction and development of refineries, as well as experience in the investment of Bologna, where shale gas reserves are estimated at this article in Bologna about 1500 billion cubic feet. Displaying a desire to enter the oil market, especially after the Syrian and the significant improvement witnessed by the investment climate in Syria in recent years.

The meeting was attended by Dr. Hassan Zeinab, Al-Din Hossam Abdo Associate Minister of Petroleum and Geological Ghzayel Jaber, head of marketing of oil and Ali Abbas, Director General of the Public Corporation for Oil and Omar Al Hamad, Director General of the Syrian Oil Company .

The end of the international tender for oil exploration in Syria .. And 12 international companies submitted their offers

Ended on last Wednesday on the eighth of this month, international tender for oil exploration and development and production in the eight new blocks, covering about 40 percent of the area of Syria announced by the Ministry of Petroleum and Mineral Resources and the General Organization of Petroleum last March.

It is located eight blocks in different parts in the north and south-east Syria, and an approximate area about 73 thousand km 2.

The announcement came in the framework of plans and programs of the Oil Ministry to increase production by expanding the exploration activities to include all the occupied Syrian and development of old fields, where it offered the ministry to new areas for exploration through a number of bids over the past years resulted in the signing of 12 contracts to explore new areas During the period from 2003 to 2007, with specialized international companies and qualified.

As they advanced 12 companies worldwide from different nationalities to their offers for this tender is the French company Total and Petro-Canada Canadian and Italy's Eni in partnership with Gulfsands British leading companies that made offers to this tender, as well as firms CNPC of China and the color of Energy - Syria Branch Canadian and Dana Gas, the UAE and HPC Tunisian and Picot Egyptian Azvenska Swedish and American IPR and Sideragon French and Flournoy Energy Oil & Gas / Flournoy Oil & Gas /.

The aim of the advertising content to the production-sharing contract to carry out all special operations for oil exploration, development and production in the region, described the book of technical conditions and pursuant to the provisions, obligations and conditions contained in the draft contract attached to the book of the conditions prescribed for this purpose. The right of the viewer to bid separately for one block or more.

The signing of a memorandum of understanding between Syria and Venezuela to complete the implementation of the joint refinery project Alfrekls

Signed and ministries of oil in Syria, Venezuela, Friday, 3/12/2010 Memorandum of Understanding for the development of operational steps to complete the refinery project Alfrekls joint studies through detailed design of the refinery project, which she could reach 140 thousand barrels per day and estimated cost of about $ 5 billion.

The Minister of Petroleum and Mineral Resources Sufian Al Alao, who signed the note on the Syrian side that the memorandum of understanding aims to document what has been agreed upon for the development of practical steps to follow up the refinery project Alfrekls where the program has been established time frame for completion of design studies and then move on to the stages of implementation and will be under this Memorandum of contract with global consulting firms through the evaluation of proposals by a joint committee to study the most appropriate selection and the best.

The minister added that the schedule notice subsequent steps to the subject of study for the conduct of this project forward as quickly as possible, pointing out that both the Syrian and Venezuelan will pay the cost of these studies in the event that the two sides of the Iranian and Malaysian did not approve it.

For his part, Minister of Energy and Petroleum of Venezuela Rafael Ramirez, the importance of implementing the directives of the leaderships of the two countries to accelerate the completion of the refinery joint pointing out that the Venezuelan side will select the best international companies specialized in the field of studies and consultations so that the end of the study before the end of the first half of next year to begin to take steps and measures following the preparation of financial studies of the project, from design to complete the two sides as soon as possible.

It is noteworthy that Syria, Iran and Venezuela, Bukhari Group of Malaysia and signed in the month of March 2008, the partnership agreement to establish a refinery for refining crude oil in the region Alfrekls east of the city of Homs and the project consists of financing and the establishment of a refinery integrated refining crude oil with a total capacity of 140 thousand barrels per day.

Attended the Engineer Hussam Abdo religion, Deputy Oil Minister, Eng Noureddine Makhlouf Director-General of the General Organization for refining and Jaber Ghzayel oil marketing head of the Office of the Council of Ministers and the Venezuelan ambassador in Damascus

Oil Minister: fact, the oil and gas in Syria is stable .. and the Declaration on the prospecting and exploration in the territorial waters beginning of the year

Said Sufian Al Alao Minister of Oil and Mineral Resources said that fact, the oil and gas in Syria is stable with high production slightly from previous years as a result there are plans to increase production and improve performance in addition to the apparent rise in the indicators of recoverable reserves in oil and gas.

The minister added in a press statement on the sidelines of a seminar the global financial crisis and its impact on oil and gas sector in the Arab States, which began its work in Damascus on Sunday, 22/11/2010 The stability of the current oil prices encouraged investors to establish projects and encouraging consumers not to search for alternative sources Energy explained that the ministry will receive special offers announce eight blocks for prospecting and exploration in wilderness areas until the end of next month and plans to announce that prospecting and exploration in the Syrian territorial waters at the beginning of next year.

He referred to the existence of projects for regional oil and gas through the presence of the Arab gas pipeline, which links between Syria, Lebanon, Jordan and Egypt, stressing that it will be delivered part complementary to link this line with the Turkish gas network during the month of March next year and the project will be linked with a network of European gas during the next year.

Indicating that the operational procedures for the implementation of vital projects and promising with Iraq began by announcing the request for a consultant to prepare studies and technical conditions for the implementation of projects on the principle of the / P or T / and include two lines for the transfer of Iraqi oil exports through Syrian ports, where the first line capacity 5.1 million barrels per day and the second 25.1 million barrels can be increased in addition to a pipeline to transport gas .

Minister of Oil in Libya, looking to develop cooperation in the field of oil and gas

Engineer Sufian Alao Minister of Oil and Mineral Resources during a meeting in Tripoli, Dr. Shukri Mohammed Ghanem, head of the Libyan National Oil bilateral relations between the two countries in the field of oil, gas and ways of developing them. The two sides expressed during the meeting, the desire to establish joint investment projects between the two countries and cooperation through the exchange of information and experiences and implementation of training programs for cadres in Syria, Libya.

The Minister said in remarks to reporters after the meeting that he discussed with the possible participation of Ghanem, the National Endowment for oil prospecting and exploration for oil and gas in Syria as well as exchange of expertise areas of marketing and development of gas fields and the training of cadres.

He added that it was the establishment of a national training center interview in Syria to cooperate with foreign companies with experience to train cadres in the areas of oil and gas industry, explaining that it had agreed to Ghanem, a delegation from the Libyan National Oil to visit Syria in the sending of the Ministry of Oil and Mineral Resources of Syria's documentation to identify place to send young Libyans to train in Syria.

He pointed out that it was discussed during the meeting to the methods of developing the performance of the Organization of Arab Petroleum Exporting Countries OAPEC also presented the "Draft Agreement", a draft bilateral agreement in the field of oil and gas between Syria and Libya, expressing his hope to study well and will be signed at the meeting of the Council of strategic cooperation joint to be held in December next in Damascus.

For his part, Ghanem said that there is cooperation between the two countries, especially in the international conferences that are to attend and participate in such meetings of the Organization of Petroleum Exporting Countries OPEC observers in OAPEC as permanent members, pointing out that it had been discussion of the topics to be presented at the meeting of OAPEC in December next year, when formatted views on some topics related to Arab cooperation in the field of petroleum projects .. With regard to oil market conditions were discussed international oil and gas market is international.

He said Mr. Ghanem, the Minister informed him that Syria will conduct a tour of the world's gas companies to participate in the processes of exploration of gas fields in addition to cooperation in the exchange of information and the oil activity in common and open the door for Arab companies and oil services company to work in Syria.

Ghanem said about the proposed memorandum of cooperation from the Syrian side that cooperation with Syria is under agreement and that the note presented by the Minister Alao is a project of cooperation between the two countries hope to sign during the meeting of Strategic Council Top Syrian Libyan to be held in Damascus later this year.

He pointed out that the essence of this agreement is to exchange information, exchange visits and training and joint projects in the field of oil and gas

Field trip to the Minister of Oil in the Fields: the return of company: good procedures to improve the environmental situation

Company Tigris: an increase in production and transportation of oil pipelines

Planet Company: unfair treatment of oil and re-soil to life

Said Sufian Al Alao Minister of Oil and Mineral Resources said that the Ministry pays great attention to the rehabilitation and training of human resources have a constant and growing to raise the professional competence and technical, linguistic and IT to keep pace with technological and technological development in the areas of oil and gas industry different, including a positive impact on production.

The Minister, during a tour to the oil and gas fields in the province on Thursday, 14/10/2010 Hasakah that the ministry recently established an institute Tghania average oil and gas field Taym in the province of Deir al-Zour began teaching with the beginning of the current academic year in addition to the opening of the national training center developed for those working in the field of gas and the refining industry in the region of Alfrekls in the province of Homs with the aim of qualifying the largest possible number of workers in this vital sector. along with many of the existing training centers in the Deir al-Zour, Hassake and Homs.

Mr.'s oil minister that his ministry is making great efforts to apply the rules of safety and security and to address all forms of pollution in the fields of production of the Syrian Oil Company and oblige all companies operating in Syria to abide by these rules in accordance with the specifications and global measures adopted.

And visited the stations return and October Committees of the company return to the oil joint-venture with Sinopec of China, which produces about 17,500 barrels per day and a look at the reality of work and listened to a briefing about the actions taken by the company to address the diversion of gas in the air through the installation of equipment surface new and the preparation of engineering designs and technical studies necessary for a number of projects aimed at improving the environmental situation in the production sites and the minister stressed the need to commit to a program schedule for the implementation of the company's projects as soon as possible.

He also briefed on the progress of work in the fields of company Tigris Petroleum shared between the Foundation of the oil company "Gulfsands" by Britain, the company produces from the station east of ruined and Yusufiyah about 21 thousand barrels per day The company has implemented recently a line for transporting oil produced from fields along the 22 km led to dispense with the process of transport tanks and take advantage of this solution is environmentally and economically.

He visited Mr. Minister station glomerulus, a subsidiary of Planet Petroleum, a joint venture between the General Organization of the Petroleum Corporation, CNPC of China where the company produces about 14 thousand barrels per day and see the sites address the inequities of oil in order to improve environmental conditions where it is the withdrawal of the remaining oil in the vicinity of the wells and then soil treatment and returned to the natural characteristics of investable agricultural.

Participated in the round Eng Abdo Hossam El Din, Deputy Oil Minister Ali Al-Abbas, Director General of the Public Corporation for Oil and Khalid Al-ahead with Deputy Director-General of the Syrian Oil Company and the heads of boards of directors and general managers of companies, the return of the Tigris and the planet and directors of the fields.

The Minister of Petroleum and Mineral Resources Sufian Al Alao on the a Ravae and Thursday toured a field to work sites and production in the fields Aljbsp and Rmelan and companies operating there and the field life of the AFPC will also convene a meeting with the staff working in operating companies and the Syrian Gas Company in the area of Deir Al-Zour for closely at the reality of work and ways to improve it.

Include the visit of Minister of Oil stations return and October Committees of the company return to the oil and stations ravaged eastern and Yusufiya subsidiaries of the company Tigris Petroleum and the station glomerulus, a subsidiary of Planet of the oil in addition to the opening of the project and the link between the systematic compilation of gas to gas plant age and Deir al-Zour.

IMPORTANT LAWS AND REGULATIONS AFFECTING OIL AND GAS EXPLORATION

CONTRACT REGULATIONS FOR PUBLIC ESTABLISHMENTS, CORPORATIONS AND ORGANIZATIONS

Organizational Decree No. 195 / T Of 25 June 1974

DECREE NO. 195/T

President of the Republic:

-Acting upon rules of Legislative Decree no. 18 of 15 February 1974.

HEREBY DECREES:

ARTICLE NO. 1:

Contracts regulations appended hereto shall apply to all public establishments, corporations and other bodies as defined by Article no.1 of Legislative Decree no. 18 of 15 February 1974.

ARTICLE NO. 2:

With effect from the date these regulations come into force, all other contract regulations so far adopted by the bodies governed by the rules of the present regulations shall lose validity as well as all other rules that are contradictory hereto, wherever these are contained in the regulations of such bodies.

ARTICLE NO. 3:

The rules of the present regulations shall not apply to those tenders whose closing date has expired, or whose contracts were concluded before the coming into force of the present regulations.

ARTICLE NO. 4:

The Minister of Finance shall issue the executive instructions of the present regulations.

ARTICLE NO. 5:

The Minister concerned may, by his own order, set forth detailed rules in such a manner that does not run counter to the rules of the present regulations.

ARTICLE NO. 6:

This decree shall be published in the official gazette.

Damascus 25 July 1974,

CONTRACT REGULATIONS FOR PUBLIC ESTABLISHMENTS, CORPORATIONS AND ORGANIZATIONS

PART ONE DEFINITIONS

Article no. 1:

For the purpose of the present regulations, the following expressions shall have the definitions hereunder assigned to them:

1. *MINISTER:* The Minister under whose authority are the public establishments, corporation or the organization, as the case requires.

2. *CONTRACTING PARTY:* The public establishment, the corporation or the organization that signs the contract.

3. *EXPENDITURE AUTHORITY:* The person defined by Article no. 32 of Legislative decree no. 18 of 15 February 1974.

4. *PUBLIC BODIES:* The Ministries, administrations, public establishments and bodies, local administration units, municipalities, municipal concerns, public companies, organizations, mortmain (Waqf) departments and all other public bodies.

5. *UNDERTAKING:* The obligation binding the contractor to the contracting party.

6. *SUCCESSFUL TENDERER:* The party winning the tender or whose offer is approved subsequent to invitation of tenders, or who is under a contract the ratification of which has not been finalized.

7. *CONTRACTOR:* The natural or legal person who is under obligation towards the contracting party for the supply of materials or provision of services or execution of works.

8. *CONTRACT:* The set of rules binding the contractor to the contracting party and including the books of general and special conditions, specifications and all other schedules, drawings and documents related to the undertaking.

CHAPTER I PROCEDURE OF SECURING THE CONTRACTING PARTY'S NEEDS

ARTICLE NO. 2:

a) An expenditure arising from the execution of works, provision of services, purchase of materials and all other needs of the Contracting party shall be disbursed in consequence of either of the following:

1. Direct Purchase.

2. Purchase under Direct Contract.

3. Tender.

4. Enquiry for Quotations.

5. Contract by Mutual Consent.

6. Competitions.

7. Execution by trust.

b) Without prejudice to the rules of this part, the Expenditure Authority may specify the procedure to be followed to meet the required needs.

CHAPTER II DIRECT PURCHASE

ARTICLE NO. 3:

Supply of materials, provision of services or execution of works shall proceed under direct purchase in the following cases:

a) If the needs are subject to official tariffs.

b) If the purchase is to be made from a public body.

c) If the disbursement involved does not exceed ten thousand Syrian pounds, but this ceiling can be majorated to fifteen thousand Syrian Pounds by approval from the respective Minister.

ARTICLE NO. 4:

a) Direct purchase as indicated in C of preceding Article shall be made through special direct purchase committees.

b) The expenditure arising from direct purchase shall be disbursed on basis of the relevant invoice issued by the selling party, provided that the invoice shall be endorsed by the concerned direct purchase committee in respect of disbursements specified in C of foregoing Article, in order to attest that the purchases conform to the required specifications and that the prices mentioned therein are moderate and comply to prevailing prices.

c) Direct Purchase Committees shall be set up by an order of the Expenditure Authority who shall determine the number of members on each committee and its function provided that the number shall not be less than three.

ARTICLE NO. 5:

a) In urgent cases and subject to his own discretion, the Expenditure Authority may consent to the purchase of certain materials whose value does not exceed three hundred Syrian Pounds through other than Direct Purchase Committees.

b) Invoices for expenditures incurred as described in A above shall be endorsed by the expenditure authority.

CHAPTER III PURCHASE UNDER DIRECT CONTRACT

Article no. 6:

a) A direct contract is an agreement on the supply of materials or provision of services from an external source through direct communication between the parties authorized to enter into contract with a contractor by any means of communications which shall subsequently be confirmed in writing specifying the nature of service, materials, prices, quantities and method, place and terms of delivery, as well as the method of satisfying obligations arasing there from, in addition to execution warranties, and in general, everything that relates to the subject of the contract and its execution procedures and both parties, obligations.

b) The rules of this Article shall solely apply to urgent cases whose nature is left to the discretion of the expenditure Authority.

CHAPTER IV TENDER

ARTICLE NO. 7:

a) As and when the estimated value of the materials to be supplied, the services, to be provided and the works to be executed exceeds the limits stipulated above for direct purchase, a tender shall be placed and shall be applied to all cases which are not specifically excluded in the present Regulations.

b) The tender shall be based on:

1. Book of general conditions issued by order of the Minister in conjunction with the Minister of Finance in a manner that conforms to the rules of the present regulations.

2. Book of special conditions (financial, juridical and technical) incorporating all drawings, specifications and studies of the materials to be supplied, the services to be provided or the works to be executed. This book shall be countersigned by the Expenditure Authority.

3. Itemized lists of all the supplies or works as well as respective quantities in estimate on basis of recognized units, unless the expenditure Authority deems otherwise.

ARTICLE NO. 8:

a) Tender shall be announced at least fifteen days before its date in case of local tenders, and at least fifty days in case of external tenders.

b) In case calling for speed, the aforesaid period may be reduced at the discretion of the Expenditure Authority but under no circumstances may this period be less than three days for local tenders and fifteen days for external tenders.

c) The day of the tender announcement and the day of the tender meeting shall not be counted in the aforesaid period.

d) No amendment whatsoever shall be introduced to the books of conditions or sketches or any other documents on which the tender is based once the tender is announced, unless the tender is repeated.

Article no. 9: a) Tender announcements shall be published only once and in one daily newspaper at least, and in the government's tender bulletin, if any. Copies of these announcements shall also be put up at the announcement Board of the Contracting Party. Moreover, and when necessary, the tender may be announced on the radio and television or through any other

mass media. Accredited Arab representations and commercial missions abroad, or foreign missions accredited in Syria may also be notified of the external tender announcements and some of their documents.

b) The tender announcement shall contain the following data in the least:

1. Subject of the tender.

2. Place and date of submitting offers as well as the tender meeting.

3. Bid Bond and Performance Bond.

4. The party from whom the tender file can be bought and from whom tender conditions and information can be obtained.

5. Execution period of the undertaking.

6. The period the offerer shall remain bound to his quotation.

ARTICLE NO. 10:

a) Prospective tenderers will have to satisfy the following conditions:

1. He shall not be prohibited from entry into a tender or a contract with the contracting party or any other public body.

2. He shall have a commercial register or duly registered at one of the chamber of Commerce, Industry or Agriculture, as the case may be, if the prospective tenderer is not a Syrian Arab or a Palestinian resident in Syria; to the exclusion of a foreign governmental organization that has a governmental character.

3. He shall not be employed by a public body.

4. He shall not be blacklisted under the Israel Boycott Regulations.

b) The book of special conditions may stipulate certain conditions that have to be satisfied by those who desire to participate as regards financial, technical and professional qualifications.

ARTICLE NO. 11:

A prospective tenderer shall submit along with his offer the required bid bond which is specified in the book of special conditions.

Nevertheless, public bodies, or the bodies that are exempted by special Legislative texts, or foreign organizations that have a govermmental character shall not be required to furnish this bond provided such an exemption be expressly indicated in the book of special conditions or in the tender announcement.

ARTICLE NO. 12:

An offer shall be placed in three sealed envelopes which are then placed in a fourth envelope addressed to the party specified in the tender announcement and featuring the subject of the tender and the tender meeting date.

ARTICLE NO. 13:

a) The first envelope shall contain all documents attesting that conditions stipulated in Article no. 10 of the present regulations are satisfied in addition to the required bid bond.

The second envelope shall contain the technical offer and specifications. The third envelope shall contain the financial and commercial offer together with a list of unit or total prices, as the case may be.

b) An offer submitted and signed by a number of natural or legal persons shall be binding upon those signatories and offerers jointly and severally towards the Contracting Party.

ARTICLE NO. 14:

A tenderer shall indicate in his offer an address he selects in Syria.

ARTICLE NO. 15:

A tenderer shall clearly indicate in his offer, the period of time during which he undertakes to supply the materials, provide the services or execute the works subject of the tender, unless the Contracting Party has already indicated this in the books of conditions. The period of delivery may be taken as a chief element in the comparative study of the offers. The method of calculating the delivery period shall be determined in the books of special conditions.

ARTICLE NO. 16:

a) An offer shall be declined if it is found failing to meet general and special conditions books.

b) The tenderers committee may give a time limit for the tenderers to supply documents lacking in their offers except for the bid bond, the quotation, price analysis bills if such documents are required with the offer.

The tender committee, may, moreover, accept those offers which contain reservations if the tenderer agrees at the beginning of the tender meeting, and before the quotations are disclosed, to withdraw his reservations and to observe the rules of the tender books and confirms this in writing on his offer.

ARTICLE NO. 17:

a) Offers shall be submitted directly to the party specified in the announcement or sent to it by registered mail on the condition that the offer be received by this party and registered at its office before the end of the working hours of the deadline specified for submitting offers which must precede the date of the tender meeting.

b) Only one offer shall be accepted by a given tenderer and the offer which comes first in registration at the concerned party's office shall be considered. Offers may not be recovered, completed or modified after they have been registered in the said office.

ARTICLE NO. 18:

a) The tender meeting takes place at the specified time and place, and in an open session which all tenderers may attend.

b) The tender committee unseals the first envelope and examines its contents and decides to accept the offers submitted by those who satisfy the conditions set for participation in the tender and rules out the offers of those who fail to meet the set conditions. The committee then declares this to those attending and returns to them the second and third envelopes which remain sealed together with other documents submitted with the offer.

c) In such cases as there is only one tenderer or one accepted offer, the tender shall be repeated after being re-announced. Yet, the contracting party may accept the only offer submitted in the second time.

d) The committee unseals the envelopes which contain the technical offer and specifications and declares their contents to those attending the meeting and rules out the offers which contain reservations that cannot be entertained according to the books of general or special conditions.

e) In those cases that call for technical examination and scrutiny of the offers, the committee may postpone its decision to another meeting whose date shall be determined and announced to those attending the meeting. So the third envelope which contains the financial and commercial offer remains sealed until the new meeting determined for deciding over the offers.

f) The accepted offers shall be sorted out according to prices in an ascending order starting with the lowest price and the committee chairman then declares the name of the successful tenderer who has quoted the lowest price.

g) If two or more offers are equal in quoting the accepted lowest price, a new tender shall take place only between those offers and in the same meeting and under sealed envelopes. If the offers are equal again, the result is referred to the Expenditure Authority who selects one from among them.

h) Minutes of the tender meeting, including all objections reaised, shall be put down in writing and all members of the committee as well as all present tenderers shall set their hands to it, and if a successful tenderer obstains from signing, it shall not be considered. The minutes of meeting shall be an official document.

i) All documents submitted by the tenderers shall be signed only by the committee members.

Article no. 19: a) Decisions of the tender meeting shall be taken by a majourity vote of the present members. In case of equal votes, the decision shall be to the side containing the vote of the chairman of the committee.

b) The tender meeting shall be deemed legal if attended by a majority of the committee members, provided always they are not less than three including the chairman.

c) Objections raised during the tender meeting shall be decided by voting. This shall be stated in the minutes of meeting.

d) The committee's decisions which are announced to the meeting shall be deemed final.

ARTICLE NO. 20:

The Expenditure Authority may specify in advance the maximum price which can be accepted in consequence to the tender and this price shall be placed in an envelope sealed with red wax which is to be opened by the tender committee at the tender meeting but its contents shall not be announced to the tenderers. And if there are no offers that are equal to, or below this price, the committee shall ask the tenderers to quote new prices under sealed envelopes in the same meeting. This procedure may not be repeated. If the new prices are not equal to the estimated prices or exceed them by a proportion also exceeding that specified by the Expenditure Authority which is appended to the maximum price of the estimate maximum value, the committee shall declare that the tender has ended in failure.

ARTICLE NO. 21:

The Contracting party may award the tender to one or more tenderers as it deems fit whereupon a part of the order shall be placed with one contractor who may not object thereto, provided always such a procedure be stated in the book of special conditions.

ARTICLE NO. 22:

a) Minutes of the tender meeting shall be countersigned by the Expenditure Authority who may cancel the tender results for reasons justified in writing and retained in the tender file. But under no. circumstances may he revise the result reached by the tender committee.

b) In such a case the tender shall be referred to concerned authorities, if any, to examine it in light of the laws and regulations in force.

c) A successful tenderer shall not be considered a contractor unless notification is completed and he is duly notified thereof to execute the undertaking. The Contracting Party, however, may retract from execution of the tender any time before the contractor is so notified and he may not claim any indemnity therefore.

d) If no contract is concluded between the contracting party and the Contractor after the ratification of the tender, the minutes of meeting established by the Committee shall be considered a contract by and between them after the legal procedures of ratification have been completed. If the successful tenderer or his agent or representative, fails to attend the tender meeting or to sign the relevant minutes of meeting, the contractor shall be notified that his undertaking has been accepted either by registered mail or by a telegram whose contents shall be confirmed by a registered letter. Notification by either procedure followed shall be deemed to have been effected as from the date of posting the registered mail or the telegram dispatched, whichever is earlier.

e) The tender committee shall not accept any underbidding in prices, nor shall the expenditure Authority accept underbidding except under the following two conditions:

1- The reduction resulting from underbidding may not be less than 10 percent of the price under which the tender has been awarded to the successful tenderer. 2- The underbidding tenderer shall enclose his offer with the legal bonds.

ARTICLE NO. 23:

In principle the successful tenderer shall remain bound by his offer throughout the period determined fro his validity in the contract or in the Bookds of Conditions. If he does not receive the go-ahead order within this period, he shall have the right, within seven days to abandon his offer by a letter to be registered at the Contracting party's office. Otherwise, his offer's validity shall be renewed automatically for another period equal in duration to the first one.

ARTICLE NO. 24:

a) The tender committee shall be formed by order of the expenditure Authority, with the condition that one of its members shall be a staff member of the contracting Party's financial department.

b) The Expenditure Authority shall issue an order specifying the documents required to confirm that conditions are satisfied for participation in a tender, and the basis of forming tender committee and all other maters related to the tender.

CHAPTER V CALL FOR QUOTATIONS

Article no. 25:

Quotations shall be invited when it is not possible for the Contracing Party to determine integral specifications or conditions for the materials to be supplied, the works to be executed or the services to be provided, so that this party can examine the offers and select the best in quality, price and other conditions.

ARTICLE NO. 26:

Subject to the rules of subsequent articles, purchase through calls for quotations shall be governed by the rules of Article no. 8 (D), Article no. 9 (A), Articles 10,11,14,15,17,19,20,21 and Articles 23 (B,C) and Articles 22 and 24 of the present regulations.

ARTICLE NO. 27:

a) Offers shall be invited through an advertisement and/or through registered letters addressed by the Contracting Party to the largest number of prospective tenderers to examine the books of conditions, if any, and to put forward their offers within the time limits prescribed in Article no. 8 of the present regulations and subject to Article no. 9 (A) in case of an advertisement.

b) A call for quotations shall contain the following data at least:

1. Types of the required materials, works or services.

2. Deadline for submitting offers and the procedure thereof.

3. Validity of the offer.

4. Place of submitting offers.

5. A demand for details of offers with regard to specifications, prices, terms of payment, period of delivery or execution of works.

6. Other conditions that the Contracting Party deems necessary to be fulfilled.

ARTICLE NO. 28:

Offers containing certain conditions that run counter to conditions which the book of special conditions has stipulated they must not be contradicted shall not be accepted.

ARTICLE NO. 29:

a) The tender committee shall in a closed meeting examine the offers and proceed to unseal the envelope containing the supporting documents to determine the accepted offers and makes out a minutes of the meeting.

b) The committee shall then unseal the envelopes that contain the technical offers of those whose offers have been accepted. These technical offers shall be referred to a technical committee or committees appointed for the purpose by the Expenditure Authority in order to post the offers into special ledgers, study them technically and comparatively on the basis of technical value, manufacturer warranty and other guarantees submitted by the tenderers, period of execution, etc. after the technical study has been completed, the envelopes containing the financial and commercial offers shall be unsealed and the prices shall be examined and compared. The technical committee shall then put forward its complete study of the financial and technical aspects together with its recommendations to the tender committee. c) The minister may appoint a local or foreign consultant office to take over the work of the technical committee or part of it.

ARTICLE NO. 30:

a) On the strength of the technical committee's report, the tender committee shall put forward its view as to the offer that best serves the interests of the Contracting Party.

b) The Expenditure Authority shall issue his decision selecting thereby the offer that best serves the interests of the Contracting Party, in case he does not endorse the view of the tender committee, his decision shall contain his reasons for this denial.

c) The tenderer whose offer has been ultimately accepted shall be so notified by the Contracting party within seven days from the date of its ratification by concerned authorities either by registered mail or telegram to be confirmed by registered letter. In these cases notification shall be deemed effected as from the date of posting the registered mail or of the telegram dispatch, whichever earlier.

CHAPTER VI COMPETITION

ARTICLE NO. 31:

a) The Minister may choose the procedure of the competition for the purpose of having studies and sketches laid out for a certain project as and when there are good reasons requiring this procedure.

b) The competition announcement shall specify all relevant points particularly the subject matter, conditions, the procedure of deciding the winners and the method of work of the selection panel, the rewards, incentives and privileges that will be awarded to the contestants.

CHAPTER VII CONTRACT BY MUTUAL CONSENT

ARTICLE NO. 32:

The Contracting Party may enter into contract by mutual consent with any party it selects in consequence to direct communication made in compliance with the rules and Procedures outlined in the present chapter.

Article no. 33: a) A Contract by mutual consent shall not be concluded except under the following conditions:

1. When the required materials, services or works are exclusively manufactured, owned, traded, supplied, or imported by one certain person, certain company or certain party or when their prices are determined by a world stock exchange.

2. When there are important technical, financial or military reasons, or economic agreements that require a certain party to supply the materials, provide the services or execute the works.

3. When the required materials, services or works are needed for conducting research or test in such a case as calling for a specific procedure of execution.

4. When the required materials, services, or works have already been placed in tender or bid for quotation as stipulated by the present regulations but no tednerer has participated or no suitable offers have been submitted.

5. Upon the purchase of real estates when there is no public benefit admitting its expropriation.

6. Upon renting a real estate.

7. When the supply of materials, providing services or executing work is required to be performed in lieu of a defaulting or refraining contractor and at his expense, or upon cancellation of a contract.

8. In contracts involving transport or insurance policies on the shipped goods.

9. In cases calling for justifiable speed when the materials services or works cannot be so quickly ensured by the other methods.

10. When such materials, services or works are required by the Armed Forces and aim at serving such military purposes as can not be sought through other channels.

11. When contracts are concluded with public establishments or corporation or their affiliated firms without prejudice to Article no. 3 (B) of the present regulations.

12.

13. When the required materials, services, or works are needed for the completion of a certain project which is under excution through a preceding contract and if there are special technical and real necessities that require the contractor to continue performance of the new works.

14. When the materials, services or works are required for execution of works by trust.

b) The cases outlined in the preceding clause (A) shall be determined at the discretion of the Expenditure Authority.

ARTICLE NO. 34:

It only required that possible parties to a contract by mutual consent shall not be prohibited from entering into contract with the Contracting Party or with public bodies. They may be further required to satisfy all, or part of, the conditions stipulated in Article no. (10) of the present regulations and produce the supporting documents.

ARTICLE NO. 35:

a) A contract by mutual consent shall be deemed in force as of the date the contractor is notified of the go-ahead order after ratification is completed. Yet, the Contracting Party may decline to execute the contract any time before the contractor is notified of the go-ahead order and shall not be claimed of any indemnity therefore.

b) The contractor shall remain bound to his undertaking with the Contracting Party as ruled by Article no. (23) of the present regulations.

ARTICLE NO. 36:

A contract by mutual consent shall take one of the following forms: a) A contract clearly outlining the rights and obligations.

b) An undertaking stated in the book of conditions in which the contractor accepts the undertaking in accordance with agreed written conditions.

c) By correspondence that conforms to commercial forms when a contract is entered with foreign markets.

ARTICLE NO. 37:

Subject to rules in force that govern the procedure of delegating abroad personnel of the Contracting Party, and where necessity arises which the Minister determines, the Contracting Party's requirements may be obtained from foreign markets through special committees formed by order of the Minister who specifies the functions of these committees, the method of procuring the purchase and all other relevant rules without reference to the present regulations provided always that such contracts shall be ratified in compliance with perinent rules in force, if any.

CHAPTER VIII EXECUTION BY TRUST

ARTICLE NO. 38:

a) Whenever the interests of the Contracting Party so require, or whenever a speedy action so requires, or if it is not possible to have works executed through contractors, such works may be executed by trust and at the responsibility of the contracting Party.

b) In such cases as works are executed by trust, the Expenditure Authority shall issue an order of approval based on report submitted by the concerned committee and containing the motivating reasons that justify an execution by trust appended there to by the complete project file along with an estimate of the type of work, prices and other explanatory documents.

ARTICLE NO. 39:

An order approving the execution of works by trust shall be considered an implicit permission to call tenders, or conclude partial contracts by mutual consent or make direct purchase, for the supply of materials, provision of services or executing works needed for the project without prejudice to the rules of the present regulations.

CHAPTER IX BONDS & ADVANCE PAYMENTS

ARTICLE NO. 40:

a) A bid bond for each tender or call for offers shall be at the rate of (5) percent of the value estimated by the Contracting Party, or a lumpsum, and the performance bond shall be

(10) percent of the contract price.

b) The Contracting Party, subject to an approval by the Expenditure Authority, may reduce the rates of the bid or performance bonds provided that such an act be stated in the announcement and the book of special conditions. Yet in cases of direct purchase or a contract by mutual consent the bonds amounts shall be left to the discretion of the Minister as he deems fit for each case.

c) The bid and performance bond shall be in cash payable to the Contracting Party's cashier or by cheque certified by the drawee bank or trough a bank guarantee or bank transfer from a resident bank. Commercial securities can be accepted in cases of contracting with artists or artistic groups or those who provide designs or artistic works which can be considered intellectual production.

ARTICLE NO. 41:

a) Bid Bond shall be refunded by those whose offers have not been accepted. As for those unsuccessful tenderers or those with whom no contracts have been concluded, Bid Bond may be refunded once the results are declared.

b) Performance Bonds shall be released after the final acceptance of the supplies or services, but after the provisional acceptance of the works executed provided always that no obligations upon the contractor require further retention of the bonds.

ARTICLE NO. 42:

A successful tenderer shall produce the performance bond within a period of time specified in the book of special conditions and not exceeding 15 days from the date he is notified in writing that he has been awarded the undertaking, and then the furnished bid bond may be considered part of a performance bond if meanwhile the contractor furnishes the balance between the two bonds, if any.

In such cases as a bid bond was furnished in the form of a bank guarantee, the bid must be substituted by a new bank guarantee, of a value equivalent to the performance bond and the bid bond is returned to the contractor once the performance bond is furnished.

The Contracting Party shall retain the performance bond as a security for the contractor's good performance of obligations stipulated in the contract concluded with him and for deduction of any delay penalty that may occur or deduction of all other indemnities resulting from loss or damages affecting the Contracting Party in consequence to the contractor's failure to fulfill obligations.

ARTICLE NO. 43:

Advance payments may be made to contractors in accordance with relevant laws in force if the books of special conditions so stipulate.

CHAPTER X EXECUTION REMEDIES

ARTICLE NO. 44:

A contractor who fails to supply the materials, or provide the services or execute the works within the period of time determined therefore shall be charged a delay penalty specified in the contract or in the book of conditions seven though the Contracting Party suffers no damage therefrom. This delay penalty shall not be less than 0.1% per day of the global price, and the total penalties shall not, per undertaking, exceed 20% of the global price of this contract.

The book of special conditions or a contract for certain undertakings of special nature may state such a delay penalty below the said rates. The Minister may also issue an order determining those contracts whose special nature call for exemption from penalty, or determining a penalty by another form.

ARTICLE NO. 45:

In case an undertaking involves the supply of imported materials, and the relevant letter of Credit is to be opened by the Contracting Party, the contractor shall in this case submit to the Contracting Party and within the period of time specified in the book of special conditions all documents required for obtaining an import licence and for opening the letter of Credit. The contractor shall be held responsible for any delay occurring from his failure to present the documents within the period specified. Such delay shall be deemed subject to the penalties described in the book of conditions whether or not this leads to a delay of execution beyond the established period of time.

Should the contractor fail to provide the documents and information mentioned above and a period of 30 days has elapsed following the expiry of the period specified in the preceding clause, the contracting Party shall have the right to cancel contract in compliance with rules of the present regulations unless the contract or books of conditions otherwise provide.

ARTICLE NO. 46:

a) –

1. A contractor shall not be held responsible for any delay caused by the Contracting Party or by any other public body.

2. A contractor shall be released of delay penalties if he is purely a victim of force majeure which is beyond his control and only in respect of the period of delay caused by this force majeure.

3. A contractor shall be released of executing the undertaking if it becomes absolutely impossible for him to carry out the contract and if this is not due to any failure on his part but rather due to circumstances completely beyond his control.

4. If there are such unforeseen or generally exceptional circumstances or events as would make the contract execution, though not impossible, exhausting to the contractor or putting him in face of a grave loss, the contractor shall have the right to file a claim for a fair compensation.

b) –

1. The case referred to in A-1 above shall be solely resolved by the Contracting Party with the Minister's fair approval.

2. The cases referred to in A-2-.3.4 above shall be resolved by arbitration if not resolved in accordance with Regulation of settlements provided for in Legislative Decree No.18 of 15.2.1974. in case of local arbitration, the arbitrators may be authorized to promote conciliation.

ARTICLE NO. 47:

a) The expenditure Authority has the right to retract execution of an undertaking from a contractor and have it executed on his own account in either of the following cases:

1. If the contractor fails to commence execution of the undertaking at the scheduled time stipulated in the contract or books of conditions.

2. When the quantities of materials definitely refused exceed one third of the contracted quantities or two thirds of any part thereof if the contract provides for partial deliveries in consecutive lots.

3. If the Contracting Party has become certain that the contractor has committed an act of deceit, fraud or bribery.

4. If the contractor fails to fulfil his obligations or refrains from rectifying his error within the period of time specified by the contracting Party.

5. If the contractor fails to adhere to the timetable of work and it is feared he may not accomplish the contract as scheduled, particularly, where there is a technical or economic necessity for its accomplishment on the specified date, or if it is foreseen that the delay penalty would exceed the rate specified in Article no. 43 above or has already exceeded it.

6. If the contractor announces his inability to continue executing the undertaking.

b) The contractor shall be only once given notice that the undertaking would be withdrawn from him within a period of time to be specified in the relevant letter before retracting the contract as per clauses 1,2,3,4,5 of the preceding paragraph, and contractor may lodge his objections with the Contracting Party within this period. At any rate, the contractor shall remain bound to executing the work during the notice period.

c) The Minister, upon a proposition by the General Director, has the right to rescind this measure if the contractor furnishes adequate guarantees for the good performance of the undertaking and it appears that this is in the best interests of the contracting Party unless he has already given a go-ahead order to a new contractor.

ARTICLE NO. 48:

In cases where an undertaking is withdrawn, or a contractor has failed, the Contracting Party may purchase the material, have the services rendered or the works executed at the contractor's expense as following:

1. Through tender in normal cases.

2. By trust or by contract of mutual consent when a tender fails or if there is special technical or economic necessities that call for execution of works through other channels than by tender.

b) The Contractor shall be notified of the measures taken in accordance with A above.

c) If it happens that a certain amount of money was saved in consequence to execution of the undertaking in pursuance of A above, this money shall be the right of the Contracting Party.

ARTICLE NO. 49:

The book of general conditions shall state the cases where the Contracting party may intervene to support the contractor's workshops and at the latter's expense, or participate with him in their management. It shall also state the procedure of settling accounts with him and the ways exercising this authority in the said cases.

ARTICLE NO. 50:

If, after offer submission or during contract execution, there occurs a rise in prices which makes execution of obligations totally or partially exhausting to the contractor and if the contractor so applies to the Contracting Party, the arbitrators committee shall observe rules of commercial laws and norms without prejudice to the rules of Article 43 of the present regulations, and the contractor shall bear the increase resulting from price rise if it does not exceed 15 percent of the contract price.

ARTICLE NO. 51:

If there occurs after offer submission a fall in prices, the Contracting Party shall enjoy the same rights as the contractor does in accordance with the preceding Article.

ARTICLE NO. 52:

A contract shall be automatically deemed null and void in either of the following cases:

a) If the contractor dies and his personal qualifications are of due consideration in the contract. But if these qualifications are not duly considered, the contract shall not be rescinded for this same reason. Yet if the Contracting Party deems that the contractor's successor does not have the adequate securities for the good performance of the work and that the cancellation of the contract does not involve in this case any indemnity to either of the contracting parties. The bonds shall be released to the successors if there are not such obligations by the contractor as would call for their retention.

b) If the contractor goes bankrupt. c) In case of judicial Liquidation. Yet, the Contracting Party may agree that the contractor continue to fulfil his obligations if the court of law so allows.

d) If it is established that the contract has violated rules of Article 10-A4. in such a case the bonds shall be seized without prejudice to the Contracting Party's right to prosecute the contractor for indemnities to compensate for the damages affecting the Contracting Prty from such cancellation.

CHAPTER XI MISCELLANEOUS RULES

ARTICLE NO. 53:

a) Receipt of the materials, services, or works shall be acknowledged by special committees set up by the Contracting Party for the purpose, and the book of general conditions shall state the method of forming these committees and how they shall function.

b) The book of special conditions shall define the guarantees required to examine the consistency of the materials, services, or works to the contract conditions. In such cases and where necessary their receipt shall be acknowledged in two stages: provisional acceptance and final acceptance. The book of special conditions shall also state the corresponding rights and obligations in these stages.

ARTICLE NO. 54:

a) The expenditure Authority may order the increase or decrease of the contracted quantities at the same terms and prices mentioned in the contract without the necessity of concluding a new contract therefore. However the rates of increase or decrease shall be specified in the books of special conditions or in the contract, provided such rate may not exceed 25 percent of the overall value of each of the contracts for works, services, and supplies.

b) In case of increase, the contractor may be given an additional period of time proportional to the nature and volume of this specific increase only.

Article no. 55: a) A contractor whose mala fide or incompetency is established during undertakings performed in favor of the Contracting Party shall be prohibited from entering into contract with the Contracting Party by order from the Minister. This disqualification,

however, shall be temporary for a period of time not exceeding three years. But disqualification and prohibition from entering into contract with all public bodies shall be by order from the Prime Minister and at the Minister's proposition.

b) The prime Minister, as the case may be, may reconsider the orders issued under the preceding clause after the lapse of one year at least.

ARTICLE NO. 56:

a) Unless otherwise stated in the contract, a contractor shall be liable to the rules of the books of special and general conditions. The contractor's offer and all the papers and documents appended thereto shall be considered an integral part of the contract. By having merely signed the offer, a contractor shall be deemed as having perused and understood all these documents.

b) Contracts may not contain terms and conditions that do not conform to the rules of the present regulations and the book of general conditions.

ARTICLE NO. 57:

A contractor shall submit all applications and claims for cases of force majeure, unforeseen accidents or emergencies occurring during the execution of the contract or for works he considers not covered by the contract (including applications for extension of the contract period) to Contracting Party within 15 days from the date

of occurrence of the event leading to delay or causing the claim submitted by him and he shall explain the motivating reason of his application. The contractor's failure to submit his application or claim within the said fifteen days shall be deemed a waiver of his right to object, particularly his objection to delay penalties incurred on delay of execution.

ARTICLE NO. 58:

A contractor may contain a clause admitting recourse to arbitration subject to rules and conditions specified therein.

PART THREE RULES GOVERNING SALES

ARTICLE NO. 59:

A sale of services, products and works by wholesale, semi wholesale or in retail shall be effected in either of the following procedures:

1. Direct sale.

2. Sale by direct contract.

3. Sale by engagement.

4. Sale by auction.

ARTICLE NO. 60:

A direct sale may be effected if the sales are based on definite tariff according to the Operations System.

Article no. 61: a) A direct contract sale may be effected through direct communication between those persons authorized to make the sale and the buyers by any method of communication or through calls for bids provided always that direct communication shall be confirmed later in writing.

b) A direct sale contract shall define the nature of services, products, works, equipment, and commodities, as well as their prices, quantities, place, method and terms of delivery, modalities of accomplishing the obligations arising therefrom, the execution remedies, and generally everything relating to the subject of the contract and contractual obligations.

c) The cases, terms, and procedures of a sale by direct contract shall be defined in the Operation Systems.

ARTICLE NO. 62:

a) A sale by engagement may be effected when future dates are fixed for deliveries as well as conditions pertinent to the nature and form of the goods. b) The Operation System shall determine the cases, rules and terms under which a sale by engagement is made.

ARTICLE NO. 63:

a) A sale by auction may be made in either of the following cases:

1. For a sale of stationary assets.

2. For other cases where the Expenditure Authority decides to resort to auction. b) Auction may be public or under sealed envelope. c) The operations System shall define the conditions of participation in an auction, and the

documents that cover the auction and its type, and all other relevant matters.

Article no. 64: Estates that can be rented under the Contracting Party's regulations may be leased under

contract of mutual consent if the annual rent of the leased property does not exceed *ten*

thousand Syrian Pounds, but by auction if such rent exceeds this amount.

Article no. 65: A sale, or lease, to a public body may be effected by direct sale or direct contract or sale by engagement as is specified in the Operations System.

THE BOOK OF GENERAL CONDITION FOR THE UNIFORM CONTRACT REGULATION

Decree No. (450)

PART ONE GENERAL RULES

Article 1

The rules of this book shall apply on bodies coming under the rules of the uniform contract regulation.

Article 2

The rules of Part Two shall apply on import contracts, while the rules of its Part Three shall apply on works contracts.

PART TWO

Import Contracts

FIRST CHAPTER TRANSPORT & INSURANCE

Article 3

In all import contracts under which contracted materials are imported by sea, contractor should carry out sea transport for the contracted materials restrictively through the Syrian General Establishment for Maritime Shipping or under its approval, but with no prejudice to the contractor's responsibility towards the public body by virtue of the contract. No performance bonds shall be given back to him unless he delivers the public body a certificate issued by the said Establishment confirming that shipping is performed through it or under its approval and that he has paid it all due amounts.

Article 4-Air Transport:

In all import contracts under which contracted materials are imported by air, contractor should carry out air transport through the Syrian Arab Airlines or under its approval, but with no prejudice to the contractor's responsibility towards the public body by virtue of the contract. Documents required for releasing the documentary credit should include a statement issued by the Syrian Arab Airlines confirming that transport shall be performed through it or under its approval.

Article 5-Land Transport:

In all import contracts under which contracted materials are imported by land, contractor should carry out land transport according to the conditions stipulated in the books of special conditions, but with no prejudice to the contractor's responsibility towards the public body by virtue of the contract.

Article 6-Insurance:

When contracted materials are to be imported, they should be covered by risk insurance within the limits specified in the book of special conditions; such insurance shall be assumed by the public body in case of (FOB) or (CFR) purchase, and by contractor in other cases.

Article 7-Sea Transport:

Sea transport is carried out through one of the following methods:

A- FOB (on board of ship at shipping port):

The public body assumes costs of sea transport and insurance, while contractor assumes transport charges and risk liability of goods from the exporting factory till board of ship, in which case contractor should notify the public body about the arrival date of each shipment of the contracted materials to the shipping port at least one month prior to its arrival date to the said port, besides delivering that public body a statement on weights and sizes of goods along with all other data required for shipping within one month maximum from the date of his being notified of commencement order or opening the documentary credit.

B-CIF (on board of ship at quay of the destination port):

1- Contractor should procure insurance for the contracted materials restrictively through the Syrian Insurance Company from the shipping port till the destination port, but with no prejudice o the contractor's responsibility towards the public body by virtue of the contract. No performance bonds shall be given back to him unless he delivers the public body a certificate issued by the Syrian Insurance Company confirming that insurance is performed through it or under its approval and that he has paid it all due amounts.

2- In external contracts, contractor should open an irrevocable divisible transferable documentar credit to the interest of the Syrian General Establishment for Maritime Shipping for covering sea transport charges and other ensuing costs

3- Contractor should send the Syrian General Establishment for Maritime Shipping a statement on weights and sizes of goods at least two month before the first shipment date, while the Syrian General Establishment for Maritime Shipping should notify contractor on the credit amount and type of the required currency, after which he should open the credit within fifteen days from the date of being so notified. Should contractor be late in fulfilling his obligations stated in this paragraph beyond the specified dates, and then the Syrian General Establishment for Maritime Shipping shall have the right to defer the transport of the first shipment for a similar period, but with no prejudice to the contractor's commitment as regards the date of fulfilling the contract-specified obligations.

4- Contractor should notify the Syrian General Establishment for Maritime Shipping or its agent appointed for executing shipping about the date he defines for transporting each shipment from the shipping port at least one month before such date, besides submitting all data needed for shipping and required by the Syrian General Establishment for Maritime Shipping or its agents abroad.

C- CFR Destination Port:

Contractor assumes transport costs till the destination port, while the public body assumes insurance; sea transport is carried out as per the procedures stated in the preceding (B) paragraph.

D-Goods Delivery to the Public Body's Warehouses:

In this case, contractor carries out sea and land transport and insurance till warehouses and assumes all taxes, duties and charges due upon contracted materials till their arrival at the warehouse land, including obtaining import licenses and opening the necessary credits when required, unless it is agreed that the public body shall assume taxes and duties pursuant to the rules of Law 438 for year 1957 and its amendments. Sea transport should be performed through the Syrian General Establishment for Maritime Shipping and as per procedures stated in paragraph (B) of this article, while procuring insurance at the Syrian Insurance Company. *E*-In all cases contractor should observe all instructions and conditions defined by the Syran General Establishment for Maritime Shipping for assuring shipping well execution.

Artcle 8-Packaging:

In his offer, bidder should state goods packaging and type of the material used for packaging, whch should be according to the international rules of overseas transport. Contractor shall asume any damage upon contracted materials as a result of insufficient packaging. Pulleys, cntes and other packaging types shall be the property of the public body, unless the contract stpulates otherwise.

SECOND CHAPTER COMMITMENT EXECUTION

Aticle 9-Increasing or Decreasing Contracted Materials:

Subject to the rules of Article 62 of Contract Regulation, quantities estimated in the quantity list or estimative statements for the various works required in this contract shall be considered only as n approximate basis liable to increase or decrease as per the work requisites during execution; ettling account with contractor shall be made on the basis of the measured real quantities ictually achieved by him at work site for each of the works required from him under this contract, vhile adding or deducting the value of such increase or decrease to/from the total contract value is per the prices defined in it.

Article 10- Manufacturing Control:

The public body shall have the right to appoint a person or company (supervisor), at its own expense, to act for it in supervising manufacturing supplies and materials during manufacturing process. Supervisor shall have the right to carry out supervision, control and test processes at all times as regards diagrams, materials and manufacturing at offices and manufacturing sites belonging to contractor or factories employed by him, and to reject what he deems as contrary to the technical conditions; such rejection cases should be notified in writing to contractor or the manufacturing company, besides being notified to the public body; contractor shall replace rejected materials with others meeting all the required conditions. Supervisor or any other person representing the public body shall have the right to freely enter during work hours all places in which contractor or owners of factories employed by him manufacture or store any of the import parts.

THIRD CHAPTER RECEIVING

Article 11-Purpose of Receiving:

The purpose of receiving the contracted materials is to check the quantity and quality conformity of the presented materials to the contracted materials, as well as the conformity of the specifications of such materials to those required or specified in the contract, besides ensuring contractor's well execution of his required obligations. A- Contractor should deliver materials to the contract body at the place defined for such delivery

under the contract, or notify it in writing that materials are ready for delivery at the place specified for that under the contract.

B- After that, the public body shall notify contractor in writing on the date it has set for receiving and the names of the receiving committee, or on the name of the body it has charged with carrying our receiving outside Syria and invite him to attend the receiving process, or duly authorize whoever he likes to do so.

C- At the date specified for receiving, the receiving committee shall review contract and its file, and after knowing quantities, types and specifications of the required materials and being sure that contractor has been notified of the receiving date, it shall check and examine the presented materials and ascertain their integrity, flawlessness and conformity to specifications specified in contract, contractor's offer and correspondences exchanged between him and the public body, and generally in all the file documents and documents deemed part of the contract. In case of assigning another body outside the Syrian territories to perform receiving process, receiving materials should be done as per the conditions defined in the receiving assignment instrument according to the conditions specified in contract and books of conditions.

D- Committee or body in charge of receiving shall duly prepare a record including facts of the process of receiving materials, checking and examining them and the results of all that, in addition to the receiving hour and date, confirming the notification of contractor to attend the receiving process and the attendance or non-attendance of contractor or his legal representative, and finally the committee's recommendations justifying accepting or refusing materials, accepting part of those materials and refusing another part, ...etc. All the receiving committee or the receiving-authorized body shall sign the said record, in addition to being signed by contractor or his legal representative in case of attending the receiving process; in case of the latter's refusal to sign, the same record should mention that, and in all cases a copy of the receiving record shall be sent to contractor.

E- The public body shall notify contractor a written brief of the receiving record in case of non-attending the receiving process or refusing to sign the said record.

F- In case of signing the receiving record with reservation, refusing to sign it or non-attending the receiving process, contractor shall have the right to object to the contents of the said record within ten days from the date of his signing record with reservation or from being notified a written brief of the receiving record; the public body shall study such objection and advise objector about the result; in case of submitting no objection within the above-mentioned period, contractor shall be deemed to have accepted the public body's viewpoint.

G- In cases other than paying by virtue of a documentary credit, it is not permitted to pay out the value of contracted materials unless after preparing the said record and being approved by the concerned paymaster. Moreover, it is not allowed to give back all types of performance bonds or release the various guarantees unless after the final receiving, which should be carried out after the end of the guarantee period stipulated in this book or the books of special conditions and submitting a quittance from the concerned financial circles.

Article 13-Guarantee of Imports:

Contractor shall guarantee submitting imports as per specifications, characteristics and technical data on the basis of which contracting has been concluded; such guarantee shall include all contracted materials against any flaw or defect in design, manufacture or material, as well as against any defect or malfunction resulting from bad composition, in addition to including the well functioning of the supplies subject of contract for the specified guarantee period, provided such guarantee period shall be defined in the announcement, the book of special conditions and contract according to the nature and type of materials to be supplied.

Article 14-Contractor's Responsibilities:

In addition to the above and as a result of examining and testing made during receiving, contractor shall guarantee the exact conformity of imports to the technical conditions, contract conditions and the books of special conditions and their being free of defects and flaws, irrespective of whether the public body, its representatives or supervisor have prepared specifications, diagrams and plans related with setting up or mounting imports, approved that, supervised works at the factory or mounting places, controlled materials and manufacturing and endorsed shipping all or part of those imports.

FOURTH CHAPTER CONTRACT EXECUTION SANCTIONS

Article 15- Delay Penalties:

A- The delay penalty stipulated in the book of special conditions shall be imposed in case contractor delays submitting contract-subject materials beyond the dates set for that or submits materials contrary to the contract conditions and specifications without replacing them within the defined periods.

B- In case contractor, thirty days after the expiry of the period set for fulfilling obligation, does not submit contracted materials or an evidence of possessing them, then the public body shall have the right, with no need for any notice or warning, to buy contracted materials at his account, either through tendering, consensual contracts or on assignment, besides imposing the delay penalties as per the rules of item (A) of this article. The minister in person may, in necessary cases estimated by him, warn the contractor failing to perform his obligations within a period he defines- but not less than two days- without observing the said thirty-day notice; at the end of such warning, the public body starts taking the above-mentioned procedures.

C- Amounts due upon contractor resulting from delay penalties, price differences resulting from buying at his account or the various purchase expenses shall be collected from contractor's performance bonds; and in case these are insufficient, contractor shall be sued for such difference as per the legal rules in force.

D- Contractor shall have no right to claim price differences from the public body in case of any decrease in the costs of buying at his account; rather, such difference shall be considered as a right acquired by the public body.

Article 16-Rejecting Imports:

The public body shall have the right to reject all or part of the presented materials in case of being wholly or partly inconsistent with contract specifications or having any defect or shortage. In such case, the public body shall have the right to withhold rejected materials and keep them at contractor's responsibility and cost till he replaces or completes them within the period specified for him, and it may deliver them to the contractor against a financial bond. The delay penalties stipulated in the preceding article shall remain operative against that contractor till the date of delivering materials as per the specifications agreed upon in contract.

PART THREE WORKS CONTRACTS

First Chapter Work Management & Execution

Article 17-Work Program:

Within ten days from the date specified to commence working, contractor should submit to the public body a written program elucidating procedures and steps he wishes to adopt in project execution and defining terms during which he expects to finish each of the general stages included in contract. The public body shall have the right to request making any adjustment on that program required to its interest within the limits of contract rules and in harmony with the period set for executing the total works; contractor should abide by such amended program and observe it during execution, and he should not depart from such limits or change any part unless under the written approval of the public body. Should contractor not submit such required program within the defined period, then the public body shall have the right to have him abide by the program set by it under its option after notifying him such a program.

Article 18-Workmanship & Execution Precision:

All works required under contract should be executed in conformity to the requirements of technical charts and specifications and the public body's instructions as regards technical precision and workmanship. Contractor should immediately remove or pull down each work rejected by the public body due to `any defect, shortage, inexactness or inconsistence with the requirements of technical charts and specifications and the instructions of the engineer in charge of conditions, and he should repair or renovate that at his own cost as required to become acceptable. The public body may decide to accept such work but with deducting an amount of its price equaling the value of such flaw or defect, provided such flaw or defect is not gross and does not lead to breach the integrity of the installation as far as the technical and investment aspects are concerned. Should contractor, or his agent, refuse or delay removing or repairing rejected works which the public body, based upon its interest, has deemed unacceptable with deduction, as well as if contractor delays doing that within the period set for him in writing for that purpose, then the public body shall have the right to have the said works repaired, removed or renovated as it deems fit and deduct all costs it incurs in this regard from contractor's payable amounts.

Article 19-Materials & Necessaries Contractor Should Submit:

A- Contractor shall be responsible at his own cost for submitting all materials, necessaries, equipment and tools and all other technical fittings needed for carrying out all required works under the contract. All those materials, necessaries and fittings brought to the work site should be of the best quality and consistent with all the technical conditions and specifications required from him under the contract.

B- All materials, necessaries, equipment and tools brought by contractor shall be considered, since arriving to the work site, as retained to the interest of the project; they should not be used except in the works required under the contract, and contractor shall have no right to dispose of them or move them, whether wholly or partly, outside the workshop unless under the public body's written approval.

C- Contractor should take all measures necessary for securing the continuity of supplying materials and needs required for all project works in the form and quantities that ensure good and regular work progress as per the program approved by the public body, with no interruption nor delay; in some special cases, the public body may require presenting some materials and needs within a period defined in the book of special conditions.

D- Should the public body find that the materials, necessaries, equipment and tools brought by contractor for use in the project are unfit for work or inconsistent with the contract conditions, then it shall have the right to refuse accepting them and request removing them out of the work site and replacing them. In this case contractor should immediately remove them out of the work site and replace them at his own cost by other suitable kinds accepted by the public body, and should he refuse or delay removing or replacing such rejected materials within the set period, then the public body shall have the right to do that at his expense however that costs. Contractor shall have no right to claim any damage, loss, compensation, extending contract term due to procedures taken by the public body by virtue of the rules of this article.

E- The public body may, at the contractor's expense, examine any of the materials brought for use in the contract works through any technical laboratory in Syria or in another country whenever it deems that necessary.

F-The public body shall give contractor all documents that enable him to buy and receive materials and necessaries which distribution is restricted to public bodies, within quantity and term limits specified in contract or as estimated later by the public body; the use of such materials and necessaries shall be done under the public body's supervision and control.

Article 20-Materials, Necessaries & Tools Presented by Public Body:

A- In case there is a text in the contract or the books of special conditions obliging the public body to submit any of the materials and necessaries required for performing any contract part, the public body shall undertake delivering that to contractor gradually and regularly as per the work progress requirements. Such delivery shall be in the site explicitly defined in the said text; otherwise, such delivery to contractor shall be from the public body's warehouse located in the center of the governorate in which executing contract works is carried out.

B- Contractor should take care of keeping, transporting and guarding materials and necessaries received from the public body and use them exactly and carefully in contract works; he should keep a special record for them stating method, quantities and place of successive and regular use of each part of them in works. In case of any subsequent shortage, deformation or defect of those materials and necessaries as a result of contractor's negligence or misuse due to utilizing them contrary to charts, technical conditions or instructions given to him by the public body, then contractor should make for the resulting shortage or replace the deformed or defected quantity at his own cost however that amounts to.

C- Contractor should submit written applications to the public body stating now and then the quantity of materials and needs the public body has undertaken to submit and as required for works and the dates of submitting them, at least twenty days before the actual need for them in order to avoid any delay in their arrival and consequently any work progress interruption.

Article 21-Disparity & Errors in Instructions & Charts:

A- Prior to executing any contract part, contractor should check and ascertain the validity of charts and their conformity to each other as well as to all requirements of the book of technical conditions, price and quantity lists and other rules. He should ask the public body to correct any disparity, contradiction, shortage or error he may detect in those charts, technical conditions, statements or instructions given to him (whether such instructions are in writing or in drawing, and whether attached to contract or given to contractor later during contract execution). In such cases, contractor should abide by the final written instructions, which the public body asks him to follow during execution in this subject.

B- Should contractor not refer to the public body in writing as regards any disparity, contradiction or shortage in the charts and technical conditions, and then after executing all or part of the works, an error unacceptable or unavoidable appears in any of the works stated in contract as a whole or in details, contractor shall assume the responsibility of the consequences of correcting, pulling down or reconstructing the part affected by such error, and he should remove such error consequences at his own account however the costs are

C- The public body is responsible for the correctness of designs submitted by it, as regards both the technical and accounting aspects.

Article 22-Work Times:

Executing works required under the contract shall be carried out during daytime for one work shift in all days of the week excluding official holidays defined under applicable regulations, except in special cases requested or approved by the public body in writing, but subject to the rules of the Labor Law. Should contractor wish to work extra hours or during official holidays, he should apply for that in writing to the public body, which has the right to approve or refuse such request without showing reasons; in case of approving, the public body shall have the right to oblige contractor to pay compensations for officials, employees and workers for securing work control in the workshop during such extra times in a reasonable way; paying compensations for extra hours by contractor shall be through the public body's accountant or financial manager as the case is and as per legal established rules; contractor should also secure the necessary lighting for ensuring well work progress according to the conditions requested or approved by the public body.

Article 23-Procedures of Protecting Souls, Properties & Works:

Contractor shall assume the responsibility of taking all measures necessary and sufficient for preventing the occurrence of any damage or loss during contract execution upon any part of the ongoing works, needs, materials, supplies, movable or immovable properties found in the work site, whether such works or properties belong to contractor, the public body, other contractors or sub-contractors working at the site, or through theft, fire, natural and weather phenomena and the like. Contractor should also take all measures necessary for safeguarding the souls of workers, employees, people and animals, whether directly related with the contract works or not, against any damage or injury incurred upon them during contractor's execution of contract works. In case of any such damage, contractor shall be liable for removing, renovating or repairing such damaged part at his own expense, besides being responsible for paying all material compensations resulting from the occurrence of any of the said damages, losses or injuries to the damaged body, whether the direct cause of the occurrence of such damages is his own negligence or that of his agents or those working at his work sites. Contractor should observe all instructions deemed necessary by the public body for protecting souls and properties and safeguarding them against damage, spoil, fire and loss at work site; but none of those instructions shall relieve contractor from his absolute responsibility in making his measures taken for this purpose sufficient for preventing the occurrence of any such damages, losses and injuries that may happen during working.

Article 24-Hygiene Measures, Maintaining Order & Municipality Peripheral Spaces:

A- During executing works required under the contract, contractor should take all the hygiene measures requested by the public body or imposed upon him by the Ministry of Health at work site to keep it clean throughout contract execution. He should erect temporary latrines sufficient for site workers, besides maintaining and keeping them healthy and clean throughout work period, and removing them after completing work.

B- Contractor should ensure keeping order at work site throughout contract execution by means of securing periodic control in cooperation with the security forces; he should inform the concerned authorities upon any accident occurrence for taking the necessary measures, in addition to abiding by all free safety peripheral spaces and special regulations imposed by the related municipality or any other official body concerning any of his contract works, how to dispose of the residues of pulling down and digging operations and how to avoid hindering use of all nearby roads and passages during execution. Contractor shall be responsible for paying any compensation that may result from his violation of these regulations.

Article 25-Property of Relics & Materials Extracted from Work Site:

A- The property of any relics or materials considered of economic value extracted from or found in the work site shall accrue to the state. Contractor shall take all the necessary measures for safeguarding such antiquities and materials against any breakage, deformation, shortage or damage till delivering them to the concerned official body and receiving its instructions on how to use or dispose of them. Upon finding out such pieces of archeological or historical value, contractor shall immediately notify the public body and the General Directorate of Antiquities and cease working in the related area till receiving the necessary instruction on them.

B- In works related with contract subject, contractor should use all materials and debris extracted from or found in the work site if considered usable by the public body; the value of such materials shall be estimated based upon the price analysis table presented by contractor and deducted from amounts due to him, unless the contract explicitly stipulates otherwise

Article 26-The Public Body's Representative During Execution:

Engineers and supervisors entrusted with controlling and supervising execution of works by the public body shall be considered as its representatives in controlling all matters related with the validity of applying contract rules and executing charts, technical specifications and instructions it issues to contractor during execution.

For achieving this purpose, contractor should provide those engineers and supervisors appointed by the public body all necessary facilities to enable them carry out their duties in the best manner, and he should work by virtue of all instructions and remarks they issue under the contract rules; he shall be responsible for providing them with temporary offices at work site suitable for making those engineers and supervisors perform all official duties required from them till completing works.

Article 27-Inspecting Works & Examining Materials:

A- The public body or its authorized deputy, as well as any related official, shall have the right to enter work site at any time to supervise execution progress in workshops, plants and outside shops preparing or manufacturing any works, necessaries or materials related with any part of contract works; contractor should provide all the required facilities and help to enable them perform examination, checking and inspection as they deem necessary.

B- At any time defined by the public body or any of the related officials, contractor should uncover any part of the works which has been covered to enable them examine and check execution validity; in case the result of such examination shows that the revealed works have been correctly executed under the contract rules and that they have been covered under the public body's approval, then the public body shall pay all the uncovering and re-covering costs; but should the examination result show that the work has been done contrary to charts, technical specifications and the engineer's instructions, or in case it becomes established that the revealed part, despite being correctly executed, has been covered prior to obtaining the written approval of the public body, then contractor shall assume all uncovering and recovering costs as well as the responsibility of the work inconsistent with the required conditions. Should contractor refuse or fail to do the required uncovering within the period set by the public body, then the public body shall have the right in such case to do the required uncovering and deduct all ensuing all costs from contractor's account regardless of such uncovering result.

C-The public body or its representatives shall pay visits to the work site within reasonable periods to check work progress as they deem to be in harmony with the interest of the project, and the public body shall assume the expenses of such visits; but as for visits and checks that the public body has to do upon the contractor's request to check works already examined, then the public body shall have the right to charge contractor their costs and deduct them from his account.

Article 28-Contractor's Deputies & Controller During Execution:

A- During contractor's absence from work site, he should appoint his deputy in charge of regulating and executing contract and works as per the instructions given by the public body or any of its representatives during work for achieving the necessary requirements; such deputy should stay at work site throughout execution hours, besides being fully authorized by the contractor to act for him during his absence in all matters related with executing contract conditions.

B- The public body, in projects deemed by it to be of special technical nature, may stipulate that one of the controllers deputized by contractor for regulating and executing the rules of the concluded contract should be an engineer, a matter that should be stated in the books of special conditions.

C- The deputy and the controllers appointed by the contractor to supervise execution of the works on his behalf in all cases should be of good conduct, having enough expertise and technical competence of the works required in the contract. The contractor should, before appointing the deputy or the controllers to supervise on the execution of the contractor on his behalf at work site, inform the public body in writing on their names and their technical qualifications to get its approval on their appointment. The public body has the right to accept or refuse such appointment without mentioning the reasons. It is not permitted to change the appointed deputy or controllers except after getting the written approval of the public body.

D- The authorized deputy should be present at work site during execution working hours to get the instructions of the public body or any of its representatives during their visit to the worksite. The absence of the contractor's deputy from the worksite during the usual working hours without getting the prior approval of the public body shall be considered as discrepancy. In such case the public body may deduct from the contractor's due amounts five hundred Syrian pounds as minimum per each day of his absence. The special conditions books may state deduction of higher amount depending on the nature of the project.

Article 29-Employees, Workers & Professionals:

A- In execution of the works, the contractor shouldn't employ workers, artisans, employees and professionals who have no competence or good manners. The public body shall have the right to ask the contractor to take out any of the emloyees including the controller and the deputy from the worksite if it ,as its estimate, finds them incapable for the work. In such case, the contractor is allowed to reinstate those refused persons only after getting written approval of the public body. Using this right by the public body doesn't entitle the contractor to disclaim his general responsibilities or to claim any compensation, defect or damage incurred upon him as a result of that.

B- The employment conditions of the workers and employees for execution of contract's works should be in conformity with regulations of Labour law and International Labour Convention No. 94 set forth in Syrian Arab Republic , and contractor has to act according to regulations of this law and convention as well as he has to apply the Social Securities Law.

Article 30-Concession of Contract and Sub-contracts: The contractor shall not have the right to concede any work or any part thereof regarding the

works for which the contract is concluded to achieve and shall not have all or part of them entrusted to or sub-contracted with other persons such as sub-contractors but after having already

obtained a prior approval of the public body. Contractor's obtaining of such approval shall in no

case mean binding the public body to enter into any kind of relationship with these sub

contractors, nor shall it release the contractor from his technical, administrative, legal and penal

obligations and responsibilities imposed upon him towards the public body under provisions of

THE CONTRACT *SECOND CHAPTER EMERGENT CASES DURING EXECUTION*

Article 31-Quantities and Prices:

A- Quantities estimated in the quantity list or estimative statements for the various works required in this contract shall be considered only as an approximate basis liable to increase or decrease as per the work requisites during execution; settling account with contractor shall be made on the basis of the measured real quantities actually achieved by him at work site for each of the works required from him under this contract.

B- The prices stated in the Prices List on basis of which the contract is concluded shall include the wages and expenses of the workers as a whole, prices of the materials necessary for execution all works, as well as the legal fees and taxes, costs of transport, guarding, sentry wastes and profits and all various responsibilities incurred upon the contractor with all necessary tools, equipment, temprorary premises and all what is required to deliver the works in satisfatory and acceptable way whether it is stated clearly in the drawings, technical specifications and plrices list or tacitly comprised.

Article 32- The Amendments:

A-The public body shall, when necessary, have the right to ask for any amendment, correction, omition or adding any of the works required in the contract whether that resulting in decrease or increase in quantities of these works required in the contract. In all cases, the contractor shall be responsible to execute all amendments or corrections required from him by written orders during work progress with no delay. Should the contractor be delay in carrying out such amendments during the time period specified for him, the public body shall have the right to carry out this amendment on his charge and it will deduct from his payable amounts all expenses spent in this regard whatever they may be.

B- Any amendment or altering in any part of the contract works required in the drawings, specifications and quantity list shall be carried out only on the basis of written request or prior approval of the public body. And if the contractor carries out any amendment or altering for any part of contract works without obtaining the approval of the public body, the public body shall have the right to refuse it or ask for correction as required at the contractor's cost whatever the expenses may be. Moreover, if the public body finds that it possible to keep on such amendment or altering with no correction, it shall have the right to consider that as contribution without paying any amount to the contractor at settling the accounts.

C- If the amendments required by the public body during the work call for pulling down, removal or making any altering for any work executed as per the provisions of the contract, the public body has to pay to the contractor cost of the wrecked part or expenses of the alteration necessiated for the required pulling down or removal or alteration.

Article 33-Calculation of Compensation:

The calculation of compensation provided for in Art /63/ of Contracts Regulation shall be effected by a special committee formed by the paymaster. The contractor and the public body have to render it all the necessary information for studying the circumstances and the conditions surrounding the execution of the work. As well, both parties shall have to provide a statement for all the losses and damages assumed by either with explaining the reasons of such losses. If this committee finds that the losses and damages claimed by contractor are the result of his dereliction or breach in execution of any of his obligations or from his carelessness or non availability of the means nesecessary for him or from his mismanagement or his delay in carrying out the works during the time period set in the contract for unjustified reasons, he will not be granted any compensation in all these cases. The contractor shall not have the right to cease the execution of the works in all the cases provided for in Art./63/ of Contracts Regulation, otherwise he will be considered responsible for all damages and losses caused to the management due to this stoppage and he will lose the right to ask for any compensation.

Article 34-The Additional Works Not Stated in the Contract:

A- When the execution of works requires carrying out additional works not taken into account in the contract or changing the sources and kinds of some materials mentioned therein, the public body has to ask the contractor to carry out these works and he has to immediately start the execution. The prices of these materials shall be determined by agreement betweeen the two parties. But if the execution of these additional works doesn't need top urgency, the public body will not give an order for execution same but after it agrees with the contractor on the prices pursuant to a contract annex. Every work carried out by the contractor before getting a written order from the public body will be considered as a contribution by him.

B- If the public body has not charged the contractor to execute the additional works according to what is mentioned in above mentioned paragraph, it has to execute these additional works directly by itself by trust or to charge the contractor to carry out these works for its account against paying a commission not exceeding 10% of total actual costs required for execution of the work or to charge a third party to carry out such works and then the contractor has to render all the facilities and assistance necessary for the third party during execution of the additional works.

C- When the prices of additional works agreed on differ from the prices mentioned in the contract, the public body has to carry out an inventory for the works executed by the contractor included in the original contract. The contractor will be called to attend the inventory process on a date specified by the public body. But if he or his deputy doesn't attend, he will be considered as having accepted the inventory results.

Third Chapter Paying Out the Value of Works

Article 35- Measurment of the Works:

A- The works that are done under the provisions of the contract shall be measured gradually during execution and at completion of every stage of the project and before covering any part of the works not possible to be uncovered and measured after being covered. The two parties have to agree on the dates on which the measurements will be taken and that will be in their presence or in presence of their authorized representatives and they have to sign on. The contractor has to provide, on his cost, all necessary workers and facilities to carry out the necessary measurements.

B- When it is necessary, the public body has the right to ask the contractor or his authorized deputy to attend to the worksite on a date it specifies for carrying out the measurements of the achieved works. If the contractor or his deputy fails to be present at the site at the specified date, the public body shall have the right to take the measurements by itself and the contractor will have no objection on the correctness of the taken measurements.

C- All the works achieved as per the contract on basis of the units registered next to in the quantity list and the statements will be measured geometrically according to the technical methods applicable in Ministry of Housing & Building, in order to deduct as the openings from all the volumes and spaces and the wastes and damaged parts will not taken into consideration unless otherwise stipulated explicitly in the contract. Any increase in quantities or dimensions carried out by the contractor without a written demand or approval from the public body will not be taken into account upon carrying out the measurements.

D- In case of any dispute arising between the contractor and the public body regarding the obtained measurements, the public body has to settle it within a period not exceeding 48 hours from date of carrying out the measurements. It is not permitted to cover any part of the works subject of the dispute only after the public body will pronounce its final decision for this dispute or give its approval. The public body's decision in this concern will be considered as decisive and binding.

Article-36. Monthly Payments:

A. The public body shall make out for the contractor monthly statements of the works and preparations achieved by him. These statements shall contain the following: 1-The works completely executed which value is estimated as per their prices set in the contract. 2-The works not completely executed which value is estimated on basis of their prices set in the contract, while taking into consideration the extent of their execution. 3-The brought supplies prepared at the worksite, their quantities to be at rate of 80% of total of what were actually prepared of them and were conformity with the contract's provisions. Their value is to be estimated on basis of the current price of these supplies at time of making out the statement and their price estimated in the price analysis list, whichever is less. At time of payment, 5% against the outstandings mentioned in Article /38/ of this book shall be deducted from the statements value. And if the public body is obliged to spend any amount of these outstandings on contractor's account, it should complete the outstandings to be 5% of total of what has been spent for the contractor by deduction from his payable amounts, if any, or by claiming him to pay according to the valid legal regulations, as may be the case.

B- For the cases where the contractor is delay in his work progress at the speed and activity set in the schedule agreed upon, or the executed works are inconsistent with the contract provisions regarding the accuracy and conformity with the drawings and specifications, the public body has the right to deduct an amount from his monthly statements to be in proportion to the delay penalty or to the extent of the defect caused to the work.

C- Listing of the works and supplies in the monthly statements and settlement of their value don't, in no case, mean the approval of the public body on accepting them finally or waiver of any of its rights stipulated in this book or the contract, and the public body shall have the right to review the calculation of these payments and to settle any error or omission that may appear.

D- Contractor's signature on the monthly statements means his appoval on all what has been mentioned therein and every objection or reserve in this concern should be provided within ten days as from date of signing them with reserve.

E- The statements shall be paid out during 15 days as from date of submitting them to the management accountancy or the concerned financial management as may be the case, complete with their documents and legal conditions. Any delay in paying out after expiry of mentioned period not caused by the contractor shall be definitely added to the period of the contract.

Article 37-Final Settlement:

A- The final statement shall be made out within six months as from date of provisional receiving. The contractor will be called to sign this statement by a letter from the public body and he has to sign with reserve or without reserve during ten days from date of being called. If he signs without reserve, that means that he has accepted the contents of the final statement and that by receiving the value of this statement, he has collected all his payable amounts and he has no claim against the public body regarding this contract except what is related to the outstanding mentioned in the following Article 38. But if he signs with reserve, he has to state his reservations once for all in a clear detailed note mentioning the reasons of the reservation supported with all the evidential documents during twenty days from the date of calling him to sign; otherwise his reservation will be considered null and void. The public body will disregard any reservation provided by the contractor after submitting above mentioned note and will be considered as if not submitted. The contractor who refuses to sign the statement will be dealt with as who signs with reserve.

B- If any amount, debt or financial obligation becomes, pursuant to the contract rules, payable to the public body from contractor and not paid by him on request, the public body shall have the right to deduct it from the due amounts or those to be payable to the contractor and will be deducted directly from the statements and transferred to the benefit of the public body whether as per this contract or another contract out of his bonds or outstandings. If that is insufficient, it can collect the remaining amounts as per the law regulations applicable in this concern.

Article 38- Outstandings:

A- The amounts deducted by the public body as per the regulations of Article 36 from all the payments due to the contractor for the achieved works and provided supplies will be considered as outstanding kept by the public body till the works required in the contract are received and accepted finally.

B- The out standings will be returned to the contractor after having delivered the project finally, providing a quitance from the financial directorates, making sure of conformity of all achieved project works with the required conditions and non-appearance of any defect or shortage in these works till the final delivery.

C- The public body shall have the right to deduct from the outstandings the amounts spent for completing any shortages and executing any works in behalf of the contactor based on its authorized powers as per the contract. Before returning the outstandings to the contractor, the public body has to deduct any penalty or compensation incurred on him according to the provisions of the contract and this book.

D- During the provisional receiving, if the public body finds that the works achieved by the contractor have been executed satisfactorily and in conformity with the required specifications, it has to refund to the contrator at accounts' liquidation an amount not exceeding half of the outstandings in addition to bonds subject to paragraph/B/ of article /47/ of Contract Regulation and it will keep a reserve amount not exceeding 50% of the outstandings to be used till date of final delivery of the project.

Chapter Fourth Receiving

Article 39- Provisional and Final Receiving:

A- The contractor has to inform the public body by a written letter through the party supervising execution the date on which the works required from him under contract have been completed and on which he is ready to deliver the project to the public body provisionally. The party supervising execution has to provide the above mentioned letter with a footnote stating that these works have been actually or have'nt been completed on the date set by the contractor. Should there be any shortage, defect or discrepancy to the contract provisions in the works and necessaries to be delivered, the public body shall have the right to refuse receiving and to ask the contractor to complete these shortages, repair the defects and remove the discrepancies before considering such provisional delivery possible. If these shortages, defects and observed discrepancies are of the determined kind or can be repaired fairly easily and the exploitation of the project is possible, the public body, if it finds that for its interest, shall receive the works achieved according to the contract's provisions and record the shortages, defects and observed discrepancies with special reservation in order to either be completed and executed by the contractor during a time period specified for him or to deduct an amount from his payable amounts equalling, as per the public body estimate, the value of these shoratges and defects to be completed by the public body at the time it deems suitable.

B- If the public body decides to receive the works with reserve or without reserve, the receiving will be in force as from the date specified by the contractor for receiving, as per a written letter registred properly at the public body unless it appears that the works are not actually ready for receiving at that date.

C- Before delivering the completed works provisionally, the contractor has to remove, at his expense, all residues, debris and waste materials and clean all spots and dirts by the way accepted by the public body.

D- If any remarks about repairs or defects are mentioned in the provisional receiving protocol, the contrator is charged to carry them out during the guaranty period or during a period specified by the receiving committee. In such cases, the contractor shall bear the wages of the supervisors and controllers supervsing the execution of above mentioned repairs during the actual period of repair.

E- The final delivery of the project will be after one year as from date of the provisional receiving. The contractor shall remain responsible towards the public body during this period for any new defect or shortage that may appear in the achieved and provisonally received works during this period. He has to assume all costs of repairing and removing of these new defects and shortages. Maintenance of the project will be on his account no matter the expenses will be. Repair of the damages that may result from misuse of the achieved works by the public body during this period is not included in the responsibility of this maintenance.

F- All the remaining outstandings will be refunded to the contractor after completion of the final receiving, and the project will be considered as completed after settlement of its related accounts.

G- In addition to his responsibility during the guaranty period set in Paragraph (E) above mentioned, the contractor shall remain responsible during ten years for any basic defect appearing in the installations that may affect their soundness and be the result of bad execution or the contractor fraud.

H- The receiving committee shall be formed by an adminstrative order issued by the concerned paymaster including at least one technical member.

FIFTH CHAPTER PENAL SANCTIONS

Article 40- The procedures taken in case of discrepancies or failure in execution of the contract:

A- If the contractor ceases the works with no logical reason accepted by the public body and if the public body deems that the contractor has lagged, failed, neglected or been incapable in execution of any work required in the contract or has acted contrary to the contract provisions, it shall warn him on the necessity to be more careful and active and to abide by the regulations and conditions imposed on him during a period not less than five days except in urgent cases, stating in this warning the kind of negligence or failure or the committed discrepancies.

B- The warning sent by the public body shall be considered as a document confirming the ocurrance of the failure or the negligence or the discrepancy under consideration, unless the contractor provides during three days from date of notifying him the warning enough proofs to convince the public body that his failure or negligence is due to acceptable excuses.

C- If the warning period ends and the contractor has not perform the request of the public body to accerelate the work and to abide by the contract's provisions, then the public body shall have the right to take the following procedures: 1- It shall, on behalf of the contractor and at his expense, increase the number of the workers

and employees whatever their occupation or specializations and to purchase the materials and necessaries and carry out all arrangements it deems necessary to ensure the work progess as per the speed, accuracy , conditions and specifications required in the contract. The contractor has to pay all the costs and expenses born by the public body in this concern without having the right for objection on any of the procedures, prices or wages according to which the works have been executed and the materials purchased. Should the contractor delay or refuse to pay these costs and expenses , the public body shall have the right to pay them to their owners on his behalf with no delay and to deduct them from his due amounts or to collect them as per Article 37 of this book.

2- It shall give the order to stop the work at any part in which discrepancy has occurred and it will not allow the contractor to proceed in the work in this part except only after he removes or repairs the said discrepancy and abides by all regualtions stipulated in the contract. In such case, the contractor should not claim any material compensation or extension of contract's period due to stopping the work in this way.

Article 41- Delay Penalties:

Should contractor be delay in completing all works required from him under the contract in a satisfactory way, and he has not delivered them provisionally to the public body during the period specified in the book of special conditions or specified as per the provisons of this book, he shall assume (in addition to the other procedures taken by the public body as per Article 40 of this book due to the delay) a financial penalty, which rate is specified in the book of special conditions provided the daily penalty will not be less than one per thousand (0.001) of the total amount of the contract, and the total penalty for one undertaking will not exceed 20% of its total amount. All that will need no warning or notice as the mere delay will be considered as substitue for it.

Article 42- Provisions of Withdrawing Execution of Works:

A- When the public body decides to withdraw execution of all or some of the works as per the Contracts Regualtions, it will call the contractor to be present at a date specified by it to participate in measuring all the works that have been achieved till date of withdrawal and in carrying out a complete inventory for all the machines, tools and necessaries brought by him to the work site and all the provisional installations achieved by him. If the contractor refuses to attend or to send his deputy or to sign the statement after being arranged, the public party has to perform the work by itself and to send a copy of the inventory and measurement list to the contractor by registered mail to state his objections on it during ten days from date of notification. After the elapse of this period, the public body shall not accept any objection in this concern.

B- When withdrawing works, the public body shall cease paying out any amount due or may be due to the contractor for the works he has achieved or the necessaries he has brought to the worksite and it has to prevent giving back the bonds and outstandings belonging to the contractor, with its right to dispose or retain or use of some or all the tools, machines, Equipments, necessaries and the temporary installations brought to the work sites or installed at in the way it deems suitable to the interest of the project without being responsible for any losses or damages incurred upon contractor due to this retention, use or disposal. The public body shall continue the retention of these things after the works are achieved if it finds that as guaranty for its rights incurred on the contractor, but if a third-party provides documents of fixed date prior the contract's date proving his property for any of these retained things, the public body shall pay him its charge as from date of withdrawing the works according to the current prices or to the conditions agreed on previously with the contractor whatever is better for the public body.

C-The contractor shall bear all expenses and costs incurred by the public body for execution of the withdrawn works as well as all the losses and damages that may be incurred upon it as a result of performing these works.All statements provided by the public body regarding what it has spent shall be considered correct, and the contractor should have no objection on these expenses or on any of the prices, charges and miscellaneous costs spent for completing works and purchasing materials and necessaries and executing all other imposed obligations as per the contract's provisions whatever their value could be. The public party shall have the right to fine the contractor in addition to what is mentioned above with some or all his bonds or outstanding as penalty against the defect and damage caused to the public body due to withdrawing works execution.

D- The contractor should follow up the progress of the works executed by the public body but if such follow up appears to hinder and disturb the works progress, the public body should prevent him to do that for indefinite period as the interest of the works requires.

E- If the final calculation results show that total expenses of the works achieved by the public body on contractor's account including the administrative expenses don't exceed the amounts that could be due to the contractor if he had achieved them by himself at the prices stated in the contract, the resulting savings will be belong to the public body and the contractor shall have no right in claiming them. But in this case the public body will pay to the contractor the same charges for his materials, machines, equipement and provisional installlations for the period the public body uses them and within the limits of the resulting savings.

F- Before deducting any delay penalty from the provisional statements or deciding to withdraw the works from the contractor, the public body shall take its decision concerning the requests of the contractor as regards his delay in execution, a matter on which the public body shall have the final word.

Article 43- Partnership Between Contractors:

When the works are assigned to partner contractors, all these contractors shall be cosidered jointly and severally responsible towards the public body for all that is related with contract execution and all resulting obligations and provisions. The public body shall deal legally with any of those contractors as a representative for the rest of partners. Moreover, it shall have the right to consider any of them responsible towards it for receiving and executing the instructions or for bearing all the financial and legal liabilities resulting from contract. All correspondences, clarifications and other procedures, whatever they are, issued by one of those contractors regarding the contract works shall be considered binding on the other contractors.

President of the Republic Bashar al- Assad

GENERAL CONDITIONS ISSUED BY MINISTRIAL ORDER NO. 349 DATED 24 APRIL 1980

PART ONE DEFINITIONS

ARTICLE NO. 1:

Each of the following expressions, as incorporated in these regulations, has the meaning set beside it: THE MINISTER: minister of Petroleum and Mineral Resources. *CONTRACTING PARTY:*

Syrian Petroleum Company.

SYSTEM OF CONTRACTS:

System of Contracts issued by legislative Decree no. 195 dated 25 July 1974.

BIDDER:

Natural or Artificial person who has submitted a duly made offer for contracting. UNDERTAKING: The obligation of the contractor towards the Contracting Party.

CANDIDATE CONTRACTOR:

Is the one on whom the bidding has settled, or the one whose bid is accepted through demand for Price offers, or the one who is bound with a contract with the Contracting Party which has not been ratified yet.

CONTRACTOR:

Is the natural or artificial person who has been obligated with contract towards the Contracting Party.

CONTRACT:

Set of provisions and documents (including Books of General and Special Conditions, Specifications, Plans, Designs and Tables) and all other documents of the contracts with which the Parties of the contract are bound.

PART TWO GENERAL PROVISIONS

Article no. 2: a) Bidder must include in his offer his selected domicile in the **Syrian Arab Republic**.

b) Contractor should specify his selected domicile in **Damascus** or at **Site** of **work.**

c) All notifications, correspondences, Admin-istrative and Legal notices and summons which are sent by registered mail, telegraph and telex to the Contractor or to his Agent or Legal Representative at his selected domicile or which are delivered to either one of them are considered legally correctly notified. The Contractor is considered legally notified with such correspondences Notifications and notices as follows: 1- Immediately, if they are delivered to him or to his Agent or to his legal Representative. 2-**Within 48 hours** from date of sending if they are sent by Cable or Fax. 3-**Within 5 days** for domestic contracts and **10 days** for external contracts from date of

depositing same at the Post if are sent by registered mail. If notification as mentioned above can not be made for any reason whatsoever, the contracting Party is then entitled to post one copy of said documents in its advertising board and the Contractor is thus considered notified of same. The entries of contracting

party are considered as evidence of notification without the need to obtain his signature on same. Article no. 3: The Bidder is held bound by his offer for the whole period specified in books of Special

Conditions and Announcement. Article no. 4: The Contractor is considered apprised of obligations, delay penalties and fines when they fall due according to the contract or the books of Special Conditions without the need to take any legal action or proceedings. Article no. 5: The Contractor is liable for all taxes and fees provided for in the laws and Regulations in force including contract stamp fee and advertising charges unless otherwise agreed upon in accordance with valid laws and regulations. Subject to the provisions of exempting certain public entities from taxes and fees, it is possible in contracts of external supplies to include Special Conditions relating to: 1- Making one of the contracting parties bear customs fees and their attachments, various harbor fees, fees on import licences and fees levied on entry of the goods into the country and their clearance. 2- Making one of the contracting parties liable for consequences of amending the fees mentioned in above item or effects of imposing new fees. c) It is possible in external contracts to provide that the Contracting Party shall bear wholly or partly various taxes and fees which are incurred originally on the contractor. Article no. 6: The Contracting Party is entitled without recourse to legal proceedings to deduct all expenses and penalties incurred on the contractor by provisions of the contract from the amounts due to him or which shall become due to him, or recover or deduct same from his security deposits. Article no. 7: If the works are awarded to contract partners, all such contractors shall be held jointly and severally responsible towards the contracting party for all matters of contract execution and obligations and verdicts thereof. The Contracting Party can legally deal with any one of such contractors as being representative of the other partners. It is also entitled to consider any one of them responsible before it, to receive and execute instructions or to bear all financial and legal charges resulting from the contract. All correspondences and other explanations of any kind issued by any one of such contractors concerning the contract's works shall obligate all other contractors. Article no. 8: No Contractor is entitled to surrender all or part of his contract to persons, companies, organizations or any other entity not mentioned in the contract, except by prior written approval of the Contracting Party. In such a case, the original contractor remains liable jointly and severally with the new contractor / contractors for all obligations and guarantees assigned on his part by the contract. If the Contractor does not abide by provisions of this article, the execution of contract is withdrawn from him and provisions of Article (50) of this book are applied on him. Article no. 9: If the contracting Party's Authority and functions (relating to purpose for which the contract was concluded) are transferred to any other public entity, then all rights, obligations, and mutual undertakings between the two parties are automatically transferred to the new entity and the Contracting Party shall advise the Contractor of this in writing. Article no. 10: The Contractor should execute all written orders and instructions notified to him by the Contracting Party of its representative. If he sees that such orders and instructions exceed limits of his contractual obligations, he must submit his objections, reservations and demands ensuing from said orders and instructions within ten days from date of their notification to him, otherwise subject to being unaccepted.

ARTICLE NO. 11:

a) Contractor is not permitted to make any alteration, change, postponement, omission or amendment in the works stated in the contract except with prior written approval from the contracting party.

b) The Contracting Party is entitled during period of contract executing, to ask the contractor in writing to make certain amendments. If such changes obstruct the contractor's fulfillment of his obligations, he should inform the Contracting Party in writing which would decide whether the changes should or should not be made and notify the

contractor as such. All this during the period stated in the Book of special Conditions or the contract.

c) Differences and periods resulting from changes requested by the Contracting party shall be subject of agreement between the two parties.

ARTICLE NO. 12:

The Contracting Party may approve to resort to arbitration if so provided in the contract and in accordance with procedures followed in the Syrian Administrative Courts. Arbitration Committee is constituted by decision of the Minister as follows:

Councilor from the State Council to be named by Head of this Council or a judge named by Minister of Justice (as President) and membership of an Arbitrator for each of the 2 Parties. The said decision shall specify subject of the dispute and committee's compensation within limits of legal provisions in force.

The Committee is entitled to obtain assistance from specialists and experts whose compensations shall be fixed by decision of the Minister at the suggestion of the committee.

It may be provided in external contracts to resort to arbitration on terms other than those stated in previous paragraphs (A) and (B).

The losing party shall bear that part of expenses and fees of arbitration which is equal to percentage of his loss.

ARTICLE NO. 13:

A Calculation of compensation stated in Articles: (50 and 51) of Contract's System to be made by the Arbitration Committee mentioned in Article no. (12) above. Both Parties shall submit to this committee all information required to study all circumstances and conditions of the work during its executing. Both Parties should also submit a statement of their respective losses. If it appears to this Committee that the losses and damages asked by the Contractor have resulted from his default or violation in execution of any of his obligations or from non-availability of his necessary means or from his mismanagement or delay in completing the works within the period specified in the contract for unjustified reasons, then the Committee should not award him any compensation in all cases. The Contractor is not entitled to stop execution of the works in all cases mentioned in Article no. (50) of System of Contracts; otherwise he will be held responsible for all damages and losses falling on the Contracting Party because of such stoppage and he loses the right to claim any compensation.

ARTICLE NO. 14:

Syrian Legislation is the sole reference in all matters related to correctness of the contract and interpretation and application of its provisions as well as in every dispute arising from its executing.

ARTICLE NO. 15:

Provisions of System of Contacts shall apply in all matters not provided for this book.

PART III SUPPLY CONTRACTS

SECTION – I– TRASNPORTATION

ARTICLE NO. 16: MARITIME TRANSPORTATION:

Sea Transportation shall be made through the Syrian General Maritime Establishment which may grant exception to transport by other means.

If such exception is obtained transport must be made aboard ships not listed on the blacklist and according to technical terms guaranteeing safety of arrival of materials. The Contractor must observe all instructions and conditions specified by the said Establishment and the Maritime Agencies Company as follows: a) ***The goods are delivered FOB (on board the ship at port of shipment):***

The contracting Party shall bear costs of sea transport and insurance while contractor bears transport charges and risks on the goods from the exporting factory unit aboard the ship.

The Contractor must in this case notify the Contracting Party of date of arrival of each shipment of contracted materials to port of shipment one month at least prior to such date.

He should also notify the Contracting Party a statement of the goods, their weights, volumes and all other information necessary for shipment during one month maximum from date of being notified of opening the documentary letter of credit. b) ***CIF delivery of goods (on quay of port of destination):***

1- Contractor must insure the materials contracted on exclusively through the Syrian General Establishment for Maritime Transport from port of shipment to port of destination without reducing the contractor's liability towards the other party in accordance with the Contract's provisions.

Final deposits shall not be returned to the contractor until he has presented to the Contracting Party a certificate from the said Establishment confirming that shipment was made through it or with its permission or that he had paid to it all its due amounts.

2- The Contractor in external contracts should open a documentary divisible, negotiable and irrevocable L/C in favour of the Syrian General Organization for Maritime Transport to cover sea freight charges and other expenses involved thereon.

3-Contractor should notify said Organization a statement of the goods, their weights and Owners at least two months prior to date of the first shipment and the said Organization must notify him of the amount of the L/C and the currency of payment and contractor shall have to open the L/C within (15) days from date of his notification. If the contractor delays execution of his obligations mentioned in this paragraph

beyond their fixed dates, the said Maritime Organization may delay transport of the first shipment for similar period, without this affecting the contractor's commitment with date fulfilling the obligations fixed in the contract.

4- The Contractor should notify the said Maritime Organization or its nominated Agent in order to exefcute the shipment on the date he specifies for transport of each shipment from port of shipment at least one month prior to that date. He should also provide all necessary information for shipping which are requested by said Syrian Maritime Organization or its Agents abroad.

c) C+F Landed(on quay of port of destination).

Contractor bears costs of transport up to port of destination landed. The insurance remains liability of the Contracting Party and Maritime transport is done according to procedures stated in the previous paragraph (B). d) ***Delivery of Goods in Warehouses of Contracting Party:***

The Contractor in this case is responsible for sea and land transport and insurance up to the warehouses of the Contracting Party.

And he bears all taxes, fees and expenses involved on contracted materials up to their arrival on land of warehouses including obtaining the necessary import licences and opening the documentary credits where necessary, unless it is agreed that the Contracting Party bears the taxes and fees.

Sea Transport and insurance must be done through the Syrian General Organization for Maritime Transport and sea transport to be accomplished according to terms mentioned in paragraph (B) of this Article. e- At any rate the Contractor should take into consideration all instructions and conditions which

are specified by the Syrian General Organization for Maritime Transport or its accredited

Agent to guarantee the good execution of shipment.

ARTICLE NO. 17: AIR TRANSPORT:

Air transport should be made on planes of the Syrian Airlines or by its permission provided these planes fulfill all the technical conditions required for safety arrival of materials, along with

observing provisions of Israel Boycott office.

ARTICLE NO. 18: LAND TRANSPORT:

Land transport should be made by means of transport possessing all technical conditions

required for safety arrival of the materials. Article no. 19: Insurance: Imported contracted materials must be insured against all risks, within the limits specified in Book of Special Conditions. Insurance is borne by the Contracting Party if the purchase is on FOB or C+F basis, and by the contractor in other cases. Article no. 20: Packaging: Method of packaging the goods and type of materials used in packing should be in accordance with the International Rules of sea or air or land distant transport. The Contractor shall be liable for every damage on the Contracted goods resulting from insufficient packing. Reels, boxes and other packing items shall be ownership of the Contracting Party unless otherwise stated in the contract.

SECTION – II – EXECUTION OF OBLIGATION

Article no. 21: Increasing Or Decreasing Of The Quantities

CONTRACTED FOR:

The Contracting Party is entitled to increase or decrease the quantities contracted on in accordance with the provisions of Article no. (54) of System of Contracts and within the percentage specified in the books of Special Conditions or the contract provided it does not exceed 25% of contract's value and at prices of contract itself.

Article no. 22: Control of Making and Preparation of Contracted

MATERIALS:

The Contracting Party may at its own expense appoint a natural or unnatural person as "supervisor" to represent it in supervising the manufacturing of required equipment and materials to be sure of good manufacturing, with the right to do so at places of manufacture whether they belong to Contractor or the factories accredited by him. Such supervisor may refuse what he deems to be contrary to the technical conditions, provided he notifies the contractor or manufacturers in writing of cases of rejection as well as the Contracting Party. The Contractor must replace the rejected materials with others which fulfil all technical conditions.

The supervisor or any other person representing the Contracting Party is entitled to enter freely during working hours into all places of work where the Contractor (Manufacturer) makes or stores the supplies or any part thereof.

The supervisor is not entitled to exempt the contractor from any of his contractual obligations, nor does he have the right to order execution of any work which may delay delivery of the contracted materials or lead to payment of additional sums by the Contracting Party or introduce any modifications unless such is included in the contract.

SECTION – III – ACCEPTANCE

ARTICLE NO. 23: ACCEPTANCE: A*) PURPOSE OF ACCEPTANCE:*

Is to ascertain conformity of delivered supplies with those contracted on in quantity, quality

and technical specifications and to make sure of good execution by the contractor of his

OBLIGATIONS. B) *METHOD OF ACCEPTANCE:*

1- Acceptance of contracted supplies is done by an Acceptance Committee constituted by a decision of Head of the Contracting Party and should include one technical member and one from the finance department at least. If acceptance is to be out side Syrian territories, said party may form one or more acceptance committee or delegate one of the entities, individuals or companies to do so on its behalf. The contractor should be notified of this in writing.

2- Contractor must deliver the contracted supplies to the Contracting Party at the place specified for delivery in the contract, provided he notifies it in writing, prior to a period to be stated in the contract, of readiness of materials for delivery at the place so agree in the contract.

3- At the fixed time for acceptance, the Acceptance Committee examines the contract file and after knowing quantities and specifications and types of required supplies, it examines the submitted supplies checks them and ascertains their perfectness and being free from default and in conformity with conditions and specifications specified in the contract.

4- The Committee or entity charged with acceptance shall make an orderly report of minutes containing facts of process of receiving, checking and examining the supplies and results thereof as well as hour and date of acceptance, and notification to the contractor to attend acceptance process and his presence or presence of his legal representative or their absence. Finally justified recommendations of the Committee to accept submitted supplies, reject them or accept a part thereof and reject the other part, or accept the supplies with reservation on certain matters. The report of minutes shall be signed by all its members or by the entity delegated to make the acceptance as well as by the Contractor or by his legal representative if he is present. If the latter refuses to sign or in case of his absence, the report should so indicate. At any rate, a copy of acceptance report shall be sent to the contractor.

5- If the contractor signs the minute's report with reservation or he is absent, he is entitled to object to said report's contents, within maximum of ten days from date signing with reservation or from date notifying him in writing of the summary of the report.

The contracting Party shall study this objection and notify the contractor of the result. If the Contractor dose not object within the above period he is considered to have accepted

the views of the Contracting Party. But if he refuses to sign the minutes he is considered accepting its contents without having any right for objection to this.

6- Value of contracted supplies shall not be paid except after making this report and having it accepted by the Disbursing Master, nor is it allowed to return final security deposits and release various guarantees except after final acceptance which must be made after expiration of period of guarantee stated in this book.

ARTICLE NO. 24: GUARANTEE OF SUPPLIES:

The Contractor guarantees providing the supplies in accordance with specifications, properties and technical statements on the basis of which contracting was made. Such guarantee shall cover all contracted supplies against every default or deficiency in design or manufacture or supply as well as against all damages and deficiency resulting from faulty installation. It also covers good working of the equipment subject of the contract throughout the period of guarantee stipulated therein.

ARTICLE NO. 25: CONTRACTOR'S RESPONSIBILITIES:

In addition to the aforementioned, the Contractor shall guarantee – as a result of tests and trials run during the acceptance – the exact conformity of supplies with the technical conditions and contract conditions and books of Special Conditions.

If must also guarantee that no defaults or deficiencies shall appear therefrom in spite of the fact that the Contracting Party or its representatives has prepared the specifications, plans and drawings of construction and installation of the supplies or had approved them or supervised the works at the factory and places of installation or supervised the materials and manufacturing of supplies and allowed their shipment wholly or partially.

SECTION – IV – ASSURANCES OF CONTRACT EXECUTION

ARTICLE NO. 26: DELAY PENALTY:

If Contractor delays delivery of contract materials beyond the dates fixed or provided materials not conforming with conditions and specifications agreed upon and does not replace them before such dates, the delay penalty stated in the contract and book of Special Conditions shall be imposed on him with no need for any notice.

b) If the Contractor fails to deliver the contracted materials after expiration of 30 days from date fixed for fulfillment of obligation, the Contracting Party is entitled with no need for a notice, to purchase the contracted materials at contractor's expense considering him defaulting by any of the methods stated in the System of

Contracts, in addition to imposition of delay penalties as per paragraph (A) of this Article. The Disbursing Master is himself entitled in the cases he deems necessary at his discretion to serve notice to the defaulting contractor to fulfil his obligation within a period he fixed without abiding by the mentioned 30 days period provided it is not less than three days. After end of the notice period, the Contracting Party shall take the above mentioned proceedings.

Sums incurred on the Contractor from delay penalties, price differences of purchasing expenditures shall be collected from his earnings and final deposits and suspended sums belonging to him. If these are insufficient, he is asked to pay the balance according to legal provisions in force.

The Contractor is not entitled to ask the Contracting Party to pay price differences which may result from purchase of materials at his expense, as this price difference shall be Considered an acquired right of the Contracting Party.

ARTICLE NO. 27: REJECTION OF SUPPLIES:

The Contracting Party is entitled to reject all or some of the provided materials if they were wholly or partially in violation of the agreed specifications or if they had any defect or deficiency. The Contracting Party may in this case seize the rejected materials and hold them at responsibility and expense of the contractor until he replaces or completes same during the period it specifies for him. It may also deliver such materials to him against a financial guarantee.

Delay Penalties stated in the previous Article remain valid against the contract up to date of delivery of materials in accordance with the specifications agreed on in the contract.

PART IV CONTRACTS OF WORKS

SECTION – I– MANAGEMENT AND EXECUTION OF THE WORK

ARTICLE NO. 28: WORK PROGRAM:

The Contractor must submit to the Contracting Party within maximum of ten days from signing the contract a written program containing measures and steps he will take for executing the project and the periods during which he expects to complete each important stage comprised in the contract.

The Contracting Party shall advise the Contractor of its approval of such program within ten days from date of being notified of this program or ask the Contractor to modify it within that period, as its interest requires, within the provisions of the contract and to be appropriate with the time fixed for total works.

The Contractor shall comply with the approved program during execution and is not allowed to overstep its limits or change any part thereof except with the written consent of the Contracting Party.

If the Contractor does not submit the required program during the specified period, the Contracting Party may then obligate him with its own program, after he is so notified of same in due manner.

ARTICLE NO. 29: PERFECTION OF WORK AND EXECUTION:

Execution of all works required in the contract should conform with plans, technical specifications and Administration's instructions as far as technical perfection and good workmanship are concerned. The Contractor must remove or demolish every work rejected by the Contracting Party because of any defect or deficiency or imperfection in such work, or nonconformity with said plans, specifications or instructions of the Contracting Party.

The Contractor must reinstate it to its required condition and according to the specifications at his own expense. It is up to the Contracting Party to accept such work in its present condition after deducting a sum from its value equal to the defect, damage or deficiency provided they are not enormous or do not infringe on safety of the plants from the technical and investment points of view.

If the Contractor or his Agent fails to remove or repair the rejected works which the Contracting Party has refused to accept as aforementioned and if the Contractor fails to do so within the period specified for him in writing for this purpose. The Contracting Party is then entitled to repair, remove or renew the works in the manner it deems and to deduct all expanses it has incurred therefrom from the Contractor's credits and frozen funds.

Article no. 30: Materials, Accessories, Equipment Required From the

CONTRACTOR:

The Contractor is responsible for providing at his own expense all materials, accessories, equipment, tools and various other technical apparatuses necessary for completion of all required works as stated in the contract. All such materials, accessories, equipment and apparatuses prepared for the work site should be of the best types and should fulfil all the technical conditions and specifications as required by the Contract.

All materials, accessories, equipment and instruments prepared by the contractor shall be considered, when they arrive at the work site, reserved for the interest of the project and cannot be used except for the works and jobs required in the contract.

The Contractor does not have the right to transfer or dispose of same or part thereof outside the workshop except with a written approval of the Contracting Party.

The Contractor should take all necessary measures to insure continuity of providing the materials and accessories required at all stages of the Project in the manner and quantities which guarantee orderly progress of work as per program ratified by the Contracting Party without interruption or delay. In certain special cases the Contracting Party may obligate the contractor to provide the materials and accessories during a period specified in book of Special Conditions.

If the Contracting Party finds the above mentioned materials, accessories equipment and instruments for use in the project not suitable for the work or not in conformity with books of Special Conditions or the contract, it is entitled to refuse acceptance of same and asks for their replacement and the contractor must in this case remove them immediately from the work site and replace them at his own expense with other suitable types acceptable to the Contracting Party.

If the contractor fails or delays transfer or replacement of rejected items within the period fixed for him, the Contracting Party may then do so at his expense no whatever the costs are, and the contractor is not entitled to claim any damages or losses or compensation or extension of the contract period because of the measures taken by Contracting Party in accordance with provisions of this paragraph.

The Contracting Party is entitled to examine at the contractor's expense, any materials prepared for use in the works and jobs contained in the contract by any technical laboratory in Syria or in one of the other countries whenever it sees necessity for this.

The Contracting Party shall give the contractor those documents which enable him to buy and receive those materials and requirements which are subject to System of Controlled Distribution or which are available exclusively at the State; all within limits of quantities required by stages of the execution.

Article no. 31: Materials, Accessories and Tools Submitted by the

CONTRACTED PARTY:

In case there is any provision in the contractor or in the book of Special Conditions which obligates the Contracting Party to submit any materials, accessories and tools required for completing any part of the contract, the contracting Party shall deliver such item to the Contractor gradually and systematically to requirements of Progress of work. Delivery shall be at the site explicitly fixed in the said provisions.

If no specific site is mentioned for delivery, the delivery shall be made at Contracting Party's warehouses in the province where the contract's works are carried out or its nearest warehouse from the center of the work.

Contractor should safeguard the materials, accessories and tools he receives from the Contracting Party and care for them also during their transport and their protection and use them with diligence and care in the execution of the contract's work. He should keep a special record which states manner, quantities and place of use of each part thereof in the works gradually and systematically.

In case shortage, defect or damage in these above items after their receiving because of the contractor's negligence, mismanagement or violation of the plans and technical conditions or instructions given to him by the Contracting Party, he is obligated to replenish the occurring shortage or replace the defective or damaged quantity at his own expense no matter what they amount to.

The Contractor shall submit written requests to the Contracting Party in which he states from time to time the requirements of current works for materials and accessories which the Contracting Party was obligated to provide and specified dates of this providing. This should be done at least 15 days before such dates.

The Contracting Party may in certain cases include in books of Special conditions an obligation by the contractor to insure the materials, accessories, tools and equipment which are provided by the Contracting party in the Contract – with the Syrian Insurance Company during the period from their delivery to the Contractor and their final use in contract's works and jobs.

ARTICLE NO. 32: DISPARITY AND ERRORS IN INSTRUCTIONS AND PLANS:

Before starting the execution of any part of the contract, the contractor should check and make sure of the correctness of the plans and their conformity with each other as well as required by book of technical conditions and table of quantities and prices and other provisions. He should ask the Contracting Party to correct any disparity, contradiction, deficiency or error he may find in these plans or technical conditions or statements or instruction given to him whether written, drawn and whether attached with the contract or given to the contractor later during execution. In such cases, contractor should work as per final written instructions which the Contracting Party asks him to follow in this regard during execution.

If the Contractor does not communicate with Contracting Party in writing concerning any disparity, contradiction or deficiency in the plans and technical conditions and an error appears which cannot be accepted or corrected in any of the works of the contract in whole or in part, the contractor will be held responsible to correct, demolish, complete or reconstruct that part affected with the defect and he must remove that defect at his own expense no matter what the costs are.

ARTICLE NO. 33: WORKING HOURS:

Execution of contract's work is done in one shift during the day on all week days except weekly holidays and official holidays stipulated by regulations in force in the Syrian Arab Republic, except in the Special cases required or approved by the Contracting Party in writing and provided provisions of the Labour Law are observed. If the Contractor wished to work overtime or during weekly and official holidays, he should submit a written request to the Contracting Party which is entitled to accept or reject such request without need to show causes.

If approved, the Contracting Party can obligate the contractor to pay compensation for the staff and employees and workers to secure reasonable control of work in the workshop during overtime hours provided that payment of overtime compensation by the contractor is done through the Contracting Party's Accountant according to legitimate procedure.

The Contractor is also required to provide the necessary lighting to guarantee good working in accordance with the terms required or approved by the Contracting Party.

ARTICLE NO. 34: PROTECTION MEASURES FOR PEOPLE, FUNDS, WORKS AND PLANTS:

Contractor is responsible for taking all necessary and sufficient measures to prevent occurrence of any damage or loss on any part of current works, materials, accessories and equipment during execution of the contract and generally in all movable and immovable properties at site of work, whether such works or properties belong to the contractor or the Contracting Party or others, or subcontractors working at the site. The Contractor shall be responsible for losses and damages arising from his failing to take the measures mentioned above or from his negligence whether such damages has resulted from direct deterioration, collapse, theft, fire or weather and natural conditions and the like.

The Contractor must also take all required measures to protect lives of workers, employees, residents and animals whether or not directly related to works of the contract from any damage or injury falling on any of them during the execution by the contractor of such works. In case of occurrence of such damages, the contractor shall be responsible for removing them and renovating or repairing the damaged part at his own expense as well as for payment of all incurred material compensation resulting from such damages, losses or injuries to the injured party, whether the direct cause of such damages was his negligence or that of his agents or that of those working at sites of his work.

The Contractor must conclude an insurance contract with the Syrian Insurance Company covering his civil liability towards other parties from execution of the works. Article no. 35: Sanitary Measures, Keeping Order, and Observance of

MUNICIPAL CODES:

In the execution of the work required from him in the contract, the Contractor shall take all sanitary measures required by the Contracting Party or imposed by the Sanitary Regulations of municipal Codes for keeping the works Site clean throughout execution period. He must erect temporary toilets sufficient for all working at the site as well as have them maintained and kept in clean hygienic condition throughout period of work and removing them after its completion.

Contractor shall keep order at the work site, the duration of contract execution, in cooperation with the Security Authorities and shall advise concerned department if any incident occurs, in order to take the required proceedings. He shall observe all Regulations imposed by the concerned municipality or any other competent official authority regarding any of his works included in the contract and concerning disposal of remains of demolishing and digging operations and shall ensure continued utilization of all neighboring roads and passages during execution. The Contractor shall be responsible for paying every compensation resulting from his violation of these regulations.

ARTICLE NO. 36: OWNERSHIP OF ANTIQUITIES AND MATERIALS FOUND AT THE

Site of Work: All archaeological pieces of materials of economic value extracted at the work site shall be ownership of the State.

The Contractor must take all measures to preserve these relics and materials for preventing any breakage, deformity, damage or diminishing on them until they are delivered to the competent official authority, or receiving its instructions on method of using or disposing of them.

When finding such pieces of historic or economic value, the contractor must inform the Contracting Party and the General Directorate of Antiquities and should discontinue the work in the area until receiving necessary instruction about them.

The Contractor shall use in the works related to the contract all materials and debris found or extracted at the work site which the Contracting Party decided its suitability for use.

Value of such materials shall be estimated on basis of table of price analysis submitted by the Contractor and shall be deducted from amounts due to him unless the contract clearly stipulates otherwise.

ARTICLE NO. 37: SUPERVISION OF WORKS AND INSPECTION OF MATERIALS:

a) Engineers and Supervisors charged by the Contracting Party with responsibility for contract and supervision of works executing as well as accredited engineering offices shall be considered as its representatives in supervision of the true application of contract's provisions and executing plans technical specifications and the instructions it issues to the contractor during the work. To achieve this purpose the contractor shall provide those engineers and supervisors appointed by the Contracting Party all necessary facilities to enable them discharge their duties in the best way and he shall work according to instructions and observations which they issue in accordance with the provisions of the contract, provided that such oral instructions are documented in writing from the Contracting Party during one week at most.

The contractor is responsible for providing temporary offices at the work site which are suitable and sufficient for the discharge of the engineers and supervisors of all official duties up to end of the works.

The Contracting Party or its delegates and those concerned officials have the right to enter the work site at all times to supervise the execution process as well as enter into factories, workshops and commercial shops which prepare or manufacture any equipment, accessories or materials related to any part of the contract's works. The contractor shall provide all necessary facilities and assistance to enable them to examine, check and test as they see necessary.

The Contractor shall not cover any part of the works except with permission from the Contracting Party or its supervising representative after having them examined. The Contractor must at any time fixed by the Contracting Party or any concerned official uncover any part of the works which was covered to enable them examine and check its sound execution.

If it appears as a result of examination that the examined works were correctly executed according to contract's provisions and that their covering was made with approval of the Contracting Party, the latter shall pay costs of examination and recovering.

But if it appears as a result of the examination that the work is not conforming with the plans and technical specifications and the supervising engineer's instructions, or if it is confirmed that the examined part, although correctly executed, was covered before obtaining permission of the Contracting Party, then the costs of examination and recovering are borne by the Contractor in addition to his responsibilities for violation of the works to the required conditions. If the Contractor refuses and fails to make the required inspection during the period stipulated for him by the Contracting Party, the Contracting Party may in this case make such inspection in due manner and deduct all costs thereof from account of the Contractor regardless of result of inspection.

The Contracting Party or its representatives shall visit the work site over reasonable periods to inspect progress of work as it deems compatible with the interest of the project.

The Contracting Party shall bear costs of such visits, however for visits and inspections which it is compelled to make at request of the contractor, to inspect works which has previously been inspected, the Contracting Party is entitled to have them borne by the Contractor and deduct them from his account.

ARTICLE NO. 38: CONTRACTOR'S AGENTS DURING EXECUTION:

When absent from the work site the Contractor must appoint a responsible Agent to follow-up execution of contract provisions and to act according to instructions of the Contracting Party or any of its representatives during the work to achieve its requirements.

The said agent should stay at the work site throughout hours of continuity of executing and should be delegated with full authority by the Contractor in his absence concerning all that is related to the contract execution.

In project of special technical nature, the Contracting Party may at its discretion require the Contractor to have one of his delegated supervisors to be an Engineer for supervising the organization and execution of the contract's provisions.

The agent and Supervisors appointed by the Contractor to supervise the work execution on his behalf must be always of good reputation and sufficient experience and technically qualified in the type of works of the contract.

Before appointing such Agent or Supervisors at site of work the Contractor shall advise the Contracting party in writing of their names and their technical qualifications to obtain its approval on their appointment.

The Contracting Party has the right to accept or reject this appointment without having to show reasons, and the appointed agent and supervisors cannot be changed except with written approval of the Contacting Party.

The authorized Agent shall remain at the work site during working hours of execution to receive instruction of the Contracting Party or its representatives when they make visits to the work site.

Absence of the contractor's Agent from the work site during normal working hours without advance approval of the Contracting Party, shall be considered a violation for which the Contracting Party may deduct a specified sum to be fixed in the book of special conditions for each day in which the said Agent is absent.

Article no. 39: Employees, Workers, Professionals and Specialists:

In carrying out the contract's works, the Contractor shall only employ those workers, labourers, employees, professionals and specialists who satisfy efficiency and good conduct requirements.

The Contracting Party may ask the Contractor to remove any of above personnel including the Supervisor and Agent from the work site if it found them unfit for work in its discretion.

In such a case, the Contractor may not reinstate those rejected except with a written approval from the Contracting Party.

The use of the Contracting Party of this right does not entitle the Contractor to shrink from his responsibilities in the contract or to claim any compensation or loss or damage which may occur as a result of that.

The Contractor shall not employ or provide work to any of the Contracting Party's workers in any capacity whatsoever; if he does not abide by this clause, the execution of the contract is withdrawn from him and provisions of Article no. (50) of this book shall be applied against him in addition to depriving him of contracting with the Contracting Party for one year at least.

Terms of employment of workers with the Contractor in the contract's works should be in agreement with the provision of the labour law and the International Labour Agreement no. 94 valid in the Syrian Arab Republic. The Contractor must work in accordance with said law and Agreement and apply law of Special Securities in all cases.

SECTION – II– EMERGENCY CONDITIONS DURING EXECUTION

ARTICLE NO. 40: QUANTITIES AND PRICES:

Quantities stated in "Tables of Quantities" and in the "Estimated Statements" for various works required by the contract shall be only on approximate basis subject to increase or decrease in accordance with the related provisions of Article no. (54) of the System of Contracts and in books of Special Conditions, as per work requirements during execution. Accounting with the Contractor shall be on basis of actually achieved quantities, which were measured at work site for each of the works required of him by the contract.

Prices stated in the price list at which it was contracted shall be fixed and include and cover all wages, labour force expenses and values of all materials required for finishing the works as well as their fees, taxes, costs of transport, keeping, protection, depreciation, profits and all liabilities which may be incurred on the Contractor; also his requirements for tools, instruments, equipment, temporary plants and all which is required to deliver the works in a satisfactory and acceptable manner; whether this was clarified in the plans or technical specifications and price

– list or implicit understood therefrom. All this unless the book of special conditions and the

contract provide otherwise.

ARTICLE NO. 41:

The Contracting Party has the right to ask for making any modification correction, omission

or addition to any of the works required by the contract whether this leads to decrease or increase in the quantities of these estimated works. In all cases, the Contractor shall be obligated to carry out without delay all modifications or changes demanded of him by written orders during the work progress. If the Contractor delays the execution of such modifications or alteration during the specified period, the Contracting Party may do so at his expense and deduct the costs incurred no matter what they are from his account subject to provisions of Article no. (21) of this book.

No modification or change shall be made in any part of the contract's works required in the plans, technical Specifications and table of Quantities unless they are done on the basis of a written request or approval by the Contracting Party. Every change which the contractor makes in any part of the contract's works without obtaining the Contracting Party's approval shall give it the right to reject same or demand its correctness in required manner at the expense of the

Contractor whatever the costs are. If the Contracting Party finds it possible to keep such

change as it is without correction, it is entitled to consider it as a contribution for which it shall

pay nothing to the contractor when making the accounting.

c) If modifications asked by the contracting Party during the work require demolishing, removing or modifying a work which was completed according to contract's provisions, then the Contracting Party should reimburse the Contractor value of the demolished part or cost of modification required.

ARTICLE NO. 42: EXTRA WORKS NOT MENTIONED IN THE CONTRACT:

a) If execution of works requires performing additional jobs not mentioned in the contract or changing sources and types of certain materials mentioned therein, the Contracting Party may ask the Contractor to do such works and he should immediately embark on execution and specify prices of such materials by agreement between the tow parties. If, however, execution of these additional works does not require full urgency, the Contracting Party does not give order for their execution except after reaching an agreement on their prices with the Contractor, and every work performed by the latter before obtaining a written order from the Contracting Party shall be considered as his own contribution.

a) If the Contracting Party does not commission the Contractor to do the extra work as stated in the previous paragraph, it may itself execute such works directly through the "Trust Way" or ask the Contractor to do these works for its account in return for a commission of no more than 10% of total actual costs which the execution of works requires, or still charge a third party to do these works. The Contactor should then offer all necessary facilities and assistance to the third party during his execution of the additional works.

b) When prices of the additional materials agreed upon are different from the prices stated in the contract, the contracting Party shall make a stocktaking of the works of the original contract which were completed by the Contractor. This shall be made in accordance with provisions of paragraph (A) of Article no. (40) of this book.

SECTION – III– DISBURSEMENT OF VALUE OF THE WORKS

ARTICLE NO. 43: MEASUREMENT OF WORK EXECUTION:

a) Execution works shall be measured and calculated gradually during execution in accordance with provisions of the contract, namely at the end of each specific stage of the project and before covering any part of the works which cannot be inspected, measured and calculated once it is covered. The two parties shall agree on the dates on which measurement and calculation of the works shall take place in their presence or presence of their accredited representatives and shall be signed by them. The Contractor shall provide at his expense all works and facilitaties required for this purpose.

b) The Contracting Party is entitled, when necessary, to ask the Contractor or his authorized agent to come to the work site on the date it fixed in order to measure and calculate the finished works. If the Contractor or his agent fails to be at the work site on the date fixed the Contracting Party may do the measurements and calculation by itself and the Contractor does not have the right of objection to the correctness of these measurements and calculations.

c) All works finished according to the contract shall be measured and calculated on the basis of the recorded units including Table of Quantities and surveys by engineering measurement in accordance with the technical methods followed at Ministry of public Works and Water Resources, so that all opening shall be deducted from volumes and areas, and damaged pieces shall be disregarded unless the contract provides explicitly to the contrary. Every increase in Quantities and dimensions made by the contractor without a written request from the contracting party or with its approval shall be disregarded.

d) Every dispute arising between the Contractor and representatives of the Contracting Party concerning current measurements and calculations shall be decided by the Contracting Party within no more than one week from the following day on which the dispute arose. No part of the disputed works shall be covered until after the Contracting Party had issued its final decision on the subject of dispute or its approval, and its decision in this regard shall be final and binding.

e) Works executed contrary to the contract's provisions shall not be included in the calculation and measurement and their value shall not be disbursed unless an agreement on them is reached between the two parties.

Article no. 44: Monthly Payments: a) The Contracting Party shall prepare for the Contractor monthly statements of the works and preparations finished by him, which include the following:

1. Completely finished works which value is to be estimated as per the prices stated for them in the contract.

2. Works not finally finished which value shall be estimated as per the prices for them in the contract along with taking into account degree of their completion.

3. Preparations made ready at the work site, their quantities are calculated at 80% of their total actually made ready, provided they conform to the terms of the contract. Value of these preparations shall be estimated on basis of their current price at time of making the inspection and the price assigned to them in the price Analysis Table, whichever is less, not taking into account the preparations in excess of those required.

From account of the above mentioned Statements (5%) shall be deducted as "frozen sums" as per Article no. (46) of this book.

If the Contracting Party resorts to spend any sum from those suspended or frozen amounts at the expense of the contractor the latter must replenish it until it reaches (5%) of total disbursed to him, namely by way of deducting from his credits, if has such, or by calling on him to pay in accordance with legal procedures in force.

b) If the contractor is lagging in conducting his work with the speed and diligence estimated in the agreed program, or in those cases where executed works do not agree with the accuracy and conformity with plans and specifications as required by the contract, the Contracting Party is then entitled to deduct a sum from his monthly statements which is commensurate with the delay penalty or with degree of defect which occurred in the works.

c) Inscription of the works and preparations on the monthly statements and payment of their value does not in any case mean their final acceptance by the Contracting Party or waiving any of its rights stated in this book or in the contract concerning the works and the preparations. The Contracting Party is entitled through out validity of the contract and period of guarantee to review account of payments and adjust any error or mission which may appear therein.

d) The Contractor's signature on the monthly statement without reservation means his approval of all its contents. Every objection in this regard should be made in writing within ten days from date of his signing on the statement with reservation. His reservation is not considered if he dose not submit his objection during the mentioned period.

e) Disbursement of statements submitted from the Technical Department is made within (15) days from date of their presentation to the competent financial directorate, provided they are fully documented and satisfy their legal requirements. Every delay in disbursing after expiration of said period not caused by the

Contractor shall be automatically added to the period of contract. Article no. 45: Final Settlement: a) Final statement should be prepared within six months from date of temporary acceptance. The contractor is invited by a letter from the Contracting Party to sign with or without reservation within ten days from his invitation date. If he signs without reservation he is considered as having accepted the contents of the final statement and by receiving value of such statement he shall be considered as having received all amounts due to him with no further claims on the Contracting Party concerning the contract except for the suspended amounts discussed in Article no. (46) of this book. But if signed with reservation, he should state his reservation in one time in a clear detailed memorandum containing the clauses of reservation together with all documentation papers during twenty days from date of his signature, otherwise his reservation is considered null and void; after submitting

this memorandum no reservation is accepted from the Contractor. However, if the contractor is absent from attendance in spite of his notification duly to sign the statement, then the proceedings made in his absence shall be considered correct and he is considered as accepting the contents of the statement and no objection from him is heard. The Contractor who refuses to sign shall be treated as having signed without reservation. b) If in accordance with the provisions of the contract a sum or debt or an obligation is owed by the Contractor to the Contracting Party and the contractor does not pay the same on demand, then the Contracting Party is entitled to deduct same from the credits of the Contractor or from the same sums which will be owed to him or to directly deduct from the statements and remitted in favour of the Contracting Party, whether this is in connection with the present contract or with any other contract or from the securities or suspended sums belonging to the Contractor. If all this is not sufficient, it may collect the balance in accordance with valid legal procedures. Article no. 46: Frozen Sums (Suspensed Amounts): a) Sums deducted by the Contracting Party in accordance with Article No. (44) of this book from value of all payments owed to the Contractor for completed works and supplied preparations shall be considered as suspended amounts kept in cash until the final delivery of the works required by the contract in a satisfactory manner. b) Suspended sums are returned to the Contractor after he had made final delivery of the project and confirmation that the completed works in the project conform with the required conditions and that no defect or deficiency appears in these works up to the final acceptance. c) The Contracting Party is entitled to deduct from the suspended amounts those sums it spends on making up any deficiencies or for completion of any works on behalf of the Contractor by virtue of the powers authorized to it by this book. Before returning these sums to the Contractor, the Contracting Party is entitled also to deduct delay penalties or fines of compensations imposed on the Contractor in accordance with the provisions of the contract and this book. d) If at provisional acceptance the Contacting Party finds that the works completed by the Contractor were satisfactorily finished and fulfil the required descriptions, then it can return at liquidation of accounts a sum not exceeding half the suspended sums in addition to the retuned securities subject to paragraph (B) of Article No. (41) of System of Contracts and accept to retain a sum not exceeding 50% (fifty percent) of the suspended sums as reserve amount which can be disposed of on date of final acceptance of the project.

SECTION – IV– ACCEPTANCE

ARTICLE NO. 47: PROVISIONAL AND FINAL ACCEPTANCE:

a) The Contractor should advise the Contracting Party, by a letter to be registered in its chancery of the date on which the works required of him in the contract were finished and the date when he is ready to deliver the project to the Contracting Party on a provisional basis. The Contracting Party should forward this letter within one week maximum from its registration date to the Executive Supervisory unit in order to see if the works were actually finished on the date specified by the Contactor or on another date. The Contracting Party is entitled to refuse acceptance of the works or requirements being delivered if it finds in them any shortage, defect or violation of contract conditions and to ask the Contractor to make up these shortages and repair the defects and remove the violations before considering the provisional acceptance as possible. If the shortages, deficiencies, defects and violations are found by the Contracting Party to be a specific type or can easily be repaired with possibility of utilizing the project, it may accept the works completed in accordance with contract's provisions and register a special reservation on the observed shortages, defects, violations so that they are either completed and corrected by the contractor during a period fixed for him by the Contracting Party or have a sum deducted from his credits which is equal, in Contracting Party's estimation to the value of these defects and shortages, which it would then complete by itself at the time it sees fit.

b) If the Contracting Party decided to accept the works with or without reservation, the acceptance shall be considered valid from the date fixed by the Contractor for such acceptance as per a letter registered duly with the Contracting Party unless it appears that the works were not actually ready for acceptance on that date.

c) Before delivering the completed works on a provisional basis, the Contactor must remove all debris, remanents and unwanted soil and take away all spots and dirts at his own expense in the way considered satisfactory by the Contracting Party.

d) If the provisional acceptance reports contain observations of repairs or defects, the contractor is charged to complete same within period of guarantee or during a period fixed by the acceptance Committee, and he shall have to bear, in such cases, wages of Supervisors who supervise the above mentioned repairs throughout period of repair.

e) The project shall be delivered on a final basis after one full year from date of the provisional

acceptance, if no other period was agreed upon. The Contractor shall remain responsible towards the Contracting Party throughout this period for any defect or new deficiency which may appear in the completed works which have been provisionally accepted during that period. He shall have to pay for all requirements of repair and removal of these defects, completion of the new shortages and project's maintenance whatever they amount to at his own expense. Repair of damages arising from the Contacting Party's misuse of the completed works during that period shall be outside the above maintained maintenance responsibility.

f) Suspended amounts or their Balance shall be returned to the Contactor upon final acceptance, after completion of settlement of all accounts of the project, it will be considered as finished.

g) In addition to Contactor's responsibility during the guarantee period stated in paragraph (E) above he shall remain responsible for (10) years for any basic subsequent defect which may affect their safety having been the result of the Contactor's fraud of their bad execution.

h) The Acceptance Committee shall be constituted by the Disbursing Master provided it includes amongst the members at least one technical and one member from the finance department.

SECTION – V– PENALTY CLAUSES

ARTICLE NO. 48: PROCEEDINGS IN CASE OF VIOLATION OR DEFAULT IN

Executing the Contract: a) If the Contractor stopped the works without a reasonable cause accepted by the Contracting Party, or if the latter finds that the Contactor had slowed, neglected, defaulted or been unable in executing any of the works required of him by the Contractor, or if he had, during execution of the work, violated any of the contractor's provisions, it may notify him of necessity to multiply his interest and activity and to abide by the provisions and conditions required of him. The Contractor must make up for this during a maximum period of five days from notifying him, except for urgent situations in which the Contracting Party may specify a shorter period for this make up, and the Contracting Party should state in the warning notice the type of negligence or default or violations which occurred. b) The notice served by the Contracting Party shall be considered a document confirming occurrence of the default, negligence or violation unless the contractor submits, within three days from date of notification, sufficient proofs to the satisfaction of the Contracting Party that default or negligence was caused by a justified excuse. c) If the period of notice expires before the Contractor's fulfillment of the Contracting Party's demands for expediting the work and abiding by the terms of the contract, the Contracting Party is then entitled to take the following proceedings:

1. Performing the following on behalf and at the expense of the Contractor: increasing the number of workers and employees of whatever specialty and occupation; purchasing materials, accessories and requirements: and taking all measures it deems necessary to insure the accuracy, conditions and descriptions of the work process as required by the

2. contract. The Contractor is obligated to pay all costs and expenses incurred by the Contracting Party in this regard and shall have no right of objection to any of the measures, prices or wages on the basis of which the Contracting Party executes the works. If the Contractor fails to pay these costs and expenses, the Contracting Party shall be entitled to pay them to these concerned on his behalf, without delay and shall have them deducted from his earnings, suspended sums and securities. If the latter are not sufficient, the amounts shall be collected in accordance with laws and regulations in force.

2. The Contracting Party is entitled to order suspension of work in any part in which observed violation occurs and not to allow the Contractor to continue the work in that part expect after removing or correcting that violation and abiding again by all provisions of the contract. The Contractor may not in such a case make any claim for material compensation or for extension of contract duration because of suspension of work in such manner.

ARTICLE NO. 49: DELAY PENALTIES:

In case the Contractor is late in completing all the works required of him by the contract beyond the fixed date, a delay penalty shall be imposed on him as provided in contract, and in addition to the proceedings mentioned in the previous Article, without need for any notice or notification since the delay is by itself considered as standing in its stead.

ARTICLE NO. 50: WITHDRAWING THE CONTRACT EXECUTION AND ITS PROVISIONS:

Withdrawing the contract execution from the Contractor means execution at his expense of all

or part of the works directly by the Contracting Party by the "Trust Method" or through another

Contractor considering that this shall not set a limit on the responsibilities and obligations

imposed on the Contractor by provisions of the contract.

a) When the Contracting Party decides to withdraw execution of all or part of the works according to provisions of System of contracts, it invites the Contractor to attend a meeting on a date it fixes in order to participate in measurement of all the works completed up to date of withdrawal and for making a complete stocktaking of all machines, equipment, instruments, accessories, materials, and apparatuses which the Contractor had brought to the work site as well as all temporary plants which he had installed there. If the Contractor refuses to attend or to delegate an agent on his behalf or if he declines to sign the statement (manifest) after its preparation, the Contracting Party is then entitled to do the job by itself and shall send a copy of the prepared stocktaking and list of measurements to the Contractor by registered mail in order to make his objections within (ten) days from date of his notification. After expiry of this period, the Contracting Party shall not accept any objection in this regard.

b) Upon withdrawing execution of the works, the Contracting Party may stop disbursement of any sum owed or shall be owed to the Contactor for works which he had completed or accessories he had brought to the work site and to prevent returning of securities and suspended money to him and to dispose with some or all the instruments, machines, equipment, accessories, temporary plants brought to the work site or installed there or to test and utilize them in the way it sees fit to the interest of the project without being responsible for any losses of damages which may be caused to the Contractor as a result of this seizure, use or disposal. The contracting Party may continue seizure of all these items after completion of the works, if it finds in this a guarantee for its rights incurred on the Contractor. But if another person proves his ownership of any of the seized items with documents bearing a fixed date preceding that of the contract, the Contracting Party may pay him their rents from the date on which the withdrawal of the works took place in accordance with the terms previously agreed on with the Contactor and at the current prices if no such previous agreement existed with the Contractor.

c) Contractor shall bear all costs and expenses sustained by the Contracting Party for completion of the withdrawn works as well as all losses and damages which it suffers as a result of its performance of these works. All the statements submitted by the Contracting Party concerning these expenditures shall be considered correct and the Contractor has no right to make objection on these expenditures or on any of the prices, wages and miscellaneous expenses disbursed to complete the works, purchase of materials and accessories and carrying out of all other obligations

imposed by the contract no matter how much they amount to. In addition to the above mentioned, the Contacting Party may penalize the Contractor with some or all of his securities or suspended sums as a sort of penalty against the loss and damage it has suffered because of withdrawing the execution of works.

d) If as a result of the final accounting it appears that the total of costs of works done by the Contracting Party at the expense of the Contractor, including the Administration expenses, is less than that sum which the Contractor would have been entitled to, had he himself performed them at the prices stated in the contract, then the saving realized shall belong to the Contracting Party and the contactor shall not be entitled to claim it, knowing that in such a case the Contracting party pays to Contractor "like rent" for the instruments, machines, equipment and temporary plants which belong to him for the period of the use by the Contracting Party within the limits of the realized saving.

e) During execution of the withdrawn works, the Contracting Party is entitled to return all or some of the remaining parts to contractor's charge, if it is convinced of removal of the causes which led to such withdrawal of the works.

GENERAL CONDITIONS ISSUED BY MINISTRIAL ORDER NO. 349 DATED 24 APRIL 1980

PART ONE DEFINITIONS

ARTICLE NO. 1:

Each of the following expressions, as incorporated in these regulations, has the meaning set beside it: THE MINISTER: minister of Petroleum and Mineral Resources. *CONTRACTING PARTY:*

Syrian Petroleum Company.

SYSTEM OF CONTRACTS:

System of Contracts issued by legislative Decree no. 195 dated 25 July 1974.

BIDDER:

Natural or Artificial person who has submitted a duly made offer for contracting. UNDERTAKING: The obligation of the contractor towards the Contracting Party.

CANDIDATE CONTRACTOR:

Is the one on whom the bidding has settled, or the one whose bid is accepted through demand for Price offers, or the one who is bound with a contract with the Contracting Party which has not been ratified yet.

CONTRACTOR:

Is the natural or artificial person who has been obligated with contract towards the Contracting Party.

CONTRACT:

Set of provisions and documents (including Books of General and Special Conditions, Specifications, Plans, Designs and Tables) and all other documents of the contracts with which the Parties of the contract are bound.

PART TWO GENERAL PROVISIONS

Article no. 2: a) Bidder must include in his offer his selected domicile in the **Syrian Arab Republic**.

b) Contractor should specify his selected domicile in **Damascus** or at **Site** of **work.**

c) All notifications, correspondences, Admin-istrative and Legal notices and summons which are sent by registered mail, telegraph and telex to the Contractor or to his Agent or Legal Representative at his selected domicile or which are delivered to either one of them are considered legally correctly notified. The Contractor is considered legally notified with such correspondences Notifications and notices as follows: 1- Immediately, if they are delivered to him or to his Agent or to his legal Representative. 2-**Within 48 hours** from date of sending if they are sent by Cable or Fax. 3-**Within 5 days** for domestic contracts and **10 days** for external contracts from date of

depositing same at the Post if are sent by registered mail. If notification as mentioned above can not be made for any reason whatsoever, the contracting Party is then entitled to post one copy of said documents in its advertising board and the Contractor is thus considered notified of same. The entries of contracting

party are considered as evidence of notification without the need to obtain his signature

on same. Article no. 3: The Bidder is held bound by his offer for the whole period specified in books of Special

Conditions and Announcement. Article no. 4: The Contractor is considered apprised of obligations, delay penalties and fines when they fall due according to the contract or the books of Special Conditions without the need to take any legal action or proceedings. Article no. 5: The Contractor is liable for all taxes and fees provided for in the laws and Regulations in force including contract stamp fee and advertising charges unless otherwise agreed upon in accordance with valid laws and regulations. Subject to the provisions of exempting certain public entities from taxes and fees, it is possible in contracts of external supplies to include Special Conditions relating to: 1- Making one of the contracting parties bear customs fees and their attachments, various harbor fees, fees on import licences and fees levied on entry of the goods into the country and their clearance. 2- Making one of the contracting parties liable for consequences of amending the fees mentioned in above item or effects of imposing new fees. c) It is possible in external contracts to provide that the Contracting Party shall bear wholly or partly various taxes and fees which are incurred originally on the contractor. Article no. 6: The Contracting Party is entitled without recourse to legal proceedings to deduct all expenses and penalties incurred on the contractor by provisions of the contract from the amounts due to him or which shall become due to him, or recover or deduct same from his security deposits. Article no. 7: If the works are awarded to contract partners, all such contractors shall be held jointly and severally responsible towards the contracting party for all matters of contract execution and obligations and verdicts thereof. The Contracting Party can legally deal with any one of such contractors as being representative of the other partners. It is also entitled to consider any one of them responsible before it, to receive and execute instructions or to bear all financial and legal charges resulting from the contract. All correspondences and other explanations of any kind issued by any one of such contractors concerning the contract's works shall obligate all other contractors. Article no. 8: No Contractor is entitled to surrender all or part of his contract to persons, companies, organizations or any other entity not mentioned in the contract, except by prior written approval of the Contracting Party. In such a case, the original contractor remains liable jointly and severally with the new contractor / contractors for all obligations and guarantees assigned on his part by the contract. If the Contractor does not abide by provisions of this article, the execution of contract is withdrawn from him and provisions of Article (50) of this book are applied on him. Article no. 9: If the contracting Party's Authority and functions (relating to purpose for which the contract was concluded) are transferred to any other public entity, then all rights, obligations, and mutual undertakings between the two parties are automatically transferred to the new entity and the Contracting Party shall advise the Contractor of this in writing. Article no. 10: The Contractor should execute all written orders and instructions notified to him by the Contracting Party of its representative. If he sees that such orders and instructions exceed limits of his contractual obligations, he must submit his objections, reservations and demands ensuing from said orders and instructions within ten days from date of their notification to him, otherwise subject to being unaccepted.

ARTICLE NO. 11:

a) Contractor is not permitted to make any alteration, change, postponement, omission or amendment in the works stated in the contract except with prior written approval from the contracting party.

b) The Contracting Party is entitled during period of contract executing, to ask the contractor in writing to make certain amendments. If such changes obstruct the contractor's fulfillment of his obligations, he should inform the Contracting Party in writing which would decide whether the changes should or should not be made and notify the

contractor as such. All this during the period stated in the Book of special Conditions or the contract.

c) Differences and periods resulting from changes requested by the Contracting party shall be subject of agreement between the two parties.

ARTICLE NO. 12:

The Contracting Party may approve to resort to arbitration if so provided in the contract and in accordance with procedures followed in the Syrian Administrative Courts. Arbitration Committee is constituted by decision of the Minister as follows:

Councilor from the State Council to be named by Head of this Council or a judge named by Minister of Justice (as President) and membership of an Arbitrator for each of the 2 Parties. The said decision shall specify subject of the dispute and committee's compensation within limits of legal provisions in force.

The Committee is entitled to obtain assistance from specialists and experts whose compensations shall be fixed by decision of the Minister at the suggestion of the committee.

It may be provided in external contracts to resort to arbitration on terms other than those stated in previous paragraphs (A) and (B).

The losing party shall bear that part of expenses and fees of arbitration which is equal to percentage of his loss.

ARTICLE NO. 13:

A Calculation of compensation stated in Articles: (50 and 51) of Contract's System to be made by the Arbitration Committee mentioned in Article no. (12) above. Both Parties shall submit to this committee all information required to study all circumstances and conditions of the work during its executing. Both Parties should also submit a statement of their respective losses. If it appears to this Committee that the losses and damages asked by the Contractor have resulted from his default or violation in execution of any of his obligations or from non-availability of his necessary means or from his mismanagement or delay in completing the works within the period specified in the contract for unjustified reasons, then the Committee should not award him any compensation in all cases. The Contractor is not entitled to stop execution of the works in all cases mentioned in Article no. (50) of System of Contracts; otherwise he will be held responsible for all damages and losses falling on the Contracting Party because of such stoppage and he loses the right to claim any compensation.

ARTICLE NO. 14:

Syrian Legislation is the sole reference in all matters related to correctness of the contract and interpretation and application of its provisions as well as in every dispute arising from its executing.

ARTICLE NO. 15:

Provisions of System of Contacts shall apply in all matters not provided for this book.

PART III SUPPLY CONTRACTS

SECTION – I– TRASNPORTATION

ARTICLE NO. 16: MARITIME TRANSPORTATION:

Sea Transportation shall be made through the Syrian General Maritime Establishment which may grant exception to transport by other means.

If such exception is obtained transport must be made aboard ships not listed on the blacklist and according to technical terms guaranteeing safety of arrival of materials. The Contractor must observe all instructions and conditions specified by the said Establishment and the Maritime Agencies Company as follows: a) ***The goods are delivered FOB (on board the ship at port of shipment):***

The contracting Party shall bear costs of sea transport and insurance while contractor bears transport charges and risks on the goods from the exporting factory unit aboard the ship.

The Contractor must in this case notify the Contracting Party of date of arrival of each shipment of contracted materials to port of shipment one month at least prior to such date.

He should also notify the Contracting Party a statement of the goods, their weights, volumes and all other information necessary for shipment during one month maximum from date of being notified of opening the documentary letter of credit. b) ***CIF delivery of goods (on quay of port of destination):***

1- Contractor must insure the materials contracted on exclusively through the Syrian General Establishment for Maritime Transport from port of shipment to port of destination without reducing the contractor's liability towards the other party in accordance with the Contract's provisions.

Final deposits shall not be returned to the contractor until he has presented to the Contracting Party a certificate from the said Establishment confirming that shipment was made through it or with its permission or that he had paid to it all its due amounts.

2- The Contractor in external contracts should open a documentary divisible, negotiable and irrevocable L/C in favour of the Syrian General Organization for Maritime Transport to cover sea freight charges and other expenses involved thereon.

3-Contractor should notify said Organization a statement of the goods, their weights and Owners at least two months prior to date of the first shipment and the said Organization must notify him of the amount of the L/C and the currency of payment and contractor shall have to open the L/C within (15) days from date of his notification. If the contractor delays execution of his obligations mentioned in this paragraph

beyond their fixed dates, the said Maritime Organization may delay transport of the first shipment for similar period, without this affecting the contractor's commitment with date fulfilling the obligations fixed in the contract.

4- The Contractor should notify the said Maritime Organization or its nominated Agent in order to exefcute the shipment on the date he specifies for transport of each shipment from port of shipment at least one month prior to that date. He should also provide all necessary information for shipping which are requested by said Syrian Maritime Organization or its Agents abroad.

c) C+F Landed(on quay of port of destination).

Contractor bears costs of transport up to port of destination landed. The insurance remains liability of the Contracting Party and Maritime transport is done according to procedures stated in the previous paragraph (B). d) ***Delivery of Goods in Warehouses of Contracting Party:***

The Contractor in this case is responsible for sea and land transport and insurance up to the warehouses of the Contracting Party.

And he bears all taxes, fees and expenses involved on contracted materials up to their arrival on land of warehouses including obtaining the necessary import licences and opening the documentary credits where necessary, unless it is agreed that the Contracting Party bears the taxes and fees.

Sea Transport and insurance must be done through the Syrian General Organization for Maritime Transport and sea transport to be accomplished according to terms mentioned in paragraph (B) of this Article. e- At any rate the Contractor should take into consideration all instructions and conditions which

are specified by the Syrian General Organization for Maritime Transport or its accredited

Agent to guarantee the good execution of shipment.

ARTICLE NO. 17: AIR TRANSPORT:

Air transport should be made on planes of the Syrian Airlines or by its permission provided these planes fulfill all the technical conditions required for safety arrival of materials, along with

observing provisions of Israel Boycott office.

ARTICLE NO. 18: LAND TRANSPORT:

Land transport should be made by means of transport possessing all technical conditions

required for safety arrival of the materials. Article no. 19: Insurance: Imported contracted materials must be insured against all risks, within the limits specified in Book of Special Conditions. Insurance is borne by the Contracting Party if the purchase is on FOB or C+F basis, and by the contractor in other cases. Article no. 20: Packaging: Method of packaging the goods and type of materials used in packing should be in accordance with the International Rules of sea or air or land distant transport. The Contractor shall be liable for every damage on the Contracted goods resulting from insufficient packing. Reels, boxes and other packing items shall be ownership of the Contracting Party unless otherwise stated in the contract.

SECTION – II – EXECUTION OF OBLIGATION

Article no. 21: Increasing Or Decreasing Of The Quantities

CONTRACTED FOR:

The Contracting Party is entitled to increase or decrease the quantities contracted on in accordance with the provisions of Article no. (54) of System of Contracts and within the percentage specified in the books of Special Conditions or the contract provided it does not exceed 25% of contract's value and at prices of contract itself.

ARTICLE NO. 22: CONTROL OF MAKING AND PREPARATION OF CONTRACTED MATERIALS:

The Contracting Party may at its own expense appoint a natural or unnatural person as "supervisor" to represent it in supervising the manufacturing of required equipment and materials to be sure of good manufacturing, with the right to do so at places of manufacture whether they belong to Contractor or the factories accredited by him. Such supervisor may refuse what he deems to be contrary to the technical conditions, provided he notifies the contractor or manufacturers in writing of cases of rejection as well as the Contracting Party. The Contractor must replace the rejected materials with others which fulfil all technical conditions.

The supervisor or any other person representing the Contracting Party is entitled to enter freely during working hours into all places of work where the Contractor (Manufacturer) makes or stores the supplies or any part thereof.

The supervisor is not entitled to exempt the contractor from any of his contractual obligations, nor does he have the right to order execution of any work which may delay delivery of the contracted materials or lead to payment of additional sums by the Contracting Party or introduce any modifications unless such is included in the contract.

SECTION – III – ACCEPTANCE

ARTICLE NO. 23: ACCEPTANCE

a) Purpose of Acceptance:

Is to ascertain conformity of delivered supplies with those contracted on in quantity, quality and technical specifications and to make sure of good execution by the contractor of his obligations.

b) *Method of Acceptance:*

1- Acceptance of contracted supplies is done by an Acceptance Committee constituted by a decision of Head of the Contracting Party and should include one technical member and one from the finance department at least. If acceptance is to be out side Syrian territories, said party may form one or more acceptance committee or delegate one of the entities, individuals or companies to do so on its behalf. The contractor should be notified of this in writing.

2- Contractor must deliver the contracted supplies to the Contracting Party at the place specified for delivery in the contract, provided he notifies it in writing, prior to a period to be stated in the contract, of readiness of materials for delivery at the place so agree in the contract.

3- At the fixed time for acceptance, the Acceptance Committee examines the contract file and after knowing quantities and specifications and types of required supplies, it examines the submitted supplies checks them and ascertains their perfectness and being free from default and in conformity with conditions and specifications specified in the contract.

4- The Committee or entity charged with acceptance shall make an orderly report of minutes containing facts of process of receiving, checking and examining the supplies and results thereof as well as hour and date of acceptance, and notification to the contractor to attend acceptance process and his presence or presence of his legal representative or their absence. Finally justified recommendations of the Committee to accept submitted supplies, reject them or accept a part thereof and reject the other part, or accept the supplies with reservation on certain matters. The report of minutes shall be signed by all its members or by the entity delegated to make the acceptance as well as by the Contractor or by his legal representative if he is present. If the latter refuses to sign or in case of his absence, the report should so indicate. At any rate, a copy of acceptance report shall be sent to the contractor.

5- If the contractor signs the minute's report with reservation or he is absent, he is entitled to object to said report's contents, within maximum of ten days from date signing with reservation or from date notifying him in writing of the summary of the report.

The contracting Party shall study this objection and notify the contractor of the result. If the Contractor dose not object within the above period he is considered to have accepted the views of the Contracting Party. But if he refuses to sign the minutes he is considered accepting its contents without having any right for objection to this.

6- Value of contracted supplies shall not be paid except after making this report and having it accepted by the Disbursing Master, nor is it allowed to return final security deposits and release various guarantees except after final acceptance which must be made after expiration of period of guarantee stated in this book.

ARTICLE NO. 24: GUARANTEE OF SUPPLIES:

The Contractor guarantees providing the supplies in accordance with specifications, properties and technical statements on the basis of which contracting was made. Such guarantee shall cover all contracted supplies against every default or deficiency in design or manufacture or supply as well as against all damages and deficiency resulting from faulty installation. It also covers good working of the equipment subject of the contract throughout the period of guarantee stipulated therein.

ARTICLE NO. 25: CONTRACTOR'S RESPONSIBILITIES:

In addition to the aforementioned, the Contractor shall guarantee – as a result of tests and trials run during the acceptance – the exact conformity of supplies with the technical conditions and contract conditions and books of Special Conditions.

If must also guarantee that no defaults or deficiencies shall appear therefrom in spite of the fact that the Contracting Party or its representatives has prepared the specifications, plans and drawings of construction and installation of the supplies or had approved them or supervised the works at the factory and places of installation or supervised the materials and manufacturing of supplies and allowed their shipment wholly or partially.

SECTION – IV – ASSURANCES OF CONTRACT EXECUTION

ARTICLE NO. 26: DELAY PENALTY:

If Contractor delays delivery of contract materials beyond the dates fixed or provided materials not conforming with conditions and specifications agreed upon and does not replace them before such dates, the delay penalty stated in the contract and book of Special Conditions shall be imposed on him with no need for any notice.

b) If the Contractor fails to deliver the contracted materials after expiration of 30 days from date fixed for fulfillment of obligation, the Contracting Party is entitled with no need for a notice, to purchase the contracted materials at contractor's expense considering him defaulting by any of the methods stated in the System of

Contracts, in addition to imposition of delay penalties as per paragraph (A) of this Article. The Disbursing Master is himself entitled in the cases he deems necessary at his discretion to serve notice to the defaulting contractor to fulfil his obligation within a period he fixed without abiding by the mentioned 30 days period provided it is not less than three days. After end of the notice period, the Contracting Party shall take the above mentioned proceedings.

Sums incurred on the Contractor from delay penalties, price differences of purchasing expenditures shall be collected from his earnings and final deposits and suspended sums belonging to him. If these are insufficient, he is asked to pay the balance according to legal provisions in force.

The Contractor is not entitled to ask the Contracting Party to pay price differences which may result from purchase of materials at his expense, as this price difference shall be Considered an acquired right of the Contracting Party.

ARTICLE NO. 27: REJECTION OF SUPPLIES:

The Contracting Party is entitled to reject all or some of the provided materials if they were wholly or partially in violation of the agreed specifications or if they had any defect or deficiency. The Contracting Party may in this case seize the rejected materials and hold them at responsibility and expense of the contractor until he replaces or completes same during the period it specifies for him. It may also deliver such materials to him against a financial guarantee.

Delay Penalties stated in the previous Article remain valid against the contract up to date of delivery of materials in accordance with the specifications agreed on in the contract.

PART IV CONTRACTS OF WORKS

SECTION – I– MANAGEMENT AND EXECUTION OF THE WORK

ARTICLE NO. 28: WORK PROGRAM:

The Contractor must submit to the Contracting Party within maximum of ten days from signing the contract a written program containing measures and steps he will take for executing the project and the periods during which he expects to complete each important stage comprised in the contract.

The Contracting Party shall advise the Contractor of its approval of such program within ten days from date of being notified of this program or ask the Contractor to modify it within that period, as its interest requires, within the provisions of the contract and to be appropriate with the time fixed for total works.

The Contractor shall comply with the approved program during execution and is not allowed to overstep its limits or change any part thereof except with the written consent of the Contracting Party.

If the Contractor does not submit the required program during the specified period, the Contracting Party may then obligate him with its own program, after he is so notified of same in due manner.

ARTICLE NO. 29: PERFECTION OF WORK AND EXECUTION:

Execution of all works required in the contract should conform with plans, technical specifications and Administration's instructions as far as technical perfection and good workmanship are concerned. The Contractor must remove or demolish every work rejected by the Contracting Party because of any defect or deficiency or imperfection in such work, or nonconformity with said plans, specifications or instructions of the Contracting Party.

The Contractor must reinstate it to its required condition and according to the specifications at his own expense. It is up to the Contracting Party to accept such work in its present condition after deducting a sum from its value equal to the defect, damage or deficiency provided they are not enormous or do not infringe on safety of the plants from the technical and investment points of view.

If the Contractor or his Agent fails to remove or repair the rejected works which the Contracting Party has refused to accept as aforementioned and if the Contractor fails to do so within the period specified for him in writing for this purpose. The Contracting Party is then entitled to repair, remove or renew the works in the manner it deems and to deduct all expanses it has incurred therefrom from the Contractor's credits and frozen funds.

Article no. 30: Materials, Accessories, Equipment Required From the

CONTRACTOR:

The Contractor is responsible for providing at his own expense all materials, accessories, equipment, tools and various other technical apparatuses necessary for completion of all required works as stated in the contract. All such materials, accessories, equipment and apparatuses prepared for the work site should be of the best types and should fulfil all the technical conditions and specifications as required by the Contract.

All materials, accessories, equipment and instruments prepared by the contractor shall be considered, when they arrive at the work site, reserved for the interest of the project and cannot be used except for the works and jobs required in the contract.

The Contractor does not have the right to transfer or dispose of same or part thereof outside the workshop except with a written approval of the Contracting Party.

The Contractor should take all necessary measures to insure continuity of providing the materials and accessories required at all stages of the Project in the manner and quantities which guarantee orderly progress of work as per program ratified by the Contracting Party without interruption or delay. In certain special cases the Contracting Party may obligate the contractor to provide the materials and accessories during a period specified in book of Special Conditions.

If the Contracting Party finds the above mentioned materials, accessories equipment and instruments for use in the project not suitable for the work or not in conformity with books of Special Conditions or the contract, it is entitled to refuse acceptance of same and asks for their replacement and the contractor must in this case remove them immediately from the work site and replace them at his own expense with other suitable types acceptable to the Contracting Party.

If the contractor fails or delays transfer or replacement of rejected items within the period fixed for him, the Contracting Party may then do so at his expense no whatever the costs are, and the contractor is not entitled to claim any damages or losses or compensation or extension of the contract period because of the measures taken by Contracting Party in accordance with provisions of this paragraph.

The Contracting Party is entitled to examine at the contractor's expense, any materials prepared for use in the works and jobs contained in the contract by any technical laboratory in Syria or in one of the other countries whenever it sees necessity for this.

The Contracting Party shall give the contractor those documents which enable him to buy and receive those materials and requirements which are subject to System of Controlled Distribution or which are available exclusively at the State; all within limits of quantities required by stages of the execution.

Article no. 31: Materials, Accessories and Tools Submitted by the

CONTRACTED PARTY:

In case there is any provision in the contractor or in the book of Special Conditions which obligates the Contracting Party to submit any materials, accessories and tools required for completing any part of the contract, the contracting Party shall deliver such item to the Contractor gradually and systematically to requirements of Progress of work. Delivery shall be at the site explicitly fixed in the said provisions.

If no specific site is mentioned for delivery, the delivery shall be made at Contracting Party's warehouses in the province where the contract's works are carried out or its nearest warehouse from the center of the work.

Contractor should safeguard the materials, accessories and tools he receives from the Contracting Party and care for them also during their transport and their protection and use them with diligence and care in the execution of the contract's work. He should keep a special record which states manner, quantities and place of use of each part thereof in the works gradually and systematically.

In case shortage, defect or damage in these above items after their receiving because of the contractor's negligence, mismanagement or violation of the plans and technical conditions or instructions given to him by the Contracting Party, he is obligated to replenish the occurring shortage or replace the defective or damaged quantity at his own expense no matter what they amount to.

The Contractor shall submit written requests to the Contracting Party in which he states from time to time the requirements of current works for materials and accessories which the Contracting Party was obligated to provide and specified dates of this providing. This should be done at least 15 days before such dates.

The Contracting Party may in certain cases include in books of Special conditions an obligation by the contractor to insure the materials, accessories, tools and equipment which are provided by the Contracting party in the Contract – with the Syrian Insurance Company during the period from their delivery to the Contractor and their final use in contract's works and jobs.

ARTICLE NO. 32: DISPARITY AND ERRORS IN INSTRUCTIONS AND PLANS:

Before starting the execution of any part of the contract, the contractor should check and make sure of the correctness of the plans and their conformity with each other as well as required by book of technical conditions and table of quantities and prices and other provisions. He should ask the Contracting Party to correct any disparity, contradiction, deficiency or error he may find in these plans or technical conditions or statements or instruction given to him whether written, drawn and whether attached with the contract or given to the contractor later during execution. In such cases, contractor should work as per final written instructions which the Contracting Party asks him to follow in this regard during execution.

If the Contractor does not communicate with Contracting Party in writing concerning any disparity, contradiction or deficiency in the plans and technical conditions and an error appears which cannot be accepted or corrected in any of the works of the contract in whole or in part, the contractor will be held responsible to correct, demolish, complete or reconstruct that part affected with the defect and he must remove that defect at his own expense no matter what the costs are.

ARTICLE NO. 33: WORKING HOURS:

Execution of contract's work is done in one shift during the day on all week days except weekly holidays and official holidays stipulated by regulations in force in the Syrian Arab Republic, except in the Special cases required or approved by the Contracting Party in writing and provided provisions of the Labour Law are observed. If the Contractor wished to work overtime or during weekly and official holidays, he should submit a written request to the Contracting Party which is entitled to accept or reject such request without need to show causes.

If approved, the Contracting Party can obligate the contractor to pay compensation for the staff and employees and workers to secure reasonable control of work in the workshop during overtime hours provided that payment of overtime compensation by the contractor is done through the Contracting Party's Accountant according to legitimate procedure.

The Contractor is also required to provide the necessary lighting to guarantee good working in accordance with the terms required or approved by the Contracting Party.

ARTICLE NO. 34: PROTECTION MEASURES FOR PEOPLE, FUNDS, WORKS AND PLANTS:

Contractor is responsible for taking all necessary and sufficient measures to prevent occurrence of any damage or loss on any part of current works, materials, accessories and equipment during execution of the contract and generally in all movable and immovable properties at site of work, whether such works or properties belong to the contractor or the Contracting Party or others, or subcontractors working at the site. The Contractor shall be responsible for losses and damages arising from his failing to take the measures mentioned above or from his negligence whether such damages has resulted from direct deterioration, collapse, theft, fire or weather and natural conditions and the like.

The Contractor must also take all required measures to protect lives of workers, employees, residents and animals whether or not directly related to works of the contract from any damage or injury falling on any of them during the execution by the contractor of such works. In case of occurrence of such damages, the contractor shall be responsible for removing them and renovating or repairing the damaged part at his own expense as well as for payment of all incurred material compensation resulting from such damages, losses or injuries to the injured party, whether the direct cause of such damages was his negligence or that of his agents or that of those working at sites of his work.

The Contractor must conclude an insurance contract with the Syrian Insurance Company covering his civil liability towards other parties from execution of the works. Article no. 35: Sanitary Measures, Keeping Order, and Observance of

MUNICIPAL CODES:

In the execution of the work required from him in the contract, the Contractor shall take all sanitary measures required by the Contracting Party or imposed by the Sanitary Regulations of municipal Codes for keeping the works Site clean throughout execution period. He must erect temporary toilets sufficient for all working at the site as well as have them maintained and kept in clean hygienic condition throughout period of work and removing them after its completion.

Contractor shall keep order at the work site, the duration of contract execution, in cooperation with the Security Authorities and shall advise concerned department if any incident occurs, in order to take the required proceedings. He shall observe all Regulations imposed by the concerned municipality or any other competent official authority regarding any of his works included in the contract and concerning disposal of remains of demolishing and digging operations and shall ensure continued utilization of all neighboring roads and passages during execution. The Contractor shall be responsible for paying every compensation resulting from his violation of these regulations.

ARTICLE NO. 36: OWNERSHIP OF ANTIQUITIES AND MATERIALS FOUND AT THE

Site of Work: All archaeological pieces of materials of economic value extracted at the work site shall be ownership of the State.

The Contractor must take all measures to preserve these relics and materials for preventing any breakage, deformity, damage or diminishing on them until they are delivered to the competent official authority, or receiving its instructions on method of using or disposing of them.

When finding such pieces of historic or economic value, the contractor must inform the Contracting Party and the General Directorate of Antiquities and should discontinue the work in the area until receiving necessary instruction about them.

The Contractor shall use in the works related to the contract all materials and debris found or extracted at the work site which the Contracting Party decided its suitability for use.

Value of such materials shall be estimated on basis of table of price analysis submitted by the Contractor and shall be deducted from amounts due to him unless the contract clearly stipulates otherwise.

ARTICLE NO. 37: SUPERVISION OF WORKS AND INSPECTION OF MATERIALS:

a) Engineers and Supervisors charged by the Contracting Party with responsibility for contract and supervision of works executing as well as accredited engineering offices shall be considered as its representatives in supervision of the true application of contract's provisions and executing plans technical specifications and the instructions it issues to the contractor during the work. To achieve this purpose the contractor shall provide those engineers and supervisors appointed by the Contracting Party all necessary facilities to enable them discharge their duties in the best way and he shall work according to instructions and observations which they issue in accordance with the provisions of the contract, provided that such oral instructions are documented in writing from the Contracting Party during one week at most.

The contractor is responsible for providing temporary offices at the work site which are suitable and sufficient for the discharge of the engineers and supervisors of all official duties up to end of the works.

The Contracting Party or its delegates and those concerned officials have the right to enter the work site at all times to supervise the execution process as well as enter into factories, workshops and commercial shops which prepare or manufacture any equipment, accessories or materials related to any part of the contract's works. The contractor shall provide all necessary facilities and assistance to enable them to examine, check and test as they see necessary.

The Contractor shall not cover any part of the works except with permission from the Contracting Party or its supervising representative after having them examined. The Contractor must at any time fixed by the Contracting Party or any concerned official uncover any part of the works which was covered to enable them examine and check its sound execution.

If it appears as a result of examination that the examined works were correctly executed according to contract's provisions and that their covering was made with approval of the Contracting Party, the latter shall pay costs of examination and recovering.

But if it appears as a result of the examination that the work is not conforming with the plans and technical specifications and the supervising engineer's instructions, or if it is confirmed that the examined part, although correctly executed, was covered before obtaining permission of the Contracting Party, then the costs of examination and recovering are borne by the Contractor in addition to his responsibilities for violation of the works to the required conditions. If the Contractor refuses and fails to make the required inspection during the period stipulated for him by the Contracting Party, the Contracting Party may in this case make such inspection in due manner and deduct all costs thereof from account of the Contractor regardless of result of inspection.

The Contracting Party or its representatives shall visit the work site over reasonable periods to inspect progress of work as it deems compatible with the interest of the project.

The Contracting Party shall bear costs of such visits, however for visits and inspections which it is compelled to make at request of the contractor, to inspect works which has previously been inspected, the Contracting Party is entitled to have them borne by the Contractor and deduct them from his account.

ARTICLE NO. 38: CONTRACTOR'S AGENTS DURING EXECUTION:

When absent from the work site the Contractor must appoint a responsible Agent to follow-up execution of contract provisions and to act according to instructions of the Contracting Party or any of its representatives during the work to achieve its requirements.

The said agent should stay at the work site throughout hours of continuity of executing and should be delegated with full authority by the Contractor in his absence concerning all that is related to the contract execution.

In project of special technical nature, the Contracting Party may at its discretion require the Contractor to have one of his delegated supervisors to be an Engineer for supervising the organization and execution of the contract's provisions.

The agent and Supervisors appointed by the Contractor to supervise the work execution on his behalf must be always of good reputation and sufficient experience and technically qualified in the type of works of the contract.

Before appointing such Agent or Supervisors at site of work the Contractor shall advise the Contracting party in writing of their names and their technical qualifications to obtain its approval on their appointment.

The Contracting Party has the right to accept or reject this appointment without having to show reasons, and the appointed agent and supervisors cannot be changed except with written approval of the Contacting Party.

The authorized Agent shall remain at the work site during working hours of execution to receive instruction of the Contracting Party or its representatives when they make visits to the work site.

Absence of the contractor's Agent from the work site during normal working hours without advance approval of the Contracting Party, shall be considered a violation for which the Contracting Party may deduct a specified sum to be fixed in the book of special conditions for each day in which the said Agent is absent.

Article no. 39: Employees, Workers, Professionals and Specialists:

In carrying out the contract's works, the Contractor shall only employ those workers, labourers, employees, professionals and specialists who satisfy efficiency and good conduct requirements.

The Contracting Party may ask the Contractor to remove any of above personnel including the Supervisor and Agent from the work site if it found them unfit for work in its discretion.

In such a case, the Contractor may not reinstate those rejected except with a written approval from the Contracting Party.

The use of the Contracting Party of this right does not entitle the Contractor to shrink from his responsibilities in the contract or to claim any compensation or loss or damage which may occur as a result of that.

The Contractor shall not employ or provide work to any of the Contracting Party's workers in any capacity whatsoever; if he does not abide by this clause, the execution of the contract is withdrawn from him and provisions of Article no. (50) of this book shall be applied against him in addition to depriving him of contracting with the Contracting Party for one year at least.

Terms of employment of workers with the Contractor in the contract's works should be in agreement with the provision of the labour law and the International Labour Agreement no. 94 valid in the Syrian Arab Republic. The Contractor must work in accordance with said law and Agreement and apply law of Special Securities in all cases.

SECTION – II– EMERGENCY CONDITIONS DURING EXECUTION

ARTICLE NO. 40: QUANTITIES AND PRICES:

Quantities stated in "Tables of Quantities" and in the "Estimated Statements" for various works required by the contract shall be only on approximate basis subject to increase or decrease in accordance with the related provisions of Article no. (54) of the System of Contracts and in books of Special Conditions, as per work requirements during execution. Accounting with the Contractor shall be on basis of actually achieved quantities, which were measured at work site for each of the works required of him by the contract.

Prices stated in the price list at which it was contracted shall be fixed and include and cover all wages, labour force expenses and values of all materials required for finishing the works as well as their fees, taxes, costs of transport, keeping, protection, depreciation, profits and all liabilities which may be incurred on the Contractor; also his requirements for tools, instruments, equipment, temporary plants and all which is required to deliver the works in a satisfactory and acceptable manner; whether this was clarified in the plans or technical specifications and price

– list or implicit understood therefrom. All this unless the book of special conditions and the

contract provide otherwise.

ARTICLE NO. 41:

The Contracting Party has the right to ask for making any modification correction, omission

or addition to any of the works required by the contract whether this leads to decrease or increase in the quantities of these estimated works. In all cases, the Contractor shall be obligated to carry out without delay all modifications or changes demanded of him by written orders during the work progress. If the Contractor delays the execution of such modifications or alteration during the specified period, the Contracting Party may do so at his expense and deduct the costs incurred no matter what they are from his account subject to provisions of Article no. (21) of this book.

No modification or change shall be made in any part of the contract's works required in the plans, technical Specifications and table of Quantities unless they are done on the basis of a written request or approval by the Contracting Party. Every change which the contractor makes in any part of the contract's works without obtaining the Contracting Party's approval shall give it the right to reject same or demand its correctness in required manner at the expense of the

Contractor whatever the costs are. If the Contracting Party finds it possible to keep such

change as it is without correction, it is entitled to consider it as a contribution for which it shall

pay nothing to the contractor when making the accounting.

c) If modifications asked by the contracting Party during the work require demolishing, removing or modifying a work which was completed according to contract's provisions, then the Contracting Party should reimburse the Contractor value of the demolished part or cost of modification required.

ARTICLE NO. 42: EXTRA WORKS NOT MENTIONED IN THE CONTRACT:

a) If execution of works requires performing additional jobs not mentioned in the contract or changing sources and types of certain materials mentioned therein, the Contracting Party may ask the Contractor to do such works and he should immediately embark on execution and specify prices of such materials by agreement between the tow parties. If, however, execution of these additional works does not require full urgency, the Contracting Party does not give order for their execution except after reaching an agreement on their prices with the Contractor, and every work performed by the latter before obtaining a written order from the Contracting Party shall be considered as his own contribution.

a) If the Contracting Party does not commission the Contractor to do the extra work as stated in the previous paragraph, it may itself execute such works directly through the "Trust Way" or ask the Contractor to do these works for its account in return for a commission of no more than 10% of total actual costs which the execution of works requires, or still charge a third party to do these works. The Contactor should then offer all necessary facilities and assistance to the third party during his execution of the additional works.

b) When prices of the additional materials agreed upon are different from the prices stated in the contract, the contracting Party shall make a stocktaking of the works of the original contract which were completed by the Contractor. This shall be made in accordance with provisions of paragraph (A) of Article no. (40) of this book.

SECTION – III– DISBURSEMENT OF VALUE OF THE WORKS

ARTICLE NO. 43: MEASUREMENT OF WORK EXECUTION:

a) Execution works shall be measured and calculated gradually during execution in accordance with provisions of the contract, namely at the end of each specific stage of the project and before covering any part of the works which cannot be inspected, measured and calculated once it is covered. The two parties shall agree on the dates on which measurement and calculation of the works shall take place in their presence or presence of their accredited representatives and shall be signed by them. The Contractor shall provide at his expense all works and facilities required for this purpose.

b) The Contracting Party is entitled, when necessary, to ask the Contractor or his authorized agent to come to the work site on the date it fixed in order to measure and calculate the finished works. If the Contractor or his agent fails to be at the work site on the date fixed the Contracting Party may do the measurements and calculation by itself and the Contractor does not have the right of objection to the correctness of these measurements and calculations.

c) All works finished according to the contract shall be measured and calculated on the basis of the recorded units including Table of Quantities and surveys by engineering measurement in accordance with the technical methods followed at Ministry of public Works and Water Resources, so that all opening shall be deducted from volumes and areas, and damaged pieces shall be disregarded unless the contract provides explicitly to the contrary. Every increase in Quantities and dimensions made by the contractor without a written request from the contracting party or with its approval shall be disregarded.

d) Every dispute arising between the Contractor and representatives of the Contracting Party concerning current measurements and calculations shall be decided by the Contracting Party within no more than one week from the following day on which the dispute arose. No part of the disputed works shall be covered until after the Contracting Party had issued its final decision on the subject of dispute or its approval, and its decision in this regard shall be final and binding.

e) Works executed contrary to the contract's provisions shall not be included in the calculation and measurement and their value shall not be disbursed unless an agreement on them is reached between the two parties.

Article no. 44: Monthly Payments: a) The Contracting Party shall prepare for the Contractor monthly statements of the works and preparations finished by him, which include the following:

4. Completely finished works which value is to be estimated as per the prices stated for them in the contract.

5. Works not finally finished which value shall be estimated as per the prices for them in the contract along with taking into account degree of their completion.

6. Preparations made ready at the work site, their quantities are calculated at 80% of their total actually made ready, provided they conform to the terms of the contract. Value of these preparations shall be estimated on basis of their current price at time of making the inspection and the price assigned to them in the price Analysis Table, whichever is less, not taking into account the preparations in excess of those required.

From account of the above mentioned Statements (5%) shall be deducted as "frozen sums" as per Article no. (46) of this book.

If the Contracting Party resorts to spend any sum from those suspended or frozen amounts at the expense of the contractor the latter must replenish it until it reaches (5%) of total disbursed to him, namely by way of deducting from his credits, if has such, or by calling on him to pay in accordance with legal procedures in force.

b) If the contractor is lagging in conducting his work with the speed and diligence estimated in the agreed program, or in those cases where executed works do not agree with the accuracy and conformity with plans and specifications as required by the contract, the Contracting Party is then entitled to deduct a sum from his monthly statements which is commensurate with the delay penalty or with degree of defect which occurred in the works.

c) Inscription of the works and preparations on the monthly statements and payment of their value does not in any case mean their final acceptance by the Contracting Party or waiving any of its rights stated in this book or in the contract concerning the works and the preparations. The Contracting Party is entitled through out validity of the contract and period of guarantee to review account of payments and adjust any error or mission which may appear therein.

d) The Contractor's signature on the monthly statement without reservation means his approval of all its contents. Every objection in this regard should be made in writing within ten days from date of his signing on the statement with reservation. His reservation is not considered if he dose not submit his objection during the mentioned period.

e) Disbursement of statements submitted from the Technical Department is made within (15) days from date of their presentation to the competent financial directorate, provided they are fully documented and satisfy their legal requirements. Every delay in disbursing after expiration of said period not caused by the

Contractor shall be automatically added to the period of contract. Article no. 45: Final Settlement: a) Final statement should be prepared within six months from date of temporary acceptance. The contractor is invited by a letter from the Contracting Party to sign with or without reservation within ten days from his invitation date. If he signs without reservation he is considered as having accepted the contents of the final statement and by receiving value of such statement he shall be considered as having received all amounts due to him with no further claims on the Contracting Party concerning the contract except for the suspended amounts discussed in Article no. (46) of this book. But if signed with reservation, he should state his reservation in one time in a clear detailed memorandum containing the clauses of reservation together with all documentation papers during twenty days from date of his signature, otherwise his reservation is considered null and void; after submitting

this memorandum no reservation is accepted from the Contractor. However, if the contractor is absent from attendance in spite of his notification duly to sign the statement, then the proceedings made in his absence shall be considered correct and he is considered as accepting the contents of the statement and no objection from him is heard. The Contractor who refuses to sign shall be treated as having signed without reservation. b) If in accordance with the provisions of the contract a sum or debt or an obligation is owed by the Contractor to the Contracting Party and the contractor does not pay the same on demand, then the Contracting Party is entitled to deduct same from the credits of the Contractor or from the same sums which will be owed to him or to directly deduct from the statements and remitted in favour of the Contracting Party, whether this is in connection with the present contract or with any other contract or from the securities or suspended sums belonging to the Contractor. If all this is not sufficient, it may collect the balance in accordance with valid legal procedures. Article no. 46: Frozen Sums (Suspensed Amounts): a) Sums deducted by the Contracting Party in accordance with Article No. (44) of this book from value of all payments owed to the Contractor for completed works and supplied preparations shall be considered as suspended amounts kept in cash until the final delivery of the works required by the contract in a satisfactory manner. b) Suspended sums are returned to the Contractor after he had made final delivery of the project and confirmation that the completed works in the project conform with the required conditions and that no defect or deficiency appears in these works up to the final acceptance. c) The Contracting Party is entitled to deduct from the suspended amounts those sums it spends on making up any deficiencies or for completion of any works on behalf of the Contractor by virtue of the powers authorized to it by this book. Before returning these sums to the Contractor, the Contracting Party is entitled also to deduct delay penalties or fines of compensations imposed on the Contractor in accordance with the provisions of the contract and this book. d) If at provisional acceptance the Contacting Party finds that the works completed by the Contractor were satisfactorily finished and fulfil the required descriptions, then it can return at liquidation of accounts a sum not exceeding half the suspended sums in addition to the retuned securities subject to paragraph (B) of Article No. (41) of System of Contracts and accept to retain a sum not exceeding 50% (fifty percent) of the suspended sums as reserve amount which can be disposed of on date of final acceptance of the project.

SECTION – IV– ACCEPTANCE

ARTICLE NO. 47: PROVISIONAL AND FINAL ACCEPTANCE:

a) The Contractor should advise the Contracting Party, by a letter to be registered in its chancery of the date on which the works required of him in the contract were finished and the date when he is ready to deliver the project to the Contracting Party on a provisional basis. The Contracting Party should forward this letter within one week maximum from its registration date to the Executive Supervisory unit in order to see if the works were actually finished on the date specified by the Contactor or on another date. The Contracting Party is entitled to refuse acceptance of the works or requirements being delivered if it finds in them any shortage, defect or violation of contract conditions and to ask the Contractor to make up these shortages and repair the defects and remove the violations before considering the provisional acceptance as possible. If the shortages, deficiencies, defects and violations are found by the Contracting Party to be a specific type or can easily be repaired with possibility of utilizing the project, it may accept the works completed in accordance with contract's provisions and register a special reservation on the observed shortages, defects, violations so that they are either completed and corrected by the contractor during a period fixed for him by the Contracting Party or have a sum deducted from his credits which is equal, in Contracting Party's estimation to the value of these defects and shortages, which it would then complete by itself at the time it sees fit.

b) If the Contracting Party decided to accept the works with or without reservation, the acceptance shall be considered valid from the date fixed by the Contractor for such acceptance as per a letter registered duly with the Contracting Party unless it appears that the works were not actually ready for acceptance on that date.

c) Before delivering the completed works on a provisional basis, the Contactor must remove all debris, remanents and unwanted soil and take away all spots and dirts at his own expense in the way considered satisfactory by the Contracting Party.

d) If the provisional acceptance reports contain observations of repairs or defects, the contractor is charged to complete same within period of guarantee or during a period fixed by the acceptance Committee, and he shall have to bear, in such cases, wages of Supervisors who supervise the above mentioned repairs throughout period of repair.

e) The project shall be delivered on a final basis after one full year from date of the provisional

acceptance, if no other period was agreed upon. The Contractor shall remain responsible towards the Contracting Party throughout this period for any defect or new deficiency which may appear in the completed works which have been provisionally accepted during that period. He shall have to pay for all requirements of repair and removal of these defects, completion of the new shortages and project's maintenance whatever they amount to at his own expense. Repair of damages arising from the Contacting Party's misuse of the completed works during that period shall be outside the above maintained maintenance responsibility.

f) Suspended amounts or their Balance shall be returned to the Contactor upon final acceptance, after completion of settlement of all accounts of the project, it will be considered as finished.

g) In addition to Contactor's responsibility during the guarantee period stated in paragraph (E) above he shall remain responsible for (10) years for any basic subsequent defect which may affect their safety having been the result of the Contactor's fraud of their bad execution.

h) The Acceptance Committee shall be constituted by the Disbursing Master provided it includes amongst the members at least one technical and one member from the finance department.

SECTION – V– PENALTY CLAUSES

ARTICLE NO. 48: PROCEEDINGS IN CASE OF VIOLATION OR DEFAULT IN

Executing the Contract: a) If the Contractor stopped the works without a reasonable cause accepted by the Contracting Party, or if the latter finds that the Contactor had slowed, neglected, defaulted or been unable in executing any of the works required of him by the Contractor, or if he had, during execution of the work, violated any of the contractor's provisions, it may notify him of necessity to multiply his interest and activity and to abide by the provisions and conditions required of him. The Contractor must make up for this during a maximum period of five days from notifying him, except for urgent situations in which the Contracting Party may specify a shorter period for this make up, and the Contracting Party should state in the warning notice the type of negligence or default or violations which occurred. b) The notice served by the Contracting Party shall be considered a document confirming occurrence of the default, negligence or violation unless the contractor submits, within three days from date of notification, sufficient proofs to the satisfaction of the Contracting Party that default or negligence was caused by a justified excuse. c) If the period of notice expires before the Contractor's fulfillment of the Contracting Party's demands for expediting the work and abiding by the terms of the contract, the Contracting Party is then entitled to take the following proceedings:

1. Performing the following on behalf and at the expense of the Contractor: increasing the number of workers and employees of whatever specialty and occupation; purchasing materials, accessories and requirements: and taking all measures it deems necessary to insure the accuracy, conditions and descriptions of the work process as required by the

2. contract. The Contractor is obligated to pay all costs and expenses incurred by the Contracting Party in this regard and shall have no right of objection to any of the measures, prices or wages on the basis of which the Contracting Party executes the works. If the Contractor fails to pay these costs and expenses, the Contracting Party shall be entitled to pay them to these concerned on his behalf, without delay and shall have them deducted from his earnings, suspended sums and securities. If the latter are not sufficient, the amounts shall be collected in accordance with laws and regulations in force.

3. The Contracting Party is entitled to order suspension of work in any part in which observed violation occurs and not to allow the Contractor to continue the work in that part expect after removing or correcting that violation and abiding again by all provisions of the contract. The Contractor may not in such a case make any claim for material compensation or for extension of contract duration because of suspension of work in such manner.

ARTICLE NO. 49: DELAY PENALTIES:

In case the Contractor is late in completing all the works required of him by the contract beyond the fixed date, a delay penalty shall be imposed on him as provided in contract, and in addition to the proceedings mentioned in the previous Article, without need for any notice or notification since the delay is by itself considered as standing in its stead.

ARTICLE NO. 50: WITHDRAWING THE CONTRACT EXECUTION AND ITS PROVISIONS:

Withdrawing the contract execution from the Contractor means execution at his expense of all

or part of the works directly by the Contracting Party by the "Trust Method" or through another

Contractor considering that this shall not set a limit on the responsibilities and obligations

imposed on the Contractor by provisions of the contract.

a) When the Contracting Party decides to withdraw execution of all or part of the works according to provisions of System of contracts, it invites the Contractor to attend a meeting on a date it fixes in order to participate in measurement of all the works completed up to date of withdrawal and for making a complete stocktaking of all machines, equipment, instruments, accessories, materials, and apparatuses which the Contractor had brought to the work site as well as all temporary plants which he had installed there. If the Contractor refuses to attend or to delegate an agent on his behalf or if he declines to sign the statement (manifest) after its preparation, the Contracting Party is then entitled to do the job by itself and shall send a copy of the prepared stocktaking and list of measurements to the Contractor by registered mail in order to make his objections within (ten) days from date of his notification. After expiry of this period, the Contracting Party shall not accept any objection in this regard.

b) Upon withdrawing execution of the works, the Contracting Party may stop disbursement of any sum owed or shall be owed to the Contactor for works which he had completed or accessories he had brought to the work site and to prevent returning of securities and suspended money to him and to dispose with some or all the instruments, machines, equipment, accessories, temporary plants brought to the work site or installed there or to test and utilize them in the way it sees fit to the interest of the project without being responsible for any losses of damages which may be caused to the Contractor as a result of this seizure, use or disposal. The contracting Party may continue seizure of all these items after completion of the works, if it finds in this a guarantee for its rights incurred on the Contractor. But if another person proves his ownership of any of the seized items with documents bearing a fixed date preceding that of the contract, the Contracting Party may pay him their rents from the date on which the withdrawal of the works took place in accordance with the terms previously agreed on with the Contactor and at the current prices if no such previous agreement existed with the Contractor.

c) Contractor shall bear all costs and expenses sustained by the Contracting Party for completion of the withdrawn works as well as all losses and damages which it suffers as a result of its performance of these works. All the statements submitted by the Contracting Party concerning these expenditures shall be considered correct and the Contractor has no right to make objection on these expenditures or on any of the prices, wages and miscellaneous expenses disbursed to complete the works, purchase of materials and accessories and carrying out of all other obligations

imposed by the contract no matter how much they amount to. In addition to the above mentioned, the Contacting Party may penalize the Contractor with some or all of his securities or suspended sums as a sort of penalty against the loss and damage it has suffered because of withdrawing the execution of works.

d) If as a result of the final accounting it appears that the total of costs of works done by the Contracting Party at the expense of the Contractor, including the Administration expenses, is less than that sum which the Contractor would have been entitled to, had he himself performed them at the prices stated in the contract, then the saving realized shall belong to the Contracting Party and the contactor shall not be entitled to claim it, knowing that in such a case the Contracting party pays to Contractor "like rent" for the instruments, machines, equipment and temporary plants which belong to him for the period of the use by the Contracting Party within the limits of the realized saving.

e) During execution of the withdrawn works, the Contracting Party is entitled to return all or some of the remaining parts to contractor's charge, if it is convinced of removal of the causes which led to such withdrawal of the works.

EXECUTIVE INSTRUCTIONS NO.6 DATED 26/07/1998 FOR THE IMPLEMENTATION OF INVESTMENT LAW NO.10/1991

ARTICLE 2 - BENEFICIARIES FROM THE LAW

Benefitting from Investment Law shall be projects of economic and social development that are to be approved by the Council and which are established with local or foreign capital, or both, by natural or juristic persons identified as follows:

1. Syrian Arab citizens residing in the Syrian Arab Republic and those who are treated as such.

2. Expatriate Syrian Arab citizens whether they retain their original nationality or have obtained the nationality of the host country.

3. Nationals of Arab and foreign states.

4. Juristic persons who will be licensed by the Council to launch enterprises under the rules of investment law.

ARTICLE 3 - INVESTMENT FIELDS

Economic and social development projects mentioned in Article 3 of Investment Law shall mean those enterprises which are created under its rules in the following areas:

1. Agricultural enterprises in both plant and animal production areas and all other activities and works related, connected or complementary thereto such as the construction of greenhouses, refrigerated storage facilities and facilities for the sorting, packing and packaging of fruits and vegetables whether those are the produce of the same enterprise or other enterprises.

2. Enterprises for the processing of agricultural (plant or animal) products.

3. Industrial enterprises that may be created by the private or joint sector.

4. Transport enterprises.

5. Projects that may be approved by the Council in areas other than the above-mentioned.

ARTICLE 4 - BASICS AND CRITERIA FOR THE COUNCIL TO GRANT APPROVAL

For a project to benefit from Investment Law the Council shall decide its approval of it in light of the following considerations:

1. The project must be in line with the state development plan.

2. The extent of the project's use of available local resources, its contribution to the growth of Domestic Product and to the opening up of more job opportunities.

3. The project's potentials in promoting exports and rationalizing imports.

4. The project's usage of modern up-to-date machinery and technology that meet the needs of the national economy.

5. The value of the project's fixed assets (machinery, vehicles, instruments, equipment, tools, installations, non-touristic transport means and all other production means which are definitely, not temporarily imported) that will be invested solely and exclusively in the project must not be less than ten million Syrian pounds or the equivalent in foreign currency calculated at the exchange rate of neighboring countries as per the bulletin of exchange rates issued by the Commercial Bank of Syria.

6. The Council of Ministers may change the afore-said minimum value by a decision signed by the Prime Minister.

7. All machinery, instruments, tools, equipment, non-touristic transport means and all other production means imported solely and exclusively in favour of projects created under this law must be brand-new, not second-hand nor reconditioned.

ARTICLE 10 - POWERS OF THE INVESTMENT BUREAU

Within the extent of its specialization, the Investment Bureau has the following tasks to perform:

1. It receives and registers applications for investment which are referred to the Council by the concerned authorities. It has to update the information and data required for every application in close cooperation and coordination with the various competent authorities, and to prepare a file for each application. Copies of such files must be handed out to the chairman and members of the Council three days at least before the meeting of the Council.

2. It keeps a special record for the invested funds brought from abroad in the form of foreign currency or assets in kind or rights which are already adopted by the Council. On the basis of this record the Bureau may issue a certificate testifying each share of the invested capital in conformity with the registered data. Such certificate shall be signed by the Bureau Director who takes the responsibility thereof.

3. It receives investors' complaints and seeks to remedy them. It helps the investors get the required permits and licenses from the concerned authorities for their enterprises and helps them follow up implementation. It receives investors' suggestions and opinions on investment issues and project implementation and refers them to the Council.

4. It records minutes of the Council meetings and its decisions and follows up their implementation with the various authorities of concern. It must keep records of the Bureau's performance with regard to implementation of Investment Law in such a manner as to ensure the good and sound implementation. Besides, it must collect, classify and study report and data of the enterprises including their balance sheets and their profit-and-loss accounts and present to the council periodical report thereof.

5. It must study the draft by-laws of joint-stock limited liability companies created under Investment Law. It must also study the draft amendments of those by-laws and transmit those drafts and studies to the Council to consider approval thereof.

6. It must publish leaflets, booklets and other publications in Arabic and a foreign language about investment in the Syrian Arab Republic according to the Council's directives.

7. It has to cooperate with the various organizations in the public, private and joint sectors for the launching of publicity campaigns to acquaint Syrian expatriates and nationals of Arab and foreign states with investment opportunities available in the Syrian Arab Republic under Investment Law, taking directives in this regard from the Council.

8. In coordination with the Ministry of Economy and Foreign Trade and Ministry of Finance, it evaluates the foreign capital.

9. It has the power to agree to the projects having the required touristic transport means as they deserve under the Council's Decision No.308 dated 05/08/1992 and amendments.

10. It has the power to agree to the projects having required communication means (telephone, telefax, telex) as they deserve under the Council Decision circulated by letter No.33/1/33 dated 15/02/1992 and the Decision circulated by letter No.404/1/33 dated 13/06/1994.

11. It studies and handles the following cases:

- It studies and handles applications filed with it for an extension of the period of execution of the projects created under Investment law without prejudice to Article 13 of the said law with regard to the period of exemption.

- It studies and approves applications filed with it concerning transfer of ownership, wholly or partly, of the approved projects in compliance with the rules of Investment Law and relevant Council decisions.

- It studies and handles applications filed with it for altering the legal status of the projects.

- It studies and handles applications filed with it for changing the projects' purposes and production capacity, which if carried out do not entail any change in the projects' costs in the light of the study made by concerned ministry. All measures taken in this respect shall be incorporated in a decision to be signed by the Prime Minister, chairman of the Higher Investment Council, and notified by the Bureau to the concerned party.

12. The Bureau Director invites Investment Directors in the various concerned ministries to periodical meetings inorder to follow up implementation of investment projects created under Investment law and to observe stages of execution of each and to exchange opinions on the manner of handling investors' issues referring those which require decisions to respective ministries or to the Council for the adoption of the necessary procedure.

13. It performs any other tasks assigned to it by the Council.

ARTICLE 12

All public authorities, departments and establishments shall have the obligation to extend all possible assistance and facilitate things to investors for the purpose of accomplishing formalities without delay. They also have the obligation of providing answers to questions and querries posed by the Bureau within one week from the dof filing the questions or querries.

ARTICLE 14 - EXEMPTIONS, ADVANTAGES AND FACILITIES

On the opening of bank accounts in foreign currency:

A. in addition to the facilities provided for by the currency laws and regulations in force, the investor has the right to open in favour of his project created under

B. Investment Law an account in foreign currency with the Commercial Bank of Syria which will have to be credited with :

1. 100% of the project capital paid in foreign currency and loans obtained in foreign currency as well.

2. 75% of the revenues obtained in foreign currency as a result of exportation and services, the remaining 25% of those revenues shall be sold to the Commercial Bank of Syria at the exchange rate specified in Article 4 above.

This said bank account shall be debited with the sums of money in foreign currency paid to cover the burdens, needs and requirements of the project such as:

1. Value of the machinery, vehicles, equipment, cars and all other materials needed for the creation, operation, development and expansion of the enterprise.

2. Value of raw and semi-processed materials and other auxiliary materials required for production.

3. Value of spare parts and costs of reconditioning worn-and-torn machinery.

4. The installments of paying back loans and interest rates due on loans borrowed in foreign currency in favour of the enterprise.

5. The due interest rates and profits authorized for transfer abroad each year in favour of expatriate Syrians and nationals of Arab and foreign states who have transferred into the country in foreign currency the value of their shares and stakes through a bank based in the Syrian Arab Republic or by any of the means approved by the Currency Bureau in conformity with the regulations in force.

6. Also to be debited in the said account are the dues authorized for transfer abroad through the Commercial Bank of Syria in favour of workers in the project who are not Syrian nor treated as Syrians.

7. Sums of money due on the project which have to be paid by transfers abroad in foreign currency through the Commercial Bank of Syria on the basis of authentic documents.

8. The expenses that have to be paid in foreign currency in the Syrian Arab Republic.

9. Insurance premiums which the enterprise must pay in foreign currency.

10. Remunerations due to members of companies' boards of directors who are not Syrian nor treated as such.

11. The Bureau must be notified by the Commercial Bank of Syrian of the sums of money that are being transferred.

12. The enterprise bears full responsibility towards making available the foreign currency that meets its needs by lawful means and no official party in the Syrian Arab Republic can have the obligation of providing any sum of money in foreign currency in favour of the enterprise or its owners.

ARTICLE 15

The investor has the right to invest the foreign currency he possesses inside the country, or the foreign currency existing abroad which he lawfully brings into the country in financing the projects created under Investment Law, or in contributing to the capital of enterprises or in purchasing shares. For such investment the investor is kept safe from any liability that falls under any clause of criminal law in force.

ARTICLE 16

1. The bank where the investors' funds are deposited in conformity with Article 16-A of Investment Law shall have the obligation of placing those deposits at their disposal upon demand and it shall take all necessary measures that ensure such action.

2. The bank shall calculate interest on the sums of money deposited with it in foreign currency for the account of the enterprise on the basis of current interest rates.

3. The investor may deposit some of his foreign currency assets in a frozen account at the Commercial Bank of Syria.

4. The bank shall deliver to the investor a cheque book special for investors which must be used solely and exclusively in favour of the enterprise.

5. The Commercial Bank of Syrian shall transfer all the project's burdens requirements and needs in foreign currency in harmony with these instructions.

6. The investor who opens a foreign currency account with the Commercial Bank of Syria in conformity with the currency regulations in force in favour of his project that is created under Investment Law may recover the balance of the money which was lawfully brought into the country and deposited in an account opened at the Commercial Bank of Syria after his project has been completely executed and all its needs and operation costs as well as cost of its raw material, spare parts and operating capital have been paid in full in foreign currency.

The investor, moreover, may have this balance transferred abroad if he is a Syrian living abroad or a non-resident national of an Arab or foreign country provided that the project owner remains under the obligation of ensuring the availability of the foreign currency needed to cover future needs of the project through lawful bank channels.

ARTICLE 17

1. For the benefit of his enterprise, the investor may borrow loans in local currency from state-owned banks against the guarantee of his private money existing in the Syrian Arab Republic in conformity with those banks' regulations.

2. The investor shall bear all material and legal consequences resulting from foreign and local loans which he has taken or will take upon himself including payment of both installments and interest in harmony with the laws and regulations in force and neither the state nor any other public body shall have the obligation of providing guarantees of whatever kind to any party whatsoever be it local or foreign. Such loans shall not be insured by the Arab Organization for Investment Guarantee or any other organization.

ARTICLE 19

- Without being restricted to rules of prohibiting, restricting and monopolizing importation and rules of direct importation and rules of Currency Regulations, the enterprises may import:

1. All required machinery, vehicles, equipment, hardware, working cars including buses and minibuses destined to service the enterprises and other materials needed for the creation, development and expansion of the enterprises.

2. Touristic service cars.

3. All materials and requirements needed for the enterprise operation (raw materials, processed and semi-processed materials and all materials needed for production operations which can be considered part of the final product and one of its components).

- The enterprise imports specified in item 1 of this Article shall be exempted from taxes, fiscal fees and municipal rates, customs duties and other fees provided that those imports are solely and exclusively used for the purposes of the enterprise.

- The enterprise may not relinquish any of the imports specified in A-1 above without a prior approval from the Council. Subject to this approval, those imports can be abandoned after the payment of all taxes and fees assessed on them in their current condition including the tax on capital profits as stipulated in Article 32 of Investment Law and in compliance with the regulations in force.

Furthermore , non of the imports mentioned in A-1 and 2 above may be relinquished, nor may they be used in other than the enterprise purposes unless the Council agrees thereto and accepts justified reasons for this action.

Excluded from the rules of this Article are the packing materials of the imports(pallets, drums, ..etc) the left-overs, wastes and exhaust of the manufacturing process in harmony with the internationally recognized rates.

In implementing the rules of Article 12-A of Investment Law, imports shall mean all imported machinery, vehicles, equipment, hardware, working cars, buses and mini-buses required to service the enterprises and all other materials needed for the creation, development and expansion of the enterprises.

ARTICLE 20

1. Enterprises belonging to individuals or companies other than joint sector companies and their profits and dividends shall be exempted from all taxes levied on income, and from real estate and vacant plots of land taxes (including the tax on machinery revenues) occurring on the enterprises properties possessed for accomplishing thepurposes and tasks for a period of five years as from the date of actual production or date of exploitation according to the nature of the enterprise.

2. Joint-sector companies in which the public sector possesses not less than 25 % of whose capital created under Investment Law shall take the form of Societe Anonym joint-stock company or limited liability company. Such companies and their shares profits, dividends and monies shall be exempted from all taxes levied on income and from real estate and vacant plots of land taxes (including taxes on machinery revenues) occurring on the enterprises properties possessed for accomplishing their purposes and tasks for seven years as from the date of actual production or date of exploitation according to the nature of each of its projects created under Investment Law.

3. In the process of implementing clauses A and B of this Article, the date of actual production or exploitation shall mean the date when commercial investment or production commences.

4. For the purpose of implementing Article 14 of Investment Law, the period of creating an investment project commences on the date when the decision providing for the creation of a joint-sector company, joint-stock company or limited liability company is issued. For enterprises belonging to other natural or legal persons the period of founding the enterprise commences on the date when the Higher Investment Council gives its approval mandating the creation of such enterprises.

ARTICLE 21

By a decision from the Council an additional period of two years shall be added to the exemption period stated in Article 13 of Investment Law if the total revenues resulting from exports of the enterprise's commodities and services actually transferred into the Syrian Arab Republic through Syrian Banks exceed 50% of its total production achieved during the original exemption period calculated at the end of the period.

ARTICLE 22

Joint sector companies created under Investment Law excluding all other companies shall be exempted from the stamp fees required on the issuance of its shares.

FREE ECONOMIC ZONES REGULATIONS

I. PROFILE:

1.   The Establishment was created by virtue of Legislative Decree No.18 of 1971, and the regulations governing its investment were ratified by Decree No.84 of 1972.

FUNCTIONS:

a. Management and investment of the free zones, construction of warehouses and storage units, looking after their development in a manner that leads to growth and prosperity.

b. Putting forward proposals for the creation of new free zones or for the cancellation of free zones.

c. Organizing the activities of free zones ensuring coordination so that the national economy is better served, and international trade exchanges are promoted and generally taking care of whatsoever is related to the management and investment of free zones.

DEVELOPMENT:

The first decade of the establishment's work can be described as the phase when construction works were completed in the free zones of Damascus, Adra, the airport, Aleppo, Lattakia and Tartous, which were also provided with all the necessary facilities and services needed for the zones investment.

The second decade was characterized by persistent and endless work for accomplishing their organizational structure. Laws were thoroughly studied and re-adjusted so that this new experience could be placed on the right track. However, substantial development has been seen in recent years in the investment activity of the free zones.

A remarkable increase has been noticed in the movement of goods admitted or exited. Trade exchanges were promoted to higher levels, which was positively reflected in the volume of the Establishment's foreign currency income and the increase of earnings gained from the private facilities that have come up with it.

WHAT IS A FREE ZONE?

It is a part of the national territory having borders and walls that separate it from the customs jurisdiction. It has a status similar to a foreign territory as far as the laws of foreign trade exchange and customs barriers are concerned. Yet, all laws and regulations governing security, public morals, public health, combatting smuggling are applied to those zones. From this point of view goods and commodities are admitted into free zones quite freely, exempted from customs duties and taxes and free from restrictions and economic regulations that are valid inside the country. Consequently, all types of goods are imported into the free zones and re-exported quite freely to Arab and foreign countries. But once such goods are to enter Syria, then all the laws and regulations in force in Syria are applicable.

CREATION OF A FREE ZONE:

The job of creating a free zone is the charge of the General Establishment of Free Zones, which erects walls around it, provides all facilities required such as administration buildings, warehouses, sheds, yards, machinery and equipment as well as access through roads, sewage, electricity, water and telephone lines. It is also in charge of guarding and insuring the goods placed therein.

TYPES OF INVESTMENT IN A FREE ZONE:

COMMERCIAL AND INDUSTRIAL:

It is the type of investment where a certain plot of land assigned for building is used by the investor for the purpose of setting up the building on it, or the investor uses a building or yard which are inside the free zone, and provided with all the facilities of roads, sewage, electricity - .etc. for the purpose of initiating an industrial project thereon, or for storing goods inside the constructions erected on the land assigned for building, or inside the already constructed building, or still in the yards as the nature of the material permits, or according to availability of space.

This investment is made against an annual fee for long-term tenancy not exceeding 15 years in the case of a piece of land used for the construction of a building for commercial activity, or not exceeding 20 years in the case of a piece of land used for the construction of building for industrial activity. Tenancy of buildings and yards is subject to annual contracts with time limits, namely not exceeding 5 years for a building used industrially, and 3 years for a building used commercially. Those contracts, however, are renewable upon expiry by mutual consent of the two parties, and against a new tenancy fee which is determined each year by a decision passed by the board of directors. The second party in such transactions is described as the Investor.

DEPOSIT:

This means the storage of goods at the warehouses, sheds and yards which are set up at the free zone by the Establishment and whose ownership reverts to the Establishment after the expiry of the long-term tenancy contracts signed with the investors who do not desire renewal, or for one reason or another the contracts were terminated. The goods are stored against a fee specified in the relevant investment regulations. However, owners of the goods may concede their ownership to a third party, which should be done in the presence of the zone officers. Goods may also undergo a process of converting such as packaging or canning inside the warehouses provided that the zone management's approval is obtained beforehand. In this type of activity the concerned person is called a depositor.

ESTABLISHMENT OF BANKING FACILITIES INSIDE THE FREE ZONE:

The Establishment's investment regulations permit the setting up of banking facilities inside the free zones so that the various activities carried out in them could be properly financed, and banking services could be offered to the investors. Unfortunately, this activity has not commenced yet, pending the issuance of the special tenancy regulations for banks inside free zones.

FREE MARKETS:

The investment regulations permit the establishment of free markets inside the free zones in addition to duty free shops in the principal cities of the country as well as civilian airports and seaports. Consequenlly, licences have been granted to a number of investors authorizing them to sell their goods by the piece inside the free zones of Adra, Damascus and Lattakia in the same way as the sale is conducted in duty free shops where commodities are sold to transit travellers or to passengers on international flights who are re-exporting the goods or to members of diplomatic or consular missions or others who are treated as such. The general rules of free zones are applied to those markets.

V. THE PRESENT FREE ZONES:

The free zones currently functioning are in Damascus, Adra, Damascus International Airport, Aleppo , Lattakia and Tartous. A brief account on each follows hereunder:

DAMASCUS FREE ZONE:

It is situated in the heart of the city, behind the General Directorate of Customs. Its surface area is 88.5 donums with an area of 72 donums set aside for investment. The activities carried out in this zone cover commercial activity (storage in private facilities), deposite in general warehouses, industrial activity, retail sales to transit passengers and to diplomats as per regulations for free markets. All the areas are tenanted for investment.

ADRA FREE ZONE:

It is situated on the Damascus-Baghdad highway 35km to the north-east of Damascus. It can be accessed also by a railway line. Thus goods can be transported to and from it by train. Its walled areas total 731 donums with various activities carried out there. Certain industries have been set up in this zone and there are storage units, two market places for the trade of foreign cars, one of which has 45 sections and the other 33. All the sections are tenanted, although there are some spaces which have not yet been invested. Furthermore, there are certain waerhouses and yards placed at the disposal of the customs directorate for the storage of goods awaiting clearance.

DAMASCUS AIRPORT FREE ZONE:

It lies in the western end of the airport with a total area of 24 donums and all facilities assigned for investment are used for both commercial and industerial activities.

LATTAKIA FREE ZONE:

Situated about 7 kms from Lattakia port on the road junction, it has an area for the first stage totalling 282 donums provided with all facilities and services. Both commercial and industerial activities are practhere and there are still some spaces ready for investment.

ALEPPO FREE ZONE:

It lies 18 kms to the north of Aleppo near the village of Musellemieh having a total area of 1117 donums. The total area of walled spaces for the first stage is 320 donums accessed by a railway line for the transport of cargo to and from it. In fact the train gets to the edge of warehouses. Both commercial and industrial activities are practised in the zone though there are still wide areas which have not been invested. Part of its warehouses and yards is placed at the disposal of the customs authority for storage of goods that await clearance.

TARTOUS FREE ZONE:

Situated on the Tartous-Lattakia highway, the free zone is actually very close to Tartous port separated from it by a gateway for admission and exit of goods and cargo between it and the port. Its surface area totals 436 donums and it is provided with all facilities and services. Investment in it tilts more towards commercial activity as a large part of the area is used for the storage of cars, iron, and timber. But there are some big industerial enterprises. The zone has the advantage of being very close to the port of Tartous, thus the expenses on formalities and transport from the port to it and vice versa have been greatly reduced because carrying goods to it from the port is direct, needing no formalities. Goods can move on from the vessel to the free zone or vice versa.

The greatest part of areas assigned for investment have been tenanted and only a very small part remains ready for tenancy.

VI. Fees Levied by the Establishment:

a. Tenancy Fee: This fee is levied from investors who sign contracts of tenancy for a certain place inside the investment area of the free zone. It is defined by the area unit (square meter) per annum and must be paid whether or not the place is used. It becomes due once the place is handed over to the investor usable and free of any occupancy. This fee differs according to type of tenancy, commercial or industrial, and according to nature of the section, (prepared for construction, already constructed, or open yard). It also differs from one free zone to another.

b. Deposit fee: It is levied from those persons who deposit their goods for storage in free zone warehouses, defined by weight unit (ton) and for the whole period of storage in the zone's warehouses. It differs from one section to another depending on the nature of the place (roofed warehouses, sheds, yards). It also differs according to the nature of the goods to be stored (commodities, cars), or the value or specific density of the merchandise. Consequently, wherever a tenancy fee is applied, a deposit fee is not, and vice versa.

c. Re-export fee: This fee is levied by the Establishment in return for the benefits which the investor or depositor gets from the advantages and facilities provided by the free zones. It is due on all goods exited from the free zones either for local consumption or for re-export abroad. It differs according to the type of tenancy (commercial or industerial) and is specified at a small percentage of the value of goods manufactured, or stored or deposited in the free zones.

d. Fees against services: In addition to the above, the Establishment levies other fees in return for services it provides at the request of the investor or depositor such as crane charges, weigh-bridge charges, water, electicity, telephone , fees on desistation, fees on documents requested and fees for administrative service,..etc.

VII. THE ESTABLISHMENT'S REVENUES:

REVENUES:

Statistics show a remarkable increase in the Establishment's revenues over the past years as a result of an increase of investment, which eventually showed a rise in the Establishment's earnings of foreign currency as well as Syrian currency. The following table shows the income in the period 1993 – 1997 (in thousand S.P.)

	1993	1994	1995	1996	1997
Income covered by foreign currency	198.948	261.491	250.738	281.203	349.863
Income in S.P.	43.521	45.577	49.070	44.541	40.624
Total	242.473	307.068	299.808	325.744	390.487

Revenues in foreign currency resulting from the Establishment's activities for the period 1993 – 1997 are shown in the following table (thousand dollars)

1993	1994	1995	1996	1997
4.385	5.666	5.392	6074	7.156

Profits:

The Establishment achieved during the same five-year period as above remarkable profits earned annually which are shown in the follwing table (in thousand S.P.)

1993	1994	1995	1996	1997
95.591	128092	131.326	138.435	168.036

MOVEMENT OF GOODS:

The remarkable development of investment activity in free zones showed itself in the movement of goods coming into, or leaving the free zones, in all categories of investment, industrial, commercial and general warehouses. The table hereunder gives figures of the goods movement during the past five years:

Year	Weight (ton)	Value (thousand S.P.)
1993	1.029.426	20.896.043
1994	1.452.335	46.422.748
1995	1.095.138	55.791.041
1996	1.222.821	43.015.861
1997	1.962.710	38.549.532

INVESTMENT LICENSES:

In response to potential investors' requests, the Establishment on an annual basis sets up additional spaces for investment. It is noteworthy to point out that all places of Damascus and airport free zones are completely used up and those in Tartous free zone are more or less used up. This situation has prompted the Establishment to take the necessary measures and prepare the needed studies for the setting up of new free zones. The following table shows the newly licensed areas and number of new investors who use areas in the free zones during the same five-year period:

	1993	1994	1995	1996	1997
New areas (sq.m.)	72.146	114.577	78.099	60.299	106.560
Number of new Investors	85	90	136	90	96

OPERATION REGULATIONS OF FREE ZONE IN SYRIAN ARAB REPUBLIC

LEGISLATIVE DECREE NO. 18 ON THE FUNDAMENTAL REGULATIONS OF THE ESTABLISHMENT

The President of the Republic
Pursuant to the rules of the provisional constitution
Pursuant to decision no.18 issued by the council of ministers on 18.2.1971

ENACTS as follows:

Article 1
There shall be created a public establishment that enjoys the status of a juristic person and has a financial and administrative autonomy to be called the public establishment of free zones in the Syrian Arab Republic attached to the minister of economy and foreign trade.

The establishment shall be considered to be an establishment of an economic character and shall be governed in its dealing with third party by the provisions of the law of commerce.

The head office of the establishment shall be in the city of Damascus and the establishment may set up branches in other Syrian cities if and when necessary.

Article 2
The Establishment shall assume the following duties:

To run and operate the free zones, to set up such warehouses and stores as may be necessary for such free zones, and to develop them so as to contribute to the growth and prosperity of these zones.

To propose such projects so as to set up or to cancel free zone.

To organize the functions of the free zones and to coordinate their activities so as to serve economy and to develop international trade exchange.

To exercise all such powers that has been exercised by such bodies operating the free zones except such powers in relation to the affairs of customs control.

Generally to handle all matters concerning the management and operation of the free zones.

The Establishment shall observe such provisions and conditions concerning customs and currency control and shall provide such constructions as may be necessary for this purpose.

Article 3
The Establishment shall have a board of directors to be set up and its powers to be defined as provided for in the fundamental regulations.

The Establishment shall be run by a general manager to be appointed by a decree and his powers shall be defined in the fundamental regulations.

Article 4
The Fundamental regulations, the numerical strength and the operation regulations of the Establishment shall be issued by a decree with the approval of the Economic committee and these regulations may embody exclusions from the provisions of the laws and regulations in force.

The other regulations of the Establishment shall be issued by an order from the minister of economy and foreign trade on a proposal by the board of directors provided that the approval by the minister of finance of the financial regulations shall be obtained.

Pending the issue of the regulations referred to in the two preceding clauses the internal, financial and appointment and employment regulations in force at present in the free zones shall continue to be in force in so far as they are not contrary to the provisions of this legislative decree.

Article 5
The Establishment shall follow the state financial year and shall keep its accounts in line with the principles of business accounting. The funds of the Establishment shall be considered as public funds for the purpose of the application of the provisions of the law of economic sanctions.
Article 6
For financing the Establishment depends in particular on:

Dues, rents and charges for temporary tenancy and services as defined in the operation regulations.

The appropriations annually set aside by the state for the Establishment.

Loans from third party.

Article 7
As regards court proceedings the Establishment shall be relieved from giving in a deposit in all such cases a deposit is required to be given in by law.

Article 8
There shall be transferred to the Establishment the free zones created prior to the issue of this legislative decree together with such constructions existing in such free zones. These constructions, the land attached thereto, their equipment and their value shall be determined by an agreement made for this purpose between the minister of finance and minister of economy and foreign trade.

Article 9
With due observance of the legal provisions in force persons in the employ of the free zones existing at the date of the coming into force of this legislative decree may be transferred or seconded to the Establishment by an order from the board of directors upon an agreement with the minister of finance and the government service in which such persons work.

Article 10
All provisions contrary to this legislative decree shall be deemed to be automatically amended.

Article 11
This legislative decree shall be published in the official Gazette and shall come into force immediately upon its issue.

Damascus, 23.12.1390 h.

18.02.1971 A.D.

President of the Republic

Decree No. 84

The President of the republic,

Pursuant to the rules of legislative decree no. 18 of 18.2.1971,

Enacts as follows:

Article 1
The operation regulations of free zones and duty free shops in the Syrian Arab Republic and its annex containing the operation tariffs shall be endorsed and shall be applied to all free zones and duty free shops in the country.

Article 2
The provisions contrary to these regulations shall be repealed.

Article 3
This Decree shall be published and shall be notified to whomsoever necessary for implementation.
Damascus, 24.11.1391 H.

10.01.1972 A.D.

President of the Republic

OPERATION REGULATIONS OF FREE ZONES IN SYRIAN ARAB REPUBLIC

General Provisions

Article 1

The following expressions shall have the meanings hereby assigned to them:

The Establishment: The public establishment of free zones

The board: The Board of directors of the establishment

The director: the General director of the establishment

Article 2

These regulations shall apply to all free zones and duty free shops that are set up or will be set up in the Syrian Arab Republic.

Article 3

The establishment shall have the exclusive power to operate all free zones and duty free shops and the board may upon a proposal by the director assign the duty to operate the markets to another administration upon such conditions as may be set by the board.

Article 4

The establishment shall have a right of priority over all movable and immovable property of the establishment's debtors lying within free zones and duty free shops.

Article 5

Free zones and duty free shops shall be governed by the laws and regulations concerning security, morals, public health and antismuggling.

ADMISSION OF GOODS

Article 6

Foreign goods of any description whatsoever, irrespective of their origin or source, shall be allowed to be admitted into and exited out of free zones and duty free shops, to the exclusion of the customs zone, and shall in this case be not subject to foreign trade regulations and shall not be chargeable to customs duties and taxes.

Domestic goods or goods that have become as such by placement for consumption shall be allowed to be admitted into free zones and duty free shops shall be governed by the regulations in force in this respect.

Goods lying in the free zone shall be allowed to be admitted into the customs zone to be placed for local consumption in accordance with the laws and regulations in force.

Article 7

As an exception to the provisions of article 6 the following goods shall be prohibited from being admitted into free zones and markets under pain of seizure without any indemnity, apart from such other legal measures as are provided for in the laws in force.

Goods of Israeli origin or source, goods prohibited to be imported under Israel boycott regulations and goods from such states with which economic dealing is prohibited.

Narcotics of any description and their derivatives to the exclusion of such narcotics and derivatives for medicines and pharmaceutical industry.

Arms, ammunitions and explosives of any description whatsoever to the exclusion of hunting arms and their ammunitions.

Rotten or inflammable materials as shown on such tables issued and upon such conditions specified by the establishment satisfy the requirement of public security, health and safety.

Article 8
The status of the free zone shall not preliminary require within the boundaries of this zone any measures to be taken by the customs other than such measures for the detection of goods prohibited from being admitted under the provisions of article 7 of these regulations in agreement and cooperation with the establishment whereupon the establishment shall report to the customs any and all things in violation of the provisions of the said article the establishment's officials or employees may perceive.

Article 9
Goods shall be admitted into the free zone on the strength of an application to be submitted by the person concerned or his legal representative showing the origin, source, nature, type, weight and value of the goods as well as the type, trademark, numbering and number of the parcels, and the application shall contain a declaration by the applicant to the effect that he is cognizant of the provisions of these regulations and all rules concerning the operation of free zones and undertakes to observe and comply with them.

Admission shall be as follows:

Admission by land:

From inside or outside the country: the customs formality accompanying the goods shall be attached to the application in question.

Admission by sea:

From outside the country direct into the free zone in the same seaport.

The original copy of the shipping manifest shall be attached to the documents and bills of lading.

If the destination of the goods is an inland free zone, apart from the manifest, the documents and bills of lading referred to in the preceding clause shall be attached to the customs formality.

From a Syrian seaport into a free zone in another Syrian seaport or an inland free zone admission shall be subject to the same conditions referred to in the preceding clause.

Article 10
The Establishment shall submit to the customs lists of all materials admitted into or exited from the free zone within 36 hours.

Article 11
When goods are admitted into or exited from the free zone, they shall be entered into the admission and exit registers prepared by the establishment in such approved regular forms which shall contain all such data of the relevant goods as set out in article 9 and all such data that may facilitate the identification of the goods.

Article 12

The goods admitted into the free zone shall be deposited in general roofed warehouses, and where there are no places in such warehouses, they shall be put under sheds or, otherwise, in open yards, with due regard as far as possible to the nature of the goods. There shall be put in open yards in particular:

Such goods that are impossible to put in sheds or roofed warehouses by reason of shape, size or weight, and are not affected by atmospheric conditions.

However, if the goods are affected by such conditions, the owners of the goods or their legal representatives shall take the necessary precautions for their protection.

The Establishment may take, without being bound, at the expense of the owners of the goods, at its sole discretion, the precautionary measures in question, and shall, in exercising this right, advise the persons concerned of the measures that have been taken and the quantum of expenses due within 48 hours, and the owners of the goods shall have the right to apply to the Establishment in writing to lift such precautionary measures at their own responsibility.

Such goods whose owners apply for their deposit in such a manner especially when the warehouses and sheds are full provided that the owners of such goods shall submit a prior declaration in writing to the effect that such a deposit is at their own responsibility.

Article 13
There shall be deposited in free zones the goods whose particulars and types are set out in the applications for admission and the owners of such goods shall be held responsible for the correctness of the statements that have been submitted and for any fault or fraud that may be found therein.

HANDING & TAKING OVER

Article 14
The goods shall be handed over to the establishment if and when they are admitted into such places other than the private tenancy according to the following procedures there shall be registered in the presence of the owner of the goods or his legal representative the parcels that have been admitted according to their types, marks and numberings, the damaged and suspicious parcels shall be sorted out, weighed and plumbed, an outturn report shall be made under the signature of the representative of the establishment and the person concerned, and there shall be entered in the outturn report any contradiction between the statements and documents on the one hand and the goods that have been taken over on the other hand. Goods in bulk or goods impossible to count shall be admitted as a whole according to their relevant documents and a reference shall be made in this respect in the outturn report.

If the person concerned declines to sign the outturn report or enters a reservation as to the facts established therein and fails to approach the court of urgent affairs within a maximum period of 3 days as from the date of the outturn report, this outturn report shall have full effect and force as if it had been signed without any reservation.

Article 15
Handing and taking over shall be as follows:

Goods of identical units : by number or weight on the basis of the carton.

Goods in bulk or goods impossible to count: according to the relevant documents without counting or weighing (i.e. as a whole as they have been received).

Other goods: by number without weight.

The Establishment shall not be responsible upon handing and taking over the goods referred to in clause (2) for weight and number as well as the goods referred to in clauses (1) and (3) for number even if this is given in the documents of the goods unless the owner of the goods asks the Establishment for handing and taking over be made on the basis of actual weight. In this case the expenses for weighing upon admission and exit shall be borne by the owner of the goods and the properties and nature of the goods, the method of packing and other circumstances that may have an effect of the weight of the goods, increase or decrease, shall be taken into consideration, whereupon the Establishment shall not be held responsible for any shortage in weight as a result of such circumstances.

WAREHOUSE WARRANTS

Article 16
The owner of the goods that have been deposited shall be given at his own request a nominal warehouse warrant or a receipt to order. Both shall be extracted from a book with counterfoil in which there shall be entered:

The name, surname, calling and service address of the depositor.

The number and date of admission of the goods into the general warehouses.

The name and nationality of the carrier vessel, if and when necessary, or any other means of transport.

The type of insurance and the sum insured.

The number, marks and condition of the parcels and place of depositing.

The type of the goods declared, the contents of the parcels and their weight.

The depositor of the goods shall be solely held responsible for the correctness of these particulars.

Article 17
The goods for which a warehouse warrant or a receipt to order is given shall be deposited in one place. The holder of the warrant or receipt shall have the right to divide the quantity deposited into several independent parts and to apply for the warrant or receipt to be replaced by a number of warrants or receipts equal to the number of the parts of the goods provided that the necessary measures shall be taken to distinguish these parts and to prevent their being mixed if and when necessary.

Article 18
The nominal warehouse warrants shall not be endorseable. The goods for which nominal warrants have been given shall be assigned before the establishment according to such instructions as may be issued by the establishment provided that both the assignor and the assignee or their respective legal representatives shall appear and the warehouse warrants of the goods that have been assigned shall be returned for the issue of new warrants in the name of the new owner in substitution.

Article 19
In case of the loss of the nominal warehouse warrant another warehouse warrant in replacement may be given or the goods subject of the warrant may be handed over to the person in whose name they are entered against a receipt along a declaration in writing of the loss of the warrant.

Article 20

Prior to the registration of the assignment and the issue of a new warehouse warrant to the assignee the applicant shall pay all fees chargeable on the goods assigned up to the date of the registration of the assignment.

Article 21

The depositor shall have the right to endorse the receipt to third party with no need to obtain the approval of or to notify the establishment and the endorser's obligations in respect of the goods shall devolve on the endorsee.

All notifications and notices shall be served by the establishment on the depositor and the goods that are the property of the depositor or the ultimate endorsee shall remain as a security for all the establishment's entitlements.

Article 22

In case of the loss of the receipt to order neither a replacement may be issued nor the goods may be handed over save by decision from the competent court and the establishment shall be under no responsibility in consequence.

Article 23

Endorsement shall transfer the ownership of the goods and all rights and obligations of the endorser in respect of the goods shall devolve on the endorsee.

Article 24

The depositing of the goods in the free zone shall not primarily be limited to a specified period except in such cases that necessitate the exit of the goods by reason of their very nature or the failure by their owners to pay such amounts as may be due to the establishment from them or their violation of the provisions of these regulations.

Article 25

The establishment shall have the right, as the exigencies of operation may be require, move, with approval of the persons concerned, the goods from the place where they are lying to another place as the establishment may deem appropriate. Anyhow the establishment may remove, at the expense of the persons concerned, the goods that may be found deleterious to the neighborhood, public health or to the constructions of the establishment.

Article 26

The establishment shall arrange for the insurance of the goods deposited in the warehouses and yards against fire risks and civil liability. This insurance shall be obligatory.

The establishment shall recover from the owners of the goods deposited the insurance premiums appropriate to the value of the goods deposited and duration of depositing.

Article 27

The establishment shall take such care as may be necessary to safeguard the goods deposited in the free zone and shall take such measures necessary for their maintenance. If it appears that the goods are susceptible to destruction or that the damage to the goods or to other goods by reason of the damage to the goods in question has become grave at the discretion of the establishment, then the establishment shall have the right to serve a notice in writing by registered mail to the person concerned to remove the goods out of the free zone within such a time limit as the establishment may set as the case may be, and in default the establishment shall have the right in agreement with the administration of customs to sell or to destroy such goods.

The establishment may take such measures as may be necessary to protect the goods, to re-pack the parcels that have suffered damage and change or repair the covers at the expense of the owner of the goods if and when the establishment may so deem necessary with the approval of the person concerned, and the establishment shall have the right to carry out such works spontaneously at the expense of the persons concerned if and when the establishment may so deem necessary.

The waste of the goods as a result of probing, packing and collection by reason of loose parcels shall be handed over to the owners provided that they shall pay for their collection and sweeping and for the bags and containers packed therein if and when necessary.

The establishment shall dispose as the establishment may wish in its own interest with the waste of the goods that have not been identified.

Article 28
The establishment shall not be responsible for blemish, damage or defect by reason of the nature of the goods, the form of their packing, their unpacking, and the ambient temperature or humidity throughout the period of depositing. Further the establishment shall not be responsible for damage by reason of strikes, commotion, riots, war operations and different sorts of force major as well as by reason of harmful animals the establishment have to fight.

The establishment shall be held responsible for damage to the goods if it is established that such damage is a result of any act or negligence on the part of its officials, employees or workers, or the bad condition of its warehouses or their being not suitable for storage, on the strength of a decision issued by the competent court of law. The board may reach an amicable settlement to indemnify for the damage without recourse of the court of law.

Article 29
There shall be allowed to be set up and to be carried out freely in the free zones with a prior license from the establishment different industries, plants and all converting processes. They are as an example not by way of limitation division, sorting, forming, processing, packing, packaging, mixing, purifying, cleaning, lubricating, distilling, acidifying, hammering, breaking, crushing, marking, placing and changing trademarks.

The above operations shall be primarily carried out in places of special operations and the establishment may allow some of such operations be carried out in its general warehouses, yards or in such places prepared for this purpose if and when the establishment finds it possible.

DUTIES AND FEES

Article 30
The board shall have the right to endorse and set fees for such services that have not been envisaged in the tariff.

The board shall have the right to increase or to decrease the fees as set out in the tariff annexed to these regulations at a rate not over than 50%. The new fees shall apply to all beneficiaries.

The decisions adopted by the board under the provisions of (a) and (b) shall be published in the official Gazette.

Article 31
The establishment shall collect the following fees as set in the tariff of free zones annexed to these regulations:

Porterage and handling fees.

Storage fee.

Tenancy fee.

Entry fee.

Insurance fee.

Assignment fee.

Fee for other services and for use of equipment and plant.

Article 32
The establishment shall carry out porterage and handling operations and shall collect from the owner of the goods the fee on the basis of weight in package or on the basis of actual weight as the case may be.

As regards goods in bulk that are impossible to count, the fee shall be collected on the basis of the weight as given in the documents (manifest, customs declaration, or shipping document) whether porterage by hand labor by vehicles and equipment in the following cases:

Case 1: Transport of the goods from the quay or the entrance of the free zone to the allocated place inside the zone and their stowing and stacking according to their types and marks.

Case 2: Transport of the goods from the warehouses or yards of the free zone to the quay or the inspection room and their loading after survey for transport outside the free zone.

Case 3: Taking over the goods alongside the means of transport inside the free zone, their depositing at the allocated place in the warehouses or yards inside the free zone and their stowing and stacking according to their types and marks.

Case 4: Transport of the goods from the warehouses or yards in the free zone and their delivery alongside on board the means of transport inside the free zone.

Case 5: Unloading the goods from a means of land transport and onloading on board another means of land transport.

Article 33
The establishment shall collect from the owner of the goods fees for all porterage operations that are not within the definition in the previous article. They cover collecting, re-packing, changing and repair covers, weighing, sorting, handling, and such other services relating to porterage as defined in the tariff.

Article 34
If the owner of the goods applies for porterage or another service and then he withdraws his application in whole or in part, the establishment shall have the right, if the necessary measures have already been taken, (according to the circumstances), to collect a porterage fee at a maximum rate or 50% for the entire quantity handled by labour.

Article 35
The establishment shall collect storage fee for such goods deposited in such warehouses inside the free zone other than the warehouses occupied by tenants throughout the whole period of their stay in the warehouses without any period of exemption.

The storage fee shall be calculated on the basis of the gross weight, number or volume as set in the tariff.

Article 36

The establishment shall collect a tenancy fee for such private places as defined in the contracts made with the persons concerned. If and when tenancy fee is chargeable, the establishment shall not collect storage fee for such goods deposited in the private places of the tenants.

Article 37

The establishment shall collect a duty at a flat rate in respect of such goods admitted into the free zone.

Article 38

The establishment shall collect an assignment fee each time the goods, contracts of commercial or industrial tenancy, or vehicles and means of transport are assigned.

Article 39

The establishment shall collect from the persons concerned fees for the different materials, services, certificates or copies of documents the establishments provides at request and charges for the use of machines and equipment.

Article 40

The fees shall be chargeable for the whole period of the stay of the goods in the free zone up to the date of their actual exit.

The board shall fix, upon a proposal from the director, the dates for the payment of the fees and advances to be paid by the persons concerned on account of the fees.

The establishment shall have the right, if there is a delay on the part of the persons concerned for more than 6 months in paying such fees, to sell the goods by public auction following the service of a notice in writing and the lapse of a period of 15 days as from the date on which the persons concerned have been served the said notice.

As regards goods that have a small value, the establishment shall have the right, if and when the fees are not paid on the dates on which they become due and payable, to sell such goods by public auction after the persons concerned are served a notice and after the lapse of the time limit referred to above. Sale shall be effected on the basis of the customs status in the free zone.

Article 41

If a dispute arises between the establishment and the persons concerned over the question of fees and charges, the persons concerned shall pay the amount claimed by the establishment and shall then have the right to appeal administratively to the competent authority in the establishment and to have recourse, if and when necessary, to the competent court of law.

Article 42

It is a condition precedent to the refunds of the difference in fees and charges erroneously collected that the difference shall be greater than five Syrian pounds and that an application in writing shall be filed within a maximum period of 6 months as from the date of collection.

Article 43

The establishment shall draft the forms of tenancy contracts and shall define the conditions of such tenancy. These contracts shall be considered temporary tenancy contracts and shall not be governed by the provisions of the law of rent.

The maximum period of the temporary tenancy contract shall be:

One year in respect of open places intended to be occupied for storage purposes without erecting buildings or installing industrial equipment.

Fifteen years in respect of open places intended to be occupied for the purpose of erecting buildings for storage.

Twenty years in respect of open places intended to be occupied for the purpose of erecting buildings for converting industries and processes.

The ownership of the buildings and appurtenances shall devolve on to the establishment after the expiry of the period as specified in the tenancy contracts.

These contracts shall be renewed, after the expiry of their period, from year to year for a rent to be paid in advance and to be fixed by mutual agreement unless the person concerned expresses his intention in writing not to renew the contract three months before the expiry of the term.

Article 44

If the establishment finds that the person concerned has suspended his activity for two consecutive years of five years at intermittent intervals without a lawful excuse, the establishment shall have the right, with the approval of the board, to determine the contract or to refuse the renewal of the contract, and this shall be attended by all consequences attending the expiry of the initial period of the contract.

Article 45

The industrial operation in free zones shall be mainly oriented for export. There may be allowed with the approval of the ministry of economy and foreign trade, upon a proposal by the establishment, the admission of a percentage of the exports of such industries into the Syrian markets by way of exclusion from the foreign trade laws and regulations and from the restrictions imposed on import except such restrictions relating to the limitation or restriction of import to a public sector body. For this portion of production there shall be granted automatic import licenses with no need to transfer the value abroad and this portion of production shall be exempt from duties pro rata the local materials incorporated in manufacture.

Article 46

It shall be observed that the industries set up in free zones shall not lead to the imitation or competition of such industries in the country except in such where they enter into a partnership with local industries .priority shall be given to the following industries with due regard to the industrial strategy and the requirements of the development plans in the Syrian Arab Republic:

Industries for which local raw materials or locally manufactured components are available.

Industries that integrate with locally existing industries.

New industries that are not locally existing and depend on modern technical production.

Industries that meet the need of local consumption and help to dispense with import from abroad.

Industries that help to employ a greater number of hand labour.

Article 47

The prospective tenant shall submit an application to the establishment in which he shall specify the purpose of tenancy, the types of goods intended to be stored or converted , the places intended to be occupied, and the buildings or the industrial enterprises and equipment he wishes to erect or set up thereon provided that the prospective tenant shall be residing in the city or town in which the free zone is situate, or shall have therein a service address or a representative.

Applications for tenancy submitted by foreign natural or juristic persons shall not be allowed unless such persons have established a head office or a branch in the Syrian Arab Republic or unless such persons have a representative who is a Syrian Arab Citizen.

In this latter case the application shall be accompanied by a copy of the contract made between the two parties provided that this contract shall, anyhow, be registered in accordance with the domestic laws.

The area of the land intended to be occupied by the prospective tenant shall not be more than 10% of the area allocated for private tenancy inside the free zone.

Article 48
The contracts made between the two parties shall specify the mode and dates of payment of the tenancy fee. There shall be collected from the prospective tenant a tenancy fee for at least one year in advance. As regards contracts for less than one year, the fee shall be collected in advance for the whole term of the contract.

Article 49
The director shall determine the applications submitted for tenancy of land for storage and the board shall determine, upon a proposal by the director, the applications submitted for tenancy of land to set up industrial enterprises.

Buildings and industrial enterprises shall be set up on the land tenanted as indicated on the drawing with all roads and means for protection from fire risks upon an approval by the establishment. There shall be observed the technical procedures as to storage, converting and manufacturing and any modification in these drawings shall be subject to an approval from the establishment.

Article 50
The tenants of private places shall observe and comply with the rules for protection from fire and explosion. Insurance shall cover civil liability to such an extent at the discretion of the establishment and shall be made with accredited insurance companies. This insurance shall be obligatory at the expense of the tenants.

Article 51
The goods shall be forwarded to the private places in the free zone at the request of the tenants provided that these goods shall be for the tenants or that these goods are regularly assigned to them. Further these goods shall be relevant to the purposes for which the place has been allocated in the tenancy contract and shall be entered in the registers of the places tenanted. Goods shall be chargeable in case of the violation of any of the conditions referred to herein to a double storage fee.

Article 52
If the tenants of the private places violate the provisions of these regulations or the terms of the tenancy contracts made with them , the establishment shall address a notice to them to remedy the violation within such a time limit as specified in the notice. In default to remedy the violation within the time limit as set in the notice, the establishment shall have the right , with the approval of the board , to rescind the contracts and to specify a reasonable period for eviction. In this case the buildings shall become the property of the establishment with no indemnity. If the persons concerned fail to remove their goods, machines and equipment within the stated time limit, the establishment shall have the right to do so at their own expense and the goods, machines and equipment shall be stored at their own expense in the general warehouses and yards.

Article 53

The tenants of private places shall be responsible for all damage caused by them, their representatives or their subordinates, or by reason of their enterprises or goods to other buildings or enterprises or the goods lying therein inside and outside the free zone, and their observance of the safety rules imposed on them shall not release them from liability.

Article 54
The tenants of private places shall keep and maintain registers to enter the incoming and outgoing goods. These registers shall be maintained in such forms as specified by the establishment.

Article 55
The tenants of private places shall keep and maintain records of the names and number of their employees and workers and the date of their employment in the free zone and lists thereof shall be sent direct to the establishment. All amendments to the particular of the records, increase or decrease, shall be notified to the establishment. The tenants shall hand each of their employees and workers a sign in such a uniform model to be specified by the establishment to carry the name of the employer and the number of the warehouse or the industrial enterprise and to be put on the arm when on duty inside the free zone. These signs shall be left with the establishment's watchmen at the gates of the free zone when they exit.

The tenants of private places shall be responsible for the behavior of their employees and workers. The establishment shall have the right to prevent any of such employees and workers from entering into the free zone if and when such person violates the regulations of work therein.

Article 56
The establishment may allow the tenants of private places to assign to third party the right of tenancy of the land they occupy and the enterprises erected on such land within the following conditions:

Assignment shall be made before the competent official of the establishment.

A new contract shall be made between the assignee and the establishment and shall be subject to all terms of the former contract with the assignor.

The assignment fee as set in the tariff of fees shall be paid.

Article 57
The tenants of private places who carry on an industrial activity in the free zone shall keep and maintain special records of the industrial machines used in such places to enter their admission and exit, with certain records assigned for machine from the domestic market, and there shall be entered therein such particulars as may be necessary such description, number, mark, origin, value, destination, type and such other useful data.

Article 58
The goods that have been admitted into the private places and have undergone converting processes shall be entered in special records to give all necessary clarifications of the converting, mixing and manufacturing processes and to show the type of the materials that have been used in the new production, their quantities, their origin and all such relevant data, and shall be cleared in such other records and registers referred to in these regulations. The products that have been converted or manufactured in the free zone shall carry the expression "free zone in ..." in a product the board resolves to be relieved from this expression.

FREE MARKETS

Article 59

The establishment may establish free markets inside the free zones, in the main cities in the country, in civil airports and in seaports.

The duty free shop shall consist of commercial stores for the wholesale or retailsale of foreign and national goods to passengers in transit and international passengers for re-export, diplomatic and consular corps, and the like, and the general rules of free zones shall apply to these duty free shops in with the nature of their composition and the purpose for which they have been established.

The establishment shall specify the types of goods, the sale conditions and the means of control in agreement with the administration of customs and the administration of the airport as the case may be provided that sale shall be in such acceptable foreign currency.

The operations allowed in the free markets shall be limited to the sorting, packing, division and grading operations and such operations as may be necessary for preservation.

Article 60
The body assigned the duty by the establishment to operate the duty free shop shall be responsible towards the establishment for all violations and faults committed direct by the said body, its agents or its subordinates.

EXIT OF GOODS

Article 61
Goods shall be exited from the free zone upon an application in writing by the person concerned to the establishment and the application shall show the type of the goods, their origin, and the number and types of parcels.

If the goods have undergone any of the converting or manufacturing operations referred to in these regulations, all clarifications of the operation in question shall be given, further, in case of mixing or new production, the types and sources of the parcels mixed shall be given, so that the customs service would be in a good position to exercise control and to compute the customs duties that may be chargeable on such materials.

Article 62
In exiting the goods the following shall be observed:

The fees due to the establishment for such goods shall be paid and the relevant customs formalities shall be channeled.

The nominal warehouse warrants or the receipts to order referred to in these regulations shall be returned.

The delivery orders and such other documents shall be produced, if and when necessary, according to such instructions issued by the establishment.

The goods shall be removed to the inspection room for survey and customs formalities. This room shall be set up at the expense of the establishment at such place to be agreed on with the administration of customs. This room shall be under the joint watchman service of both the establishment and the customs.

The owner of the goods or his representative shall sign a note in acknowledgement of receipt.

Article 63
If and when a parcel is opened for customs inspection or at the request of the person concerned, the soundness of the parcels shall be verified before opening, so that if it appears that a parcel is suspicious a customs report shall be made in cooperation with the establishment. If no customs report is made, this parcel that has been opened is considered to be intact. In this case the

establishment shall not be responsible for any discrepancy that may transpire in the contents of the parcels when opened.

OPERATION OF BANKS

Article 64
Banking enterprises may be licensed to be established within free zones to exercise functions in financing different commercial and industrial activities and operations and in rendering different bank services as may be required for the activities of the operators in these zones.

Article 65
There shall be specified by an order from the board the tenancy fee and duration.

Article 66
The board shall formulate the provisions concerning the operation of banks, especially the provisions:

To regulate the granting of loan

To specify the capital and reserve of the bank

To specify the bank operations allowed

To specify such date and information to be submitted to the establishment to verify the sound standing and activity of the bank

To specify the role of the establishment in exercising control and supervision of the bank operations

To regulate the liquidation of the bank

To specify the securities to safeguard the rights of the customers of the bank and the provisions for the regulation of the operation of bank

To specify the violations, fines and administrative penalties.

In formulating such provisions there shall be observed that they are consistent with the purpose of creating free zones and the nature of operation without due observance of the provisions of laws governing bank operations in the country.

GENERAL & MISCELLANEOUS PROVISIONS

Article 67
Foreign goods shall not be allowed to be consumed in the free zones for personal use before payment of such customs duties and other taxes and duties chargeable.

Further residence in free zones shall not be allowed save by a special permission from the establishment as may be required for running the work.

Article 68
All national and foreign vessels may arrange for the supply of all marine equipment as they may require from the free zone.

National and foreign vessels, load over 150 net marine tons, may arrange for the supply of foodstuffs, cigarettes, drinks, oil, and all materials as necessary for their machines from the free zone. The establishment shall have the right suspend the supply operation if and when fraud and abuse are established.

Article 69

Any person who enters into the free zone, or deals with it, or uses its constructions and facilities shall observe and comply with these regulations.

Article 70

No person shall be allowed to enter into the free zone unless he holds a special permit from the director of the free zone for this purpose to the exclusion of the customs guards and the competent customs officials if and when necessary for the exigencies of work.

Article 71

Working hours and procedures to enter into and exit from the free zone shall be specified by the director of the establishment.

STRATEGIC AND PRACTICAL INFORMATION FOR CONDUCTING BUSINESS

MAJOR MINISTRIES

The following is a list of selected ministries and government institutions which foreign businessmen may come into contact with.

OFFICE OF THE PRIME MINISTER

Shahbander Street, Damascus
Tel. 2226000/1/2; Tel. 2210212

INVESTMENT OFFICE

Baghdad Street, Damascus
Tel. 4410448; Tel. 4412039

MINISTRY OF AGRICULTURE AND AGRARIAN REFORM

Jabri Street, Hejaz Square, Damascus
Tel. 2213613/4; Tel. 2219874

MINISTRY OF COMMUNICATIONS

Parliament Street, Damascus
Tel. 2227033/4; Tel. 2221133/4/5

MINISTRY OF ECONOMY AND FOREIGN TRADE

Maysaloun Street, Damascus
Tel. 2213513/4/5; Tel. 2224932

MINISTRY OF EDUCATION

Shahbander Street, Damascus
Tel. 2227033/4; Tel. 2221133/4/5

MINISTRY OF ELECTRICITY

Kouwatly Street, P.O. Box 4900, Damascus
Tel. 2223086; Tel. 2229654; Tel. 2228334; Tel. 2228915

MINISTRY OF FINANCE

Tajreeda Square, P.O. Box 13136, Damascus
Tel. 2219603; Tel. 2216300/1/2/3

GENERAL DIRECTORATE FOR CUSTOMS

Palestine Street, P.O. Box 329, Damascus
Tel. 2215900/1; Tel. 2217900; Tel. 2215751

MINISTRY OF FOREIGN AFFAIRS

Shora, Muhajireen, Damascus
Tel. 3331200/1/2/3

MINISTRY OF HOUSING AND UTILITIES

Yousef Azmeh Square, Damascus
Tel. 2224194/5/6/7; Tel2217570/1/2

MINISTRY OF INDUSTRY

Maysaloun Street, P.O. Box 12835, Damascus
Tel. 2231845; Tel. 2231834; Tel. 3720959

MINISTRY OF INFORMATION

Dar Al-Baath, Mezzeh Autostrad, Damascus
Tel. 6622141/2/3/4; Tel. 6617616/94/24

ARAB ADVERTISING ORGANIZATION

Moutanabbi Street, P.O. Box 2842Damascus
Tel. 2225219/20/21

MINISTRY OF INTERIOR

Al-Marjeh, Damascus
Tel2211001; Tel. 2220100

MINISTRY OF OIL AND MINERAL RESOURCES

P.O. Box 40, Al-Adawi, Damascus
Tel. 4455972; Tel. 4445610

SYRIAN PETROLEUM COMPANY

Moutanabbi Street, P.O. Box 2849 Damascus
Tel. 3120044

MINISTRY OF SOCIAL AFFAIRS AND LABOUR

Yousef Al-Azmeh Square, Damascus

MINISTRY OF SUPPLY AND INTERNAL TRADE

Salhiyeh, Damascus
Tel. 2219044; Tel. 3720599; Tel. 2219241

MINISTRY OF TOURISM

Kouwatly Street, Damascus
Tel. 2210122; Tel. 2215916

MINISTRY OF TRANSPORT

Abou Roumaneh, Damascus
Tel. 3336801/2/3

MINISTRY OF ECONOMY AND FOREIGN TRADE

TASKS OF MINISTRY OF ECONOMY AND FOREIGN TRADE

The tasks assigned to the Ministry of Economy and Foreign Trade since it was created by Legislative Decree No. 82 of 30.06.1947 have experienced some changes enacted over the following years through various legislative instruments.

When decree No. 2804 was issued on 17.12.1969 , those tasks acquired more clarity and became better defined in terms of specialization, highlighting as it does the basic and fundamental role of the Ministry in the following domains:

1. Taking part in the drawing out of the state's economic policy .

2. Preparing the required legislation relevant to foreign trade and granting the necessary permits and licenses.

3. Concluding trade and economic cooperation agreements with Arab and foreign states.

4. Drawing out the country's monetary and banking policies as well as policies of savings, loaning and insurance and following up their implementation.

5. Overseeing the banking system, the system of the insurance establishment as well as foreign trade establishments.

6. Supervising the works of the General Establishment for Cotton Ginning and Marketing, the activities of the General Organization of Tobacco, the General Organization of Free Zones, and the General Establishment for the Damascus International Fair.

7. Looking after investment issues, encouraging, promoting and developing investment regulations.

8. Completing all procedures of importation and exportation for the public, private and mixed sectors.

9. Supervising the organization of exhibitions locally and abroad.

10. Establishing trade centers and commercial representation offices that promote Syrian products in external markets.

The Ministry of Economy and Foreign Trade accomplishes the afore-said tasks in addition to various other tasks connected with its special and significant position in the management of the economy and foreign trade through a number of directorates and offices which form in their combination the backbone of the central administration to which is linked a vast network of directorates existing in the governorates of the Syrian Arab Republic besides a number of establishments and banks affiliated with the Ministry but having their financial and administrative independence supported by their own by-laws.

However, in order to give a clear view of the administrative and organization structure that enables the Ministry of Economy and Foreign Trade to perform its active role and accomplish the tasks assigned to it , we find it useful to outline the following:

THE CENTRAL ADMINISTRATION

Directorate of:

1. The minister's own office.

2. Administration and finance.

3. Arab relations.

4. International relations and organizations.

5. Monetary and banking business, Insurance and savings.

6. Planning, statistics and follow up.

7. Foreign Trade.

8. Internal control.

9. Organizations of productive nature affairs.

10. Organizations of commercial nature affairs.

11. International fairs and exhibitions.

12. Economic affairs.

13. Commercial representation and export promotion.

14. Secretariat of export committee.

15. Export bureau.

16. Investment affairs.

ECONOMIC DIRECTORATES IN THE GOVERNORATES

Damascus- Damascus Country Side- Aleppo- Homs- Hama- Lattakia- Tartous- Hasakeh- Dara'a- Al-Sweida- Al-Rakka- Idleb- Al-Kunaitra- Deir Ez-Zor.

ORGANIZATIONS

1. General Organization of Free Zones.

2. General organization of Tabacoo.

3. Public organization for cotton ginning and marketing.

4. General organization of Damascus International Fair.

5. Geza.

6. Sayarat (vehicles).

7. Maaden (metals).

8. Gota.

9. Saydaliah (pharmacy).

10. Naseej (textiles).

BANKS

1. Central Bank Of Syria.

2. Commercial Bank Of Syria.

3. Real Estate Bank.

4. Public Loaning Bank.

5. Industrial Bank.

6. Agricultural Bank.

7. Syrian General Establishment for insurance.

COMPANIES

1. George and Anton Ginajeh

2. Machines, Electricity and agriculture (Mercedes)

3. Al-Niser for industry and commerce

4. Industrial and Agricultural Production Market in Aleppo: minister of economy and foreign trade was designated, by decree no. 2563 of 1962, as a trustee of the market's fund.

AGREEMENTS SIGNED WITH FOREIGN STATES ON PROTECTION AND GUARANTEE OF INVESTMENT

State	Type of Agreement	Date of Signing	Instrument of Ratification and Date	Remarks
United States of America	Exchanged Notes on Manner of Guaranteeing American Investments in Syria	09.08.1976	Legislative Decree No.33 dated 01.08.1977	
Swiss Federation	Accord on Encouraging and protecting Investments	22.06.1977	Legislative Decree No.24 dated 12.07.1978	Most Favoured Nation
France	Agreement on Reciprocal Encouragement and Protection of Investments	28.11.1977	Legislative Decree No.30 dated 31.07.1978	Most Favoured Nation
Federal Germany	Agreement on Reciprocal Encouragement and Protection of Investments	02.08.1977	Legislative Decree No.34 dated 11.09.1978	Most Favoured Nation
Pakistan	Accord on Reciprocal Encouragement and Protection of Investments	25.04.1996	Law No. 5 dated 02.07.1997	
People's Republic of China	Accord on Reciprocal Encouragement and Protection of Investments and	09.12.1996	Law No. 11 dated 04.08.1998	Protocol treats investment formalities and the transfers resulting

	Appended Protocol			from investment
Indonesia	Accord on Reciprocal Encouragement and Protecting Investments and Appended protocol	27.06.1997	Law No. 19 dated 31.12.1996	Most Favoured Nation. Protocol regulates transfers resulting from investment
Iran	Accord on Reciprocal Encouragement and Protection of Investments	05.02.1998	Legislative Decree No.3 dated 11.02.1998	Most Favoured Nation
Belorussia	Accord on Reciprocal Encouragement and Protection of Investments	11.03.1998	Legislative Decree No.8 dated 04.08.1998	

TRADE AGREEMENTS SIGNED WITH FOREIGN STATES

State	Type of Agreement	Date of Signing	Instrument of Ratification and Date	Remarks
Russian Federation	Technical, Economic and Commercial Cooperation	15.04.1993	Law No. 11 dated 22.06.1993	
Bulgaria	Trade	02.05.1974	Legislative Decree No.54 dated 24.07.1974	New trade agreement was initialed by the two states on 13.03.1996
Hungary	Syrian side notified Hungarian side of its decision to nullify the trade agreement of 1974			New trade agreement has been initialed by the two sides
Albania	Trade	17.06.1979	Decree No.1252 dated 08.02.1980	
Cuba	Trade	27.03.1974	Decree No.167 dated 24.07.1974	It provides for exemption from Consular legalization. New trade agreement was initialed on .03.1998
Poland	Trade	20.08.1974	Decree No.303 dated 04.12.1974	
Czech	Syrian side nullified the trade agreement of 1975 signed with Czechoslovakia when the latter broke			The two sides have not agreed to signing new trade agreement

	up as of 01.01.1993			
Slovak	Long term trade agreement	29.08.1995	Law No. 7 dated 03.07.1996	
Romania	Trade	13.04.1993		
Korea	Trade	28.06.1982	Law No.5 dated 08.02.1983	It provides for exemption from Consular Legalization
Vietnam	Trade	12.05.1994	Legislative Decree No.12 dated 27.06.1994	
People's Republic of China	Trade	16.03.1982	Law No. 23 of 1982	
Byelorussia	Technical, Economic and Commercial	11.03.1998	Legislative Decree No.9 dated 04.08.1998	
Armenia	Trade	30.03.1992	Legislative Decree No.7 dated 11.07.1992	
Turkmenistan	Trade	26.03.1992	Legislative Decree No.8 dated 11.07.1992	
Kazakhstan	Trade	27.03.1992	Legislative Decree No.9 dated 11.07.1992	
Azerbaijan	Trade	28.03.1992	Legislative Decree No.10 dated 11.07.1992	
Tajikistan	Trade	19.03.1992	Legislative Decree No.11 dated 11.07.1992	
Republic of Tanzania	Trade	15.02.1974	Decree No.166 dated 15.03.1974	
Republic of Niger	Trade	26.06.1980	Decree No.2661 dated 22.12.1980	
Republic of Nigeria	Trade	17.09.1969	Decree No.242 dated 23.12.1969	
Republic of Guinea	Trade	22.01.1979	Decree No.1209 dated 23.01.1979	
Republic of Senegal	Economic, Commercial, Cultural, and Technological	04.11.1975	Decree No.589 dated 03.03.1976	
Cyprus	Long term trade agreement	23.02.1982		
Pakistan	Trade Annex to trade agreement	11.08.1969 25.04.1996	Legislative Decree No.342 dated 23.11.1969	

Sri Lanka	Trade and Payments	09.10.1966	Legislative Decree No.29 dated 09.04.1966	
Turkey	Trade	17.09.1974	Decree No.31 dated 02.12.1974	
India	Trade	09.10.1969	Decree No.345 dated 23.12.1969	
Indonesia	Trade	18.03.1976	Decree No.1220 dated 09.07.1977	
Argentina	Trade	06.09.1989		
Grenada	Trade	22.01.1980	Decree No.1144 dated 27.05.1980	
Chile	Trade	27.02.1990	Legislative Decree No.12 dated 24.05.1990	
Iran	Trade	21.08.1996	Decree No.241 dated 10.11.1997	
European Union	Cooperation	18.01.1977	Legislative Decree No.14 dated 05.07.1977	

INVESTMENT CLIMATE

OPENNESS TO FOREIGN INVESTMENT

The Syrian government has adopted a hesitantly positive attitude toward foreign investment in recent years. However, most representatives of foreign firms find Syria's business environment a difficult one.

The government has passed three key pieces of legislation since1985 to encourage foreign investment. In 1985, the SARG issued" Decision 186" to encourage investment in tourism. In1986, the government issued "Decree 10" to encourage the establishment of joint-venture agricultural companies.

In June 1991, as part of its overall reform program to encourage the private sector, the government passed a new investment law--"Law Number 10"-- to promote investment in all sectors of the economy. The new law offers the same incentives to local and foreign investors. Specifically, companies that receive licenses under the new law are accorded duty free privileges for the import of capital goods and materials necessary for a project, including vehicles, and a tax holiday for the first five years of operation. Companies that export over 50 percent of their products enjoy seven year tax holiday.

All applications for investment under the law must be screened and vetted through the Higher Council for Investment. The council meets at least once every two months. Membership includes the Prime Minister, and the Ministers of Economy, Agriculture, Transportation, Supply, Industry, Planning, Finance, and the Director of the Investment Bureau. No definitive criteria for approving investment is made explicit under the new law, but the council is more likely to approve a project if it:

- Maximizes the use of local resources

- Utilizes advanced technologies

- Boosts exports

- Creates jobs

- Advances the government's development plans

Most foreign investment in Syria is in the energy sector. Beginning in the late 1980s, the government actively courted international oil companies to sign concession agreements to explore for oil. In 1990, twelve foreign firms had operations in Syria, but today, only three remain. Western firms departed because of disappointments over dry wells, rising costs, and friction with the Syrian government over contractual terms.

Foreign oil company representatives have mentioned several difficult aspects of doing business in Syria, citing both Syrian and U.S. government policies and restrictions.

- In past exploration and production contracts, the SARG required foreign oil companies to use the unfavorable official rate of11.2 Syrian pounds (SP)/USD versus the neighboring country rate of 43.5 SP/USD and the offshore rate of 49-52 SP/USD for all business transactions with Syrian individuals and companies. Recently however, faced with the departure of most exploration companies, the SARG decided that all new contracts be at the neighboring country rate.

- The SARG requires that export and import licenses be obtained for every single item imported and then re-exported, regardless of value. Several company representatives recalled that documentation for even minor items, such as paint cans and used spark plugs, had to be kept to prove to customs officials that they had not been illegally re-exported or sold locally. Likewise, foreign companies must acquire temporary permits for each item of equipment intended for temporary use and subsequent re-export (i.e. drilling rigs) to avoid paying import duties. These permits can be difficult to extend if the company's service contract has expired, and fit wants to keep the equipment in-country for stand-by usage. Delays in the re-export of equipment after a temporary permit expires has drawn heavy fines.

- In the absence of an adequate infrastructure in Syria, such as telecommunications, maintaining contact with field crews became costly as companies leased expensive, dedicated lines from the Syrian Telecommunications Establishment at the official exchange rate. However, as of August 1, 1996, the government began to apply the neighboring country rate, thereby reducing costs.

- USG foreign policy sanctions and individual validated licensing requirements imposed on "dual use items" such as computer equipment and oil exploration technology, including global positioning indicators, make work difficult. Also mentioned was the "Grassley Amendment ," another USG sanction on Syria, that prevents U.S. companies from taking advantage of foreign tax credits on loyalties paid to the SARG.

- In April 1996, Congress enacted new Antiterrorism legislation affecting financial transactions with Syria.

According to the final regulations, all financial transactions between U.S. persons or entities and the Government of the Syrian Arab Republic are authorized unless the transaction constitutes a donation to the U.S. person or entity, or the U.S. person or entity recipient knows or has reasons to know that the transfer poses a risk of furthering terrorist acts in the United States. Additional information is available from the Department of Treasury's Office of Foreign Assets Control, at (202) 622-2520.

RIGHT TO PRIVATE OWNERSHIP

All major private investment projects must be licensed. Over the past few years, the Syrian government has steadily opened sectors, formerly reserved to government monopolies, to private sector investment. Key sectors opened since 1994 included flour milling, sugar refining, and cement manufacturing. The Prime Minister has stated publicly that the Higher Council of Investment, which he chairs, is open to any and all proposals for investment, in any industry and on any scale. Nevertheless, state enterprises withal competing interest in a proposed project are routinely consulted by the Investment Council.

The standard of competitive equality is not applied to private enterprises competing with state enterprises in a number of important areas. For example, although a number of state banks, such as the Real Estate and Industrial Bank, are authorized to loan local currency to help finance private sector projects, state enterprises continue to have privileged access to local credit and exclusive access to official foreign exchange loans from the Commercial Bank of Syria. However, private companies can sometimes access offshore financing. Likewise, according to local business sources, state enterprises have priority in the allocations of commodities and material produced by other state enterprises. Public sector firms also appear to have greater access to public services, such as telecommunications and electricity.

The government has rejected "privatization" of state enterprises as a viable strategy because of the unmarketability of most state enterprises and the continued dependence of the national workforce on public sector employment.

PROTECTION OF PROPERTY RIGHTS

Syria's legal system recognizes and facilitates the transfer of property rights, including intellectual property rights. Under its own law, the Syrian government has raided shops known to pirate computer software. In April 1995, the Syrian government announced its intention, in principle, to join the Paris Union for the International Protection of Industrial Property. The government also stated that it is considering joining the 1967 Stockholm Intellectual Property Rights Agreement.

The following information details the specific legal protections for patents, copyrights, and trademarks:

Patents: These are issued for fifteen year periods, provided the invention has been utilized within two years after the patent was granted.

Copyrights: Most books printed in Syria are in Arabic and by Arab authors. However, instances of copyright infringement especially of Arabic translations of English texts, have occurred. Pirated records, cassettes, and videos are widely available.

Despite government efforts, pirated computer software is also readily available. The amount of lost revenue is probably minimal. In any event, enforcement and the associated litigation would-be, if not impossible, extremely costly compared to any positive benefits that may result.

The motion picture industry estimates the home video market in Syria is 100 percent pirated, and is also concerned with unauthorized hotel video performances, which are said to be common. However, only a few hotels have internal video systems.

Additionally, 100 percent of both Arab and non-Arab commercial music products are pirated. Given the lack of technical sophistication of Syrian industry and strict government control of communications and data processing, infringements on new technologies are note problem.

Trademarks: These may be registered for ten-year periods. The first applicant is always entitled to registration.

PERFORMANCE REQUIREMENTS AND INCENTIVES

Apart from specifying a minimum investment of ten million Syrian pounds, the new investment law has no formal performance requirements. For example, foreign investors are not required to employ a fixed proportion of local labor, although there are reports that informal guidelines are negotiated on a case-by-case basis during the licensing process. Investors' access to foreign exchange is limited as it's a function of the value of a company's exports.

Proprietary information may also have to be disclosed for project approval. The Ministry of Supply has the authority to set prices and/or profit margins for products destined for the local market, buts far, foreign investors have not encountered problems as a result of this practice. Under Investment Law 10, there are additional incentives for investment in rural areas and for those companies that use local raw materials.

Prior to coming to Syria, all U.S. citizens must obtain an entry visa which may be procured from the Syrian embassy in Washington. Although there are no discriminatory or excessive visa, residence, or work permit requirements, if an individual wishes to remaining Syria longer than 14 days, that person must register with the government and acquire a temporary residence permit (in addition to the entry visa). The Syrian government will not grant entry to persons with passports bearing an Israeli visa or entry/exit stamp, or to persons born in the Gaza region or of Gazan descent.

REGULATORY SYSTEM

The Syrian regulatory system is not oriented toward promoting competition either among private firms or between private and state enterprises. Regulations enforced by the Ministry of Supply are aimed at promoting consumer protection by preventing hoarding and price gouging.

Nevertheless, to foster competition, the government has put public sector enterprises on notice that they will no longer be permitted to monopolize whole sectors, particularly if private capital, whether foreign or domestic, can be attracted to finance needed projects. As for fiscal and welfare regulations, such as tax, labor, safety, and health laws, these appear to been forced without discrimination. Bureaucratic procedures for licensing and necessary documentation move slowly and require official approval from many levels within the government. In this regard, under-the-table payments are often required as corruption is endemic at nearly all levels of government.

The absence of organized capital, foreign exchange, and financial markets continues to be an important impediment to private investment, both domestic and foreign. In 1994, the parliament approved legislation authorizing the re-opening of the Damascus stock market; however, it still awaits the President's approval. The government continues to impose strict foreign exchange controls on private sector operations outside the specific concessions granted under the new investment law to operate self-funding foreign exchange accounts at the Commercial Bank of Syria.

CORRUPTION

Syrian laws prohibit corruption and accepting money donations. The Central Commission for Control and Inspection is responsible for criminalizing such actions. Both the briber and the recipient will be subject to imprisonment and/or confiscation of property. Occasionally, newspapers publish lists of government employees who were fired for "reasons related to integrity". However, incomes are so low in the public sector that some fringe benefits are unofficially accepted as means of direct compensation, especially in government procurement, investment licensing, and obtaining importation approval.

LABOR

The private sector has been able to recruit both skilled and professional labor. On the other hand, state enterprises have difficulty attracting qualified personnel, due to low salaries. To resign their positions, public sector employees must obtain permission, which is often difficult.

The government-controlled Syrian General Federation of Trade Unions(GFTU) oversees all aspects of union activity. The GFTU is affiliated with the International Confederation of Arab Trade Unions. In the public sector, unions do not normally bargain collectively on wage issues, but there is some evidence that union representatives participate with the representatives of the employer and Ministry of Labor in establishing sect oral minimum wages.

In a country whose major industries are state-owned, workers make up the majority of each board of directors and union representatives are always included on those boards. They also monitor and enforce compliance with the labor law. In the private sector, unions are active in monitoring compliance with the laws and ensuring workers' health and safety. The unions, under the law, can undertake negotiations for collective contracts with employers, but there is no information available on whether such contracts envision that unions can also sue and be represented in court. The government has continued to resist the abolition of the Minister of Labor's power over collective contracts. Organized unions do not seem to have a role in the receptivity of foreign investment.

EFFICIENT CAPITAL MARKETS AND PORTFOLIO INVESTMENT

Policies do not facilitate the free flow of financial resources. Capital can be brought into the country, but must be exchanged at the unfavorable exchange rate which is about 20% less than the free market rate. On the other hand, repatriation of capital remains a problem because foreign investors do not have access to foreign exchange. Investors wishing to repatriate their funds are expected to generate foreign currencies from their exports.

There are no foreign banks operating in Syria. Furthermore, all Syrian banks are government-owned and offer only basic banking services. Local and foreign investors may acquire small loans from local banks through very complicated and impractical procedures.

Legal, regulatory, and accounting systems are consistent with international norms in theory. In reality, however, local businesses do not comply with these regulations in order to avoid confiscator tax rates.

There are no stock or bond markets in Syria.

CONVERSION AND TRANSFER POLICIES

The new investment law sets no limits on the inflow of funds. Beneficiaries under the law are permitted to open foreign exchange accounts with the Commercial Bank of Syria. An investor must deposit100 percent of all foreign exchange capital and hard currency loans secured by the project, and 75 percent of export earnings. Outward capital transfers and profit remittances are prohibited, unless approved by the Prime Minister or sanctioned under the new investment law or a specific arrangement, as in the case of production sharing agreements concluded with oil exploration companies.

Under Law 10/1991, invested capital may be repatriated after five years from the project completion date (six months, if the project fails due to events beyond the control of the investor), and profits remitted on an annual basis.

Expatriate employees are permitted to transfer abroad 50 percent of their salaries, and 100 percent of severance pay. In the case of foreign oil companies, "cost recovery" of exploration and development expenditures misgoverned by formulas specifically negotiated in the applicable concession agreement.

Foreign oil partners in production sharing joint-ventures with the state oil company report delays in the recognition of "cost recovery" claims, although such payments are eventually approved.

The private sector has had no access to official foreign reserves since 1984. Under the new investment law, all foreign exchange operations must be generated from company operations and transacted through the investor's foreign exchange account at the Commercial Bank of Syria. No mechanism exists in the parallel "gray" foreign exchange market, funded from permitted private sector retained export earnings, for the repatriation of capital and profits.

Strict foreign exchange restrictions are enforced outside the concessions granted under law 10/1991. The export of capital requires the approval of the Central Bank, as does overseas borrowing. Foreign companies operating outside the new investment law may transfer capital only in accordance with the special agreements, usually in the form of a presidential decree, which allow their operation in Syria.

EXPROPRIATION AND COMPENSATION

There have been no expropriations of private property for public use since the 1960s. Although protection against expropriations not explicitly stated in the new investment law, older investment laws include such clauses, which presumably remain valid and applicable under the new investment law.

DISPUTE SETTLEMENT

Few investment disputes have occurred during the past several years. The few that have transpired have typically been settled(often with long delays) through negotiations or via arbitration clauses in contracts. While a number of U.S. suppliers have asserted claims against state enterprises for non-payment on goods and services delivered, the Syrian government, working closely with the Commercial Bank of Syria, has taken steps since early 1995to settle some of these debts on a case by case basis.

Property and contractual rights are protected by the constitution and enforced by law. However, there is considerable government interference in the court system and judgments by foreign courts are generally accepted only if the verdict favors the Syrian government. Although a written bankruptcy law exists, it is not applied fairyland creditors may or may not salvage their investment. Monetary judgments in such cases are made in the local currency which can not be converted to a hard currency.

The government accepts binding international arbitration of investment disputes between foreign investors and the state in cases where the investment agreement or contract includes such a clause. Otherwise, local courts have jurisdiction. Syria is neither a member of the International Center for the Settlement of Investment Disputes nor of the New York Convention of 1958 on the recognition and enforcement of foreign arbitral awards.

BILATERAL INVESTMENT AGREEMENTS

Syria is a safe environment for personal security, and the country has enjoyed over 25 years of political stability. However, with the economy and progress in the Middle East peace process stalled, and uncertainty over succession of the aging President Asad, future stability is an area of concern.

Syria and the U.S. signed an investment guarantee agreement on August 9, 1976 that protects investments from nationalization and confiscation. Similar agreements were also signed with Germany, France, and Switzerland. In addition, since the Gulf War, a number of bi-national committees have been established with Gulf Arab countries to explore private and mixed joint-ventures.

U.S. investment is not eligible for OPIC and other types of insurance programs due to Syria's inclusion on the list of state supporters of terrorism. For the same reason EXIM Bank, small business administration, and commodity corporation financing is not available for U.S.exports to Syria. USAID assistance to Syria was terminated in1983.

FOREIGN DIRECT INVESTMENT STATISTICS

Official foreign investment statistics by country are not available. According to press stories, some 1476 projects valued at about326 billion Syrian pounds (approximately USD 6.5 billion at the offshore rate centered in Beirut) have been approved under the new investment law since its issuance in 1991 and through May1996. However, only a small percentage of approved projects have even begun construction much less operation.

TRADE AND PROJECT FINANCING

BANKING SYSTEM

Syria's government-controlled banking system consists of five banks: The Commercial Bank of Syria, the Agricultural Cooperative Bank, the Industrial Bank, the Real Estate Bank, and the People's Credit Bank. The Central Bank of Syria oversees banking operations and manages the money supply. According to Syrian bank regulations, only the Central Bank and the Commercial Bank may engage in international transactions and hold foreign exchange deposits outside Syria. Within Syria, only the Commercial Bank may sell Syrian pounds for foreign currencies. Except for a few exemptions, unused Syrian pounds cannot be sold back to the Commercial Bank. Moreover, Law24 of 1986 criminalizes the private exchange of foreign currencies and Syrian pounds.

Besides monopolizing the exchange of foreign currencies, the Syrian government maintains one of the last remaining fixed, multiple exchange rate systems in the world. At present the government exchanges money at four different rates, ranging from the "official" rate of 11.2 SP/USD, to the "neighboring country" rate of 43.5 SP/USD. However, virtually all transactions occur at either the "neighboring country" rate, the "offshore" rate, negotiated in the free markets of Amman or Beirut, which ranges between 49 and 52 SP/USD, or the "export dollar" rate, which ranges between 52 and 57 SP/USD.

HOW TO FINANCE EXPORTS/METHODS OF PAYMENT

In general, private Syrian traders finance imports from their own resources or through their own credit. Contracts with the private sector are negotiated on an individual basis with little or no interference from the government. All documentary transactions for imports must be by a letter of credit opened at the Commercial Bank of Syria. Typically, the Bank requires the importer to cover100 percent of the transaction from his own resources offshore or from funds generated by exports. Syrian importers often require that one of the following two clauses be added to the preformed invoices and bills of lading as payment conditions, "free of payment" or "180-day credit facilities."

In this case, the importer pays through his offshore bank, either cash in advance, or via L/C, and the bill of lading is then sent to the Commercial Bank of Syria. In such instances, U.S. exporters are well advised to avoid delayed payment or the "cash against documents" mechanism, since the U.S. exporter has no protection under such a transaction and the Commercial Bank of Syria has no authority to release funds under such a clause.

Moreover, the importer could simply walk away from the contract even after the goods are shipped.

Alternatively, an importer may use foreign exchange earned from exports (export dollars) and deposit it in the Commercial Bank of Syria. The foreign exchange used to cover an L/C opened at the Commercial Bank may be his own, or purchased in an informal secondary market.

In March 1994, the Syrian government transferred several importable goods from the list of items that can be financed from offshore accounts to the list of items that must be purchased with export dollars. Whatever the source of funding, it is strongly recommended that U.S. exporters sell their goods to Syrians under" cash in advance" or "confirmed irrevocable letters of credit" until a satisfactory relationship with the Syrian importer has been established.

For its contracts, the government will open an L/C only after the contractor has posted a ten percent performance bond to ensure that goods will be delivered within the stated time of delivery, free of defects, and identical to the offer in both quality and quantity.

Posting these bank guarantees has been a constraint for U.S. firms wishing to do business in Syria because suppliers' banks often lack correspondence arrangements with the Commercial Bank of Syria. Again, U.S. commercial financing is not a practical way to do business with Syrian firms because foreign exchange impediments make it impossible to guarantee a loan or credit facility for a Syrian beneficiary.

TYPES OF AVAILABLE FINANCING AND INSURANCE

Because Syria remains on the list of state supporters of terrorism, Eximbank financing and insurance is unavailable to U.S. exporters. For the same reason, USAID is not present in Syria.

Moreover, the World Bank will not fund projects in Syria because of unpaid arrears on Syria's debt to that institution. However, Syria has received some project financing from Japan, the EU, and various Arab national and multinational institutions. Projects financed include upgrading the national telephone system, construction of several electrical power plants, and the purchase of earthmoving equipment.

Syrian Banks with correspondent U.S. banking arrangements:

- Central Bank of Syria

- Commercial Bank of Syria

U.S. Banks in New York with known correspondent Syrian banking arrangements:

- Arab American Bank, New York

- Bank of New York, New York

- Morgan Guarantee Trust Company, New York

- Credit Lyonnais, New York

- Citibank, New York

USEFUL ADDRESSES

- **General company for fruits and vegetables**

 Damascus P.O.Box: 5603
Tel 5422926-5422824-5422928
Fax 5423001
Tlx: 411914,412734
Cable :KHODAR
Products: Vegetables, Fruits, Fresh, Fruits, and Dehydrated

- **General Establishment For Food Industries**

Damascus P.O.Box :105
Tel :2225290-2234426-2234428
Fax :224537
Products: Soda , Conservatives, Jams, Arak, Oil, and Biscuits

---

- **General Establishment For Tobacco**

Damascus P.O.Box :616
Tel :2323125-2323126
Fax : 2233805
Tlx :411301   Cable :MONTAB
Products :Tobacco Tobacco Wholly , (Tombac)

- **General Company Leather Industries**

Damascus   P.O.Box :2994
Tel 5121808-5121809-5121810
Tlx :411628
Cable :AHZEAH
Products :Leather Footwear for men & women

- **General organization for fish**

Jableh
Tel :821677-833112-831367
Fax :831367
Tlx :451025
Products :FISH , CARP, FISH ,TILAPIA

- **General Establishment For Cows**

For additional analytical, business and investment opportunities information,
please contact Global Investment & Business Center, USA
at (703) 370-8082. Fax: (703) 370-8083. E-mail: ibpusa3@gmail.com
Global Business and Investment Info Databank - www.ibpus.com

Hama, P.O.Box :48
Tel :410985
Fax :422984
Products: Meat frish, (Frezian,Holoshtin)

- **General Company For Matches ,Chipbord**

 Damascus   P.O.Box :2672
Tel :5435734
Fax : 5437337
Tlx :41526 KEBRET SY
Cable :KEBRET-Damascus
 Products :Matches ,Playwood, Chipboard ,Pencils (Graphite & Color)

- **General Establishment For Foreign Trade Of Food & Chemical Materials**

Damascus ,Jumhuryah St.
P.O.Box :893
Tel: 2218919-2225421
Fax:2226927
Productes: Cotton Linters,Onion (dried)

- **General Organization For Sugar**

Homs   P.O.Box :4290
Tel :227600-227602- Damascus 2212329
Fax :237899
Tlx :441123-441006 GOFS Cable :GOFS
PRODUCTS :MOLASSES,YEST DRY ,AL-COHOL, MEDICAL

- **"Orient" Company For Underwear**

Damascus   P.O.Box :1100
Tel :5436001-5436003
Fax :5436000
Tlx :412436 O.U.M.C.SY
Products :Ccoton Underwear

- **General Establishment For Cereal Processing And Trade**

Damascus   P.O.Box :4106
Tel :2238364-2238397-2237818
Fax :2232368
Tlx :412511-411027-411391
Cable :HOBOB-Damascus
 Products: :Seed Of Lentils ,Lentils, Chick-Peas ,Barley

- **CARPET MANUFACTURING GENERAL CORPORATION**

Damascus   P.O.Box :1400
Tel :8880100 –8816973
Fax :8887002
Tlx :412514 CARP
Cable :CARPETCO
Products :Carpets , Woolen

- **HAMA COTTON YARN COMPANY**

Hama   P.O.Box :11
Tel :511092-551093-511091
Fax :511096
Tlx :431037 HAYC
Cable :GHAZEL Hama
Products :Cotton Carded Or Combed

- **Dry Battery Fabric**

Damascus   P.O.Box :3120
Tel: 6311643-8880789
Fax:2123375
Products: Dried battery

- **GENERAL ESTABLISHMENT FOR TIRES PRODUCTIONS**

Damascus   P.O.Box :12175
Tel :2210355 -2778808
Fax :2247499
 Poducts :Carpets, hand-made rug , carpets, hand made woolen , knit Faber. wool/fine hair

- **GENERAL ESTABLISHMENT FOR TIRES PRODUCTIONS**

Hama, Salamyah rood
Tel:424533-424532
Fax:424531
Tlx:431039
Products:Tires (different kinds)

- **General Company For Asphalt**

Lataquia   P.O.Box :6
Tle: 473121-475826
Fax : 475674
Tlx :451150
Cable :ASPEL
Products :,Nat. Asphalt Bituminous Mixtures Raw Stones

- **General Establishment For Porcelain**

Syria,Hama
P.O.Box : 161
Tel :510896-510996
Fax :511707
PRODUCTS : Porcelain , SANITARY WARE

- **General Organization For Poultry**

Damascus   P.O.Box :5597
Tel :2211968 -2212876
Fax :2217473
Tlx :412423 G.O.P. SYR
Cable :G.O.P. Damascus
Products :POULTRY LIVE, POULTRY FRESH
,EGGS BIRDS IN SHELL (HATCHING) ,EGGS BIRDS IN SHELL (TABLE)

- **Productive Projects Administration**

Damascus   P.O.Box :4703
Tel :2131499-212990-3314790
Fax :2205210
Tlx :412914 SY PRODUC
Products :, ,HONEY (flowred),HONEY (zalloo) ,MEDICAL PLANETS

- **General Establishment For Panting & Chemical Industries**

P.O.Box:1276
Tle : 5435511-5435512
Fax:5431088
Tlx:411299
Products Paints (deferent)

- **General Establishment For Chemical Industries**

Damascus
Tle:2127654-2123363
Fax :2128289
Products :Sport & leather shoes,Plastic houses, Chinaware

- **General Establishment For Engineering Industries**

Damascus
P.O.Box: 3120
Tle :212825-2122650
Fax :2123375
Products: Refrigerators, Household, Appliances, color TV Telephone sets, Cables

- **General Establishment For Textile Industries**

Fardous St.,Damascus
P.O.Box : 620
Tel :2216200-2215624-2215262
Fax :2216021
Tlx:411011
Products :Cotton yarns, Cotton Fabric, Socks , wool Carpets

- **General Establishment For Cleaners chemical Industry**

Damascus, Adra
P.O.Box: 682
Tel : 5810163- 5810164
Fax : 581062
Tlx : 412694 jecoda
PRODUCTS: Cleaners (Powders & Liquid), selphonic aside

- **General Electric Motors Manufacturing Company**

Lataquia   P.O.Box :190
Tel :421850 -421533
Fax :410761
Tlx :451090
Cable :MOTORS
Products :ELICTRICAL CABLE,TRANSFORMER (FLORESANT)

- **GENERAL COMPANY FOR Tanning**

Damascus ,Zablatani road
P.O.Box : 2019
Tel: 457840-454863
Fax : 4424935
Products :Raw & processed leather,leather jacets.

- **General Company For Transformation Industry**

Damascus P.O.Box :2803
Tel :6714574
Fax :6714572
Products :Sanitary Paper (For Baby & Women

TRAVEL TO SYRIA

SYRIA – US STATE DEPARTMENT SUGGESTIONS

COUNTRY DESCRIPTION: The Syrian Arab Republic has a developing, mixed-sector economy. The ruling Ba'th party espouses a largely secular ideology, but Islamic traditions and beliefs

provide a conservative foundation for the country's customs and practices. The constitution refers to Islamic jurisprudence as a
principal source of legislation, but the legal system remains influenced by French practice. Tourist facilities are widely available, but vary in quality depending on price and location. The workweek in Syria is Saturday through Thursday. The U.S. Embassy is open Sunday through Thursday.

ENTRY REQUIREMENTS: A passport and a visa are required. Visas must be obtained prior to arrival in Syria. Entry to Syria is not granted to persons with passports bearing an Israeli visa or entry/exit stamps, or to persons born in the Gaza region or of Gazan descent. Entry into Syria via the land border with Israel is not possible. Foreigners who wish to stay 15 days or more in Syria must register with Syrian Immigration by their 15th day in Syria. Americans between the ages of 18 and 45 who are of Syrian birth or recent descent are subject to the Syrian compulsory military service requirement, unless they receive an exemption from the Syrian Embassy in the United States prior to their entry into Syria. An AIDS test is not required for foreigners prior to arrival in Syria. However, tests are mandatory for foreigners (age 15 to 60) wishing to reside in Syria. The AIDS test must be conducted in Syria at a facility approved by the Syrian Ministry of Health. A residence permit will not be issued until the absence of the HIV virus has been determined. Foreigners wishing to marry Syrian nationals must also be tested for HIV. For further entry information, travelers may contact the Embassy of the Syrian Arab Republic, 2215 Wyoming Ave. N.W., Washington, D.C. 20008, tel. (202) 232-6313.

American citizens are cautioned that the Syrian government rigidly enforces restrictions on prior travel to Israel. Travelers with Israeli stamps in their passports, Jordanian entry cachets or cachets from other countries which
suggest prior travel to Israel, or the absence of any entry stamps from a country adjacent to Israel which the traveler has just visited, will cause Syrian immigration authorities to refuse the traveler admission to Syria. In one case in 1998, a group of American citizen travelers suspected of traveling to Israel were detained overnight for questioning.

Although Syria is a signatory to the Vienna Convention, consular notification and access to arrested Americans is problematic. Syrian officials generally do not notify the American Embassy when American citizens are arrested. When the American Embassy learns of arrests of Americans and requests consular access, individual police officials have, on their own initiative, responded promptly and allowed consular officers to visit the prisoners. However, security officials have also in the past denied Embassy requests for consular access.

MILITARY SERVICE: Syrian-American males of draft age who are planning to visit Syria are strongly urged to check with the Syrian Embassy in Washington concerning their requirement for compulsory military service. Even Americans who have never resided in or visited Syria before may be considered Syrian and required to complete military service if their fathers were Syrian. Possession of a U.S. passport does not absolve the bearer of this obligation.

IRAQ: Syrian security officials are sensitive about travel to Iraq. There have been past instances of Iraqi-Americans or Americans believed to have traveled to Iraq being detained for questioning at ports of entry/exit.

MEDICAL FACILITIES: Basic medical care and medicines are available in the principal cities of Syria, but not necessarily in outlying areas. Doctors and hospitals often expect immediate cash payment for health care services. The Medicare/Medicaid program does not always provide for payment of medical services outside the United States. U.S. medical insurance is not always valid outside the United States. Supplemental medical insurance with specific overseas coverage, including a provision for emergency evacuation, has proven useful. Information on health problems can be obtained from the Centers for Disease Control and Prevention at 1-877-FYI-

---

TRIP (1-877-394-8747), fax: 1-888-CDC-FAXX (1-888-232-3299), or on the Internet at http://www.cdc.gov.

INFORMATION ON CRIME Crime is generally not a serious problem for travelers in Syria. The loss or theft of a U.S. passport abroad should be reported immediately to local police and the nearest U.S. Embassy or Consulate. Useful information on safeguarding valuables, protecting personal security, and other matters while traveling abroad is provided in the Department of State pamphlets, A Safe Trip Abroad and Tips for Travelers to the Middle East and North Africa. They are available from the Superintendent of Documents, U.S. Government Printing Office, Washington, D.C. 20402, via the Internet at http://www.access.gpo.gov/su_docs, or via the Bureau of Consular Affairs home page at http://travel.state.gov.

Syria is included on the Department of State's list of state sponsors of terrorism. There is no record of terrorist attacks against Americans in Syria and Syrian government officials have repeatedly stated their commitment to protect Americans. However, a number of terrorist groups which oppose U.S. policies in the Middle East have a presence in this country.

CUSTODY/FAMILY ISSUES: Children under the age of eighteen whose fathers are Syrian must have the father's permission in order to depart Syria, even if the mother has been granted full custody by a Syrian court. Women in Syria are often subject to strict family controls; on occasion families of Syrian/American women visiting Syria have attempted to prevent them from leaving the country. This can be a particular problem for young single women of marriageable age. Finally, although this occurs only rarely, a Syrian husband is permitted to take legal action to prevent his wife from leaving the country, regardless of her nationality.

DRUG PENALTIES: U.S. citizens are subject to the laws and legal practices of the country in which they travel. Penalties for possession of even small amounts of illegal drugs for personal use are severe in Syria. The penalty in Syria for growing, processing or smuggling drugs is the death penalty, which may be reduced to a minimum of 20 years imprisonment.

TRAFFIC SAFETY AND ROAD CONDITIONS: Driving in Syria requires great caution. Although drivers generally follow traffic signs and signals, they often maneuver aggressively and show little regard to vehicles traveling behind them. Lane markings are usually ignored. Unlike the U.S., vehicles within Syrian traffic circles must give way to oncoming traffic. Pedestrians must also exercise caution. Parked cars, deteriorating pavement, and guard posts present obstacles on sidewalks, often forcing pedestrians to walk in the street.

CURRENCY REGULATIONS: Syrian currency cannot be exchanged for any other currency except at government-approved exchange centers within Syria. Travelers must declare all foreign currency when they enter Syria. Amounts in excess of $5,000 (US) [or $2,000 (US) for those holding dual Syrian-American
nationality] are subject to confiscation upon leaving Syria.

AVIATION SAFETY OVERSIGHT: As there is no direct commercial air service by local carriers at present, or economic authority to operate such service, between the U.S. and Syria, the U.S. Federal Aviation Administration (FAA) has not assessed Syria's Civil Aviation Authority for compliance with international aviation safety standards for oversight of Syria's air carrier operations. For further information, travelers may contact the Department of Transportation within the U.S. at 1-800-322-7873, or visit the FAA Internet home page at http://www.faa.gov/avr/iasa/index.htm. The U.S. Department of Defense (DOD) separately assesses some foreign air carriers for suitability as official providers of air services. For information regarding the DOD policy on specific carriers, travelers may contact DOD at 618-256-4801.

Y2K INFORMATION: As a consequence of the so-called Y2K "bug," on or about January 1, 2000, some automated systems throughout the world may experience problems, including unpredictable system malfunctions. In countries that are not prepared, the Y2K problem could affect financial services, utilities, health
services, telecommunications, energy, transportation and other vital services. American citizens who are traveling to any country during this time period should be aware of the potential for the disruption of normal medical services. Travelers with special medical needs should consult with their personal physician and take appropriate precautions. While travelers do not necessarily need to alter their travel plans, being informed and prepared for possible disruptions is prudent.

Syria is not heavily reliant on computerized systems and is working with the international community to minimize any impact as a result of Y2K. While Syria appears to be generally prepared to deal with the Y2K problem, remediation and contingency planning continue. Critical systems in sectors such as aviation, water distribution and chlorination, electricity generation and distribution, maritime transport and telecommunications are either expected to be Y2K-compliant, or are based on manual or non-date-dependent systems. Syrian officials acknowledge the potential for unexpected problems and said they are preparing contingency plans in all critical sectors. Without further remediation, interest payments on current accounts at the Commercial Bank of Syria may also be affected. U.S. citizens traveling to or residing in Syria in late 2004 or early 2000 should be aware of these potential difficulties.

It is difficult to predict the severity or duration of Y2K-related disruptions. U.S. citizens in Syria should take practical precautions, anticipate the potential for disruptions to their daily activities, and be prepared to cope with the impact of such disruptions. Information about personal preparedness and Y2K is available in the Department of State Worldwide Public Announcement of July 26, 2004, which is accessible on the Department of State, Bureau of Consular Affairs home page at http://travel.state.gov/y2kca.html.

Aviation and Y2K: The Department of Transportation is heading an international Year 2000 civil aviation evaluation process to review information on Y2K readiness in aviation based on reports to the International Civil Aviation Organization and other available sources. The Federal Aviation Administration is working with the industry and its international partners to encourage sharing of Y2K readiness and contingency planning information so that air carriers will be able to make appropriate decisions. Consult your airline about contingency plans in the event of unforeseen Y2K-related delays, cancellations, or disruptions. See the Department of Transportation Y2K home page at http://www.dot.gov/fly2k for updated information on Y2K and aviation issues.

As January 1, 2000, draws nearer, we will provide updated information available to us about important Y2K issues in Syria on the Consular Affairs home page at http://travel.state.gov/y2kca.html.

REGISTRATION/U.S. EMBASSY LOCATION: U.S. citizens are encouraged to register at the U.S. Embassy and obtain updated information on travel and security within Syria. The U.S. Embassy in Damascus, Syria, is located in Abu Roumaneh, Al-Mansur St. No. 2; P.O. Box 29. Telephone numbers are (963) (11) 333-2814, 332-0783, 333-0788, and 333-3232. Fax number is (963) (11) 331-9678.

BUSINESS CUSTOMS

TRAVEL ADVISORY AND VISAS

1. Personal entry requirements

Passport: Required
Visa: Required
Health & Immunization: Certificates are required of all travelers arriving from infected areas. There are not currently any AIDS test requirements for short-term visitors to Syria. The Syrian government will not grant entry to persons with passports bearing an Israeli visa or entry/exit stamp, or to persons born in the Gaza region or of Gazan descent.

2. Embassy information

Syrian Embassy in the United States:
Address: Embassy of the Syrian Arab Republic,
2215 Wyoming Ave., Washington, D.C. 20008
Telephone: (202) 232-6313, Fax: (202)234-9548

U.S. Embassy in Syria:
Address: Abou Roumaneh, 2 Al-Mansour Street, P.O. Box 29,
Damascus, Syria
Telephone: 963-11-3332814/3330416/3330788, Fax: 963-11-2247938

HOLIDAYS

Syrians will observe the following holidays

July 15	(Prophet's Birthday)1/
October 6	(Tishrin War)
December 25	(Christmas Day)
January 1	(New Year's Day)
January 29-31	(Al-Fitr Holiday)1/
March 8	(Revolution Day)
March 21	(Mothers' Day)
April 7-10	(Al-Adha Holiday)1/
April 12	(Easter)
April 17	(Independence Day)
April 19	(Orthodox Easter)
April 29	(Muslim New Year)1/
May 1	(Labor Day)
May 6	(Martyr Day)
July 5	(Prophet's Birthday)1/
October 6	(Tishrin War)
December 25	(Christmas Day)

1/ Based on lunar calendar. Exact date to be confirmed.

SYRIA, THE CIVILIZATION AND HISTORY

Syria is an ancient Tourist country. It is the land of continuous and uninterrupted history. It has known most of the prophets and conquerors. It is the land on which greatest empires accumulated.

This has not affected its inhabitants who were sometimes known as Amorites and sometimes the Arameans, but were all the time known as Arab who remained trade mediators all over the world and emissaries combining human education and cooperation.

This land does not only embody human efforts and hopes, including the civilization above and beneath it, but it was a landmark of antiquity throughout all ages. It was also eternal paradise in all times, and dreamful desert covered by sand dunes around abandoned cities that have once ruled the near east region as a whole. It is a land of dense forests that almost prevented sunshine to beam over their feet. It is also a beautiful coastline that curves along soft-sanded shores, and it is a superior climate that is affected by mountains, forests, sea and desert making tourism and enjoyment. It is first and for all the country of human being who has turned cooper into artistic tools and mud into embroidered containers, whereby changing the shepherd life into a stable agricultural life which witnessed the construction of cities and civilizations.

It is the land of the Arabs who introduced the alphabet in the form of language and simplified writing that has turned to be political and trade apparatus through the world conveying thought from era to era.

It is the land of the Arabs who accomplished all these achievements and who are currently leading a civilized process and dignity under a wise and inspiring leadership.

The Syrian Arab republic is located in the western part of Asia overlooking the Mediterranean Basin. Its area is 184,000 square Kilometers with 12 million inhabitants.

It is surrounded by Turkey from the north, Iraq from the east, Jordan from and Palestine from the south and the Mediterranean sea and Lebanon from the west.

Syrian is known for being a land containing many historical ruins. The national Museum in Damascus is famous for the valuable historical belonging. It is similar to an active exhibition showing evidences of human development on the Syrian territories.

There, one can find astonishing ruins with stands for Syrian oriental ruins and other ruins belonging to the Greek, Roman, and Byzatine eras as well as Arab and Islamic ruins.

It also contahall, whichis a symbol of beauty. In Damascus also, there is the Ommayad Mosque, which is viewed as one of the marvelous Arab architecture. Beside it lies the tomb of Salah din al-Ayyouby in another area in the city, lies the Takiyeh Suleimanieh with its wonderful engraving and architecture.

Al-Azim palace is also a touritic gift of Damascus where the straight street extends with nearby churches of Saint Hanania and Saint Paul in the palace vicinity, lie the old markets of Damascus, which reflect the flavor of an oriental history, in addition to a large number of Monastries, churches, mosques, schools, gates, inns and old beautiful Damascus houses.

In the outskirts of Damascus, there is the site of Sayeda Zeinab, grand daughter of prophet Mohammad and Koukab the place where Saint Paul viewed, there is also Maalola historical city with its Monastry which is considered one of the oldest Christian Monastries in the world. Then comes Sydnaya town, which still maintains its famous monastry. In Aleppo to the north, which is a city full of touristic places, there stands Aleppo citadel with all its great landmarks and the wonderful museum, which contains most valuable historical richness.

In this city, one can also find old oriental markets, which enjoy a special charming attraction derived from its famous industries. There are also numerous oriental houses, mosques, inns, and Bathrooms. In the outskirts of Aleppo, stands Saint Simon citadel with its historical church and monastry and to the southwest also stands the famous historical city of Ebla which goes back to the third thousand B.C. This old city is considered one of the oldest civilization centers where a prosperous kingdom was established.

Homs city, which is located to the north of Damascus, is famous with Zennar church which contains the belt of virgin Mary and Khaled Bin Al-Walid mosque where the tomb of this great leader lies. In Hums province (Muhafazet) lies crac de chevaliers, one of the greatest military castles of the middle ages.

The historical city of Palmyra, the capital of the great Arab queen of Zennobia, is located in the central Syrian desert. This city became famous worldwide because of its historical temples, pillars and engravings which are kept in Palmyra museum and under the city's cemetries, status and the arches of victory.

In Hama city there is Al-Azem palace which is an immitation of Al-Azem palace of Damascus. It was turned into a museum containing ruins and precious belonging.

Hama waterwheels still stand as giants defying the burdens of the time and carrying water from the orontes river to the surrounding plantations and nursaries.

In Bosra, located in Derra muhafazet south of Damascus, lies the Roman stadium with its unique theater and Bosra Islamic citadel. In this town there is a number of Roman ruins that have been recently discovered.

In Sweidaa, east of Bosra, a collection of Roman, Arab, and Islamic ruins scatter in nearly Shahba, Al-Hiet, Al-Hiyat, Zukeir, and Ariqa. There, you can also find Salkhad citadel, which lies on a big hill overlooking the plateaues of Salkhad in addition to landmarks of antiquity scattered here and there.

The Syrian coastal area comprises Lattakia and Tartous Muhafazets with their fascinating landscape and Furullouq Forests and Kassab area, which contains wonderful Arab and crusade citadels and castles. It also contains Ugarit city in Ras Shamra near Lattakia, where the oldest alphabet known in the world was found. On the Syrian coast, soft sand shores stretch. It is one of the places where tourists can enjoy their time fautastically throughout the year.

In Al-Raqqa and Deir Ezzor muhafazet east of Syria, lies the Rusafa of Hicham Bin Abdul Malik, which turns the sun beams to the Rainbw colors on its walls. This place is very away from Jaaber citadel which floats inside Al-Assad lake formed by the great Euphrates Dam. Other historical sites which lie along the banks of the Euphrates river are Mary, Doura, Orobos, Halabieyeh, Zilbiyeh, and Al-Rahba citadel in Al-Mayadin town.

In general, Syria with its beautiful summer resorts, fruit trees and fresh air has been bestowed with all natural beauty and weather variance which make the country a fascinating place.

The people of Syria, who have been famous for hospitality and generosity throughout history, now invite you to get acquainted with the consecutive civilization erected over this beautiful land. They also open their arms and hearts to embrace all Arab and foreign tourists to see on spot the Syria of civilization and glory and to view the Syria of president Hafez Al-Assad, the country of loving, fraternity and peace.

FORMALITIES TO ENTER AND LEAVE SYRIA

- All individuals who wish to travel to Syria must posses a valid passport .

- Passports must contain a valid entry visa for Syria , delivered by the Syrian embassy or consulate accredited to the country of the holder of passport .

- If there is not a Syrian mission in the country of the passport holder, a visa can be obtained at any Syrian foreign mission or upon arrival at the Syria border .

- A collective visa, free of charge , is given to tour groups consisting of ten persons or more . This visa is attached to a list of the members of the tour group ; however , each individual in the tour group must also carry a valid passport .

- If the duration of an individual's stay in Syria exceeds fifteen days, he or she must contact the Syrian authorities to obtain an extension of stay on his or her passport .

- Passports must not contain an Israeli visa .

- The cost of a visa is a calculated on the basis of the current reciprocal relationship between Syria and the country of the passport holder .

- Travellers do not need an exit visa if the duration of their stay in Syria does not exceed fifteen days .

CUSTOMS REGULATIONS FOR TRAVEL

- Clothing and personal effects which are accompanying travellers are exempt from customs and do not need to be declared .

- The following consumable materials accompanying travellers are exempt from customs but must be declared :

- One litre of eau de Cologne

- One litre of an alcoholic beverage .

- Two hundred cigarettes or fifty cigars or two hundred grams of tobacco .

- The following products accompanying travellers must be declared , but are exempt from customs on the condition that they are used and that the travellers agrees that the goods will leave Syria with him or her :

- photographic camera

- video camera , for non-professional use .

- pair of binoculars

- portable musical instrument

- portable tape recorder

- baby carriage or stroller

- portable typewriter

- camping equipment

- individual sports equipment

- bicycle

- small iron for pressing clothing

- medical instruments that are commonly carried by a doctor

- toilet accessories

- travelling blankets and sleeping bags .

Customs agent at the Syrian border are permitted , according to their personal judgement , to authorise the entry of other objects for personal use mentioned above.

To bring a car to Syria , the owner must carry an international driver's licence , an international grey card , and a triptych . A car can stay in Syria for three to four months , on one or more trips .

Cars that are fuelled by diesel can stay in Syria for four months , but the driver must pay an entry tax . For more information , please contact the Syrian customs authorities . Cars that run on gasoline do not require an entry tax .

It is possible , in all cases , to acquire detailed information concerning customs , transit formalities and recent change to customs regulations from Syrian embassies and consulates , and from the customs offices located on the Syrian boeder .

IMPORTANT TO REMEMBER WHEN IN SYRIA

Don't accept food in a social setting the first time it's offered. It's polite to   decline at least once before accepting.

Do offer a guest food or drink several times (as he or she may decline the first offer)

Do feel free to talk politics with your guests, but don't hammer home a point or be insensitive to local and national traditions. Feel free to debate issues such as   democracy, the price of coffee, etc., but don't say negative things about the ruler of the country, even if asked. Syrians feel very upset about their country's negative reputation. They will spend a lot of time defending their country's good name.

Don't admire a specific item in a host's home or office - or the host may feel obliged to give it to you, something neither of you really wants. Keep your compliments general.

Do expect to see Syrian women riding on the back of motorbikes, wearing jeans and fashionable clothes. Not all will be veiled or covered in black. Don't assume that there is anything unusual about men walking arm in arm or hand in hand. Men are much more physically affectionate with their male friends and relatives than men are in the West

Do be careful at security checkpoints when traveling inside Syria. Move slowly and obey the authorities. Don't expect your phone conversations to be private (the phones may be bugged).

Don't point at people or use your hands to give direction, as to do so is considered rude. Also, be careful that the soles of your shoes don't show when you're sitting.

Do make appointments and be on time, but don't be offended by a lack of punctuality by others. Also, don't be offended if the person you're meeting for business conducts other business during "your" appointment. Don't show irritation when everything stops five times a day for prayers. Do shake hands and say marha-bah, keif halak, when greeting people. Don't expect stores, offices or markets to be open on Friday, the Muslim Sabbath (the work week is Saturday through Thursday).

Do take along a small gift when invited to a home (don't bring liquor, or artwork that contains images of people).

Don't inquire about a host's wife. If you meet her, shake hands only if she offers   hers first.

Do be sure to dress appropriately (no bare arms or legs) when visiting a mosque and remove your shoes before entering. However, you should carry your shoes with you during your visit, as thieves have been known to steal shoes left at the mosques' entrances.

Don't let two days go by without visiting a hammam. The spa treatment is basic, but the atmosphere and prices are unbeatable.

Do choose Damascus's Omayyad Mosque over Aleppo's and Aleppo's suq and citadel over Damascus's if time is limited.

Don't photograph veiled women (unless permission is granted first), airports, military establishments or bridges.

Don't talk business during social visits with a business host.

Do attend one of the numerous cultural festivals if you get the chance.
Don't exchange money in the black market. Its illegal, unsafe and the exchange   rate is not that much higher than in banks. And don't exchange more money than you have to if you are crossing over from the Turkish land border. The rate is lousy.

Don't pass anything (especially food) with your left hand.
Do take along toilet paper. But don't flush it: Place it in the basket provided next to the toilet.

Don't be surprised if, when you shake your head side to side to mean "no," it's interpreted as meaning "I don't understand." If you want to say "no," shake your head upward, while making a "tut" sound.

Don't go beyond the iconostasis when visiting an Orthodox church.
Don't drink or smoke in public during Ramadan, the Islamic holy month.
Do expect to see pictures of President Assad and his late son Basil on every storefront, office, street lamp and car in the country.

Do expect to see old Buicks and Dodges from the 1940s and '50s still working as shared taxis on the routes to Beirut and Amman.

Don't be surprised if it seems like every time you turn around you're tipping someone. Pay is low, and tipping is expected nearly everywhere.

MONEY & COSTS

Currency: Syrian pound (£S)
Relative costs:

Budget meal: US$1-4
Moderate restaurant meal: US$5-10
Top-end restaurant meal: $10-15

Budget room: US$4-10
Moderate hotel: US$10-20
Top-end hotel: US$200 and upwards

Syria is still a pretty cheap place to visit, but it's definitely getting more expensive. It is possible (but you'd have to be pretty desperate) to get by on US$15-20 a day, if you're prepared to sleep in fleabags and live on felafel and juice. If you'd prefer to stay in a room with its own bathroom and eat in restaurants once a day, you'll need to budget about US$30-40 a day.

Cash is king in Syria, but travelers' checks, of course, are safer. There's no commission for changing cash, but you'll pay per transaction for checks. You're unlikely to get a cash advance on your credit card, but plastic is   increasingly accepted by bigger hotels and stores, and for buying air tickets or renting cars.

Tipping is the oil that keeps the Middle East running smoothly. Waiters in better restaurants expect a tip, and if you don't give one they'll probably short change you anyway. People who open doors for you and people who carry your luggage will also expect a tip, but it's up to you to decide if it's worth it. Bargaining is integral when buying souvenirs - you won't have to try very hard to get the asking price halved.

HOW TO GET THERE

Syria has two international airports, one 35km (22mi) south-east of Damascus, the other just north-east of Aleppo. Both have regular connections to Europe, the Middle East, Africa and Asia. Flights tend to be quite expensive. There's a departure tax of about US$5.

Buses run between Aleppo or Damascus and Istanbul (Turkey), between Damascus and Amman (Jordan), Damascus and Beirut or Tripoli (Lebanon) and Damascus and Riyadh (Saudi Arabia). Trains go from Aleppo to Istanbul and from Damascus to Amman. Service taxis also run from Damascus to most of the neighboring countries. You can bring your own vehicle into Syria, but you will need a carnet de passage and local third-party insurance. If you prefer the ferry, there's a weekly service from Lattakia for Alexandria (Egypt) via Beirut. In summer, the ferry also stops in Cyprus.

GETTING AROUND

There are internal flights between Damascus and Aleppo, Qamishle, Lattakia and Deir ez-Zur. Syria's road network is excellent, and buses are frequent and cheap - most Syrians use the bus, as very few have their own car. Distances are short and most trips take under four hours. Bus types include the traditional coach, minibuses and Japanese vans known as microbuses. Service taxis operate on the major bus routes but are considerably more expensive than microbuses.

Syria's trains are a modern lot, made in Russia. They're cheap and punctual, but the stations are usually a fair way out of town. The main line connects Damascus, Aleppo, Deir ez-Zur, Hassake and Qamishle, with a secondary line along the coast. There are a few car rental companies in Syria, but rates are around 50% higher than in the West and petrol is expensive and hard to find. Syrians drive on the right.

SUPPLEMENTS

BASIC   EXPLORATION CONTRACT

SELECTED CONTACTS

FOREIGN EMBASSIES

EUROPEAN UNION

DELEGATION OF THE EUROPEAN COMMISSION

P. O. Box 11269, Abou Roumaneh, Rue Chekib Arslan, Immeuble du
Patriarcat Grèc Catholique, Damascus
Tel. 3327640; Tel. 3327641; Fax 3320683

REPUBLIC OF AUSTRIA

P. O. Box 5634, Rue Chafic Al-Mouàyd, Immeuble Sabri, Malki Damascus
Tel. 3327691; Tel. 337528; Fax 3329232

COMMERCIAL SECTION

Tel. 2124616; Tel. 2124771

KINGDOM OF BELGIUM

P.O. Box 31, Rue Ata Ayoubi, Immeuble Hachem, Damascus
Tel. 3332821; Tel. 3338098; Fax 3330426

KINGDOM OF DENMARK

P.O. Box 2244, Rue Chekib Arslan, Abou Roumaneh Immeuble du
Patriarcat Grèc Catholique, Damascus
Tel. 3331008; Tel. 3337853; Fax 3337928

REPUBLIC OF FINLAND

P.O. Box 3893, Malki West, Hawakir, Immeuble Yacoubian, Damascus
Tel. 3338809; Tel. 3338670

REPUBLIC OF FRANCE

P.O. Box 769, Rue Ata Ayoubi, Damascus
Tel. 3327992/3/4/5

COMMERCIAL SECTION

1st, Cham Palace Hotel, Rue Maysaloun, Damascus
Tel. 2213414; Tel. 2213987

FEDERAL REPUBLIC OF GERMANY

P.O. Box 2237, 53 Rue Ibrahim Hanano, Immeuble Kotob, Damascus
Tel. 3323800/1/2; Fax 3323812

REPUBLIC OF GREECE

P.O. Box 30319, Mezzeh, east Villas, Opp. Al-Farabi Gardens, Damascus
Tel. 2233009; Tel. 2233035

COMMERCIAL SECTION

P.O. Box 3792, Rue Ata Ayoubi, Damascus
Tel. 3338258

RUSSIAN FEDERATION

Rue Omar Ben Al Khattab, Damascus
Tel. 4423155; Tel. 4423156

COMMERCIAL SECTION

Tel. 3712238; Tel. 3718884; Fax 3710243

SWITZERLAND

P.O. Box 234, Rue Mehdi Ben Baraka, Damascus
Tel. 3715474; Tel. 3321137

REPUBLIC OF ITALY

P.O. Box 2216, 82 Avenue Al-Mansour, Damascus
Tel. 3332621; Tel. 3338338; Tel. 3332537; Fax 3320325

KINGDOM OF NETHERLANDS

P.O. Box 702, Rue Abou Roumaneh, Damascus
Tel. 3336871; Tel.. 3337661; Tel. 3338069;
Fax. 3339369

KINGDOM OF SPAIN

Rawda Al-Jallah, Immeuble Al-Kabbani, Damascus
Tel. 3332126; Tel. 3335178

COMMERCIAL SECTION

61 Hidjaz Al-Jadid, Rawda, Damascus
Tel. 3330015; Tel. 3333619S

KINGDOM OF SWEDEN

P.O. Box 4266, Rue Chekib Arslan, Abou Roumaneh,
Immeuble du Patriarcat Catholique, Damascus
Tel. 3327261/1/2/3

UNITED KINGDOM OF GREAT BRITAIN AND NORTHERN IRELAND

P.O. Box 37, Malki, Rue Kurd Ali, Immeuble Kotob, Damascus
Tel. 3712561/2/3; Fax 3713592

IRELAND, PORTUGAL AND LUXEMBOURG

Not currently represented through their own embassies in Syria. Queries
should be addressed to embassies in neighbouring countries or the
appropriate ministry of foreign affairs.

COMMONWEALTH OF AUSTRALIA

P.O. Box 3882, Mezzeh, East Villas, 128/A Rue Al Farabi Damascus

Tel. 6664317; Tel. 6660238; Fax. 6621195

CANADA

P.O. Box 3394, Mezzeh Autostrad, near Razi Hospital, Damascus
Tel. 2236892; Tel. 3330535; Tel. 3332409

PEOPLE'S REPUBLIC OF CHINA

83 Rue Ata Ayoubi, Damascus
Tel. 3339594; Tel. 2247968

JAPAN

P.O. Box 3366, Rue Mehdi Ben Baraka, Damascus
Tel. 3338273; Tel. 3332553; Tel. 3339781; Fax. 3335314

HASHEMITE KINGDOM OF JORDAN

Abou Roumaneh, Rue Al Aljalaà, Damascus
Tel. 3334642; Tel. 3339313

RUSSIAN FEDERATION

Rue Omar Ben Al Khattab, Damascus
Tel. 4423155; Tel. 4423156

COMMERCIAL SECTION

Tel. 3712238; Tel. 3718884; Fax 3710243

SWITZERLAND

P.O. Box 234, Rue Mehdi Ben Baraka, Damascus
Tel. 3715474; Tel. 3321137

TURKEY

58 Avenue Ziad Bin Abou Soufian, Damascus
Tel. 3331411; Tel. 3334253; Tel. 3331370

COMMERCIAL SECTION

Tel. 3333142

UNITED STATES OF AMERICA

P.O. Box 29, Rue Al Mansour, Damascus
Tel. 3332315; Tel. 3332814; Fax. 2247938

COMMERCIAL SECTION

Tel. 3714108

MINISTRIES

SYRIAN CABINET

Cabinet of Ministers

(Includes Ministries of state and of State for Cabinet and Services Affairs)
Shahbandar Street
Tel 2226001, 2221000, 2110212
Tlx. 411020

Ministry of the Interior
Al Bahsah Street

Tel. 2238682
　　 2238683
Fax 2246921
Tlx. 412752

Ministry of Housing and Utilities
Al-Salheyeh, Yousef
Azmeh Square

Tel 3722552
　　 2217571
　　 2217572
　　 3722552
Fax 2217570

Ministry of Information
Mezzeh Autostrad,
Dar al Ba'th Building

Tel 6664600
　　 6664601
Fax 6620052
Tlx. 412620

Ministry of Economy and Foreign Trade
Maysaloun Street

Tel   2213514
　　 2213515
Fax. 2225695
Tlx. 411982

Ministry of Construction
and Building
Sa'dallah al-Jaberi
Street in Front of
the Mail Center

Tel. 2223595
　　 2227966
　　 2223196
　　 2223597

Ministry of Al Awkaf
Rukeneddin

Tel. 4419079
　　 4419080
Fax. 419969

Ministry of Education

Al Mazraa,
Al Shahbandar
Square

Tel. 4444703/4/2
　　 4444800
Fax. 4420435
Tlx. 421959

Ministry of Higher Education
Al Rawda, Kasem
Amin Avenue

Tel. 3330700/1/2/3
Fax. 3337719

Ministry of Supply and Internal Trade
Al Salheyeh

Tel. 2219044
　　 2219241
Fax. 2219803
Tlx. 411908

Ministry of Culture
Al Rawda, George
Haddad Street

Tel   3331556
　　 3338633
　　 338600
Fax 3320804
Tlx. 411944

Ministry of Foreign Affairs
Muhajereen,
Shora Avenue

Tel. 3331200/4
　　 3337200
Fax. 3320686
Tlx. 411975
　　 419123

Ministry of the Interior
Al Shuhadaa Square

Tel. 2211001
　　 2219401
Fax.2223428

Ministry of Defense

Omayad Square

Tel. 7770700
880980
3710980
3720936

Ministry of Environment
Al Salheyeh

Tel. 2222600/1/2/3/4
Fax. 3335645
Tlx. 412686

Ministry of Irrigation
Fardoss Street

Tel. 2212741
2221400
Fax. 3320691
Tlx. 411059

Ministry of Agriculture and Agrarian Reform
Sa'dallah Al Jaberi
Street

Tel. 2213613
2222513
Fax. 2244078
2244023
Tlx. 411643

Ministry of Tourism
Kwatli Street,
Barada bank

Tel. 2210122
2237940
Fax. 2242636
Tlx. 411672

Ministry of Social Affairs and Labor
Al Salheyeh, Yousef
Azmeh Square

Tel. 2210355
2225948
Fax.2247499

Ministry of Health
Parliement Street

Tel. 3339600/1/2
Fax. 2223085
Tlx. 412655

Ministry of Industry
Maysaloun Street

Tel. 2231834
Fax. 2231096
Tlx. 411115

Ministry of Justice
al-Nasre Street

Tel. 2214105
2220302
Fax. 2246250

Ministry of Electricity
Kwatli Street

Tel. 2223086
2229654
Fax.2223686
Tlx. 411938

Ministry of Finance
Al Sabee Bahrat Square, Baghdad Street.

Tel. 2219600/1/2/3
Fax. 2224701
Tlx. 411932

Ministry of Communications
Al Salheyeh

Tel. 2227033/34
Fax. 2246403
Tlx. 411933

Ministry of Oil and Mineral Resources
Adawi, Insha'at

Tel. 4445610
4451624
Fax 4457786
Tlx. 411006

Ministry of Transport
Al Jalaa Street

Tel. 3336801/2/3
Fax. 3323317
Tlx. 411994

SELECTED GOVERNMENT AND BUSINESS CONTACTS

Syrian Petroleum Company (SPC)
Contact Name: Dr. Muhammad Khaddour
Contact Title: Director General
Address: Fardos, Mutanabi St., P.O. Box

2849, Damascus, Syria
Telephone: 2227095, 2227007, 2226984, 2226245

Fax: 2225648
Telex: 411031 sypco SY

Al-Furat Petroleum Company (AFPC)
John Darley
General Manager
Mazzeh, Writers' Union Building, P.O. Box 7660, Damascus,
Telephone: 6183333
Fax: 2238104, 2244010
Tlx: 412088 SY or 412089 SY

Syrian Petroleum Transport Company
Mohammad Douba
Director General
P.O. Box 13, Banias, Syria/ P.O. Box 51, Homs, Syria/ P.O. Box 310, Damascus, Syria
Telephone: (43) 711300
Fax: (43) 710418
Tlx: 441012 scot SY

Public Establishment for Power Generation and Distribution
Zeki Odeh
Director General
P.O. Box 3386, Damascus, Syria
Telephone: 2227981, 2229654, 2223086, 2228334, 2246472
Fax: 2229062
Tlx: 411056 syrlec SY

General Organization for Engineering Industries
Issa Dawood
Director General
P.O. Box 3120, Damascus, Syria
Telephone: 2123438, 2121889, 2121824, 2121825
Fax: 2123375
Tlx: 411035 SY

Syrian Telecommunications Corporation (STE)
Makram Obeid
Director General
Mezzeh, Damascus, Syria
Telephone: 2240300, 6122210
Fax: 2242000
Tlx: 411015 gentel SY

General Organization for Cement and Building Material
Ahmad Al-Hamo
General Director

Mazzeh, Western Villas, P.O. Box 5265, Damascus, Syria
Telephone: 6117666, 6117444, 611333, 6118444, 6117503
Fax: 6117111
Tlx: 411369 SY

General Organization for Textile Industries
Hussein Al-Zu'bi
Director General
P.O. Box 620, Damascus, Syria
Telephone: 2216200, 2227158
Fax: 2216201
Tlx: 412036 nasige SY

General Organization for Chemical Industries
Zaid Al-Hariri
Director General
Baramkeh, P.O. Box 5447, Damascus, Syria
Telephone: 2127654, 2123363, 2122743, 2122917, 2122362
Fax: 2128289
Tlx: 419145 SY

General Organization for Food Industries
Ali Kamel Salman
Director General
P.O. Box 105, Damascus, Syria
Telephone: 2225290, 2225291
Fax: 2245374
Tlx: 419154 SY

Ministry of Health
Dr. Iyad Chatti
Minister of Health
Najmeh Square, Parliament Street, Damascus, Syria
Telephone: 3339602, 3333801, 3311020/1/2/3
Fax: 3311114

Foreign Trade Organization for Machinery and Equipment (SAYARAT)
Muhammad Salim Dalloul
General Director
P.O. Box 3130, Damascus, Syria
Telephone: 2218223, 2218156, 2232190, 2232199
Fax: 2211118
Tlx: 411036 SY

Country Trade Associations/ Chambers of Commerce

The Federation of Syrian Chambers of Commerce and Industry:
President: Dr. Rateb Shallah
P.O. Box 5909
Damascus, Syria
Telephone: 3337344, 3311504
Fax: 963-11-3331127

Damascus Chamber of Commerce
President: Dr. Rateb Shallah
P.O. Box 1040
Damascus, Syria
Telephone: 223-2348, 223-2360, 2211339,
2218339
Fax: 963-11-222-5874

Damascus Chamber of Industry
President: Dr. Yahya Hindi
P.O. Box 1305
Damascus, Syria
Telephone: 222-2205, 221-3475, 221-5042,
221-3475
Fax: 963-11-224-5981

Aleppo Chamber of Commerce
President: Mr. Mohammad Saleh Al-Mallah
P.O. Box 1261
Aleppo, Syria
Telephone: 963-21-238-236, 238-237
Fax: 963-21-213-493

Aleppo Chamber of Industry
President: Mr. Muhammad Oubari
P.O. Box 1859,
Aleppo, Syria
Telephone: 963-21-620-600/1/2, 639-700
Fax: 963-21-620-040

Homs Chamber of Commerce and Industry
President: Mr. M. Walid Tuleimat
P.O. Box 440
Homs, Syria
Telephone: 963-31-228-605, 231-000
Fax: 963-31-224-247

Hama Chamber of Commerce and Industry
President: Mr. Abd Al-Salam Al-Sabe'
P.O. Box 147
Hama, Syria
Telephone: 963-33-233-304, 517-700
Fax: 963-33-517701

Latakia Chamber of Commerce and Industry
President: Mr. Kamal Ismail Al-Assad
P.O. Box 124
Latakia, Syria
Telephone: 963-41-239-530
Fax: 963-41-238-526

Country Market Research Firms

The Syrian Consulting Bureau
Dr. Nabil Succar
P.O. Box 12574, Damascus, Syria
Tel: 2225946
Fax: 2231603

Commerce and Engineering Consultants
Mr. Ramez Raslan
Malki, P.O. Box 6136, Damascus, Syria
Tel: 3733956, 3730771
Fax: 3733955

Consulting, Management, and Contracting Company
Mr. Hani Sawaf
P.O. Box 3858, Damascus, Syria
Tel: 3331226
Fax: 3333031

Financial, Economic, & Consulting Services
Dr. M. Ayman Midani
P.O. Box 7825, Damascus, Syria
Tel: 3316075
Tlx: 411044 Midani SY

FOREIGN EMBASSIES IN SYRIA

Name of Embassy	Address	Telephone
Argentina	Al-Rawda	3334167
Armenia	Abu-Roumaneh	3711357
Spain	Abu-Roumaneh	3332126

Australia	Mezzeh - Farabi Str.	6664317
Germany	Malki - Hanano Str.	3323800
U.S.A	Abu-Roumaneh	3332315
Iran	Mezzeh - Autostrad	2227675
Italy	Malki - al-Mansour Str.	3332537
Pakistan	Mazzeh - Farabi Str.	6662391
Brazil	Al-Rawda	3337770
U.K.	Malki - Kurd ali Str.	3712561
Belgium	Abu-Roumaneh	3332821
Czech	Mezzeh - Farabi Str.	3331383
Greece	Mezzeh - Farabi Str.	2123009
Turkey	Al-Rawda	3331383
Russia	Omar ben Al-khattab Str.	4423156
Romania	Abu-Roumaneh	3327570
Sweden	Abu-Roumaneh	3327261
Switzerland	Omar ben Al-khattab Str.	3311871
China	Malki - al-Mansour Str.	3339594
France	Affif Atta-Ayoubi Str.	3327993
Cyprus	Abu-Roumaneh	3332919
Canada	Mezzeh - Autostrad	6116870
Cuba	Mezzeh Al-Rashid Str.	3339624
Austria	Mezzeh - Farabi Str.	6624732
India	Malki Square	3719580
Netherlands	Abu-Roumaneh	3337661
Japan	Abu-Roumaneh	3332533
United Arab Emirates	Al-Mehdi ben Barakeh Str.	3330308
Jordan	Abu-Roumaneh	3334642
Tunisia	Mezzeh East Villas	6617509
Algeria	Al-Rawda	3334548
Saudi Arabia	Abu-Roumaneh	3334914
Sudan	White Bridge	2247046

Qattar	Abu-Roumaneh	3327451
Kuwait	Malki - Hanano Str.	3714760
Libya	Abu-Roumaneh	3333914
Egypt	Abu-Roumaneh	3332932
Morocco	Mezzeh - Farabi Str.	6620839
Yemen	Mezzeh East Villas	6622706
Mauritania	Malki Karameh Str.	3339317

SELECTED U.S. AND COUNTRY CONTACTS FOR SYRIA

SYRIAN CONTACTS

Organization: Syrian Petroleum Company (SPC)
Contact Name: Dr. Muhammad Khaddour
Contact Title: Director General
Address: Fardos, Mutanabi St., P.O. Box 2849, Damascus, Syria
Telephone: 2227095, 2227007, 2226984, 2226245
Fax: 2225648
Telex: 411031 sypco SY

Al-Furat Petroleum Company (AFPC)
John Darley
General Manager
Mazzeh, Writers' Union Building, P.O. Box 7660, Damascus,
Telephone: 6183333
Fax: 2238104, 2244010
Tlx: 412088 SY or 412089 SY

Syrian Petroleum Transport Company
Mohammad Douba
Director General
P.O. Box 13, Banias, Syria/ P.O. Box 51, Homs, Syria/ P.O. Box310, Damascus, Syria
Telephone: (43) 711300
Fax: (43) 710418
Tlx: 441012 scot SY

Public Establishment for Power Generation and Distribution
Zeki Odeh
Director General
P.O. Box 3386, Damascus, Syria
Telephone: 2227981, 2229654, 2223086, 2228334, 2246472
Fax: 2229062
Tlx: 411056 syrlec SY

General Organization for Engineering Industries
Issa Dawood
Director General
P.O. Box 3120, Damascus, Syria
Telephone: 2123438, 2121889, 2121824, 2121825

Fax: 2123375
Tlx: 411035 SY

Syrian Telecommunications Establishment (STE)
Makram Obeid
Director General
Mezzeh, Damascus, Syria
Telephone: 2240300, 6122210
Fax: 2242000
Tlx: 411015 gentel SY

General Organization for Cement and Building Material
Ahmad Al-Hamo
General Director
Mazzeh, Western Villas, P.O. Box 5265, Damascus, Syria
Telephone: 6117666, 6117444, 611333, 6118444, 6117503
Fax: 6117111
Tlx: 411369 SY

General Organization for Textile Industries
Hussein Al-Zu'bi
Director General
P.O. Box 620, Damascus, Syria
Telephone: 2216200, 2227158
Fax: 2216201
Tlx: 412036 nasige SY

General Organization for Chemical Industries
Zaid Al-Hariri
Director General
Baramkeh, P.O. Box 5447, Damascus, Syria
Telephone: 2127654, 2123363, 2122743, 2122917, 2122362
Fax: 2128289
Tlx: 419145 SY

General Organization for Food Industries
Ali Kamel Salman
Director General
P.O. Box 105, Damascus, Syria
Telephone: 2225290, 2225291
Fax: 2245374
Tlx: 419154 SY

Ministry of Health
Dr. Iyad Chatti
Minister of Health
Najmeh Square, Parliament Street, Damascus, Syria
Telephone: 3339602, 3333801, 3311020/1/2/3
Fax: 3311114

Foreign Trade Organization for Machinery and Equipment (SAYARAT)
Muhammad Salim Dalloul
General Director
P.O. Box 3130, Damascus, Syria
Telephone: 2218223, 2218156, 2232190, 2232199

Fax: 2211118
Tlx: 411036 SY

COUNTRY TRADE ASSOCIATIONS/ CHAMBERS OF COMMERCE

The Federation of Syrian Chambers of Commerce and Industry:
President: Dr. Rateb Shallah
P.O. Box 5909
Damascus, Syria
Telephone: 3337344, 3311504
Fax: 963-11-3331127

Damascus Chamber of Commerce
President: Dr. Rateb Shallah
P.O. Box 1040
Damascus, Syria
Telephone: 223-2348, 223-2360, 2211339, 2218339
Fax: 963-11-222-5874

Damascus Chamber of Industry
President: Dr. Yahya Hindi
P.O. Box 1305
Damascus, Syria
Telephone: 222-2205, 221-3475, 221-5042, 221-3475
Fax: 963-11-224-5981

Aleppo Chamber of Commerce
President: Mr. Mohammad Saleh Al-Mallah
P.O. Box 1261
Aleppo, Syria
Telephone: 963-21-238-236, 238-237
Fax: 963-21-213-493

Aleppo Chamber of Industry
President: Mr. Muhammad Oubari
P.O. Box 1859,
Aleppo, Syria
Telephone: 963-21-620-600/1/2, 639-700
Fax: 963-21-620-040

Homs Chamber of Commerce and Industry
President: Mr. M. Walid Tuleimat
P.O. Box 440
Homs, Syria
Telephone: 963-31-228-605, 231-000
Fax: 963-31-224-247

Hama Chamber of Commerce and Industry
President: Mr. Abd Al-Salam Al-Sabe'
P.O. Box 147
Hama, Syria
Telephone: 963-33-233-304, 517-700
Fax: 963-33-517701

Latakia Chamber of Commerce and Industry
President: Mr. Kamal Ismail Al-Assad
P.O. Box 124
Latakia, Syria
Telephone: 963-41-239-530
Fax: 963-41-238-526

COUNTRY MARKET RESEARCH FIRMS

The Syrian Consulting Bureau
Dr. Nabil Succar
P.O. Box 12574, Damascus, Syria
Tel: 2225946
Fax: 2231603

Commerce and Engineering Consultants
Mr. Ramez Raslan
Malki, P.O. Box 6136, Damascus, Syria
Tel: 3733956, 3730771
Fax: 3733955

Consulting, Management, and Contracting Company
Mr. Hani Sawaf
P.O. Box 3858, Damascus, Syria
Tel: 3331226
Fax: 3333031

Financial, Economic, & Consulting Services
Dr. M. Ayman Midani
P.O. Box 7825, Damascus, Syria
Tel: 3316075
Tlx: 411044 Midani SY

COMMERCIAL BANKS

Commercial Bank of Syria: Director General: Mr. Riad Hakim, YousefAl-Azmah Square, P.O. Box 933, Damascus, Syria; Telephone: 221-4508;Fax: 221-6975, 222-8524

U.S. Embassy Trade Personnel: Telephone: (963)(11) 333-3232

Anne Bodine: Economic/Commercial Attache
Donna Vandenbroucke: Economic/Commercial Officer
Jamal Aliah: Economic/Commercial Officer
Jonathan Rice: Economic/Commercial Officer

WASHINGTON-BASED USG CONTACTS

Office of Syrian Affairs
E. Candace Putnam
U.S. Department of State
Washington, D.C. 20520
Telephone: (202)647-7216
Fax: (202)647-0989

Office of Syrian Affairs
Thomas A. Sams
U.S. Department of Commerce
Washington, D.C.
Telephone: (202)482-1860
Fax: (202)482-0878

ATTORNEYS IN SYRIA

Damascus

Mazhar Anbari: Sanjakdar Street, tel: 2217017. Citizenof the SAR. Born in Damascus 1923. Graduate of Damascus Law School1948; practicing since 1948. Specializes in criminal and civilcases, insurance, and international arbitration. Former Ministerof Justice. Former Vice-Speaker of the Parliament. Former Presidentof the Syrian Bar Association. Languages: Arabic, English, and French.

Farid Arslanian: Balkis Street, telephone: 2218321 and3331676. Citizen of the SAR. Born in Turkey in 1915. Graduateof Damascus Law School. Specializes in criminal, civil, and insurancecases. Secretary General of the Committee of Damascus Bar Association.Controller, 1960-1971. Elected Deputy in the Syrian Parliament.Legal consultant since 1964 for the United Nations Relief andWorks Agency in the SAR. Languages: Arabic, French, English, Armenian,and Turkish.

Ghazi Al-Ghazzi: 69 Salhieh street, Tibi & Sulo Building,P.O. Box 4238, tel: 2224036 (office), fax: 2229798, 3327648 (home).Citizen of the SAR. Born in 1937. Graduate of Damascus Law School.Represents a number of foreign firms in Syria. Languages: Arabic,English, and French.

Jacques Hakim: Victoria Bridge, Mardam Building, P.O. Box5788. Telex 412033 Sy (drobco); tel: 2223577 (office), 3710554(home). Citizen of the SAR. Born in Damascus in 1931. Doctor ofLaw (France), graduate in economics (Economics Institute, Univ.of Colorado). Professor, Head of the Commercial Law Department, Damascus University. Practicing since 1952. Specializes in commercial,and finance cases along with international arbitration. Languages:Arabic, English, and French.

Hazem Jazzar: Salhieh Street, Cinema Amir's Building, Tel:4421069 (home), 2225286 (office). Citizen of the SAR. Born inDamascus in 1948. Graduate of Damascus Law School 1971. Has practicedlaw since 1971. Specializes in commercial and criminal cases.Languages: Arabic and English.

Zouheir Al-Midany: Abou-Roumaneh Street, tel: 2213100 (office),3332075, 3330650 (home). Citizen of the SAR. Born in Damascusin 1923. Graduate of Damascus Law School 1947. Has practiced lawsince 1947. Specializes in civil, commercial, and criminal cases.Former head of the Syrian Bar Association and former Vice-Presidentof the International Bar Union. Languages: Arabic and French.

Mamdouh Rahaby: Salhieh, Dentists' Syndicate Building,3rd floor, tel: 2221428 (office), 3332905 (home). Citizen of theSAR. Born in Damascus in 1932. Graduate of Damascus Law School1966. Specializes in civil, real estate, and commercial cases. Languages: Arabic and English.

Souheil Sarkis: 7 Fountain Square, Adel Sharaf Building,2nd floor, tel: 4428240, 4420049, telex 412464. Citizen of theSAR. Born in Damascus in 1934. Graduate of Damascus Law School1960. Has practiced law since 1961. Specializes in civil and commercialcases. Languages: Arabic, English, and French.

Sami Wardeh: Marjeh Square, Kabbani building, P.O. Box10355, tel: 2211767 (office), 3714892 (home). Citizen of the SAR.Born in Damascus in 1942. Graduate of Damascus Law School 1965.Has practiced law since 1965. Specializes in commercial and realestate cases. Languages: Arabic, French and English.

Aleppo

Miss Ghada Bismarji: Kostaki Homsi Street, Azizieh, telephone219428. Citizen of the SAR, graduate of Damascus Law School 1962. Has practiced law since 1962. Sworn translator English-Arabic,and vice-versa. Handles all types of cases. Languages: English, Arabic, French, and some Armenian.

Ihsan Kayali: Baron Street, tel: office 215811, home 219403.Citizen of the SAR. Born in Aleppo in 1925. Graduate of DamascusLaw School in 1949. Handles all cases with specialization in commercialand insurance cases. Languages: Arabic, English, and French.

Simon Bashkhamji: P.O. Box 67, Azizieh, tel: office 247074,home 217624. Citizen of the SAR. Graduate of the University ofAleppo 1969. General practice. Languages: Arabic, French, andsome English.

Homs

Mouhammad Mounir Amoudi: P.O. Box 362, tel: 223115 (office),222683 (home). Citizen of the SAR. Born in 1928. Graduate of DamascusLaw School 1949. Has practiced law since 1949. Specializes incriminal, civil, banking, and insurance cases. Languages: Arabic,French, and English.

Antoun Trabulsi: tel: 224406 (office), 225286, 224655 (home).Citizen of the SAR. Born in 1919. Graduate of Damascus Law School1940. Has practiced law since 1940. Lawyer of the Municipality of Homs. Head of Homs Bar Association. General practice. Languages: Arabic and French.

Hama

Fathallah Alloush: Al-Alamien Street, tel: 223206 (office).Citizen of the SAR. Born in Hama in 1932. Graduate of DamascusLaw School in 1955, practicing law since 1955. Specializes incivil, banking, and criminal cases. Languages: Arabic and French.

Khaled Al-Keylani: Kowatly Street, tel: 222536, 221299.Citizen of the SAR. Born in Hama in 1929. Graduate of DamascusLaw School in 1954. No specialization, handles all cases. Languages:Arabic, French, and some English.

Latakia

Hassan Makhlouf: P.O. Box 1025, tel: 338055 (office), 226089(home). Citizen of the SAR. Born in 1930. Graduate of DamascusLaw School 1960. Has practiced law since 1960. No specialization, handles all cases. Languages: Arabic, French, and English.

INTERNATIONAL AGREEMENTS

AGREEMENTS SIGNED WITH FOREIGN STATES ON PROTECTION AND GUARANTEE OF INVESTMENT

State	Type of Agreement	Date of	Instrument of	Remarks

		Signing	Ratification and Date	
United States of America	Exchanged Notes on Manner of Guaranteeing American Investments in Syria	09.08.1976	Legislative Decree No.33 dated 01.08.1977	
Swiss Federation	Accord on Encouraging and protecting Investments	22.06.1977	Legislative Decree No.24 dated 12.07.1978	Most Favoured Nation
France	Agreement on Reciprocal Encouragement and Protection of Investments	28.11.1977	Legislative Decree No.30 dated 31.07.1978	Most Favoured Nation
Federal Germany	Agreement on Reciprocal Encouragement and Protection of Investments	02.08.1977	Legislative Decree No.34 dated 11.09.1978	Most Favoured Nation
Pakistan	Accord on Reciprocal Encouragement and Protection of Investments	25.04.1996	Law No. 5 dated 02.07.1997	
People's Republic of China	Accord on Reciprocal Encouragement and Protection of Investments and Appended Protocol	09.12.1996	Law No. 11 dated 04.08.1998	Protocol treats investment formalities and the transfers resulting from investment
Indonesia	Accord on Reciprocal Encouragement and Protecting Investments and Appended protocol	27.06.1997	Law No. 19 dated 31.12.1996	Most Favoured Nation. Protocol regulates transfers resulting from investment
Iran	Accord on Reciprocal Encouragement and Protection of Investments	05.02.1998	Legislative Decree No.3 dated 11.02.1998	Most Favoured Nation
Belorussia	Accord on Reciprocal Encouragement and Protection of Investments	11.03.1998	Legislative Decree No.8 dated 04.08.1998	

Trade Agreements Signed with Foreign States :				
State	Type of Agreement	Date of Signing	Instrument of Ratification and Date	Remarks
Russian Federation	Technical, Economic and Commercial Cooperation	15.04.1993	Law No. 11 dated 22.06.1993	
Bulgaria	Trade	02.05.1974	Legislative Decree No.54 dated 24.07.1974	New trade agreement was initialed by the two states on 13.03.1996
Hungary	Syrian side notified			New trade

	Hungarian side of its decision to nullify the trade agreement of 1974			agreement has been initialed by the two sides
Albania	Trade	17.06.1979	Decree No.1252 dated 08.02.1980	
Cuba	Trade	27.03.1974	Decree No.167 dated 24.07.1974	It provides for exemption from Consular legalization. New trade agreement was initialed on .03.1998
Poland	Trade	20.08.1974	Decree No.303 dated 04.12.1974	
Czech	Syrian side nullified the trade agreement of 1975 signed with Czechoslovakia when the latter broke up as of 01.01.1993			The two sides have not agreed to signing new trade agreement
Slovak	Long term trade agreement	29.08.1995	Law No. 7 dated 03.07.1996	
Romania	Trade	13.04.1993		
Korea	Trade	28.06.1982	Law No.5 dated 08.02.1983	It provides for exemption from Consular Legalization
Vietnam	Trade	12.05.1994	Legislative Decree No.12 dated 27.06.1994	
People's Republic of China	Trade	16.03.1982	Law No. 23 of 1982	
Byelorussia	Technical, Economic and Commercial	11.03.1998	Legislative Decree No.9 dated 04.08.1998	
Armenia	Trade	30.03.1992	Legislative Decree No.7 dated 11.07.1992	
Turkmenistan	Trade	26.03.1992	Legislative Decree No.8 dated 11.07.1992	
Kazakhstan	Trade	27.03.1992	Legislative Decree No.9 dated 11.07.1992	
Azerbaijan	Trade	28.03.1992	Legislative Decree No.10 dated 11.07.1992	
Tajikistan	Trade	19.03.1992	Legislative Decree No.11 dated	

			11.07.1992	
Republic of Tanzania	Trade	15.02.1974	Decree No.166 dated 15.03.1974	
Republic of Niger	Trade	26.06.1980	Decree No.2661 dated 22.12.1980	
Republic of Nigeria	Trade	17.09.1969	Decree No.242 dated 23.12.1969	
Republic of Guinea	Trade	22.01.1979	Decree No.1209 dated 23.01.1979	
Republic of Senegal	Economic, Commercial, Cultural, and Technological	04.11.1975	Decree No.589 dated 03.03.1976	
Cyprus	Long term trade agreement	23.02.1982		
Pakistan	Trade Annex to trade agreement	11.08.1969 25.04.1996	Legislative Decree No.342 dated 23.11.1969	
Sri Lanka	Trade and Payments	09.10.1966	Legislative Decree No.29 dated 09.04.1966	
Turkey	Trade	17.09.1974	Decree No.31 dated 02.12.1974	
India	Trade	09.10.1969	Decree No.345 dated 23.12.1969	
Indonesia	Trade	18.03.1976	Decree No.1220 dated 09.07.1977	
Argentina	Trade	06.09.1989		
Grenada	Trade	22.01.1980	Decree No.1144 dated 27.05.1980	
Chile	Trade	27.02.1990	Legislative Decree No.12 dated 24.05.1990	
Iran	Trade	21.08.1996	Decree No.241 dated 10.11.1997	
European Union	Cooperation	18.01.1977	Legislative Decree No.14 dated 05.07.1977	

LIST OF BILATERAL AGREEMENTS SIGNED WITH ARAB STATES AND THE ADVANTAGES GRANTED THEREBY

State	Name & date of Agreement	Exemptions for Syrian Commodities	Exemptions for Arab Commodities
Saudi Arabia	Economic and	- Agricultural products and	- Agricultural and animal

	Trade Agreement of 1972 Still valid	livestock and the produce of natural resources are exempted from customs duties according to list No.1 appended to the agreement - Syrian industrial products are exempted from customs duties according to list No.2 appended to the agreement - Syrian industrial products as per list No.3 appended to the agreement are exempted from two thirds of customs duties.	products and livestock and the produce of natural resources are exempted from duties as per list No.1 appended to the agreement - All Saudi industrial products are exempted from duties
Kuwait	Economic and Commercial Cooperation Agreement of 1991 Still valid	- Agricultural and livestock products and the produce of natural resources are exempted from customs duties and other fees of similar effect - Syrian industrial products are exempted from duties and fees of similar effect except for the following: 1- Cast iron covering 2- Welded black steel pipes 3- oxygen gas for medical or industrial purposes	- Agricultural and livestock products and the produce of Kuwaiti natural resources are exempted from duties and fees of similar effect. - Kuwaiti industrial products are exempted from duties and fees of similar effect except for : 1- Cars. 2- Raw tobacco and byproducts. 3- cotton yarns locally produced.

Qatar	Economic and Commercial Cooperation Agreement of 1990 Still valid.	Agricultural, livestock and industrial products and raw materials that will be agreed upon in lists by the joint committee are exempted from customs duties.	Agricultural, livestock and industrial products and raw materials that will be agreed upon in lists by the joint committee are exempted from customs duties.
Bahrain	Economic and Commercial Cooperation Agreement of 1994 Still valid.	-Syrian agricultural and livestock products are exempted from customs duties and fees of similar effect. - Syrian industrial products according to lists prepared by the joint committee as stated in the agreement are exempted from customs duties and fees of similar effect.	-Bahraini agricultural and livestock products are exempted from customs duties and fees of similar effect. - Industrial products according to lists prepared by the joint committee as stated in the agreement are exempted from customs duties and fees of similar

			effect.
United Arab Emirates	Economic and Commercial Cooperation Agreement of 1990 endorsed by Syria but not endorsed by U.A.E.Consultations are underway with the U.A.E for the purpose.	No advantages of preferences or exemptions for the products of each country. Yet, the agreement provides for offering facilities that support the movement of export and import between the two countries.	No advantages of preferences or exemptions for the products of each country. Yet, the agreement provides for offering facilities that support the movement of export and import between the two countries.
Oman	Economic and Commercial Cooperation Agreement of 1991 Still valid.	Agreement does not give any performances or exemptions from customs duties.	Agreement does not give any performances or exemptions from customs duties.
Jordan	Agreement on Economic Cooperation and Regulating Trade Exchange of 1975. Minutes of meeting of the joint committee of 1986.	The 1975 agreement provides for exemption from customs duties for agricultural, livestock products and the produce of natural resources and exchanged industrial products. The two sides agreed on two lists, one for prompt implementation and the other is a guideline. The "prompt" list benefits From exemption from customs duties in each country according to certain banking arrangements , the guidelines list does not benefit from customs exemptions.	The agreement provides for total exemption from customs duties for Jordanian products.
Yemen	Trade agreement signed in 1996, ratified by Yemen, procedures of ratification in Syria are under way.	Agreement does not provide for any advantage of preference. The joint committee will discuss preferences which each party can offer for the purpose of promoting and developing trade Exchange between the two countries.	Agreement
Iraq	An agreement on economic cooperation and regulation of trade exchange, signed in 1979 (frozen at present)	All Syrian Products are exempted from customs duties. Free zone products are exempted from duties within the limits of local costs used in the manufacture of those products.	All Iraqi products are exempted from customs duties. Free zone products are exempted from duties within the limits of local costs used in the manufacture of those products.

Egypt	Trade agreement signed in 1991 (Valid)	Exemption from customs duties and relevant taxes (except local taxes and fees and taxes on sales) for the Syrian commodities and products as listed in Table A appended to the agreement. (This list contains 19 commodities)	Exemption from customs duties and relevant taxes (except local taxes and fees and taxes on sales) for the Egyptian commodities listed in Table B appended to the agreement. (This list contains 20 commodities)
Morocco	Agreement on regulating trade exchange and economic cooperation signed in1972 (Valid)	Each side treats the other side as a most favoured nation. Excluded from this condition are the relations binding either side to other countries that form with it customs union or economic unity or common market and the advantages granted by either side to facilitate cross-border trade.	Each side treats the other side as a most favoured nation. Excluded from this condition are the relations binding either side to other countries that form with it customs union or economic unity or common market and the advantages granted by either side to facilitate cross-border trade.
Libya	Agreement on regulating trade exchange and economic cooperation signed in1978 (Valid)	All Syrian agricultural, livestock products, produce of natural resources and industrial products are exempted from customs duties and other taxes and fees.	All Libyan agricultural, livestock products, produce of natural resources and industrial products are exempted from customs duties and other taxes and fees.

Sudan	An agreement on trade and economic cooperation signed in 1974 (Valid)	Exemption from customs duties and additional fees for Syrian agricultural and animal products and livestock except for a fee of 5%. - Syrian industrial products as listed in Table 1 are subject to reduced duties as explained in the said table (ranging between 10% and 100%) . - Most favoured nation.	Exemption from customs duties and additional fees for Sudanese agricultural and animal products and livestock except for a fee of 2%. - Sudanese industrial products as listed in Table 2 are subject to reduced duties as explained in the said table (ranging between30% and 100%) . - Most favoured nation.
Tunisia	Trade agreement signed in 1977 (Valid)	All Syrian products are exempted from customs duties (agricultural, animal products, livestock, produce of natural resources and industrial products).	All Tunisian products are exempted from customs duties (agricultural, animal products, livestock, produce of natural resources and industrial products).

Algeria	Trade agreement signed in 1979, valid until the concluding of a new agreement in 1997 and notes of ratification are exchanged. Ratification is being followed up.	Old Agreement: Syrian agricultural products and livestock are exempted from customs duties. - Syrian industrial products as listed in Table 1 appended to the agreement are exempted from customs duties. New Agreement: No provision for most favoured nation for either country.	Old Agreement: Algerian agricultural products and livestock are exempted from customs duties. - Algerian industrial products as listed Table 2 appended to the agreement are exempted from customs duties. New Agreement: No provision for most favoured nation for either country.
Somalia	Trade agreement signed in 1973 (valid)	Most favoured nation with regard to customs duties and other taxes and fees on imports, exports, storage, transit, unloading and shipment of goods. Excluded are: 1- Advantages and benefits granted to facilitate cross-border trade. 2- Goods of non-Syrian or non-Somali origin. 3- Advantages and benefits resulting from customs union, free trade area, common market or any special agreements.	Same advantages
Lebanon	Economic agreement signed in 1953, still valid by virtue of the provisions of agreement on social and economic cooperation and coordination of 1992 duly ratified by the two countries and being implemented by both of them	- Syrian agricultural and livestock products as listed in Table 1 appended to the agreement are exempted from customs duties. - Syrian industrial products as listed in Table 2 appended to the agreement are exempted from customs duties. -Exempted from half the duties are Syrian industrial products as listed in Table 3 appended to the agreement.	- Lebanese agricultural and livestock products as listed in Table 1 appended to the agreement are exempted from customs duties. - Lebanese industrial products as listed in Table 2 appended to the agreement are exempted from customs duties. -Exempted from half the duties are Lebanese industrial products as listed in Table 3 appended to the agreement.

MAJOR EXPORT-IMPORT PRODUCTS

EXPORT & IMPORT BY CLASSIFICATION OF COMMODITY OF S.I.T.C.(Rev.3)

EXPORT & IMPORT BY CLASSIFCATION OF COMMODITY OF S.I.T.C.(REV.3) (Quantity in tons and value in "000" S.P.)

S.I.T.C. Rev.(3)	Sections	Divisions	Description of Goods	IMPORT		EXPORT	
				Quant.	Value	Quant.	Value
	0		Food & live Animals	1296533	7374798	1382088	6957868
		"00"	Live animals other than animals of div.03	15278	709256	208	1079268
			Sheeplive, live "000 heads"	NO.5969	5396	524	989970
"001.21"		"01"	Meat & meat preparations	2309	38642	87	662
		"02"	Dairy products and birds, eggs	13061	409501	4716	75157
		"03"	Fish	2931	262230	0	0
		"04"	Cereals and cereal preparations	406988	1224086	836730	1676225
"041.0"			Wheat & meslin, unmilled	_	_	278191	652686
"043.0"			Barley unmilled	_	_	556495	998871
		"05"	Vegetables and fruit	65003	583301	454034	3632990
"054.24"			Lentils	_	_	160665	602076
"054.40"			Tomatoes fresh or chilled	"000"	1	83104	512701
"057.93"			Stone fruit n.e.s. fresh	_	_	26843	397265
		"06"	Sugar preparations & hlney	528284	2144764	34327	145266
"061.10			Sugars beet or cane	124898	479175	_	_
		"07"	Coffee, tea, cocoa, spices,and manuf.thereof	48508	1230409	20977	303235
		"08"	Feeding stuff for animals	209033	668350	30837	42500
		"09"	Miscellaneous edible products and preparations	5138	104259	172	2565
	1		beeverages and tobacco	2918	342155	6160	30065
		11	Beverages	869	33626	4178	17429
		12	Tobacco and tobacco manufactures	2049	308529	1982	12636
	2		Crude Materials, linedible except fuels	264073	1899151	1537302	2484344
		21	Hides, Skins and furskins, raw	4289	51068	598	19050
		22	Oil seeds and oleaginous fruits	26500	237286	377	440

		23	Crude rubber	6062	86100	27	701
		24	Crok and wood	148750	888039	1473	860
		25	Pulp and waste paper	13688	73637	1	35
		26	Textile fibers	4946	120872	121605	2026421
"263.10			cotton (other than linters), not carded or combed	60	8058	99708	1914002
		27	Crude fertilizers, other than those of divison 56&crude				
			mineral (excluding coal, petroleum,&precious stones)	37660	92033	1408823	305500
		28	Metalliferous & metal scrap				
				19280	209992	94	1415
		29	Crude animal and vegetable materials	2898	140124	4304	126222
	3		Mineral fuels, lubricants and related materilas	487098	1081488	1.9E+07	3.1E+07
		32	Coal,coke and briquettes	5873	14013	1070	1121
		33	Petroleum, petroleum products and related materials	373727	807741	1.9E+07	3.1E+07
"333.00			petroleom oils and oils obtained from bituminous minerals cude	"000	25	1.7E+07	2.9E+07
334.11			Motor spririt(gasolene)including aviation spirit	44	1167	467245	923933
		34	Gas natural and manufactured	107498	259734	0	0
	4		ANIMAL AND VEGETABLE OILS, FATS & WAXES	151700	1191062	6183	184024
		41	Animal oils and fats	59702	579951	18	152
		42	Fixed vegetable fats and oils crude	74765	518199	6163	183846
421.1			soya hean oil and its fractions	38005	329582		
421.49			oil and their fractions obtained solely from olives	5572	35653	28	1712
		43	animal of vegetable fats and oils, processed, waxes of				

			animal of vegetable origin, inedible mixtures of preparati				
			of animal of vegetable fats of oils. N.E.S	17233	92912	2	26
	5		chemicals and related prodcucts N.E.S	927765	7248508	12843	113382
		51	organic chemicals	140839	915114	108	1517
		52	inorganic chemicals	99835	468754	666	4346
		53	dyeing, tanning & colouring mater	19010	423452	202	1695
		54	medicianl & farmaceutical products	3262	740650	819	18786
		55	essential oils and resionoids and perfume materials,				
			toilet, polishing & cleaning preparations	10295	153877	7742	78719
		56	fertilizers (other than those of group 272)	434539	706026	4	43
		57	plastices in primary forms	181532	2693543	2868	5660
571.1			polyethylene	58672	570068	7	65
573.1			polyvinyl chloride	27062	793648	21	223
		59	chemical materials and predicts N.E.S	38453	1147092	434	2616
	6		manufactured goods classified chefly by materei	2289116	1.9E+07	89306	1222880
		61	leather, leather manufactured, N.E.S. and dressed				
			furskins	1032	10479	4285	134284
		62	ruber manufactures,n.e.s.	27799	809427	491	4120
625.1			tyres, pneumatic, new, of akind used on motor cars	1137	33847		
625.2			tyres, pneumatic, new, of akind used on buses, lor.	11790	384507	2	29
		63	cork and wood manufactures (excluding furniture	12670	89080	430	6532
		64	paper, paperboard and articles of paper pulp, of pape or				

For additional analytical, business and investment opportunities information,
please contact Global Investment & Business Center, USA
at (202) 546-2103. Fax: (202) 546-3275. E-mail: rusric@erols.com

			of paperboard	151839	957111	3435	52257
		65	textile yarn, fabrics, made-up articles, n.e.s. and				
			related products	199639	4844425	17771	885271
651.5			synthetic filament yarn not put up for retail sale	68055	1343858	35	1636
651.59			other synthetic filament yarn (other than sweing thread)	40913	1112549	1	1961
655.23			other fabrics, warp knit	70	7256	7205	399570
		66	non-metallic mineral manufactures, n.e.s.	811161	1856593	36309	38971
661.22			portland cement	627246	974419		
		67	iron and steel	984079	7832861	330	3037
676.00"			iron and steel bars, rods, angles, shapes and sections				
			(includings sheet piling)	564061	3691951	3	43
679.3			other tubes and pipes	76445	1855630	100	819
		68	non ferrous metals	15897	544185	22280	35164
		69	menufactures of metals n.e.s	85000	2248305	3975	43244
	7		machinery and transport equipment	245308	1.9E+07	9772	80734
		71	power geerating machinery and equipment	24669	2137947	28	866
		72	machinery specialized particular industries	40813	1736762	1483	25666
728.49			machinery having individual functions n.e.s.	3176	396461	192	3323
		73	metalworing machinery	2386	162472	108	1849
		74	general industrial machinery and equipment				
			n.e.s. and machine parts, n.e.s.	46960	4756336	6594	36443
741.89			other machinery, plant or equipment	639	522763	5	151
748.2			bearing housings and plain shaft bearings	4147	798097	41	524
		75	office machines and automatic data processing				

			machines	836	469026	5	109
		76	telecommunications & sound recording & reproducing	3106	854459	3	46
			apparatus & equipment				
		77	electrical machinery, apparyatus and appliances, n.e.s	43897	3308748	365	6607
			and electrical parts hereof (including non-electrical				
			counterpants, n.e.s.				
773.1			insulated wire, cable and other insulated electric	18262	1191459	45	511
			conductors, whether or not fitted with connectors,				
			optical fiber cables made up of individually sheathed,				
			whether or noyt assemble with electric conductors or				
			fitted with conductors				
		78	road vehicles (including air-cushion vehicles)	55686	5134045	1141	8626
782.1			motor vehicles for the transport of goods	28430	3268280		
		79	other transport equipment	26955	571452	45	522
	8		miscellaneous manufactured articles	30511	1398473	44689	3101932
		81	prefabricated buildings sanitary, blumbing, heating and	596	44466	150	4174
			lighting fixtures and fittings, n.e.s.				
		82	furniture and parts thereof, bedding mattresses,	628	80280	1274	26843
			supports, cushions and similar stuffed furnishings				
		83	travel goods, handbags and similar containers	1	155	1699	43495
		84	articles of apparel clothing accessories	713	26288	28650	2578520

842.00"			womens and girls coats, capes, jackets, shirts	3	209	5730	619696
846.93			shawls, scarves, mufflers mautillas, veils and the like	5	1310	8857	702152
		85	footwear	28	5873	6849	357112
		87	professional, scientific & controlling instruments &	1755	572407	26	1298
			apparatus, n.e.s				
		88	photographic apparatus, equipment and supplies and	11517	235425	58	5198
			optical goods, n.e.s. watches and clocks				
		89	miscellaneous manufactured articles n.e.s.	15273	433579	5983	85292
	9		commodities and transactions not classified	22	2527	0	2
			elsewhere in the sitc				
		91	postal packages not classified according to kind				
		93	special transactions & commodities not classified				
			according to kind				
		96	coin (other than gold coin) not being legal tender	19	2252		
		97	gold, non-monetary (excluding gold ores and	3	275	0	2
			concentrates)				
			by passengers		1523505		
			GRAND TOTAL	5695045	60385380	22196902	44886991

LARGEST EXPORTERS

- **General company for fruits and vegetables**

Damascus P.O.Box: 5603
Tel 5422926-5422824-5422928
Fax 5423001
Tlx: 411914,412734

Cable :KHODAR
Products: Vegetables, Fruits, Fresh, Fruits, and Dehydrated

- **General Establishment For Food Industries**

Damascus P.O.Box :105
Tel :2225290-2234426-2234428
Fax :224537
Products: Soda , Conservatives, Jams, Arak, Oil, and Biscuits

- **General Establishment For Tobacco**

Damascus P.O.Box :616
Tel :2323125-2323126
Fax : 2233805
Tlx :411301   Cable :MONTAB
Products :Tobacco Tobacco Wholly , (Tombac)

- **General Company Leather Industries**

Damascus   P.O.Box :2994
Tel 5121808-5121809-5121810
Tlx :411628
Cable :AHZEAH
Products :Leather Footwear for men & women

- **General organization for fish**

Jableh
Tel :821677-833112-831367
Fax :831367
Tlx :451025
Products :FISH , CARP, FISH ,TILAPIA

- **General Establishment For Cows**

Hama, P.O.Box :48
Tel :410985
Fax :422984
Products: Meat frish, (Frezian,Holoshtin)

- **General Company For Matches ,Chipbord**

 Damascus   P.O.Box :2672
Tel :5435734
Fax : 5437337
Tlx :41526 KEBRET SY
Cable :KEBRET-Damascus
 Products :Matches ,Playwood, Chipboard ,Pencils (Graphite & Color)

- **General Establishment For Foreign Trade Of Food & Chemical Materials**

Damascus ,Jumhuryah St.
P.O.Box :893
Tel: 2218919-2225421

Fax:2226927
Productes: Cotton Linters,Onion (dried)

• General Organization For Sugar

Homs   P.O.Box :4290
Tel :227600-227602- Damascus 2212329
Fax :237899
Tlx :441123-441006 GOFS Cable :GOFS
PRODUCTS :MOLASSES,YEST DRY ,AL-COHOL, MEDICAL

• "Orient" Company For Underwear

Damascus   P.O.Box :1100
Tel :5436001-5436003
Fax :5436000
Tlx :412436 O.U.M.C.SY
Products :Ccoton Underwear

• General Establishment For Cereal Processing And Trade

Damascus   P.O.Box :4106
Tel :2238364-2238397-2237818
Fax :2232368
Tlx :412511-411027-411391
Cable :HOBOB-Damascus
 Products: :Seed Of Lentils ,Lentils, Chick-Peas ,Barley

• CARPET MANUFACTURING GENERAL CORPORATION

Damascus   P.O.Box :1400
Tel :8880100 –8816973
Fax :8887002
Tlx :412514 CARP
Cable :CARPETCO
Products :Carpets , Woolen

• HAMA COTTON YARN COMPANY

Hama   P.O.Box :11
Tel :511092-551093-511091
Fax :511096
Tlx :431037 HAYC
Cable :GHAZEL Hama
Products :Cotton Carded Or Combed

• Dry Battery Fabric

Damascus   P.O.Box :3120
Tel: 6311643-8880789
Fax:2123375
Products: Dried battery

• GENERAL ESTABLISHMENT FOR TIRES PRODUCTIONS

Damascus   P.O.Box :12175
Tel :2210355 -2778808
Fax :2247499
 Poducts :Carpets, hand-made rug , carpets, hand made woolen , knit Faber. wool/fine hair

- **GENERAL ESTABLISHMENT FOR TIRES PRODUCTIONS**

Hama, Salamyah rood
Tel:424533-424532
Fax:424531
Tlx:431039
Products:Tires (different kinds)

- **General Company For Asphalt**

Lataquia   P.O.Box :6
Tle: 473121-475826
Fax : 475674
Tlx :451150
Cable :ASPEL
Products :,Nat. Asphalt Bituminous Mixtures Raw Stones

- **General Establishment For Porcelain**

Syria,Hama
P.O.Box : 161
Tel :510896-510996
Fax :511707
PRODUCTS : Porcelain , SANITARY WARE

- **General Organization For Poultry**

Damascus   P.O.Box :5597
Tel :2211968 -2212876
Fax :2217473
Tlx :412423 G.O.P. SYR
Cable :G.O.P. Damascus
Products :POULTRY LIVE, POULTRY FRESH
,EGGS BIRDS IN SHELL (HATCHING) ,EGGS BIRDS IN SHELL (TABLE)

- **Productive Projects Administration**

Damascus   P.O.Box :4703
Tel :2131499-212990-3314790
Fax :2205210
Tlx :412914 SY PRODUC
Products :, ,HONEY (flowred),HONEY (zalloo) ,MEDICAL PLANETS

- **General Establishment For Panting & Chemical Industries**

P.O.Box:1276
Tle : 5435511-5435512
Fax:5431088
Tlx:411299
Products Paints (deferent)

• General Establishment For Chemical Industries

Damascus
Tle:2127654-2123363
Fax :2128289
Products :Sport & leather shoes,Plastic houses, Chinaware

• General Establishment For Engineering Industries

Damascus
P.O.Box: 3120
Tle :212825-2122650
Fax :2123375
Products: Refrigerators, Household, Appliances, color TV Telephone sets, Cables

• General Establishment For Textile Industries

Fardous St.,Damascus
P.O.Box : 620
Tel :2216200-2215624-2215262
Fax :2216021
Tlx:411011
Products :Cotton yarns, Cotton Fabric, Socks , wool Carpets

• General Establishment For Cleaners chemical Industry

Damascus, Adra
P.O.Box: 682
Tel : 5810163- 5810164
Fax : 581062
Tlx : 412694 jecoda
PRODUCTS: Cleaners (Powders & Liquid), selphonic aside

• General Electric Motors Manufacturing Company

Lataquia   P.O.Box :190
Tel :421850 -421533
Fax :410761
Tlx :451090
Cable :MOTORS
Products :ELICTRICAL CABLE,TRANSFORMER (FLORESANT)

• GENERAL COMPANY FOR Tanning

Damascus ,Zablatani road
P.O.Box : 2019
Tel: 457840-454863
Fax : 4424935
Products :Raw & processed leather,leather jacets.

• General Company For Transformation Industry

Damascus P.O.Box :2803
Tel :6714574

Fax :6714572
Products :Sanitary Paper (For Baby & Women)

MAJOR NEWSPAPERS

Tishrin
Midan Street, P.O. Box 5452
Damascus, Syria
fax: 963-11-223-1374
phone: 224-7359, 224-7049, 889-6902/3/4.

Al-Thawra
Kaffar-Souseh Square, P.O. Box 2448
Damascus, Syria
fax: 963-11-221-6851
phone: 222-2399, 221-0850, 222-2911.

Al-Baath
Mazzeh Street, P.O. Box 9389
Damascus, Syria
fax: 963-11-662-2099
phone: 662-2142, 661-7616, 661-7683.

Golan
(the daily bulletin of official tenders)
P.O. Box 2842
Damascus, Syria
fax: 963-11-222-0754
phone: 222-5219.

Syria Times
(an English language daily newspaper targeted at the Western audience)
Midan Street, P.O. Box 5452
Damascus, Syria
fax: 963-11-223-1374
phone: 224-7359, 224-7049, 889-6902/3/4.

Commercial Bank of Syria:

Director General: Mr. Riad Hakim,

Yousef Al-Azmah Square, P.O. Box 933, Damascus, Syria; Telephone: 221-4508; Fax: 221-6975, 222-8524

U.S. Embassy Trade Personnel: Telephone: (963)(11) 333-3232

Anne Bodine: Economic/Commercial Attache
Donna Vandenbroucke: Economic/Commercial Officer
Jamal Aliah: Economic/Commercial Officer
Jonathan Rice: Economic/Commercial Officer

WASHINGTON DC - BASED CONTACTS FOR SYRIA

Office of Syrian Affairs
E. Candace Putnam
U.S. Department of State

Washington, D.C. 20520
Telephone: (202)647-7216
Fax: (202)647-0989

Office of Syrian Affairs
Thomas A. Sams
U.S. Department of Commerce
Washington, D.C.
Telephone: (202)482-1860
Fax: (202)482-0878

The Syrian for Exhibitions & International Conferences (SEIC)
P.O. Box 16046
Damascus, Syria
Tel. 963-11-613-3295
Fax: 963-11-613-3296.

United for Exhibitions and Media Services:
P.O. Box 6454, Damascus, Syria.
Tel. 963-11-331-2123
Fax: 963-11-331-2423.

The Arabian Group:
P.O. Box 2683, Damascus, Syria
Tel. 963-11-3737444/8/9
Fax: 963-11-3737446.

The International Group:
P.O. Box 35222, Damascus, Syria
Tel: 963-11-4428217
Fax: 963-11-4454510

BILATERAL AGREEMENTS SIGNED WITH ARAB STATES AND THE ADVANTAGES GRANTED THEREBY

State	Name & date of Agreement	Exemptions for Syrian Commodities	Exemptions for Arab Commodities
Saudi Arabia	Economic and Trade Agreement of 1972 Still valid	- Agricultural products and livestock and the produce of natural resources are exempted from customs duties according to list No.1 appended to the agreement - Syrian industrial products are exempted from customs duties according to list No.2 appended to the agreement - Syrian industrial products as per list No.3 appended to the agreement are exempted from two thirds of customs duties.	- Agricultural and animal products and livestock and the produce of natural resources are exempted from duties as per list No.1 appended to the agreement - All Saudi industrial products are exempted from duties
Kuwait	Economic and Commercial Cooperation Agreement of 1991 Still valid	- Agricultural and livestock products and the produce of natural resources are exempted from customs duties and other fees of similar effect - Syrian industrial products are exempted from duties and fees of similar effect except for the following: 1- Cast iron covering 2- Welded black steel pipes 3- oxygen gas for medical or industrial purposes	- Agricultural and livestock products and the produce of Kuwaiti natural resources are exempted from duties and fees of similar effect. - Kuwaiti industrial products are exempted from duties and fees of similar effect except for : 1- Cars. 2- Raw tobacco and byproducts. 3- cotton yarns locally produced.
Qatar	Economic and Commercial Cooperation Agreement of 1990 Still valid.	Agricultural, livestock and industrial products and raw materials that will be agreed upon in lists by the joint committee are exempted from customs duties.	Agricultural, livestock and industrial products and raw materials that will be agreed upon in lists by the joint committee are exempted from customs duties.
Bahrain	Economic and Commercial Cooperation Agreement of 1994 Still valid.	-Syrian agricultural and livestock products are exempted from customs duties and fees of similar effect. - Syrian industrial products according to lists prepared by the joint committee as stated in the agreement are exempted from customs duties and fees of similar effect.	-Bahraini agricultural and livestock products are exempted from customs duties and fees of similar effect. - Industrial products according to lists prepared by the joint committee as stated in the agreement are exempted from customs duties and fees of similar effect.

Country	Agreement	Syrian Products	Other Country Products
United Arab Emirates	Economic and Commercial Cooperation Agreement of 1990 endorsed by Syria but not endorsed by U.A.E.Consultations are underway with the U.A.E for the purpose.	No advantages of preferences or exemptions for the products of each country. Yet, the agreement provides for offering facilities that support the movement of export and import between the two countries.	No advantages of preferences or exemptions for the products of each country. Yet, the agreement provides for offering facilities that support the movement of export and import between the two countries.
Oman	Economic and Commercial Cooperation Agreement of 1991 Still valid.	Agreement does not give any performances or exemptions from customs duties.	Agreement does not give any performances or exemptions from customs duties.
Jordan	Agreement on Economic Cooperation and Regulating Trade Exchange of 1975. Minutes of meeting of the joint committee of 1986.	The 1975 agreement provides for exemption from customs duties for agricultural, livestock products and the produce of natural resources and exchanged industrial products. The two sides agreed on two lists, one for prompt implementation and the other is a guideline. The "prompt" list benefits From exemption from customs duties in each country according to certain banking arrangements , the guidelines list does not benefit from customs exemptions.	The agreement provides for total exemption from customs duties for Jordanian products.
Yemen	Trade agreement signed in 1996, ratified by Yemen, procedures of ratification in Syria are under way.	Agreement does not provide for any advantage of preference. The joint committee will discuss preferences which each party can offer for the purpose of promoting and developing trade Exchange between the two countries.	Agreement
Iraq	An agreement on economic cooperation and regulation of trade exchange, signed in 1979 (frozen at present)	All Syrian Products are exempted from customs duties. Free zone products are exempted from duties within the limits of local costs used in the manufacture of those products.	All Iraqi products are exempted from customs duties. Free zone products are exempted from duties within the limits of local costs used in the manufacture of those products.
Egypt	Trade agreement signed in 1991 (Valid)	Exemption from customs duties and relevant taxes (except local taxes and fees and taxes on sales) for the Syrian commodities and products as listed in Table A appended to the agreement. (This list contains 19 commodities)	Exemption from customs duties and relevant taxes (except local taxes and fees and taxes on sales) for the Egyptian commodities listed in Table B appended to the agreement. (This list contains 20

			commodities)
Morocco	Agreement on regulating trade exchange and economic cooperation signed in1972 (Valid)	Each side treats the other side as a most favoured nation. Excluded from this condition are the relations binding either side to other countries that form with it customs union or economic unity or common market and the advantages granted by either side to facilitate cross-border trade.	Each side treats the other side as a most favoured nation. Excluded from this condition are the relations binding either side to other countries that form with it customs union or economic unity or common market and the advantages granted by either side to facilitate cross-border trade.
Libya	Agreement on regulating trade exchange and economic cooperation signed in1978 (Valid)	All Syrian agricultural, livestock products, produce of natural resources and industrial products are exempted from customs duties and other taxes and fees.	All Libyan agricultural, livestock products, produce of natural resources and industrial products are exempted from customs duties and other taxes and fees.

Sudan	An agreement on trade and economic cooperation signed in 1974 (Valid)	Exemption from customs duties and additional fees for Syrian agricultural and animal products and livestock except for a fee of 5%. - Syrian industrial products as listed in Table 1 are subject to reduced duties as explained in the said table (ranging between 10% and 100%) . - Most favoured nation.	Exemption from customs duties and additional fees for Sudanese agricultural and animal products and livestock except for a fee of 2%. - Sudanese industrial products as listed in Table 2 are subject to reduced duties as explained in the said table (ranging between30% and 100%) . - Most favoured nation.
Tunisia	Trade agreement signed in 1977 (Valid)	All Syrian products are exempted from customs duties (agricultural, animal products, livestock, produce of natural resources and industrial products).	All Tunisian products are exempted from customs duties (agricultural, animal products, livestock, produce of natural resources and industrial products).

Algeria	Trade agreement signed in 1979, valid until the concluding of a new agreement in 1997 and notes of ratification are exchanged. Ratification is being followed up.	Old Agreement: Syrian agricultural products and livestock are exempted from customs duties. - Syrian industrial products as listed in Table 1 appended to the agreement are exempted from customs duties. New Agreement: No provision for most favoured nation for either country.	Old Agreement: Algerian agricultural products and livestock are exempted from customs duties. - Algerian industrial products as listed Table 2 appended to the agreement are exempted from customs duties. New Agreement: No provision for most favoured nation for either country.
Somalia	Trade agreement signed in 1973 (valid)	Most favored nation with regard to customs duties and other taxes and fees on imports, exports, storage, transit, unloading and shipment of goods. Excluded are: 1- Advantages and benefits granted to facilitate cross-border trade. 2- Goods of non-Syrian or non-Somali origin. 3- Advantages and benefits resulting from customs union, free trade area, common market or any special agreements.	Same advantages
Lebanon	Economic agreement signed in 1953, still valid by virtue of the provisions of agreement on social and economic cooperation and coordination of 1992 duly ratified by the two countries and being implemented by both of them	- Syrian agricultural and livestock products as listed in Table 1 appended to the agreement are exempted from customs duties. - Syrian industrial products as listed in Table 2 appended to the agreement are exempted from customs duties. -Exempted from half the duties are Syrian industrial products as listed in Table 3 appended to the agreement.	- Lebanese agricultural and livestock products as listed in Table 1 appended to the agreement are exempted from customs duties. - Lebanese industrial products as listed in Table 2 appended to the agreement are exempted from customs duties. -Exempted from half the duties are Lebanese industrial products as listed in Table 3 appended to the agreement.

DIRECTORY OF GEOSCIENCE ORGANIZATIONS OF THE WORLD

AFGHANISTAN

Afghanistan Geological Survey
Kabul Email: asef.anwar@gmail.com Web: www.bgs.ac.uk/afghanminerals/
Department of Mines A□airs
Ministry of Mines and Industries (MMI) Pashtunistan Square, Kabul Phone: 20-2100-309 Email: mmiafg@gmail.com, mmiafg@hotmail.com Web: www.bgs.ac.uk/afghanminerals/DMA Home.htm

ALBANIA

Geological Survey of Albania
Rruga e Kavajes, Nr.153, Tirana Phone: □4 2255 80/2225 78 Fax: □4 2294 41 Email: mimoza simixhiu@ags.com.al Web: pages.albaniaonline.net/ags/

ALGERIA

O□ce National de la Recherche G´eologique et Mini`ere (ORGM)
B.P. 102, Boumerdes 35000 Phone: □24 81 85 25/24 81 91 42 Fax: □24 81 83 79 Email: orgm@wissal.dz
Division du Service G´eologique de l'Algerie
B.P. 102, Boumerdes 35000 Phone: □24-819681 Fax: □24-817606
Direction G´en´erale des Mines
Ministry of Energy and Mining (MEM) B.P.677, Alger Gare, 80 Av. Ghermoul, Algiers Phone: □21 65 22 22 Fax: □21 65 19 04 Email: info@mem-algeria.org Web: www.mem-algeria.org

ANDORRA

Centre de Recerca en Ci`encies de la Terra (CRECIT)
Institut d'Estudis Andorrans C/La Valireta No 5, Encamp Phone: □731030 Fax: □834578 Email: crecit@andorra.ad Web: www.iea.ad/crecit/index2.html

ANGOLA

Direccao de Servicos de Geologia
Av. Ho Chi Min, Predio Geominas, C.P. 1260-C, Luanda Phone: □2-323024/324989 Fax: □2-321655/324989
Instituto Geologico de Angola
P.O.Box 1260, Luanda Phone: □2-323024 Fax: □2-323276/321655/324989 Email: igeo@netangola.com

ARGENTINA

Servicio Geol´ogico Minero Argentino (SEGEMAR)
Secretaria de Energ´ıayMiner´ıa Av. Julio A. Roca 651, piso 9 C 1067 ABB Buenos Aires Phone: 11-43493200 Fax: 11-43493198 Web: www.segemar.gov.ar/
Museo Argentino de Ciencias Naturales B. Rivadavia e Instituto Nacional de Investigaci´on de las Ciencias Naturales (MACN)
Av. Angel Gallardo 470, C1405DJR, Buenos Aires Phone: 11-4982 0306/1154/5243/4494 Fax: 11-4982 0306/1154/5243/4494 Email: info@macn.gov.ar

ARMENIA

Institute of Geological Sciences

Armenian Academy of Sciences Marshal Baghramian Avenue 24a, Yerevan 375019 Phone: □1 52 44 26 Fax: □1 56 80 72 Email: hrshah@sci.am Web: www.sci.am/
National Survey for Seismic Protection
Davidashen-Masiv 4, 375054, Yerevan Phone: □2-286494/282811 Fax: □2-151108 Email: o□ce@nssp-gov.am Web: www.nssp-gov.am/
Institute of Geophysics and Engineering Seismology
Armenian Academy of Sciences 5, Leningradyan Str. Gyumri, 377515 Phone: □41 31261 Fax: □41 31261 Email: as iges@shirak.am Web: www.sci.am/

AUSTRALIA

Geoscience Australia
G.P.O.Box 378, Canberra City, ACT 2601 Phone: 2-6249-9111 Fax: 2-6249-9999 Web: www.ga.gov.au/
CSIRO Energy Technology
CSIRO Energy Centre, P.O. Box 330, Newcastle NSW 2300 Phone: 2-4960-6000 Fax: 2-4960-6021 Web: www.det.csiro.au/
CSIRO Exploration & Mining
PO Box 883, Kenmore QLD 4069 Phone: 7 3327 4444 Fax: 7 3327 4455 Web: www.dem.csiro.au/
CSIRO Land and Water
Private Bag No.2, Glen Osmond SA 5064 Phone: 8-8303-8400 Fax: 8-8303-8590 Email: enquiries@adl.clw.csiro.au Web: www.clw.csiro.au/
CSIRO Minerals
Box 312, Clayton South VIC 3169 Phone: 3-9545-8500 Fax: 3-9562-8919 Web: www.minerals.csiro.au/
CSIRO Petroleum
PO Box 1130, Bentley, WA 6102 Phone: 8-6436-8500 Fax: 8-6436-8555 Web: www.csiro.au/petroleum
Seismology Research Centre
8 River Street, Richmond, VIC 3121 Phone: 3-8420-8999 Fax: 3-8420-8900 Email: seismology@esand.com Web: www.seis.com.au/

AUSTRIA

Geological Survey of Austria (GBA) (Geologische Bundesanstalt)
Neulinggasse 38, A-1030 Vienna Phone: 1-712 56 74 0 Fax: 1-712 56 74 56 Email: sekretariat@geologie.ac.at Web: www.geologie.ac.at/

AZERBAIJAN

Institute of Geology
Azerbaijan National Academy of Sciences 29A H. Javid av., Baku 1143 Phone: □12-497 52 86/438 62 30 Fax: □12-497 52 85 Email: gia@azeurotel.com, gia@azdata.net Web: www.gia.az
Ministry of Ecology and Natural Resources
Bahram Agayev str., 100-A, Baku 1073 Phone: □12-925907 Fax: □12-925907 Web: www.eco.gov.az/
The Republican Center of Seismic Service
Azerbaijan National Academy of Sciences AZ 1001, Baku City, Nigar Rafibeili str. 9 Phone: □12-492-34-37 Fax: □12-492-14-55 Email: seys@azeurotel.com
Geophysics and Geology Department
State Oil Company of Azerbaijan Republic (SOCAR) 83A, H. Aliyev avenue, AZ1033   Baku Phone: □12-566-6488 Fax: □12-514-1271 Email: ggi@skynet.az Web: www.socar.az/index-en.html
Azerbaijan Research Institute of Geophysics (ASERGEOFIZIKA ETI)

73, Tbilisi av., Baku, Az 1012 Phone: □12-31 05 68 Fax: □12-31 10 64 Email: geophiz@azdata.net

BAHAMAS

Department of Lands & Surveys
O□ce of the Prime Minister Bay and Armstrong Streets, P.O. Box N-592, Nassau, N.P. Phone: 242 322 2328 Fax: 242 322 5830

BANGLADESH

Geological Survey of Bangladesh (GSB)
153 Pioneer Road, Segunbagicha, Dhaka 1000 Phone: □2 8312599 Fax: □2 9339309 Email: gsb@dhaka.agni.com Web: www.gsb.gov.bd

BELARUS

Institute of Geochemistry and Geophysics
National Academy of Sciences of Belarus (NASB) 7 Academician V.F.Kuprevich Street, Minsk BY-220141 Phone: □17-264 53 15/263 41 62 Fax: □17 263 63 98 Email: geology@ns.igs.ac.by Web: igig.org.by/

BELGIUM

Geological Survey of Belgium (GSB)
Royal Belgian Institute of Natural Sciences Jenner street 13, B-1000 Brussels Phone: 2-627-0350 Fax: 2-647-7359 Email: gsb@naturalsciences.be Web: www.naturalsciences.be/geology/
Belgian Nuclear Research Centre
Boeretang 200, B-2400 Mol Phone: 14-33-2111 Fax: 14-31-5021 Web: www.sckcen.be/
The Belgian Agency for Radioactive Waste and Enriched Fissile Materials (ONDRAF/NIRAS)
Avenue des Arts 14, 1210 Brussels Phone: 2-212-1011 Fax: 2-218-5165 Email: e.biesemans@nirond.be Web: www.nirond.be/

BELIZE

Department of Geology and Petroleum
Ministry of Natural Resources and the Environment 34/36 Unity Boulevard, Belmopan City Phone: □822-2178/2651 Fax: □822-3538 Email: geology@mnrei.gov.bz Web: www.mnrei.gov.bz

BENIN

O□ce B´eninois des Recherches G´eologiques et Mini`eres (OBRGM)
Minist`ere des Mines, de l'Energie et de l'Eau (MMEE)
B.P. 249, Cotonou Phone: □21310309 Fax: □21314120 Email: OBRGM@energie.gouv.bj

BHUTAN

Department of Geology and Mines
Ministry of Trade and Industry
P.O. Box 173, Thimphu Phone: □2-323096/322879/323349 Fax: □2-323013 Email: gsbmti@druknet.net.bt Web: www.mti.gov.bt/

BOLIVIA

National Geology and Mining Survey (SERGEOMIN) (Servicio Nacional de Geolog´ia y Miner´ia)
Federico Zuazo No. 1673, esq. Reyes Ortiz, La Paz Phone: □2-326278/363765 Fax: □2-391725 Email: sergeomi@caoba.entelnet.bo

BOSNIA AND HERZEGOVINA

Geological Survey of Bosnia & Herzegovina
Ustaniˇcka 11, BIH-71210 Illidˇza-Sarajevo Phone: □33-621-567 Fax: □33-621-567 Email: zgeolbih@bih.net.ba

BOTSWANA

Department of Geological Survey
Private Bag 14, Lobatse Phone: □5330327 Fax: □5332013 Email: botsgs@gov.bw Web: www.gov.bw/

BRAZIL

Geological Survey of Brazil (CPRM) (Companhia de Pesquisa de Recursos Minerais)
Av. Pasteur, 404-Urca Rio de Janeiro-RJ-22290-240 Phone: 21-2546-0219/0456 Fax: 21-2295-6347 Email: cprm@rj.cprm.gov.br, cprmsede@df.cprm.gov.br Web: www.cprm.gov.br/

BRUNEI

Survey Department
Ministry of Development Bandar Seri Begawan BB3510 Phone: □2-382171 Fax: □2-382900 Email: survey@brunet.bn Web: www.survey.gov.bn/

BULGARIA

Geological Institute "Acad. Strashimir Dimitrov"
Bulgarian Academy of Sciences Bl. 24 Acad. G. Bonchev Street, 1113 Sofia Phone: □2-723563 Fax: □2-724638 Email: geolinst@geology.acad.bg Web: www.geology.bas.bg/
Institute of Oceanology
Bulgarian Academy of Sciences
P.O. Box 152, Varna 9000 Phone: □52-370484 Fax: □52-370483 Email: o□ce@io-bas.bg Web: www.io-bas.bg/
Geophysical Institute
Bulgarian Academy of Sciences Bl. 3, Acad. G. Bonchev Street, 1113 Sofia Phone: □2 700128 Fax: □2 9713005 Email: o□ce@geophys.bas.bg Web: www.geophys.bas.bg/
Directorate of Geology and Protection of Subsurface
Ministry of Environment and Waters 22 Princess Marie-Louise Blvd., Sofia 1000 Phone: □2-9406548 Fax: □2-9805561 Web: www2.moew.government.bg/index e.html

BURKINA FASO

Bureau des Mines et de la G´eologie du Burkina (BUMIGEB)
01 BP 601, Ouagadougou 01 Phone: □50-364802/364890 Fax: □50-364888 Email: bumigeb@cenatrin.bf Web: www.bumigeb.bf/

BURUNDI

Directorate General of Geology and Mines
Ministry of Energy and Mines
P.O. Box 745, Bujumbura Phone: □22-2278 Fax: □22-9624

CAMBODIA

General Department of Mineral Resources
Ministry of Industry, Mines and Energy 45, Preah Norodom Blvd., Phnom Penh Phone: □12-996517/23-210811 Fax: □23-362989/428263 Email: dgm@camnet.com.kh

CAMEROON

Institute for Geological and Mining Research (IRGM)
Rue Mgr Vogt, P.O. Box 4110 Nlongkak, Yaounde Phone: □222-24 30/24 41 Fax: □222-24 31
Email: irgm@iccnet.cm
Direction Mines & G´eologie
Minist`ere Mines, Eau & Energie Yaounde Phone: □23 3404 Fax: □22 3400 Email:
minmee@camnet.cm

CANADA

Earth Sciences Sector
Natural Resources Canada 580 Booth Street, Room 2064, Ottawa, Ontario KIA OE4 Web:
ess.nrcan.gc.ca/index e.php
Geological Survey of Canada, Ottawa (Headquarters)
Earth Sciences Sector 601 Booth Street, Ottawa, Ontario K1A 0E8 Phone: 613-995-0947 Email:
questions@nrcan.gc.ca Web: gsc.nrcan.gc.ca/index e.php
Geological Survey of Canada, Atlantic
1 Challenger Drive, P.O. Box 1006, Dartmouth, Nova Scotia, B2Y 4A2 Phone: 902-426-3225 Fax:
902-426-1466 Email: info-dartmouth@gsc.nrcan.gc.ca Web: gsc.nrcan.gc.ca/index e.php
Geological Survey of Canada, Pacific (Vancouver)
625 Robson St., Vancouver, British Columbia, V6B 5J3 Phone: 604-666-0529 Fax: 604-666-1124
Email: gscvan@nrcan.gc.ca Web: gsc.nrcan.gc.ca/index e.php
Geological Survey of Canada, Pacific (Sidney)
9860 West Saanich Road, Sidney, B.C. V8L 4B2 Phone: 250-363-6500 Fax: 250-363-6565
Email: info-sidney@gsc.nrcan.gc.ca Web: gsc.nrcan.gc.ca/index e.php
Geological Survey of Canada, Calgary
3303-33rd Street N.W., Calgary, Alberta T2L 2A7 Phone: 403-292-7000 Fax: 403-292-5377
Email: info-calgary@gsc.nrcan.gc.ca Web: gsc.nrcan.gc.ca/index e.php
Geological Survey of Canada, Qu´ebec
GSC-Qu´ebec, 490, rue de la Couronne, Qu´ebec, (Qu´ebec) G1K 9A9
Phone: 418-654-2604 Fax: 418-654-2615 Email: cgcq.gscq@nrcan.gc.ca Web:
gsc.nrcan.gc.ca/index e.php
Canada-Nunavut Geoscience O□ce
Geological Survey of Canada, Iqaluit
P.O. Box 2319, 626 Tumiit Plaza, Suite 202, Iqaluit, Nunavut, X0A 0H0
Phone: 867-979-3539 Fax: 867-979-0708 Email: djames@nrcan.gc.ca Web:
gsc.nrcan.gc.ca/index e.php
Canada Centre for Cadastral Management
Geomatics Canada 615 Booth Street, 5th Floor, Ottawa, Ontario K1A 0E9 Fax: 613-992-1122
Web: cccm.nrcan.gc.ca/english/index e.asp
Canada Centre for Remote Sensing
Geomatics Canada 588 Booth Street, 3rd Floor, Ottawa, Ontario K1A 0Y7 Web:
www.ccrs.nrcan.gc.ca/
Mapping Services Branch, Centres for Topographic Information
Geomatics Canada 615 Booth Street, 7th Floor, Ottawa, Ontario K1A 0E9 Phone: 800-465-6277
Fax: 613-947-7948 Email: topo.maps@NRCan.gc.ca Web: www.ccrs.nrcan.gc.ca/
Centre for Topographic Information, Sherbrooke
Geomatics Canada 2144 King Street West, suite 010, Sherbrooke, QC J1J 2E8 Phone: 800-661-
2638/819-564-5600 Fax: 819-564-5698 Email: NTDB@NRCan.gc.ca Web:
www.ccrs.nrcan.gc.ca/
Polar Continental Shelf Project
Earth Sciences Sector 615 Booth Street, 4th Floor, Ottawa, Ontario K1A 0E9 Phone: 613-947-
1601 Fax: 613-947-1611 Email: pcsp@NRCan.gc.ca Web: polar.nrcan.gc.ca/
Canadian Space Agency

6767 route de l'Aeroport, Saint-Hubert, Quebec J3Y 8Y9 Phone: 514-926-4800 Fax: 514-926-4352 Web: www.space.gc.ca/

CENTRAL AFRICAN REPUBLIC

Minist´ere des Mines, de l'´Energie et de l'Hydraulique
B.P. 26, Bangui Phone: □ 61 58 63 Fax: □ 61 60 76

CHAD

Direction des Mines et de la G´eologie
Minist`ere des Travaux Publics, des Mines et du P´etrole Djamena

CHILE

Servicio Nacional de Geolog´ıa y Miner´ıa (SERNAGEOMIN)
Av. Santa Mar´ıa 0104, Santiago, Casilla 10465 Phone: 2-7375050 Fax: 2-7771906 Email: comunicaciones@sernageomin.cl Web: www.sernageomin.cl/
Empresa Nacional de Miner´ıa (ENAMI)
MacIver 459, Santiago Phone: 2-6375278 Fax: 2-6375452 Email: webmaster@enami.cl Web: www.enami.cl/
Corporaci´on Nacional del Cobre (CODELCO)
Hu´erfanos 1270, Santiago Phone: 2-690-3935 Fax: 2-690-3059 Email: comunica@stgo.codelco.cl Web: www.codelco.com/

CHINA

China Geological Survey
24 Huangsi Street, 22 Building, Xicheng District, Beijing 100011 Phone: 10-51632828 Fax: 10-51632827 Email: Jshijin@mail.cgs.gov.cn Web: www.cgs.gov.cn
Development and Research Center
China Geological Survey
Xueyuan Road 40, Building Yan 1, Haidian District, Beijing 100083 Phone: 10-62303003 Fax: 10-62303002 Web: www.drc.cgs.gov.cn
Aero Geophysical Survey and Remote Sensing Center
China Geological Survey 31 Xueyuan Road, Haidian District, Beijing 100083 Phone: 10-82329070 Fax: 10-82329131
Tianjin Institute of Geology and Mineral Resources
China Geological Survey 4 Bahao Road, Dazhigu, Tianjin 300170 Phone: 22-24023487 Fax: 22-24023488 Email: tjigmr@public.tpt.tj.cn Web: www.tianjin.cgs.gov.cn/
Shenyang Institute of Geology and Mineral Resources
China Geological Survey 25 Beilingdajie, Shenyang 110032, Liaoning Province Phone: 24-86843110 Fax: 24-86843124 Web: www.shenyang.cgs.gov.cn/
Xian Institute of Geology and Mineral Resources
China Geological Survey 438 Youyi Road, Xian 710054, Shaanxi Province Phone: 29-87821906 Fax: 29-87821900 Web: www.xian.cgs.gov.cn/
Nanjing Institute of Geology and Mineral Resources
China Geological Survey 534 Zhongshandonglu, Nanjing 210016, Jiangsu Province Phone: 25-4600446 Fax: 25-4600446 Web: www.nanjing.cgs.gov.cn/
GSJ/AIST
Yichang Institute of Geology and Mineral Resources
China Geological Survey 37 Gangyaolu, Yichang 443003, Hubei Province Phone: 717-6331941 Fax: 717-6331867 Email: ycbgs@cgs.gov.cn Web: www.yichang.cgs.gov.cn/
Chengdu Institute of Geology and Mineral Resources
China Geological Survey 82 Beisanduan, Yihuanlu, Chengdu 610082, Sichuan Province Phone: 28-8337 1706 Fax: 28-8333 2657 Web: www.chengdu.cgs.gov.cn/
Guangzhou Marine Geological Survey

China Geological Survey 477 Huanshi Dong Rd., Guangzhou 510075, Guangdong Province Phone: 20-87755461 Fax: 20-87765102 Web: www.gmgs.com.cn/
Qingdao Institute of Marine Geology
China Geological Survey 62 Fuzhoulu, Qingdao 266071, Shandong Province Phone: 8532-5725313 Fax: 8532-5720553 Web: www.qimg.cgs.gov.cn/
Chinese Academy of Geological Sciences (CAGS)
China Geological Survey 26 Baiwanzhuang Road, Beijing 100037 Phone: 10-68335853 Fax: 10-68310894 Web: www.cags.ac.cn
Institute of Geology, CAGS
China Geological Survey 26 Baiwanzhuang Road, Beijing 100037 Phone: 10-68311293 Fax: 10-68311293
Institute of Mineral Resources, CAGS
China Geological Survey 26 Baiwanzhuang Road, Beijing 100037 Phone: 10-68327292 Fax: 10-68327263
Institute of Geomechanics, CAGS
China Geological Survey 11 Minzuxueyuannanlu, Haidian District, Beijing 100081 Phone: 10-68412303 Fax: 10-68422326 Web: www.geomech.ac.cn/
Institute of Hydrogeology and Environmental Geology, CAGS (IHEG)
China Geological Survey 2 Zhongshandonglu, Zhengding, Shijiazhuang 050803, Hebei Province Phone: 311-8021122 Fax: 311-8021225 Web: www.iheg.org.cn
Center for Hydrogeology and Environmental Geology, CGS
China Geological Survey 1305 Qiyizhounglu, Baoding 071051, Hebei Province Phone: 312-3107066 Fax: 312-3107065 Email: cgs□s@188.com Web: www.□s.cgs.gov.cn/
Institute of Geophysical and Geochemical Exploration, CAGS
China Geological Survey 84 Jinguangdao, Langfang 06500, Hebei Province Phone: 316-2212704 Fax: 316-2014156 Web: www.iggeinfo.com/
Institute of Karst Geology, CAGS
China Geological Survey 50 Qixinglu, Guilin 541004, Guangxi Phone: 773-5812943 Fax: 773-5813708 Web: www.karst.ac.cn/first.htm
National Research Center for Geoanalysis, CAGS
China Geological Survey 26 Baiwanzhuang Road, Beijing 100037 Phone: 10-68999557/68327982 Fax: 10-68998605 Email: yzc@cags.net.cn Web: nrcga.cags.ac.cn/Cshweb/Enrcg/index.asp
Chengdu Institute of Multipurpose Utilization of Mineral Resources, CAGS
China Geological Survey 5 Nansanduan, Erhuanlu, Chengdu 610041, Sichuan Province Phone: 28-8555 1383 Fax: 28-8559 4582
Zhengzhou Institute of Multipurpose Utilization of Mineral Resources, CAGS
China Geological Survey 328 Longhaixilunan, Zhengzhou 450006, Henan Province Phone: 371-8614942 Fax: 371-8614942
Institute of Exploration Technique, CAGS
China Geological Survey 77 Jinguangdao, Langfang 06500, Hebei Province Phone: 316-2096605 Fax: 316-2096506/2096827 Email: kkc@cniet.com, ranhq666@heinfo.net, mengqh@cniet.com Web: www.cniet.com/
Institute of Exploration Technology, CAGS
China Geological Survey 1 Beierduan, Yihuanlu, Chengdu 610081, Sichuan Province Phone: 28-8317 2893 Fax: 28-8317 9249 Email: info@cgiet.com
Beijing Institute of Exploration Engineering, CAGS
China Geological Survey 29 Xueyuan Road, Haidian District, Beijing 100083 Phone: 10-82321831 Fax: 10-82321882
China Institute of Geo-Environmental Monitoring
China Geological Survey 20 Dahuisi, Haidian District, Beijing 100081 Phone: 10-62173424 Fax: 10-62173426 Web: www.cigem.gov.cn/
National Geological Museum of China
China Geological Survey 15 Yangrouhutong, Sixi, Beijing 100031 Phone: 10-66176387 Fax: 10-66168870 Web: www.gmc.org.cn/

China Geological Library
China Geological Survey 29 Xueyuan Road, Haidian District, Beijing 100083 Phone: 10-82321426 Fax: 10-82319243 Email: cgl@cgl.org.cn Web: www.cgl.org.cn/
Chinese Academy of Sciences (CAS)
52 Sanlihe Road, Beijing 100864 Phone: 10-68597289 Fax: 10-68512458 Email: bulletin@mail.casipm.ac.cn Web: www.cas.ac.cn/
Institute of Geology and Geophysics, South Area (IGGCAS)
Chinese Academy of Sciences P.O.BOX 9825, Beijing 100029 Phone: 10-62008001 Fax: 10-62010846 Web: www.igcas.ac.cn/
Institute of Geology and Geophysics, North Area (IGGCAS)
Chinese Academy of Sciences P.O.BOX 9701, Beijing 100101 Phone: 10-64889084 Fax: 10-64871995 Web: www.igcas.ac.cn/
Institute of Remote Sensing Applications (IRSA)
Chinese Academy of Sciences P.O.BOX 9718, Beijing 100101 Phone: 10-64876313 Fax: 10-64876313/64889786 Email: proj@irsa.irsa.ac.cn Web: 159.226.117.4/en/index.htm
Guangzhou Institute of Geochemistry (GIGCAS)
Chinese Academy of Sciences Baishigang, Wushan, Tianhe district, Guangzhou 510640 Phone: 20-85290702 Fax: 20-85290130 Email: zhaojs@gig.ac.cn, gisof@gig.ac.cn Web: www.gig.ac.cn/
Xinjiang Institute of Ecology and Geography
Chinese Academy of Sciences 40-3 South Beijing Street, Urumqi, Xinjiang, 830011 Phone: 991-7885304/7885504 Fax: 991-3835459/7885300 Email: go□@ms.xjb.ac.cn, bsdr@ms.xjb.ac.cn Web: www.egi.ac.cn
Institute of Geographic Sciences and Natural Resources Research (IGSNRR)
Chinese Academy of Sciences Bldg.917, Datun Road, Anwai, Beijing 100101 Phone: 10-64854841/64889276 Fax: 10-64851844 Email: ign@igsnrr.ac.cn Web: www.igsnrr.ac.cn/
Nanjing Institute of Geology and Palaeontology
Chinese Academy of Sciences No.39, East Beijing Road, Nanjing 210008 Phone: 25-3282113 Fax: 25-3357026 Email: ngb@nigpas.ac.cn Web: www.nigpas.ac.cn/
Cold and Arid Regions Environmental and Engineering Research Institute (CAREERI)
Chinese Academy of Sciences 260 West Donggang Road, Lanzhou, Gansu Province 730000 Phone: 931-8875129 Fax: 931-8273894 Email: Careeri@ns.lzb.ac.cn Web: www.casnw.net/
Institute of Oceanology
Chinese Academy of Sciences 7 Nan-Hai Road, Qingdao 266071 Phone: 532-2898611 Fax: 532-2898612 Email: iocas@ms.qdio.ac.cn Web: www.qdio.ac.cn/
Institute of Soil Science
Chinese Academy of Sciences P.O.Box 821, Nanjing Phone: 25-3610462 Fax: 25-3353590 Email: iss@issas.ac.cn Web: www.issas.ac.cn/
Institute of Rock and Solid Mechanics (IRSM)
Chinese Academy of Sciences Xiaohongshan, Wuchang, Wuhan, Hubei Province 430071 Phone: 27-87199251 Fax: 27-87197386 Email: irsm@whrsm.ac.cn Web: www.whrsm.ac.cn/English/
Lanzhou Institute of Geology
Chinese Academy of Sciences 324 West Donggang Road, Lanzhou, Gansu Province 730000 Phone: 931-4960909 Fax: 931-8278667 Email: xbwang@ns.lzb.ac.cn Web: www.lig.ac.cn/
China Earthquake Administration (CEA)
No.63 Fuxing Ave. Beijing 100036 Phone: 10-68589224 Fax: 10-6810995
Center for Seismic Data and Information
China Earthquake Administration 56 Sanlihe Road, Xicheng district, Beijing 100045 Phone: 10-68530255 Fax: 10-68530226 Email: wangyi@sbd.csdi.ac.cn
Institute of Geology
China Earthquake Administration P.O.Box 9803, Dewai Qijiahuozi, Beijing 100029 Phone: 10-62009001 Fax: 10-62009003 Email: web@eq-igl.ac.cn Web: www.eq-igl.ac.cn/
Institute of Seismology
China Earthquake Administration No.40 Hongshan Celu Ave., Wuhan 430071 Phone: 27-87878210 Fax: 27-87884662 Web: www.eqhb.gov.cn/en/
Institute of Geophysics

China Earthquake Administration 5, Minzuxueyuan Nanlu, Haidian District, Beijing 100081
Phone: 10-68417744 Fax: 10-68415372 Web: www.cea-igp.ac.cn/English.files
Institute of Engineering Mechanics (IEM)
China Earthquake Administration No.9, Xuefu Road, Harbin 150080 Phone: 451-86652900 Fax:
451-86664755 Email: iemrd@iem.ac.cn Web: www.iem.ac.cn/
State Oceanic Administration (SOA)
Ministry of Land and Resources 1 Fuxingmenwai Avenue, Beijing 100860 Phone: 10-68019791
Fax: 10-68030799 Web: www.soa.gov.cn/
China Exploration & Engineering Bureau (CEEB)
Jia 16 Xibahe Dongli, Chaoyang District, Beijing 100028 Phone: □84515547 Fax: □84515466
Email: rsj@chexenb.gb.com.cn Web: www.chexenb.com.cn/
General Bureau of Geology and Exploration
China National Nonferrous Metals Industry Corporation 12B Fuxing Road, Beijing 100814 Phone:
10-68514593/4477 Fax: 10-68515367
Beijing General Research Institute of Nonferrous Metals (GRINM)
China National Nonferrous Metals Industry Corporation 2 Xinwai Street, Western District, Beijing
100088 Phone: 10-620 14488 Fax: 10-620 15019 Web: www.grinm.com/
Exploration and Development Technology Research Center
China National Petroleum Corporation (CNPC) 20 Xue Yuan Road, PO Box 910, Beijing 100083
Phone: 1-200 7522 Fax: 1-201 5420
China National O□shore Oil Corporation (CNOOC)
P.O.Box 4705, No.6, dongzhimenwai Xiaojie, Beijing 100027 Phone: 10-84521010/84521999
Fax: 10-84521044 Email: webmaster@cnooc.com.cn Web:
www.cnooc.com.cn/yyww/default.shtml
China Coal Research Institute (CCRI)
No. 5, Qingniangou Road, Hepingli, Beijing 100013 Email: webmaster@ccri.com.cn Web:
www.ccri.com.cn/e index.asp
Xi'an Branch
China Coal Research Institute 52 Yabta Road (N), Xi'an 710054 Phone: 29-7857567 Fax: 29-
7850504 Web: www.xianccri.com/
China Coal Information Institute (CCII)
State Administration of Coal Industry 35, Shaoyaoju, Chaoyang District, Beijing 100029 Phone:
10-84612550 Fax: 10-84612550 Email: ccii@coalinfo.net.cn Web:
www.coalinfo.net.cn/english.htm
Beijing Research Institute of Uranium Geology (BRIUG)
No.10, Anwai Xiaoguan Dongli, Chaoyang District, Beijing 100029 Phone: 10-
64914829/64960721 Fax: 10-64917143 Email: briug@public3.bta.net.cn
State Bureau of Surveying and Mapping (SBSM)
Ministry of Land and Resources 9 Sanlihe Road, Baiwanzhuang, Beijing 100037 Phone: 10-
68346614/68339095 Fax: 10-68311564/68339095 Email: fanbsm@public.bta.net.cn Web:
www.sbsm.gov.cn/

COLOMBIA

Instituto de Investigaci´on e Informaci´on Geocient´ıfica Minero-Ambiental y Nuclear
(INGEOMINAS)
Diagonal 53, No.34-53, Apartado Aereo 4865, Bogota, D.C. Phone: 1-2221811 Fax: 1-2220797
Email: cliente@ingeomin.gov.co Web: www.ingeominas.gov.co/

COMOROS

RecherchedelaMini`ere
B.P. 131, Moroni Phone: □744232 Fax: □733440 Email: tsaid@zdnetmail.com,
naoil@zdnetmail.com

CONGO (DEMOCRATIC REPUBLIC OF THE)

Centre de Recherches G´eologiques et Mini`eres (C.R.G.M.)
B.P. 898, 44, Avenue des Huileries, Kinshasa/Gombe

CONGO

Direction des Mines et de la G´eologie
B. P. 2124, Brazzabille Phone: □831281 Fax: □836243

COOK ISLANDS

Department of Survey and Physical Planning
Raratonga

COSTA RICA

Direcci´on de Geolog´ıa y Minas
Ministerio del Ambiente y Energ´ıa Apartado 10104, 1000 San Jose Phone: □233-2360 Fax: □233-2334

COTE D'IVOIRE

Direction des Mines et de la G´eologie
Minist`ere des Mines et de l'Energie
B.P. V 28, Abidjian Phone: □444528 Fax: □448462

CROATIA

Croatian Geological Survey
Sachsova 2, HR-10000, Zagreb Phone: □1 61 60 888 Fax: □1 61 44 718 Email: josip.halamic@hgi-cgs.hr Web: www.hgi-cgs.hr/

CUBA

National O□ce of Mineral Resources (Oficina Nacional de Recursos Minerales)
Ministry of Basic Industry Avenida Salvador Allende No.666, entre Oquendo y Soledad, Centro Habana, Ciudad de la Habana Phone: 7-8799262 Fax: 7-8732915 Email: nancy@onrm.minbas.cu
Institute of Geology and Paleontology (IGP) (Instituto de Geolog´ıa y Paleontolog´ıa)
Via Blanca y Linea del Ferrocarril, San Miguel del Padron, La Havana Phone: 7-99 5790/98 611 Fax: 7-33 3833
Instituto de Geof´ısica y Astronom´ıa (IGA)
Calle 212, No. 2906, Loronela, La Havana 11600 Phone: 271 4331/273 9497 Email: lpalacio@iga.cu Web: www.iga.cu/
National Center for Seismological Researches (CENAIS) (Centro Nacional de Investigaciones Sismol´ogicas)
Calle 17 No. 61, Vista Alegre, Santiago de Cuba 90400 Phone: 226-642521 Fax: 226-641623 Email: lasersat@ceniai.inf.cu, cenais@cenais.ciges.inf.cu
Museo Nacional Historia Natural
Obispo 61, Plaza de Armas, La Havana 10100 Phone: 7 863 9361 Fax: 7 862 0353 Email: museo@mnhnc.inf.cu Web: www.cuba.cu/ciencia/citma/ama/museo/
Centro de Investigaciones del Petr´oleo (CEINPET)
Washington No169 esq. a Churruca, Cerro, Ciudad de la Habana Phone: 7-57-7309/7341/7342 Fax: 7-66-6021 Email: lab@castrol.minbas.cu

CYPRUS

Geological Survey Department

Ministry of Agriculture, Natural Resources and Environment 1 Lefkonos, 1415 Nicosia Phone: □22409213/22409217 Fax: □22316873 Email: director@gsd.moa.gov.cy Web: www.moa.gov.cy/gsd

CZECH REPUBLIC

Czech Geological Survey (CGS) (˘
Cesk´e Geologisk´eSlu˘zby)
Klarov 3, 118 21, Praha 1 Phone: □257 089 411 Fax: □257 320 438 Email: secretar@cgu.cz Web: www.cgu.cz/
Geophysical Institute
Academy of Sciences of the Czech Republic Bocni II/1401, 141 31 Praha 4 Phone: □267 103 111 Fax: □272 761 549 Email: gfu@ig.cas.cz Web: www.ig.cas.cz/
Institute of Geology
Academy of Sciences of the Czech Republic Rozvojov´a 135, 16502 Praha 6 Phone: □233087111/233087209 Fax: □220922670 Email: inst@gli.cas.cz Web: www.gli.cas.cz/

DENMARK

Geological Survey of Denmark and Greenland (GEUS) (De Nationale Geologiske Undersøgelser for Danmark og Grønland)
Ministry of Climate and Energy Øster Voldgate 10, DK-1350 Copenhagen K Phone: 38 14 20 00 Fax: 38 14 20 50 Email: geus@geus.dk Web: www.geus.dk/

DJIBOUTI

Institut Sup´erieur d'´
Etudes et de Recherches Scientifiques et Technique (ISERST)
B.P. 486, Djibouti Phone: □352795 Fax: □354812

DOMINICAN REPUBLIC

Servicio Geol´ogico Nacional
Directorate General of Mines
Av. M´exico esq., Leopoldo Navarro, Edif. Juan Pablo duarte, 10mo. Piso, Santo Domingo Phone: 809-685-8191 Fax: 809-686-8327 Email: direc.mineria@verizon.net.do Web: www.dgm.gov.do/index.htm

ECUADOR

Direcci´on Nacional de Geolog´ıa (DINAGE)
Ministerio de Energ´ıayMinas Juan Le´on Mera y Orellana (esq.), Edificio MOP, 3er. Piso, Quito Phone: □2-2977 013/2977 012 Fax: □2-2550 018/2550 041 (Ext.3313) Email: dinage@menergia.gov.ec Web: www.menergia.gov.ec
Direcci´on Nacional de Miner´ıa (DINAMI)
Ministerio de Energ´ıayMinas Juan Le´on Mera y Orellana (esq.), Edificio MOP, 3er. Piso, Quito Phone: □2-2977 013/2977 012 Fax: □2-2550 018/2550 041 Email: jsalvador@menergia.gov.ec Web: www.menergia.gov.ec

EGYPT

Egyptian Geological Survey and Mining Authority (EGSMA)
3 Salah Salem Road, Abbasiya, 11517, Cairo Phone: 2-6828013/6855660 Fax: 2-4820128 Email: egsma@idsc.gov.eg Web: www.egsma.gov.eg/

EL SALVADOR

Servicio Nacional de Estudios Territoriales (SNET)

Ministerio de Medio Ambiente y Recursos Naturales Km. 5 textonehalf Carretera a Nueva San Salvador, Avenida Las Mercedes Phone: □2283-2246/2247 Fax: □2223-7791 Web: www.snet.gob.sv/
Centro de Investigaciones Geotecnicas
Ministerio de Obras P´ublicas Calle Antigua La Chacra, Contiguo a Talleres de DUA, San Salvador, Apartado Postal No. 109

EQUATORIAL GUINEA

Department of Mines and Hydrocarbons
Ministry of Mines and Energy Malabo, C/12 de Octubre Phone: □9 3567/7 7502 Fax: □9 3353 Email: d.shaw@ecqc.com Web: www.equatorialoil.com/

ESTONIA

Geological Survey of Estonia (EGK) (Eesti Geoloogiakeskus)
Kadaka tee 82, Tallinn, 12618 Phone: □672 0094 Fax: □672 0091 Email: egk@egk.ee Web: www.egk.ee/

ETHIOPIA

Geological Survey of Ethiopia
P.O. Box 2302, Addis Ababa Phone: □1-46 33 21 Fax: □1-46 33 26 Email: geology.institute@telecom.net.et Web: geoinfo.uneca.org/geoinfo/ethiopia/gse.html

FIJI

Mineral Resources Department
Ministry of Lands and Mineral Resources Private Mail Bag, GPO, Suva Phone: □3381611 Fax: □3370039 Email: director@mrd.gov.fj

FINLAND

Geological Survey of Finland (GTK) (Geologian Tutkimuskeskus)
P.O.Box 96, FI-02151 Espoo Phone: □20 550 11 Fax: □20 550 12 Email: gtk@gtk.fi Web: en.gtk.fi/

FRANCE

Bureau de Recherches G´eologiques et Mini`eres (BRGM)
3, Avenue Claude Gullemin, B.P. 6009, F-45060, Orl´eans Cedex 2 Phone: 2 38 64 34 34 Fax: 2 38 64 35 18 Web: www.brgm.fr/
French Research Institute for Exploitation of the Sea (IFREMER) (Institut Fran‚cais de Recherche pour l'Exploitation de la Mer)
Technopole de Brest-Iroise, BP 70 29280 PLOUZANE Phone: 2-98224040 Fax: 2-98224545 Web: www.ifremer.fr/

GABON

Direction des Mines et de la G´eologie
Minist`ere des Mines, de l'´etrole
Energie et du P´ BP 576, Libreville

GEORGIA

A.Djanelidze Institute of Geology
Georgian Academy of Sciences

M. Aleksidze str. 1, b.9, Tbilisi 380093 Phone: □32-293941/940234/335109 Email: root@geology.acnet.ge, geolog@gw.acnet.ge Web: www.acnet.ge/geology.htm
State Department of Geology of Georgia
24 Mosashvilli Street, Tbilisi 380062 Phone: □32-224040 Fax: □32-955006
M.Nodia Institute of Geophysics
Georgian Academy of Sciences 1, M. Alexidze str., Tbilisi 0193 Phone: □32-36 37 93 Fax: □32-33 28 67 Email: chelidze@ig.acnet.ge, root@geophy.acnet.ge Web: www.acnet.ge/geophy.htm
Vakhushti Bagrationi Institute of Geography
Ministry of Education and Sciences Merab Alexidze st., 1/8, Tbilisi 0193 Phone: □32-33 26 84/33 14 18 Fax: □32-33 14 17 Email: geograf@gw.acnet.ge
Institute of the Hydrogeology and Engineering Geology
Georgian Academy of Sciences 31 Rustaveli Av., Tbilisi 0108 Phone: □32-525499/527219 Fax: □32-001153 Email: bguram2@yahoo.com Web: www.acnet.ge/geohyd.htm
A. Tvalchrelidze Caucasian Institute of Mineral Resources
#85, Paliashvili str., Tbilisi 0162 Phone: □32-226 400/231 315 Fax: □32-231 315/226 981 Email: tcimr@internet.ge Web: www.caumineral.org.ge/
Seismic Monitoring Center
Nutsubidze Str. 77, 0177 Tbilisi Phone: □32-210256 Fax: □32-210276 Email: smc@seismo.ge Web: www.seismo.ge/

GERMANY

Federal Institute of Geoscience and Natural Resources (BGR) (Bundesanstalt f¨ur Geowissenschaften und Rohsto□e)
Stilleweg 2, D-30655 Hannover Phone: 511-6 43-0 Fax: 511-6 43-23 04 Email: poststelle@bgr.de Web: www.bgr.de/
Alfred Wegener Institute for Polar and Marine Research
Postfach 120161, D-27515 Bremerhaven Phone: 471-4831-0 Fax: 471-4831-1149 Web: www.awi-bremerhaven.de/
GeoForschungsZentrum Potsdam (GFZ)
Telegrafenberg A17, D-14473 Potsdam Phone: 331-288-0 Fax: 331-288-1044 Web: www.gfz-potsdam.de/
Leibniz Institute of Marine Sciences (IFM-GEOMAR) (Leibniz-Institut f¨ur Meereswissenshaften)
Wischhofstrasse 1-3, D-24148 Kiel Phone: 431-600-0 Fax: 431-600-2805 Web: www.ifm-geomar.de/

GHANA

Ghana Geological Survey
No.6, 7th Avenue, Accra, P.O. Box M 80 Phone: □21-228079/228093 Fax: □21-224676/228063 Email: ghgeosur@ghana.com

GREECE

Institute of Geology and Mineral Exploration (IGME)
Entrance C -Olympic Village -Acharnai 13677 -Athens Phone: 210-2413000-2 Fax: 210-2413440 Web: www.igme.gr/enmain.htm

GUATEMALA

Instituto Geogr´afico Nacional, "Ingeniero Alfredo Obiols G´omez"
Avenida las Am´ericas 5-76, Zona 13, CP 01013, Guatemala City Phone: □3322611 Fax: □3313548 Email: ign@ign.gob.gt
Direcci´on General de Miner´ia
Ministerio de Energia y Minas Diagonal 17, 29-78, Zona 11, Ciudad Capital Phone: □477 0382 Fax: □476 8506 Email: direminer@mem.gob.gt Web: www.mem.gob.gt

GUINEA

Direction G´en´erale des Mines et G´eologie
B.P. 295, Conakry Phone: ☐462011 Fax: ☐7752211

GUINEA-BISSAU

Direccao Geral, Geolog´ıa e Minas
Comissariado dos Recursos Naturais Bissau

GUYANA

Guyana Geology and Mines Commission (GGMC)
P.O.Box 1028, Upper Brickdam, Georgetown Phone: ☐22-52862/52865/53047/74737 Fax: ☐22-53047/52274 Email: ggmc@guyana.net.gy, ggmc@sdnp.org.gy Web: www.sdnp.org.gy/ggmc/

HAITI

Bureau of Mines and Energy (BME) (Bureau des Mines et de l'Energie)
Minist`ere des Travaux Publics Transports et Communications Delmas 19, Rue Nina #14, P.O.Box 2174, Port-au-Prince Phone: ☐246 1163 Fax: ☐240 2459 Email: mines-energie@rehred-haiti.net

HONDURAS

Direcci´on General de Minas e Hidrocarburos
Ministerio de Recursos Naturales y Ambientales Apartado Postal 981, Tegucigalpa Phone: ☐32-6721/8613/6595 Fax: ☐32-7848

HUNGARY

Hungarian Geological Survey (MGSz) (Magyar Geol´ogiai Szolg´alat)
H-1143 Budapest, Stef´ania ut 14
´Phone: 1-267-1421 Fax: 1-251-1759 Email: mgsz@mgsz.hu
Geological Institute of Hungary (MAFI)
Hungarian Geological Survey H-1143 Budapest, Stef´ania ut 14
´ Phone: 1-251-0999/0489/0689 Fax: 1-251-0703 Email: geo@mafi.hu Web: www.mafi.hu/
E¨otv¨os Lor´and Geophysical Institute of Hungary (ELGI)
Hungarian Geological Survey H-1145 Kolumbusz U. 17/23, Budapest Phone: 1-252-4999 Fax: 1-363-7256 Email: elgi@elgi.hu Web: www.elgi.hu/

ICELAND

Icelandic Geosurvey (ISOR) (Islenskar Orkurannsoknir)
Grens´asvegur 9, IS-108 Reykjav´ık Phone: ☐528 1500 Fax: ☐528 1699 Email: ogf@os.is Web: www.isor.is/
Icelandic Institute of Natural History
Hlemmur 3, P.O. Box 5320, IS-125 Reykjavik Phone: ☐590-0500 Email: ni@ni.is Web: www.ni.is/
Icelandic Meteorologic O☐ce (Vedurstofa Islands)
Bustadavegur 9, IS-150 Reykjavik Phone: ☐522-6000 Fax: ☐522-6001 Email: o☐ce@vedur.is Web: www.vedur.is/english

INDIA

Geological Survey of India
27 Jawaharlal Nehru Road, Kolkata 700016 Phone: 33-286-1641/65/73/72 Fax: 33-2286-1656 Email: geosurv@dataone.in Web: www.gsi.gov.in/
Geological Survey of India, Central Region

GSI Complex, Seminary Hills, Nagpur-440 006 Phone: 712-510226 Fax: 712-510918/511671/510036 Email: gsigdi@nagpur.dot.net.in, gsipgrs@nagpur.vsnl.net.in
Geological Survey of India, Eastern Region
GSI Complex, DK-6, Sector-II, Bidhannagar, Kolkata 700091 Phone: 33-3210817/3219379 Fax: 33-3219241 Email: gsi.ero@vsnl.com, gsicergd@vsnl.com
Geological Survey of India, North Eastern Region
Zorem Building, Nongrim Hills, Shilling-793003 Phone: 364-232406/232407/230429 Fax: 364-230233 Email: gdnergsi@sancharnet.in, nergeodata@dte.vsnl.net.in
Geological Survey of India, Northern Region
GSI Complex, Sector E'Alligunj, Lucknow 226024 Phone: 522-321510 Fax: 522-376407 Email: geodatnr@sancharnet.in, geodatnr@hotmail.com
Geological Survey of India, Southern Region
GSI Complex, Bandalguda, Hyderabad-500068 Phone: 40-4220949□4220958 Fax: 40-4220958 Email: gsisrhyd@hd2.dot.net.in, geodatasr@hotmail.com
Geological Survey of India, Western Region
GSI Complex, 15-16 Jhalana Dungri, Jaipur-302004 Fax: 141-511582 Email: geodata@sancharnet.in, geodatawr@hotmail.com
Geological Survey of India Training Institute
GSI Complex, Bandlaguda, Hyderabad-500 068 Phone: 40-24220682 Fax: 40-24220680 Email: hyd2 gsitihyd@sancharnet.in
Department of Mines
Ministry of Coal and Mines A-wing, Shastri Bhawan, 3rd Floor, New Delhi 110001 Phone: 11-3385173/3382614/3389211 Fax: 11-3386402 Web: www.mines.nic.in/ www.nic.in/ www.coal.nic.in/

INDONESIA

Geological Agency (GA) (Badan Geologi (BGL))
Ministry of Energy and Mineral Resources (MEMR)
Jln. Diponegoro No.57, Bandung 40122 / Jln. Jenderal Gatot Subroto Kav.49 Jakarta 12950 Phone: 22-7215297/ 21-5228371 Fax: 22-7216444/ 21-5228372 Email: geologi@bgl.esdm.go.id Web: www.bgl.esdm.go.id/
Secretariat for Geological Agency (SGA) (Sekretariat Badan Geologi)
Geological Agency, Ministry of Energy and Mineral Resources Jl. Diponegoro No.57, Bandung 40122 Phone: 22-7206515 Fax: 22-7218154
Center for Geological Survey (CGS) (Pusat Survei Geologi)
Geological Agency, Ministry of Energy and Mineral Resources Jl. Diponegoro 57, Bandung 40122 Phone: 22-7272601 Fax: 22-7202669 Email: contact@grdc.esdm.go.id Web: www.grdc.esdm.go.id/
Center for Geological Resources (CGR) (Pusat Sumber Daya Geologi (PMG))
Geological Agency, Ministry of Energy and Mineral Resources Jl. Soekarno-Hatta No. 444, Bandung 40254 Phone: 22-5202698 Fax: 22-5226263 Email: admin@dim.esdm.go.id Web: www.dim.esdm.go.id/
Center for Volcanology and Geological Hazard Mitigation (CVGHM) (Pusat Vulkanologi dan Mitigasi Bencana Geologi (PVG))
Geological Agency, Ministry of Energy and Mineral Resources Jl. Diponegoro No.57, Bandung 40122 Phone: 22-7214612 Fax: 22-7202761 Email: dali@vsi.esdm.go.id Web: www.vsi.esdm.go.id/
Center for Environment Geology (CEG) (Pusat Lingkungan Geologi (PMG))
Geological Agency, Ministry of Energy and Mineral Resources Jl. Diponegoro No.57, Bandung 40122 Phone: 22-7274676 Fax: 22-7206167 Email: inf@dgtl.esdm.go.id Web: www.dgtl.esdm.go.id
Marine Geological Institute (MGI)
Jl. Dr. Djunjunan 236, P.O. Box 1301 Bandung 40174 Phone: 22-6032151 Fax: 22-6017887 Email: mgidesdm@melsa.net.id, subaktian@bdg.centrin.net.id,

kapus@mgi.esdm.go.id
Meteorological and Geophysical Agency (BMG)
P.O. Box 3540 Jkt, Jl. Angkasa I No. 2 Kemayoran, Jakarta Pusat 10720
Phone: 21-4246321/6546311 Fax: 21-4246703 Email: humas@bmg.go.id Web: www.bmg.go.id
National Institute of Aeronautics and Space (LAPAN) (Lembaga Penerbangan dan Antariksa Nasional)
Jl. Pemuda Persil No.1, Jakarta Timur Phone: 21-4892802 Fax: 21-4894815 Email: bangfogan@mail.lapan.go.id Web: www.lapan.go.id/
Center for Research and Development for Oil and Gas Technology (LEMIGAS)
Jl. Cileduk Raya, Cipulir Kebayoran Lama, Jakarta Selatan 12230 Phone: 21-7394422/7394591 Fax: 21-7246150 Email: nurastuti@lemigas.esdm.go.id Web: www.lemigas.esdm.go.id/
The National Coordination Agency for Survey and Mapping (BAKOSURTANAL)
Jl. Raya Jakarta -Bogor KM. 46, Cibinong 16911, West Java Phone: 21-8753155/8753407 Fax: 21-8753366 Email: info@bakosurtanal.go.id Web: www.bakosurtanal.go.id
Research and Development Centre for Geotechnology
Indonesian Institute of Sciences (LIPI) Kompleks LIPI, Jalan Sangkuriang, Bandung 40135
Phone: 22-2507772 Fax: 22-2504593 Web: www.lipi.go.id/

IRAN

Geological Survey of Iran (GSI)
Azadi Sq., Meradj Blud., Tehran, P.O. Box 13185-1494 Phone: 21-66041981 Fax: 21-66070516
Email: international@gsi.ir Web: www.gsi.ir/

IRAQ

State Company of Geological Survey and Mining
Ministry of Industry and Minerals
P.O. Box 986, Alwiya, Baghdad Phone: ⬜1-719 5123 Email: geosurv69iraq@yahoo.com

IRELAND

Geological Survey of Ireland (GSI)
Beggars Bush, Haddington Road, Dublin 4 Phone: ⬜1-678 2000 Fax: ⬜1-668 1782 Email: gsisales@gsi.ie Web: www.gsi.ie/

ISRAEL

Geological Survey of Israel
Ministry of National Infrastructures 30 Malkhe Israel St., Jerusalem 95501 Phone: ⬜2-5314220/5314211 Fax: ⬜2-5380688/5378721

ITALY

Geological Survey of Italy (Dipartimento Difesa del Suolo)
APAT -Italian Agency for Envitonmental Protection and for Technical Services Via Curtatone, 3, 00185 Roma Phone: 06-44442324 Fax: 06-4465159 Web: www.apat.gov.it/
Institute of Geosciences and Earth Resources (IGG) (Instituto di Geoscienze e Georisorse)
National Research Council of Italy (CNR) Via G. Moruzzi, no.1, Pisa 56124 Phone: 050-3152381/4 Fax: 050-315 2323 Email: igg@igg.cnr.it Web: www.igg.cnr.it
Instituto Nazionale di Geofisica e Vulcanologia
Via di Vigna Murata 605, 00143 Rome Phone: 06-518601 Fax: 06-5041181 Web: www.ingv.it/

JAMAICA

Mines and Geology Division (MGD)
Ministry of Mining and Energy Hope Gardens, P.O. Box 141, Kingston 6 Phone: 876-927-1940 Fax: 876-927-0350/977-1204 Email: commissioner@minesandgeology.gov.jm

Oﬃce of Disaster Preparedness and Emergency Management (ODPEM)
12 Camp Road, Kingston 4, 938-2550 Phone: 876-928-5111-4 Fax: 876-928-5503 Email: odpem@cwjamaica.com Web: www.odpem.org.jm

JAPAN

Geological Survey of Japan (GSJ)
National Institute of Advanced Industrial Science and Technology (AIST) AIST Central 7, 1-1-1, Higashi, Tsukuba, Ibaraki 305-8567 Phone: 29-861-3635 Fax: 29-856-4989 Email: intl@gsj.jp Web: www.gsj.jp/
Geographical Survey Institute (GSI)
Ministry of Land, Infrastructure andTransport 1 Kitasato, Tsukuba, Ibaraki 305-0811 Phone: 29-864-1111 Web: www.gsi.go.jp/
Hydrographic and Oceanographic Department
Japan Coast Guard 5-3-1 Tsukiji, Chuo-ku, Tokyo 104-0045 Phone: 3-3541-3685 Fax: 3-3248-1250 Email: ico@cue.jhd.go.jp Web: www1.kaiho.mlit.go.jp/
Japan Agency for Marine-Earth Science and Technology (JAMSTEC)
2-15 Natsushima, Yokosuka, Kanagawa 237-0061 Phone: 468-66-3811 Fax: 468-66-5541 Web: www.jamstec.go.jp/
Japan Oil, Gas and Metals National Corporation (JOGMEC)
6F, Muza Kawasaki Central Tower, 1310 Omiya-cho, Saiwai-ku, Kawasaki, Kanagawa 212-8554 Phone: 44-520-8600/8560 Fax: 44-520-8710 Web: www.jogmec.go.jp/english/index.html
Meteorological Research Institute
Japan Meteorological Agency 1-1 Nagamine, Tsukuba, Ibaraki 305-0052 Phone: 29-853-8536 Fax: 29-853-8545 Email: tf03-mri@mri-jma.go.jp Web: www.mri-jma.go.jp/
National Institute for Environmental Studies
16-2 Onogawa, Tsukuba, Ibaraki 305-0053 Phone: 29-850-2308 Fax: 29-851-2854 Web: www.nies.go.jp/
National Research Institute for Earth Science and Disaster Prevention
3-1 Tennodai, Tsukuba, Ibaraki 305-0006 Phone: 29-851-1611 Fax: 29-851-1622 Web: www.bosai.go.jp/
Japan Aerospace Exploration Agency (JAXA)
7-44-1 Jindaiji Higashi-machi, Chofu-shi, Tokyo 182-8522 Phone: 3-3438-6000 Fax: 3-3438-6512 Web: www.jaxa.jp/index e.html
New Energy and Industrial Technology Development Organization (NEDO)
16F, Muza Kawasaki Central Tower, 1310 Omiya-cho, Saiwai-ku, Kawasaki, Kanagawa 212-8554 Phone: 44-520-5100 Fax: 44-520-5103 Email: qinf@nedo.go.jp Web: www.nedo.go.jp/
Public Works Research Institute
1-6 Minamihara, Tsukuba, Ibaraki 305-8516 Phone: 29-879-6700 Web: www.pwri.go.jp/

JORDAN

Natural Resources Authority (NRA)
Bayadir Wadi Sir, 8th Roundabout, P.O. Box 7, Amman Phone: □6-5857600 Fax: □6-5811866 Email: dirgen@nra.gov.jo Web: www.nra.gov.jo/

KAZAKHSTAN

Academy of Mineral Resources of the Republic of Kazakhstan
91 Abylay Khan Av., Almaty 480091 Phone: 3272-795950 Fax: 3272-795921
Institute of Seismology
Ministry of Education and Science Al-Farabi avenue 75, Almaty, 480060 Phone: 3272-482134 Fax: 3272-494417 Email: seismolog@itte.kz
Eastern Mining and Metallurgical Research Institute for Non-Ferrous Metals (VNIITSVETMET)

Ministry of Industry and Trade of Kazakhstan Republic Promyshlennaya 1, Ust-Kamenogorsk, 070002 Phone: 7272-473773/503460 Fax: 7272-473771 Email: VNIItsvetmet@ukg.kz Web: vcm.ukg.kz/
Institute of Metallurgy and Ore Beneficiation
Shevchenko St, 29/33, 480 100, Almaty Phone: 3272-618156/615781 Fax: 3272-614660

KENYA

Mines and Geological Department
Ministry of Environment and Natural Resources
Machakos Road, Industrial area, P.O. Box 30009-00100, Nairobi Phone: □20-558782/558034 Fax: □20-554366 Email: cmg@bidii.com Web: www.environment.go.ke/

KIRIBATI

Ministry of Fisheries and Marine Resources Developments
P.O. Box 64, Bairiki, Tarawa Phone: □21099 Fax: □21120

KOREA, DEMOCRATIC PEOPLE'S REPUBLIC OF

Institute of Geology
State Academy of Sciences Kwahak-1 Dong, Unjong District, Pyongyang Fax: □2-3814580

KOREA, REPUBLIC OF

Korea Institute of Geoscience and Mineral Resources (KIGAM)
30 Gajeong-dong, Yuseong-gu, Daejeon 305-350 Phone: 42-8683114 Fax: 42-8619720 Web: www.kigam.re.kr/
Korea Ocean Research and Development Institute (KORDI)
Ansan P.O.Box 29, Seoul 425-600 Phone: 31-400-6269 Fax: 31-406-6925 Web: www.kordi.re.kr/

KUWAIT

Kuwait Institute for Scientific Research (KISR)
P.O. Box 24885, 13109 Safat Phone: □48136100/4818630 Fax: □4830643 Email: public relations@safat.kisr.edu.kw Web: www.kisr.edu.kw/

KYRGYZSTAN

Kyrgyz Geological Survey
State Agency on Geology and Mineral Resources 2, Erkindik Ave., Bishkek 720739 Phone: □312-664901/223834 Fax: □312-660391 Email: mail@geoagency.bishkek.gov.kg
Institute of Geology
National Academy of Sciences 30, Erkindik Ave., Bishkek 720481 Phone: □312-664737 Fax: □312-664256 Email: geol@aknet.kg
Institute of Physics and Mechanics of Rocks
National Academy of Sciences 98, Mederova Str., Bishkek 720035 Phone: □312-54-11-15/54-11-28/54-11-17 Fax: □312-54-11-17 Email: ifmgp@mail.kg

LAOS

Department of Geology and Mines
Ministry of Industry and Handicrafts Khounboulom Road, Vientiane Phone: □21-212081 Fax: □21-222539 Email: dgmnet@laotel.com Web: www.dgm.gov.la/

LATVIA

State Geological Survey of Latvia

Exporta iela 5, Riga LV-1010 Phone: □7-320379 Fax: □7-333218 Email: vgd@vgd.gov.lv Web: mapx.map.vgd.gov.lv/geo3/

LESOTHO

Department of Mines & Geology
Ministry of Natural Resources
P.O. Box 750, Maseru 100 Phone: □32 3750 Fax: □31 0498

LIBERIA

Liberian Geological Survey
Ministry of Lands, Mines and Energy
P. O. Box 10-9024, Monrovia Phone: □227 490 Fax: □227 838

LIBYA

Geological Research and Mining Department
Industrial Research Center
P.O. Box 3633, Tripoli Phone: □21-691512 Fax: □21-691510

LITHUANIA

Geological Survey of Lithuania (LGT) (Lietuvos Geologijos Tarnyba)
S.Konarskio 35, LT-03123 Vilnius-600 Phone: □5-2332889 Fax: □5-2336156 Email: lgt@lgt.lt Web: www.lgt.lt/
Institute of Geology and Geography
Sevcenkos 13, 03223 Vilnius Phone: □5-2104690 Fax: □5-2104695 Email: info@geo.lt Web: www.geo.lt/

LUXEMBOURG

Service G´eologique du Luxembourg (SGL)
43, bd G.-D. Charlotte L-1331, Luxembourg Phone: □444126 Fax: □458760 Email: geologie@pch.etat.lu Web: www.pch.public.lu/

MACEDONIA

Geological Institute of Scopje
Skopje Fah 28 Phone: □2-230-873

MADAGASCAR

Direction des Mines et de la G´eologie (DMG)
Minist`ere de l'Energie et des Mines
B.P. 280 Ampandrianomby, Antananarivo 101 Phone: □20-22 418 22 Fax: □20 22 400 77 Email: dmgcentrale@blueline.mg Web: www.mem.gov.mg/

MALAWI

Geological Survey Department
Ministry of Natural Resources and Environmental A□airs Box 27, Zomba Phone: □1-524-166 Fax: □1-524-716 Email: gsdmalawi@sdnp.org.mw

MALAYSIA

Minerals and Geoscience Department
20th Floors, Tabung Haji Building, Jalan Tun Razak, Kuala Lumpur Phone: 3-21611033 Fax: 3-21611036 Email: jmgkll@jmg.gov.my Web: www.jmg.gov.my/

MALI

Direction Nationale de la G´eologie et des Mines (DNGM)
BP 223, Bamako Phone: □221-5821 Fax: □221-7174

MALTA

Environment Protection Directorate
Malta Environment & Planning Authority
P.O. Box 200 Valletta CMR 01 Phone: □21-240976 Fax: □21-224846 Email:
enquiries@mepa.org.mt Web: www.mepa.org.mt/

MARSHALL ISLANDS

Marshall Islands Marine Resources Authority
P. O. Box 860 Phone: □625-8262 Fax: □625-5447 Email: mimra@ntamar.com

MAURITANIA

Service G´eologique
Minist`ere des Mines et de l'Industrie B.P.199, Nouakchott Phone: □525-3225 Fax: □525-3225/6861

MEXICO

Servicio Geol´ogico Mexicano (SGM)
Blvd. Felipe Angeles km. 93.5-4, Col. Venta Prieta, 42080, Pachuca, Hidalgo Phone: 771-711 4016/4188 Fax: 771-711 3938 Email: dirgral@coremisgm.gob.mx Web: www.coremisgm.gob.mx/
Fideicomiso de Fomento Minero (FIFOMI)
Secretaria de Comercio y Fomento Industrial Puente de Tecamachalco No.26, Col. Lomas de Chapultepec,
C.P. 11000 Phone: 55-52499500 ext.5300 Fax: 55-52499550 Web: www.fifomi.gob.mx/

MICRONESIA

Department of Economic A□airs
P.O.Box PS-12, Palikir, Pohnpei, FM, 96941 Phone: □320-2646/5133 Fax: □320-5854 Email:
fsmdea@mail.fm

MOLDOVA

State Agency of Geology "AGeoM" (Asociat,ia de Stat "AGeoM")
Ministry of Ecology and Natural Resources 156, Metropolit Dosophtey Street, Kishinev, MD-2004
Phone: □22-750656 Fax: □22-750863 Email: ageom@starnet.md

MONGOLIA

Geology Department (Mongolian Geological Survey)
Mineral Resources and Petroleum Authority of Mongolia
(MRPAM) Builders' Square 3, State Property Building #5, Ulaanbaatar 211238
Phone: □11-327180/263701 Fax: □11-327180/310370 Email: mram@mram.mn Web:
www.mrpam.gov.mn/
Geological Information Center
Geology Department (Mongolian Geological Survey) P.O.Box 318, Tolgoid, Ulaanbaatar 37 Web:
www.mrpam.gov.mn/
Central Geological Laboratory
Songino Khairhan district, Trade Union street, Post Box 55, Ulaanbaatar 211137 Phone: □11-632904/632914/632979/632969 Fax: □11-632944 Email: cengeolab@mongol.net Web:
www.cengeolab.com/

Institute of Geology and Mineral Resources
Mongolian Academy of Sciences
P.O. Box 118, Ulaanbaatar 210351 Phone: ☐11-4 57858 Fax: ☐11-4 57858 Email: Inst
geology@arvis.ac.mn

MONTENEGRO

Geological Survey of Montenegro (JU Republiˇckl zavod za geoloˇska istraˇzivanja)
Naselje Kruˇsevac bb, 81000 Podgorica Phone: ☐81 245 453/438 Fax: ☐81 245 438 Email:
geozavod@cg.yu

MOROCCO

Geological Survey of Morocco (DirectionduD´eveloppment Minier)
Minist`ere de l'Energie, des Mines, de l'eau et de l'environnement, D´epartement de l'Energie et
des Mines
B.P. 6208, Rabat -Instituts Phone: ☐37 68 87 02 Fax: ☐37 68 87 47 Email:
a.charik@mem.gov.ma
O☐ce National des Hydrocarbures et des Mines (ONHYM)
5, avenue Moulay Hassan, B.P. 99, Rabat Phone: ☐37 23 98 98 Fax: ☐37 70 94 11 Email:
benkhadra@onhym.com Web: www.onhym.com

MOZAMBIQUE

Direc¸cˇao Nacional de Geologia
P.O. Box 217, Maputo Phone: ☐1-420797 Fax: ☐1-429216 Email: geologia@zebra.uem.mz

MYANMAR

Department of Geological Survey & Mineral Exploration
Ministry of Mines Kanbe Road, Yangon Phone: 1-52099 Fax: 1-577455
Department of Meteorology and Hydrology
PO 11061, Kava-aye, Yangon

NAMIBIA

Geological Survey of Namibia
Ministry of Mines & Energy Private Bag 13297 Windhoek Phone: ☐61-2848111 Fax: ☐61-249144
Email: gschneider@mme.gov.na Web: www.mme.gov.na/gsn/

NEPAL

Department of Mines and Geology
Ministry of Industry, Commerce & Supplies Lainchour, Kathmandu Phone: ☐1-4412065/4414740
Fax: ☐1-4414806 Email: dmg plan@infoclub.com.np, dmgdgo@infoclub.com.np
Royal Nepal Academy of Science & Technology
P.O. Box 3323, Khumaltar Lalitpur, Kathmandu Phone: 977-1-547714☐547718 Fax: ☐1-547713
Email: info@nast.org.np Web: www.nast.org.np/

NETHERLANDS

Geological Survey of the Netherlands-TNO Built Environment and Geosciences
P.O. Box 80015, NL-3508 TA Utrecht Phone: 30 256 42 56 Fax: 30 256 44 75 Email: info-
BenO@tno.nl Web: www.tno.nl/
International Institute for Geo-Information Science and Earth Observation (ITC)
Hengelosestraat 99, P.O.Box 6, 7500 AA Enschede Phone: 53-4874444 Fax: 53-4874400 Web:
www.itc.nl/

NEW CALEDONIA

Geology and Mines Bureau (ServicedelaG´eologie et des Mines)
Department of Industry, Mines, and Energy (DIMENC) BP 465, 98 845 Noum´ea Cedex Phone:
□273944 Fax: □272345

NEW ZEALAND

Institute of Geological and Nuclear Sciences Ltd. (GNS Science)
PO Box 30-368, Lower Hutt Phone: 4-5701444 Fax: 4-5704600 Web: www.gns.cri.nz/
National Institute of Water and Atmospheric Research Ltd. (NIWA)
Private Bag 99940, Auckland Phone: 9-3752090 Fax: 9-3752091 Web: www.niwa.co.nz/

NICARAGUA

Direcci´on General de Recursos Naturales
Ministerio de Fomento Industria y Comercio Costado Este Hotel Intercontinental Metrocentro,
Managua Phone: □2674551 Email: Bosco.Bonilla@mific.gob.ni Web: www.mific.gob.ni
Ministerio del Ambiente y los Recursos Naturales (MARENA)
Km 12 1/2 Carretera Norte, Frente a zona Franca, Apartado 5123, Managua Phone:
□2632615/2632831 Fax: □2632615/2632831 Email: sinia@sdnnic.org.ni Web:
www.marena.gob.ni

NIGER

Direction Recherche G´eologiques et Mini`eres
Minist`ere des Mines et de l'Energie
B.P. 11700, Niamey Phone: □73 4582 Fax: □73 2759

NIGERIA

Geological Survey of Nigeria Agency
Private Mail Bag 2007, Kaduna South 800001, Kaduna Phone: □62-232069 Fax: □62-232069
Email: gsna kaduna@yahoo.com

NORWAY

Geological Survey of Norway (NGU) (Norges Geologiske Undersøkelse)
7491 Trondheim Phone: 73-904000 Fax: 73-921620 Email: ngu@ngu.no Web: www.ngu.no/
Norwegian Petroleum Directorate
Professor Olav Hanssens vei 10, Postboks 600, N-4003 Stavanger Phone: 51876000 Fax:
51551571/51871935 Email: postboks@npd.no Web: www.npd.no/
Norwegian Geotechnical Institute (NGI)
P.O.Box 3930 Ullevaal Stadion, N-0806 Oslo Phone: 22 02 30 00 Fax: 22 23 04 48 Email:
ngi@ngi.no Web: www.ngi.no/
PETRAD-International Program for Petroleum Management and Administration
c/o Norwegian Petroleum Directorate, P.O. Box 600, N-4003 Stavanger Phone: 51876000 Fax:
51-876428 Email: petrad@petrad.no Web: www.petrad.no/

OMAN

Ministry of Petroleum and Minerals
P.O. Box 551, Muscut 113 Phone: □603333

PAKISTAN

Geological Survey of Pakistan (GSP)
Ministry of Petroleum and Natural Resources

P.O. Box No. 15, Sariab Road, Quetta Phone: 81-9211032/9211045 Fax: 81-9211018 Email: qta@gsp.gov.pk Web: www.gsp.gov.pk/
Geoscience Advance Research Laboratories
Geological Survey of Pakistan National Park Road, Shahzad Town, Islamabad Phone: 51-9255140 Fax: 51-9255136 Email: geolab@gsp.gov.pk
Hydrocarbon Development Institute of Pakistan
Plot 18, Street 6, Sector H-9/1, P.O.Box 1308, Islamabad Phone: 51-925-8301/8302 Fax: 51-925-8310 Email: hdip@apollo.net.pk, hdip@isb.compol.com Web: www.hdip.com.pk

PANAMA

Direcci´on General de Recursos Minerales
Ministerio de Comercio e Industria Apartado Postal 8515, Panam´a5 Phone: ☐36-1823/1825 Fax: ☐36-2868 Email: dgrm@sinfo.net

PAPUA NEW GUINEA

Geological Survey Division
Mineral Resources Authority (MRA)
Mining Haus, Poreporena Freeway, P.O. Box 1906, Port Moresby, National Capital District Phone: ☐321 3511 Fax: ☐321 5711 Email: hdavies@mra.gov.pg, info@mra.gov.pg Web: www.mra.gov.pg/

PARAGUAY

Direcci´on de Recursos Minerales (DRM)
Ministerio de Obras P´ublicas y Comunicaciones Calle Alberdi y Oliva, Asuncion Phone: ☐21-672 531/670 183 Fax: ☐21-672 531 Email: drm ssme@telesurf.com.py

PERU

Instituto Geol´ogico Minero y Metal´urgico (INGEMMET)
Av. Canad´a No. 1470, San Borja, Apartado 889, Lima, 41 Phone: 1-2242965/2253128 Fax: 1-2254540/2253063 Email: informacion@ingemmet.gob.pe, postmaster@ingemmet.gob.pe Web: www.ingemmet.gob.pe/

PHILIPPINES

Mines and Geosciences Bureau (MGB)
Department of Environment and Natural Resources
2/F J. Fernandez Bldg., MGB Comp. North Ave., Diliman, Quezon City 1100 Phone: 2-928-8544/8819 Fax: 2-928-8544 Email: central@mgb.gov.ph Web: www.mgb.gov.ph/
National Mapping and Resource Information Authority (NAMRIA)
Department of Environment and Natural Resources Lawton Avenue, Fort Bonifacio, Taguig City, 1638 Phone: 2-810-5466 Fax: 2-810-5468/2891 Email: oss@namria.gov.ph Web: www.namria.gov.ph/
Philippine Institute of Volcanology and Seismology
Department of Science and Technology
PHIVOLCS Building, C. P. Garcia Avenue, U. P. Campus, Diliman, Quezon City Phone: 2-4261468☐4261479/9262611 Fax: 2-9298366 Web: www.phivolcs.dost.gov.ph/
Energy Resource Development Bureau
Department of Energy (DOE) Energy Center, Merrit Road, Fort Bonifacio, Taguig 1634 Web: www.doe.gov.ph/

POLAND

Polish Geological Institute (PGI) (Pa˝nstwowy Instytut Geologiczny) ul.Rakowiecka 4, 00-975 Warszawa Phone: 22 849 5351 Fax: 22 849 5342 Email: bibliotekapig@tlen.pl Web: www.pgi.gov.pl/

PORTUGAL

National Institute of Engineering, Technology and Innovation, Center of Geologic and Mineralogic Data (INETI) (Instituto Nacional de Engenharia, Tecnologia e Inova¸c˜ao, Centro de Dados Geol´ogicos e Mineiros)
Estrada da Portela -Zambuhal, Apartado 7586, 2721-866 Alfragide Phone: ☐21 4705474/5 Fax: ☐21 4720203 Email: geral@ineti.pt Web: www.igm.ineti.pt/

QATAR

Department of Industrial Development
Ministry of Energy and Industry
P.O. Box 2599, Doha Phone: ☐832121 Fax: ☐832024

ROMANIA

Geological Institute of Romania (Institutul Geologic al Romˆaniei)
Caransebes Street, RO-012271 Bucharest Phone: 21-3177408/3181328/3181329 Fax: 21-3181326 Email: geol@igr.ro Web: www.igr.ro/

RUSSIA

All-Russian Research Institute for Hydrogelogy and Engineering Geology (VSEGINGEO)
142452, Zeleny-village, Noginsk district, Moscow region Phone: 495-521-2000 Fax: 495-913-5126
Department of Geology, Geophysics, Geochemistry and Mining Sciences
Russian Academy of Sciences (RAS) 6-25, 32a, Leninskay ave., Moscow 117993 Phone: 495-938-5544 Fax: 495-938-1928 Email: geodep@ipsun.ras.ru Web: www.ras.ru/
All-Russian Research Institute of Geological, Geophysical and Geochemical Systems (VNIIGeosystem)
Federal Agency of Mineral Resources, Ministry of Natural Resources 8, Varshavskoye Highway, Moscow 113105 Phone: 495-954-53 50 Fax: 495-958-37 11 Email: vniigeosystem@geosys.ru Web: www.geosys.ru
All-Russian Research Institute of Mineral Resources (VIMS)
Ministry of Natural Resources, Russian Academy of Sciences (RAS) 31, Staromonetny Lane, Moscow 109017 Phone: 495-951-1907 Fax: 495-959-3447 Email: vims@dataforce.net Web: www.rsoft.ru/vims/english/index.htm
Central Research Institute of Geological Prospecting for Base and Precious Metals (TsNIGRI)
Ministry of Natural Resources Varshavskoye sh., 129 B, 117545 Moscow Phone: 495-313-1818 Fax: 495-313-1818 Email: tsnigri@tsnigri.ru Web: www.tsnigri.ru
All-Russian Research Institute for Geology and Mineral Resources of the World Ocean (VNIIOkeangeologia)
Ministry of Natural Resources, Russian Academy of Sciences (RAS) 1, Angliisky ave., St-Petersburg 190121 Phone: 812-113-8379 Fax: 812-114-1470 Email: VNIIO@g-ocean.spb.ru Web: www.vniio.nw.ru/
All-Russian Research Institute of Exploration Geophysics (VNIIGeofizika)
Ministry of Natural Resources, Russian Academy of Sciences (RAS) 22 Pokrovka Str., Moscow 101000 Phone: 495-925-4513 Fax: 495-956-3938
Logachev All-Russian Research Institute of Exploration Geophysics (VIRG-Rudgeofizika)
Ministry of Natural Resources, Russian Academy of Sciences (RAS) 20, Fayansovaya Street, St-Petersburg 193019 Phone: 812-567-6803 Fax: 812-567-8741 Email: root@virg.ru Web: www.virg.ru
Siberian Institute of Geology, Geophysics and Mineral Resources (SNIIGGIMS)

Ministry of Natural Resources, Russian Academy of Sciences (RAS) 67, Krasny Prospekt, Novosibirsk 630091 Phone: 3832-21-3895 Fax: 3832-22-5740 Email: pvb@sniiggims.nsk.ru
Fersman Mineralogical Museum of Russian Academy of Sciences
Leninski Prospect, 18/2, 119071 Moscow Phone: 495-952-0067/954-3900 Fax: 495-952-4850 Email: mineral@fmm.ru Web: www.fmm.ru/
A.P. Karpinsky Russian Geological Research Institute (FGUP "VSEGEI")
Ministry of Natural Resources and Ecology of the Russian Federation 74, Sredny prospect, 199106, St. Petersburg, VSEGEI Phone: 812-321-5706 Fax: 812-321-3023 Email: vsegei@vsegei.ru Web: www.vsegei.ru/
All-Russian Research Institute of Economy and Exploration of Mineral Resources (VIEMS)
Russian Academy of Sciences (RAS) 38, 3-d Magistralnaya Street, Moscow 123853 Phone: 495-259-6988
All-Russia Petroleum Research Exploration Institute (VNIGRI)
Ministry of Natural Resources, Russian Academy of Sciences (RAS) 39, Liteiny Prospekt, St-Petersburg 191104 Phone: 812-273-4383/275-2305 Fax: 812-275-5756 Email: ins@vnigri.spb.su Web: www.vnigri.spb.ru/
Dagestan Scientific Centre, Institute of Geology (DRC)
Russian Academy of Sciences (RAS) 75, M. Yaragsky Str., 30 Makhachkala 367030 Phone: 872-262-93-95 Fax: 872-262-03-63 Email: dangeo@iwt.ru Web: www.igdncran.narod.ru
Institute of Geosphere Dynamics (IDG)
Russian Academy of Sciences (RAS) 38, Leninsky Prospekt, Bild. 6, Moscow 117979 Phone: 495-1376611/9397924 Fax: 495-1376511 Email: dir@idg.chph.ras.ru Web: idg.chph.ras.ru/
Geoelectromagnetic Research Institute (GEMRI)
Russian Academy of Sciences (RAS) P.O.Box 30, 142190 Troitsk, Moscow Region Phone: 495-7777218 Fax: 495-7777218 Email: gemri@igemi.troitsk.ru Web: www.igemi.troitsk.ru/
Scientific Geoinformation Centre (NGIC)
Russian Academy of Sciences (RAS) 11, New Arbat Street, G-19 Moscow 119019, P.O. Box 168 Phone: 495-202-1149 Fax: 495-202-9529 Email: mail@ngic.ru Web: www.ngic.ru/
Geophysical Centre (GC)
Russian Academy of Sciences (RAS) 3, Molodezhnaya Street, Moscow 119296 Phone: 495-930-0546 Fax: 495-930-0506 Email: gcras@gcras.ru Web: www.gcras.ru/
Research Institute of Comprehensive Exploitation of Mineral Resources (IPKON)
Russian Academy of Sciences (RAS) 4, Kryukovsky Tupik, Moscow 111020 Phone: 495-360-8960 Fax: 495-360-8960 Email: info@ipkonran.ru Web: www.ipkonran.ru/
Sergeev Institute of Environmental Geoscience (IEG)
Russian Academy of Sciences (RAS) 13, Ulansky Per., Bldg. 2, Centre, Moscow 101000 Phone: 495-623-31 11 Fax: 495-623-18 86 Email: direct@geoenv.ru Web: www.geoenv.ru
Institute of Experimental Mineralogy (IEM)
Russian Academy of Sciences (RAS) Chernogolovka, Institutskaya ulitsa, Moscow Region, 142432 Phone: 49652 44425 Fax: 49652 4687 Email: postmaster@iem.ac.ru Web: www.iem.ac.ru/
Institute of Geology and Exploitation of Combustible Resources (IGIRGI)
Russian Academy of Sciences (RAS) 50, Fersman Street, V-312 Moscow 117312 Phone: 495-121-9155
Institute of Geology (GIN)
Russian Academy of Sciences (RAS) 7, Pyzhevsky per, 119 017 Moscow Phone: 495-230-8029/8039 Fax: 495-951-0443 Email: gin@ginras.ru Web: www.ginras.ru
Institute of Geology of Ore Deposits, Petrography, Mineralogy and Geochemistry (IGEM)
Russian Academy of Sciences (RAS) Staromonetny per 35, Moscow 119017 Phone: 495-9517270 Fax: 495-2302179 Email: web@igem.ru Web: www.igem.ru
Institute of Lithosphere (ILS)
Russian Academy of Sciences (RAS) 22, Staromonetny per., Moscow 109180 Phone: 495-953-5588/959-0168 Fax: 495-953-5590
All-Russian Research Institute of Oil Geology (VNIGNI)

Russian Academy of Sciences (RAS) 36, Entuziastov Highway, Moscow 105118 Phone: 495-273-2651
Institute of Precambrian Geology and Geochronology (IGGD)
Russian Academy of Sciences (RAS) 2, Makarov Embankment, V-34, St-Petersburg 199034 Phone: 812-328-4701/4801 Fax: 812-328-4801 Email: admin@ad.iggp.ras.spb.ru Web: www.spbrc.nw.ru/PH/archive/!english/org/iggd.htm
International Institute of Earthquake Prediction Theory and Mathematical Geophysics (MITPAN)
Russian Academy of Sciences (RAS) Profsoyuznaya str. 84/32, Moscow 117997 Phone: 495-333-45-13 Fax: 495-333-12-55 Email: mitpan@mitp.ru Web: www.mitp.ru/
Karelian Research Centre, Institute of Geology
Russian Academy of Sciences (RAS) 11 Pushkinskaya str., Republic of Karelia, Petrozavodsk 185610 Phone: 8142-784316/786039 Fax: 8142-780602 Web: ig.krc.karelia.ru/
Kola Science Centre, Geological Institute
Russian Academy of Sciences (RAS) 14, Fersman Str., 184209 Apatity, Murmansk region Phone: 81555-79567 Fax: 81555-76481 Email: felix@geoksc.apatity.ru Web: geoksc.apatity.ru
Kola Science Centre, Mining Institute
Russian Academy of Sciences (RAS) 24 Fersman Str., 184209 Apatity, Murmansk region Phone: 815 55 7 43 42 Fax: 815 55 7 53 51 Email: isa@goi.kolasc.net.ru Web: www.kolasc.net.ru/ksc/goi/inform/goi.html
Kola Science Centre, Polar Geophysical Institute
Russian Academy of Sciences (RAS) 15, Khalturin Str., Murmansk 183010 Phone: 8152-565829 Fax: 8152-560337 Email: general@pgi.ru Web: www.kolasc.net.ru/ksc/pgi/inform/pgi.html
O.J.Shmidt United Institute of Earth Physics
Russian Academy of Sciences (RAS) 10, B. Gruzinskaya Street, D-242, GSP-5 Moscow 123995 Phone: 495-252-0726 Fax: 495-255-6040 Email: direction@ifz.ru Web: www.ifz.ru/
Oil and Gas Research Institute
Russian Academy of Sciences (RAS) 3 Gubkin street 117971 GSP1 Moscow Phone: 8-499-135-73-71 Fax: 8-499-135-54-65 Email: a.dmitrievsky@ipng.ru Web: www.ipng.ru/
Seismological Coordination and Research-Engineering Centre
Russian Academy of Sciences (RAS) 51, Ulyanovskaya Street, V-71 Moscow 109004 Phone: 495-272-3618
St-Petersburg State Institute of Mining, Laboratory of Hydrogeology and Mining Technologies on Nature Protection
Russian Academy of Sciences (RAS) 2, 21-st Line, St-Petersburg 199026 Phone: 812-218-8421
Geophysical Survey (GS)
Russian Academy of Sciences (RAS) 189 Lenin str., Obninsk, Kaluzhski region, 249020 Phone: 48439 3-14-05, 495-912-68 72 Fax: 495-334-20 02 Email: ceme@gsras.ru Web: www.ceme.gsras.ru
Kola Regional Seismological Centre, Geophysical Survey
Russian Academy of Sciences (RAS) 14, Fersman Str., Apatity 184200, Murmansk Region Phone: 81555-79663 Fax: 81555-76590 Email: admin@krsc.ru Web: www.krsc.ru/english/default.htm
The National Mining Research Center -A.A. Skochinsky Institute of Mining (IGD)
Russian Academy of Sciences (RAS) 140004 Lyubertsy-4, Moscow Region Phone: 495-554-8513 Fax: 495-554-5247
Ufa Scientific Centre, Institute of Geology
Russian Academy of Sciences (RAS) 16/2 K Marks Str., Ufa 450000 Phone: 347-272-8256 Fax: 347-273-0368 Email: ig@anrb.ru Web: www.anrb.ru/geol/index.htm
V.I.
        Vernadskii State Geological Museum
Russian Academy of Sciences (RAS) 11, bld.2, Mokhovaya Street, Moscow 103009 Phone: 495-203-5387 Fax: 495-203-4798 Email: webmaster@sgm.ru Web: www.sgm.ru
V.I.
        Vernadsky Institute of Geochemistry and Analytical Chemistry (GEOKHI)

Russian Academy of Sciences (RAS) 19, Kosygin str, Moscow 119991 Phone: 495-137 4127 Fax: 495-938 2054 Email: galimov@geokhi.ru Web: www.geokhi.ru/
Buryat Science Centre, Geological Institute
Siberian Branch of the Russian Academy of Sciences (SB RAS) 6-a, Sakhyanova Str., Ulan-Ude 670047 Phone: 3012-33-0955 Fax: 3012-33-6024 Email: burgin@eastsib.ru
Institute of the Earth's Crust
Siberian Branch of the Russian Academy of Sciences (SB RAS) 128, Lermontov Str., Irkutsk, 664033 Phone: 3952-46-4000 Fax: 3952-46-2900 Email: skl@gpg.crust.irk.ru, drf@earth.crust.irk.ru Web: www.crust.irk.ru
Vinogradov Institute of Geochemistry
Siberian Branch of the Russian Academy of Sciences (SB RAS) 1A, Favorskogo, P.O.Box 304, Str., Irkutsk, 650033 Phone: 3952-46-0500 Fax: 3952-46-4050 Email: root@igc.irk.ru
Institute of Mining
Siberian Branch of the Russian Academy of Sciences (SB RAS) 54, Krasny Prospect, Novosibirsk, 630091 Phone: 383-217-05-36 Fax: 383-217-06-78 Email: admin@misd.nsc.ru Web: www.misd.nsc.ru/
Trofimuk United Institute of Geology, Geophysics and Mineralogy (UIGGM)
Siberian Branch of the Russian Academy of Sciences (SB RAS) 3, Koptyug Ave., Novosibirsk, 630090 Phone: 3832-33-2600 Fax: 3832-33-2792 Web: www.uiggm.nsc.ru/
Institute of Geology
Siberian Branch of the Russian Academy of Sciences (SB RAS) 3, Koptyug Ave., Novosibirsk, 630090 Phone: 3832-33-2600 Fax: 3832-33-2792 Email: dobr@uiggm.nsc.ru Web: geology.uiggm.nsc.ru/ (www.uiggm.nsc.ru/)
Institute of Mineralogy and Petrography
Siberian Branch of the Russian Academy of Sciences (SB RAS) 3, Koptyug Ave., Novosibirsk, 630090 Phone: 3832-33-2406/39-6445 Fax: 3832-33-2792 Email: sobolev@uiggm.nsc.ru Web: imp.uiggm.nsc.ru/ (www.uiggm.nsc.ru/)
Institute of Geophysics
Siberian Branch of the Russian Academy of Sciences (SB RAS) 3, Koptyug Ave., Novosibirsk, 630090 Phone: 383-333-2513 Fax: 383-333-2513 Email: goldin@uiggm.nsc.ru Web: igp.uiggm.nsc.ru/eng/index.html
Institute of Petroleum Geology (IPG)
Siberian Branch of the Russian Academy of Sciences (SB RAS) 3, Koptyug Ave., Novosibirsk, 63009 Phone: 3832-33-2128 Fax: 3832-33-2301 Email: alex@petrol.uiggm.nsc.ru
Mining Institute of the North
Siberian Branch of the Russian Academy of Sciences (SB RAS) 43, Lenin Prospekt, Yakutsk, 677018 Phone: 4112-44-5930 Fax: 4112-44-5930 Email: igds@sci.yakutia.ru
Diamond and Precious Metal Geology Institute
Siberian Branch of the Russian Academy of Sciences (SB RAS) 39, Lenin Prospekt, Yakutsk 677980 Phone: 4112-33-5872/6241 Fax: 4112-33-5708 Email: geo@yakutia.ru
Amur Integrated Research Institute
Far Eastern Branch of the Russian Academy of Sciences (FEB RAS) 1, Relochny Lane, Blagoveshchensk-on-Amur 675000 Phone: 4162-42-7232 Fax: 4162-42-5931 Email: aurum@amur.ru Web: www.febras.ru/ amur.febras.ru/
Branch of Regional Geology and Hydrogeology, Amur Scientific Center
Far Eastern Branch of the Russian Academy of Sciences (FEB RAS) 2, Khmelnitsky St., Blagoveshchensk 675000 Phone: 4162-42-5522 Fax: 4162-42-3454 Email: orgig@amur.ru Web: www.febras.ru/ amur.febras.ru/
Institute of Volcanic Geology and Geochemistry (IVGG)
Far Eastern Branch of the Russian Academy of Sciences (FEB RAS) 9, Piip Blvd., Petropavlovsk-Kamchatski 683006 Phone: 41522-5-9195/9577 Fax: 41522-5-9195/9577/9130 Email: ivgg@mail.kamchatka.ru Web: www.febras.ru/
Institute of Volcanology (IV)

Far Eastern Branch of the Russian Academy of Sciences (FEB RAS) 9, Piip Blvd., Petropavlovsk-Kamchatski 683006 Phone: 41522-5-0603/9175 Fax: 41522-5-4723 Email: volcan@kcs.iks.ru Web: www.febras.ru/
Institute of Tectonics and Geophysics
Far Eastern Branch of the Russian Academy of Sciences (FEB RAS) 65, Kim Yu Chen Street, Khabarovsk 680063 Phone: 4212-22-7499 Fax: 4212-22-7684 Email: tectonic@itig.fe.ru Web: www.febras.ru/
Mining Institute
Far Eastern Branch of the Russian Academy of Sciences (FEB RAS) 51, Turgenev Street, Khabarovsk 680000 Phone: 4212-32-7927 Fax: 4212-32-7927 Email: mamaev@igd.khv.ru Web: www.igd.khv.ru/
North-Eastern Scientific Center
Far Eastern Branch of the Russian Academy of Sciences (FEB RAS) 16, Portovaya Street, Magadan 685000 Phone: 41322-3-0051 Fax: 41322-3-0442 Email: nesc@neisri.magadan.ru Web: www.febras.ru/
Far East Geological Institute (FEGI)
Far Eastern Branch of the Russian Academy of Sciences (FEB RAS) 159 Pr-t 100-letiya Vladivostoka, Vladivostok, 690022 Phone: 4232-318-750 Fax: 4232-317-847 Web: www.fegi.ru
Pacific Institute of Geography
Far Eastern Branch of the Russian Academy of Sciences (FEB RAS) 7, Radio Street, Vladivostok 690041 Phone: 4232-32-0672 Fax: 4232-31-2159 Email: geogr@tigdvo.marine.su Web: www.febras.ru/
Pacific Oceanological Institute (POI)
Far Eastern Branch of the Russian Academy of Sciences (FEB RAS) 43, Baltiyskaya Str., Vladivostok 690041 Phone: 4232-31-1400/2600 Fax: 4232-31-2573 Email: pacific@online.marine.su Web: www.febras.ru/ poi.febras.ru/
Institute of Marine Geology and Geophysics
Far Eastern Branch of the Russian Academy of Sciences (FEB RAS) 5, Nauka Street, Yuzhno-Sakhalinsk 693022 Phone: 42422-79-1517 Fax: 42422-79-1517 Email: nauka@sakhalin.ru Web: imgg.febras.ru/
A.N. Zavaritsky Institute of Geology and Geochemistry (IGG)
Ural Branch of the Russian Academy of Sciences (UB RAS) 7, Pochtovy Lane, Ekaterinburg 620151 Phone: 3432-711997 Fax: 3432-715252 Email: root@igg.e-burg.su
Institute of Mineralogy
Ural Branch of the Russian Academy of Sciences (UB RAS) Miass, Chelyabinsk Region, 456301 Phone: 35135-5-4632 Fax: 35135-5-0286 Email: imin@ural.telecom.chel.su
Institute of Geophysics (IGF)
Ural Branch of the Russian Academy of Sciences (UB RAS) 100, Amundsen Str., Yekaterinburg 620016 Phone: 3432-678-868/888 Fax: 3432-678872 Email: dir@igeoph.mplik.ru, outkin@nexcom.ru
Institute of Mining (IGD)
Ural Branch of the Russian Academy of Sciences (UB RAS) 58, Mamin-Sibiryak St., Ekaterinburg 620219 Phone: 343-350-21-86 Fax: 343-350-21-11 Email: direct@igd.uran.ru Web: www.igd.uran.ru
Institute of Geology (IG)
Komi Science Center, Ural Branch of the Russian Academy of Sciences (UB RAS) 54, Pervomaiskaya Str., Syktyvkar, Komi Republic, 167982 Phone: 8212-24-0037 Fax: 8212-24-0970 Email: institute@geo.komisc.ru
Institute of Mining
Ural Branch of the Russian Academy of Sciences (UB RAS) 78a Sibirskaya St., Perm 614007 Phone: 3422-16-7502 Fax: 3422-16-0969 Email: arc@mine.perm.su

RWANDA

Direction des Mines et de la Géologie

Minist`ere de l'Energie, de l'Eau et des Ressources Naturelles (MINIRENA) B.P.447, Kigali Phone: ☐856 38 Fax: ☐873 31 54 Web: www.minirena.gov.rw/

SAMOA

Lands and Survey Department
Main Beach Road, P. O. Box 63, Apia
Apia Observatory
Samoa Meteorology Division P.O.Box 3020, Apia Web: www.meteorology.gov.ws/

SAUDI ARABIA

Saudi Geological Survey
P.O.Box 54141, Jeddah-21514 Phone: ☐2-6198000 Fax: ☐2-6198906 Web: www.sgs.org.sa/
Deputy Ministry for Mineral Resources
Ministry of Petroleum and Mineral Resources
P.O. Box 345, Jeddah 21191 Phone: ☐2-667 4800 Fax: ☐2-667 2265 Email: deputyminister@dmmr.gov.sa Web: www.dmmr.gov.sa/

SENEGAL

Direction des Mines et de la G´eologie
Minist`ere de l'Energie et des Mines Bulding Administratif, B.P.4029, 4 Etage, Dakar Phone: ☐849 73 02 Email: dmg@primatime.sn Web: www.gouv.sn/ministeres/mem/contacts.cfm

SERBIA

Serbian Geological Institute
Bograd, Rovinjska 12, SCG Phone: ☐11-488 99 66 Fax: ☐11-488 52 96 Email: geoins@EUnet.yu, geoins@tehnicom.net
Serbian Geological Institute
Beograd, Karadordeva 48, SCG Phone: ☐11-180 931/32 83 383 Fax: ☐11-638 241 Email: hgig@beotel.yu
Geophysical Institute (NIS-Naftagas)
Batajnicki drum 18, 11080 Beograd Phone: ☐11-3163976 Fax: ☐11-3163976 Email: komsne@yahoo.com

SIERRA LEONE

Geological Survey and Mines Division
Ministry of Mineral Resources New England, Freetown Phone: ☐22 240 740/22 240 382/ 22 240 688 Fax: ☐22 241 936 Email: pabundu@yahoo.com

SINGAPORE

CPG Consultants Pte Ltd, Civil & Transportation Division
238B Thomson Road #16-00, Tower B Novena Square, Singapore 307685 Phone: 6357-4888 Fax: 6357-4188 Email: cpgcorp@cpgcorp.com.sg Web: www.cpgcorp.com.sg/

SLOVAKIA

Geological Survey of Slovak Republic (St´atny Geologick´y´ustav Dion´yza St´ura)
Mlynska dolina 1, 817 04 Bratislava

Phone: ☐2-59375147	Fax: ☐2-54771940
Email: secretary@gssr.sk	Web: www.gssr.sk/

Institute of
Geography
(Geografick´y ´
Ustav)

Slovak Academy of Sciences ˇ
Stef´anikova 49, 814 73 Bratislava Phone: ☐2-524 955 87 Fax: ☐2-524 913 40 Email:
geogsav@savba.sk Web: www.geography.sav.sk/

SLOVENIA

Geological Survey of Slovenia (GeoZS)
(Geoloski zavod Slovenije)
Dimiceva 14, 1000, Ljubljana Phone: ☐1-2809-700 Fax: ☐1-2809-753 Email: www@geo-zs.si
Web: www.geo-zs.si/
Geophysical Survey of Slovenia
Dunajska 47, 1000, Ljubljana Phone: ☐1-4787250 Fax: ☐1-4327067 Email: bojan.uran@gov.si

SOLOMON ISLANDS

Ministry of Energy, Mines & Minerals
P.O. Box G37, Honiara Phone: ☐21521 Fax: ☐25811

SOMALIA

Geological Survey Department
Ministry of Minerals and Water Resources
P.O. Box 744, Mogadishu

SOUTH AFRICA

Council for Geoscience
Privat Bag X112, Pretoria 0001 Phone: 12-841-1911 Fax: 12-841-1203/1221 Email:
njacha@geoscience.org.za Web: www.geoscience.org.za/
Council for Scientific and Industrial Research (CSIR)
P.O. Box 395, Pretoria 0001 Phone: 12 841-2911/2000 Fax: 12 349-1153 Web: www.csir.co.za/
CSIR Miningtek
P.O. Box 395, Pretoria 0001 Phone: 11 358-0079 Email: ggurtunc@csir.co.za Web:
www.csir.co.za/
CSIR Environmentek
P.O. Box 395, Pretoria 0001 Phone: 21-8882576/8413680 Email: lbarwell@csir.co.za,
pmanders@csir.co.za Web: www.csir.co.za/

SPAIN

Geological Survey of Spain (IGME) (Instituto Geol´ogico y Minero de Espa˜na)
R´ıos Rosas, 23, 28003 Madrid Phone: 91 349 5700 Fax: 91 442 6216 Email: igme@igme.es
Web: www.igme.es/
Spanish Institute of Oceanography (IEO) (Instituto Espa˜nol de Oceanografia)
Avda. del Brazil, 31, 28020 Madrid Phone: 915-974443/914-175411 Fax: 915-974770 Email:
ieo@md.ieo.es Web: www.ieo.es/
National Geographic Institute (IGN) (Instituto Geogr´afico Nacional)
General Ib´a˜nez Ibero 3, 28003 Madrid Phone: 91597 5000/7000 Fax: 91597 9758 Web:
www.mfom.es/ign/

SRI LANKA

Geological Survey and Mines Bureau (GSMB)

No.4, Galle Road, Senanayake Building, Dehiwala Phone: 11-2739307/2739308 Fax: 11-2735752 Email: gsmb@slt.lk

SUDAN

Geological Research Authority of the Sudan (GRAS)
Ministry of Energy & Mining
P.O. Box 410, Khartoum 11111 Phone: □11-777939 Fax: □11-776681 Email: info@gras-sd.com, gras@sudanmail.net Web: www.gras-sd.com/

SURINAME

Geological Mining Service (Geologisch Mijmbouwkundige Dienst)
Kleine Waterstraat 2-6, Paramaribo

SWAZILAND

Geological Survey and Mines Department
P.O. Box 9, Mbabane, H100 Phone: □404-2411/2 Fax: □404-5215 Email: geoswz dir@realnet.co.sz, geo.director@swazi.net Web: www.gov.sz/home.asp?pid=2243

SWEDEN

Geological Survey of Sweden (SGU) (Sveriges Geologiska Unders¨okning)
Box 670, SE-751 28 Uppsala Phone: 1817 9000 Fax: 1817 9210 Email: sgu@sgu.se Web: www.sgu.se/
International Geosphere-Biosphere Programme (IGBP)
The Royal Swedish Academy of Sciences Box 50005, Lilla Frescativagen 4, S-104 05 Stockholm Phone: 8-166448 Fax: 8-166405 Email: sec@igbp.kva.se Web: www.igbp.kva.se/

SWITZERLAND

Swiss Geological Survey
Federal O□ce of Topography (Swisstopo) Seftigenstrasse 264, CH-3084 Wabern Phone: 31 963 21 11 Fax: 31 963 24 59 Email: info@swisstopo.ch Web: www.swisstopo.ch/
Swiss Hydrological Survey (Hydrology Division)
Federal O□ce for Environment (FOEN) CH-3003 Bern Phone: 31 324 7758 Fax: 31 324 7681 Email: hydrologie@bafu.admin.ch Web: www.bafu.admin.ch/grundwasser/index.html?lang=en

SYRIA

General Establishment of Geology and Mineral Resources
Ministry of Petroleum & Mineral Resources
P.O. Box 7645, Damascus Phone: □11-4455426/4447755/4450507 Fax: □11-4423684

TAIWAN

CentralGeologicalSurvey(CGS)
P.O. Box 968, Taipei Phone: □2-29462793 Fax: □2-29429291 Email: cgs@moeacgs.gov.tw Web: www.moeacgs.gov.tw/english/

TANZANIA

Geological Survey of Tanzania (gst)
Ministry of Energy and Minerals
P.O. Box 903, Dodoma Phone: □26-2323020 Fax: □26-2323020 Email: madini-do@gst.go.tz Web: www.gst.go.tz/

THAILAND

Department of Mineral Resources (DMR)
Ministry of Natural Resources and Environment (MONRE) 75/10 Rama VI Road, Ratchathewi, Bangkok 10400 Phone: 2-621 9817/9698 Fax: 2-621 9820/9821/9699 Email: preecha c@dmr.go.th, cc:sommai@dmr.go.th Web: www.dmr.go.th/eng/indexeng.htm
Department of Groundwater Resources (DGR)
Ministry of Natural Resources and Environment (MONRE) 49 Soi 30, Rama VI Rd., Phayathai 10400 Phone: 2-299 3911(DL)/299 3912 Fax: 2-229 3913 Email: somkid@ddgr.go.th
Department of Mineral Fuels (DMF)
Ministry of Energy
24-26th Floor Shinawatra Tower III, 1010 Viphavadi-Ransit Road, Chatuchak, Bangkok 10900 Phone: 2791-8300/8379/8380 Fax: 2791-8378 Email: navee@dmf.go.th Web: www.dmf.go.th/dept/strategies activities eng.asp

TIMOR LESTE

National Directorate for Geology and Minerals
Geovernment Secretariat of State for Natural Resources 1st floor Fomento Building, P.O.Box 171, Dili Phone: ☐3331083 Fax: ☐3317143 Email: brizildf@yahoo.com

TOGO

General Directorate of Mines and Geology (DGMG) (Direction G´en´eral des Mines et de la G´eologie)
Ministry of Equipment, Mines, Energy, Post and Telecommunications
B.P. 356, Lome Phone: ☐221 3001 Fax: ☐221 3193

TONGA

Ministry of Lands, Survey and Natural Resources
P.O. Box 5, Nuku´alofa Phone: ☐23210 Fax: ☐23216 Email: minlands@kalianet.to Web: pmo.gov.to/

TRINIDAD AND TOBAGO

Ministry of Energy and Energy Industries
Riverside Plaza, P.O. Box 96, Port-of-Spain Phone: 868-623-6708/6719 Fax: 809-625-0306 Email: ttomener@undp.org Web: www.energy.gov.tt/

TUNISIA

O☐ce National des Mines
24 rue 8601, Zone Industrielle Charguia, 2035 Tunis Carthage Phone: ☐71-797343 Fax: ☐71-794016 Email: dsg.onm@email.ati.tn

TURKEY

General Directorate of Minerals Research and Exploration Institute of Turkey (MTA) (Maden Tetkik Arama Enstitusu Genel M¨ud¨url¨ug¨u)
MTA 06520 Ankara Phone: 312-287-3430 Fax: 312-287-9188 Email: mta@mta.gov.tr Web: www.mta.gov.tr/
Turkish Petroleum Corporation (TPAO) (T¨urkiye Petrolleri Anonim Ortakligi)
S¨og¨ut¨oz¨u Mahallesi 2. Cad. No : 86 06100
cankaya/ANKARA Phone: 312-207 2000 Fax: 312-286 9000/9001 Email: tpaocc@petrol.tpao.gov.tr Web: www.tpao.gov.tr/

UGANDA

Department of Geological Survey and Mines (DGSM)
Ministry of Energy and Mineral Development PLOT 21-29 Johnstone Road, P.O. Box 9, Entebbe
Phone: □41-320656/320790 Fax: □41-320364 Email: minerals@infocom.co.ug,
gsurvey@starcom.co.ug Web: www.energyandminerals.go.ug/

UKRAINE

Ukrainian State Geological Survey
Ministry of the Environment and Natural Resources 16, Ezhena Potye Str., Kyiv, 03057 Phone:
□44-446 1171 Fax: □44-241 8460 Email: sgeos@geoinf.ipri.kiev.ua
Ukrainian State Geological Prospecting Institute
Ministry of the Environment and Natural Resources 78, Avtozavods'ka Str., Kyiv, 04114 Phone:
□44-430 7024 Fax: □44-439 4176
Institute of Geological Sciences (IGS)
National Academy of Sciences of Ukraine (NASU) 55-b Olesya Gonchara str., Kiev-54, 01601
Phone: □44-216-9446 Fax: □44-216-9334 Email: ignnanu@geolog.freenet.kiev.ua
Institute of Geochemistry, Mineralogy and Ore Formations (IGMOF)
National Academy of Sciences of Ukraine (NASU) 34, prosp. Palladina, 34, Kiev-142, 03680
Phone: □44-424-0105 Fax: □44-424-1270 Email: zhovin@geochem.kiev.ua
Institute of Geology and Geochemistry of Combustible Minerals
National Academy of Sciences of Ukraine (NASU) 3a, Naukova St., Lviv, 79060 Phone: □322-
632209 Fax: □322-632209 Web: www.iggcm.org.ua/
Institute of Geophysics
National Academy of Sciences of Ukraine (NASU) 32, Academician Palladina Pr., Kyiv 164,
03680 Phone: □44-424 0112 Fax: □44-450 2520 Email: earth@igph.kiev.ua Web:
www.igph.kiev.ua

UNITED KINGDOM

British Geological Survey (BGS)
Kingsley Dunham Centre, Keyworth, Nottingham NG12 5GG Phone: 115-936-3100 Fax: 115-
936-3200 Email: enquiries@bgs.ac.uk Web: www.bgs.ac.uk/
British Antarctic Survey
High Cross, Madingley Road, Cambridge, CB3 0ET Phone: 1223-221400 Fax: 1223-362616
Email: information@bas.ac.uk Web: www.antarctica.ac.uk/
Centre for Ecology and Hydrology
CEH Directorate, Monks Wood, Abbots Ripton, Huntingdon, PE17 2LS Phone: 1487-772400 Fax:
1487-773467 Email: director@ceh.ac.uk Web: www.ceh.ac.uk/
Plymouth Marine Laboratory
Prospect Place, The Hoe, Plymouth, PL1 3DH Phone: 1752-633100 Fax: 1752-633101 Email:
forinfo@pm.ac.uk Web: www.pml.ac.uk/
Proudman Oceanographic Laboratory
6 Brownlow Street, Liverpool L3 5DA Phone: 151-795 4800 Fax: 151-795 4801 Email:
polenquiries@pol.ac.uk Web: www.pol.ac.uk/

UNITED STATES

U. S. Geological Survey (USGS)
100 National Center, 12201 Sunrise Valley Drive, Reston, VA 20192 Phone: 703-648-7411 Fax:
703-648-4454 Web: www.usgs.gov/
U. S. Geological Survey, International Programs
917 National Center, 12201 Sunrise Valley Drive, Reston, VA 20192 Phone: 703-648-6206 Fax:
703-648-7031/4227
U. S. Geological Survey, Central Region
Denver Federal Center., Bldg. 810, MS-150, Denver CO 80225 Phone: 303-202-4740 Fax: 303-
202-4742

U. S. Geological Survey, Western Region
345 Middlefield Road, Menlo Park, CA 94025 Phone: 650-853-8300
National Oceanic and Atmospheric Administration (NOAA)
14th Street and Constitution Ave., N.W. Washington, D.C. 20230 Phone: 202-482-6090 Fax: 202-482-3154 Email: answers@noaa.gov Web: www.noaa.gov/
National Geophysical Data Center (NGDC)
National Oceanic and Atmospheric Administration (NOAA) 325 Broadway, E/GC, Boulder, CO 80305-3328 Phone: 303-497-6826 Fax: 303-497-6513 Email: ngdc.info@noaa.gov Web: www.ngdc.noaa.gov/
National Aeronautics and Space Administration (NASA)
300 E Street, S.W. Washington, DC 20546 Phone: 202-358-0000 Fax: 202-358-0071 Web: www.nasa.gov/

URUGUAY

Direcci´on Nacional Miner´ıa y Geolog´ıa (DINAMIGE)
Hervidero 2861, C.P.11800, Montevideo Phone: ☐2-2001951/2001952 Fax: ☐2-2094905/2091120 Email: secretaria@dinamige.miem.gub.uy Web: www.dinamige.gub.uy/

UZBEKISTAN

State Committee for Geology and Mineral Resources (GOSKOMGEOLOGIYA)
11 Shevchenko St., Tashkent 100060 Phone: ☐71-2568653/2561321 Fax: ☐71-2562275/2568658 Email: geolcom@bcc.com.uz Web: www.uzgeolcom.uz
State Geological Information Centre (Gosgeolinformcentre)
11 Shevchenko St., Tashkent 100060 Phone: ☐71-2560931 Fax: ☐71-2560786 Email: gicenter@bcc.com.uz
Institute of Geology and Geophysics
Uzbekistan Academy of Sciences 49 Khodjibaev St., Tashkent, 700041 Phone: ☐71-162 65 16 Fax: ☐71-162 63 81 Email: igg@uzsci.net Web: www.academy.uz/
Institute of Seismology
Uzbekistan Academy of Sciences 3 Zulfiyakhonim St., Tashkent, 100128 Phone: ☐71-142 51 70/135 75 34 Fax: ☐71-135 75 31 Email: tashkent@seismo.org.uz Web: isas.uzsci.net/

VANUATU

Department of Geology, Mines and Water Resources
Private Mail Bag 1, GPO, Port Vila Phone: ☐22423 Fax: ☐22213

VENEZUELA

National Institute of Geology and Mining (INGEOMIN) (Instituto Nacional de Geolog´ıa y Miner´ıa)
Ministerio de Energ´ıayMinas Parque Central, Torre Oeste, Piso 8, Caracas Phone: 212-5075247/5333 Fax: 212-5754945 Email: ingeomin@uole.com Web: www.ingeomin.gob.ve/
Centro de An´alisis de Informaci´on, Geol´ogica-Minera
Torre Oeste, Parque Central, Piso 8, Caracas D.F. 1010

VIETNAM

Department of Geology and Minerals of Vietnam (DGMV)
Ministry of Natural Resources and Environment 6 Pham Ngu Lao Street, Hanoi Phone: 4-8260671/8253151 Fax: 4-8254734 Email: tranxuanhuong@dgmv.gov.vn, hopnx@dgmv.gov.vn Web: www.dgmv.gov.vn/default en.aspx?tabid=163
Institute of Geological Sciences
Vietnamese Academy of Science and Technology 84 Chua Lang Street, Dongda, Hanoi Phone: 4-775 47 98 Fax: 4-775 47 97 Email: Geoins@ncst.ac.vn
Institute of Geophysics

Vietnamese Academy of Science and Technology Hoang Quoc Viet Street, Cau Giay, Hanoi
Phone: 48352380 Fax: 48352483/48364696
Institute of Oceanography (IO)
Vietnamese Academy of Science and Technology 01 Cau Da, Nha Trang Phone: 58-59033/590036 Fax: 58-590034 Email: haiduong@dng.vnn.vn
Institute of Marine Environment and Resources (IMER)
Vietnamese Academy of Science and Technology 246 Da Nang Street, Haiphong Phone: 31-761523 Fax: 31-761521 Email: imervn@imer.ac.vn Web: www.imer.ac.vn
Institute for Marine Geology and Geophysics (IMGG)
Vietnamese Academy of Science and Technology 18 Hoang Quoc Viet Road, Nghia do, Hanoi
Phone: 4 8363980 Fax: 4 7561647 Email: Thetiepvast@Vnn.vn Web: imgg.com.vn/imgg en/
Institute of Geography
Vietnamese Academy of Science and Technology 18 Hoang Quoc Viet Road, Cau Giay, Hanoi
Phone: 4 7568643 Fax: 4 8361192 Email: nvc@netnam.vn
Vietnam Petroleum Institute (VPI)
Vietnam Oil & Gas Corporation (PETROVIETNAM) 72 Truong Chinh Street, Dong Da District,
Hanoi Phone: 4-784 3061 Fax: 4-784 4156 Email: vpi@vpi.pvn.vn Web:
www.petrovietnam.com.vn/

YEMEN

Geological Survey and Mineral Resources Board (GSMRB)
P.O. Box 297, Sanaa Phone: □ 1 211818 Fax: □ 217575 Email: gsmrb@y.net.ye Web:
www.ygsmrb.org/

ZAMBIA

Geological Survey Department (GSD)
Ministry of Mines and Minerals Development
P.O. Box 50135, Lusaka Phone: □1-251655/250056/250174 Fax: □1-251557/250056/250174
Email: gsd@zamnet.zm Web: www.zambia-mining.com/

ZIMBABWE

Zimbabwe Geological Survey
P.O. Box 210, Causeway, Harare Phone: □4-726342 Fax: □4-739601 Email:
zimgeosv@africaonline.co.zw

INTERNATIONAL ORGANIZATIONS

ASEAN Council on Petroleum (ASCOPE)
c/o PETRONAS, International Business Ventures, Level 45, Tower 1, Petronas Twin Towers,
50099 Kuala Lumpur, Malaysia Phone: 3-23314804/23313597 Fax: 3-23311203 Web:
www.petronas.com.my/ascope/
Asian Disaster Preparedness Center (ADPC)
P.O. Box 4, Klong Luang, Pathumthani 12120, Thailand Phone: 2-516 5900□5910 Fax: 2-524-5350/5360 Email: adpc@adpc.net Web: www.adpc.net/

Association of Ibero-American Geological and Mining Surveys (ASGMI) (Asociaci´on de Servicios
de Geolog´ıa y Miner´ıa Iberoamericanos)
c/o Jose Pedro Calvo Sorando, R'iacute;os Rosas, 23. 28003 Madrid, Spain, c/o Lic. Pedro
Alc´antara, Geological Survey of Argentina, Av. Julio A. Roca, 651 -piso 3. 1322 Buenos Aires,
Argentina
Phone: 91 349 5962, 11 4349 3162 Fax: 91 349 5817, 11 4349 3160 Email: jose.calvo@igme.es,
palcan@secind.mecon.gov.ar Web: www.igme.es/internet/asgmi/

Central Africa Mineral Resources Development Centre (CAMRDC)

P.O.Box 579, Brazzaville, Republic of the Congo Phone: □831916 Fax: □836243
Circum-Pacific Council (CPC)
12201 Sunrise Valley Drive, MS-917, Reston, VA 20192 Phone: 703-648-6645 Fax: 703-648-4227 Email: mredner@usgs.gov Web: www.circum-pacificcouncil.org
Commission for the Geological Map of the World (CGMW)
77, rue Claude Bernard, 75005 Paris, France Phone: 1-47-072284 Fax: 1-43-369518 Email: ccgm@club-internet.fr Web: ccgm.free.fr/

Coordinating Committee for Geoscience Programmes in East and Southeast Asia (CCOP)
CCOP Technical Secretariat, CCOP Building, 75/10 Rama VI Rd., Phayathai, Ratchathewi, Bangkok 10400, Thailand Phone: 2-644-5468 Fax: 2-644-5429 Email: ccopts@ccop.or.th Web: www.ccop.or.th/

Division of Ecology and Earth Sciences
UNESCO 1, rue Miollis, 75732, Paris Cedex 15, France Phone: 1-45684117 Fax: 1-45685822 Email: earth@unesco.org Web: www.unesco.org/science/index.shtml

Environment and Sustainable Development Division
Economic and Social Commission for Asia and the Pacific (ESCAP) 5th Floor, UN Building, Rajadamnern Nok Avenue, Bangkok 10200, Thailand Phone: 2288 1234 Fax: 2288 1059 Email: escap-esdd@un.org Web: www.unescap.org/esd/

EuroGeoSurveys-The Association of the Geological Surveys of Europe (EGS)
Rue du Luxembourg 3, B-1000 Brussels, Belgium Phone: 2-5015332/5015330/5015329 Fax: 2-5015333 Email: secretary@eurogeosurveys.org, info@eurogeosurveys.org Web: www.eurogeosurveys.org

European Space Agency (ESA)
8-10 rue Mario Nikis, 75738 Paris Cedex 15, France Phone: 1-5369 7654 Fax: 1-5369 7560 Web: www.esa.int/

International Centre for Training and Exchanges in the Geosciences (CIFEG)
B.P. 36517, 45065 Orleans Cedex 2, France Phone: 2-38 64 33 67 Fax: 2-38 64 34 72 Email: f.pinard@cifeg.org Web: www.cifeg.org/

International Hydrographic Organization (IHO)
4 quai Antoine 1er, B.P.445, MC 98011 Monaco Cedex Phone: □93 10 81 00 Fax: □93 10 81 40 Email: info@ihb.mc Web: www.iho.shom.fr/

International Union of Geological Sciences (IUGS)
c/o Geological Survey of Norway, NO-7491 Trondheim Phone: 73 90 40 40 Fax: 73 50 22 30 Email: iugs.secretariat@ngu.no Web: www.iugs.org/

Mining Policy and Reform Division
World Bank 2121 Pennsylvania Avenue, NW, Washington, DC 20433, U. S. A. Phone: 202-473-4242 Fax: 202-522-0396 Email: Pvanderveen@worldbank.org Web: www.ifc.org/, worldbank.org/

Organisation of African Geological Surveys, The (OAGS)
c/o Nthombii Mdluli Jacha, Marketing & Communications Unite, Council for Geoscience, Private Bag X112, Pretoria 0001, South Africa Phone: 12 841 1471 Email: nmdlulijacha@geoscience.org.za Web: 196.33.85.14./cgs inter/content/view/508/416/

Pacific Islands Applied Geoscience Commission (SOPAC)

Private Mail Bag, GPO, Suva, Fiji Islands Phone: ☐3381377 Fax: ☐3370040 Email: director@sopac.org Web: www.sopac.org

South Asia Geological Congress (GEOSAS) Southern and Eastern Africa Mineral Centre (SEAMIC)
c/o Hilal A. Raza, Secretary General, #18, Street 6, Sector P.O.Box 9573, Dar es Salaam, Tanzania H-9/1, Islamabad, Pakistan Phone: ☐22-2650321/2650347 Phone: 51-925-8301/8302 Fax: 51-925-8310 Fax: ☐22-2650319/2650346 Email: hdip@apollo.net.pk Email: seamic@seamic.org Web: www.seamic.org/

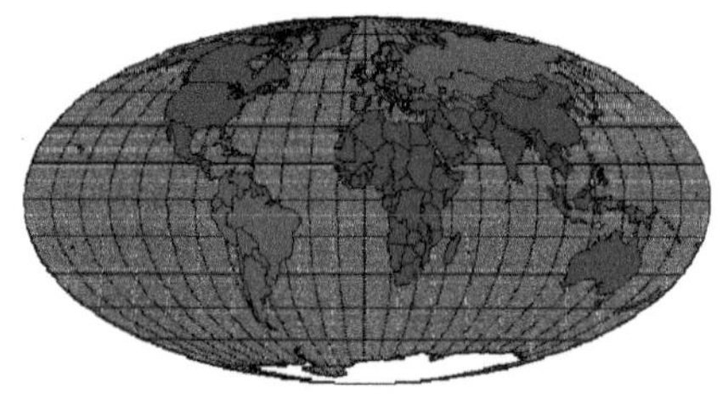

WORLD MINERAL AND MINING SECTOR INVESTMENT AND BUSINESS GUIDES LIBRARY
Price: $149.95 Each

1. Afghanistan Mineral and Mining Sector Investment and Business Guide - Strategic Information and Regulations
2. Albania Mineral and Mining Sector Investment and Business Guide - Strategic Information and Regulations
3. Algeria Mineral and Mining Sector Investment and Business Guide - Strategic Information and Regulations
4. Angola Mineral and Mining Sector Investment and Business Guide - Strategic Information and Regulations
5. Argentina Mineral and Mining Sector Investment and Business Guide - Strategic Information and Regulations
6. Armenia Mineral and Mining Sector Investment and Business Guide - Strategic Information and Regulations
7. Australia Mineral and Mining Sector Investment and Business Guide - Strategic Information and Regulations
8. Austria Mineral and Mining Sector Investment and Business Guide - Strategic Information and Regulations
9. Azerbaijan Mineral and Mining Sector Investment and Business Guide - Strategic Information and Regulations
10. Bahrain Mineral and Mining Sector Investment and Business Guide - Strategic Information and Regulations
11. Bangladesh Mineral and Mining Sector Investment and Business Guide - Strategic Information and Regulations
12. Belarus Mineral and Mining Sector Investment and Business Guide - Strategic Information and Regulations
13. Belgium Mineral and Mining Sector Investment and Business Guide - Strategic Information and Regulations
14. Benin Mineral and Mining Sector Investment and Business Guide - Strategic Information and Regulations
15. Bolivia Mineral and Mining Sector Investment and Business Guide - Strategic Information and Regulations
16. Bosnia and Herzegovina Mineral and Mining Sector Investment and Business Guide - Strategic Information and Regulations
17. Botswana Mineral and Mining Sector Investment and Business Guide - Strategic Information and Regulations
18. Brazil Mineral and Mining Sector Investment and Business Guide - Strategic Information and Regulations
19. Brunei Mineral and Mining Sector Investment and Business Guide - Strategic Information and Regulations
20. Bulgaria Mineral and Mining Sector Investment and Business Guide - Strategic Information and Regulations
21. Burkina Faso Mineral and Mining Sector Investment and Business Guide - Strategic Information and Regulations
22. Burundi Mineral and Mining Sector Investment and Business Guide - Strategic Information and Regulations
23. Cambodia Mineral and Mining Sector Investment and Business Guide - Strategic Information and Regulations
24. Cameroon Mineral and Mining Sector Investment and Business Guide - Strategic Information and Regulations
25. Canada Mineral and Mining Sector Investment and Business Guide - Strategic Information and Regulations
26. Cape Verde Mineral and Mining Sector Investment and Business Guide - Strategic Information and

Regulations
27.   Cayman Islands Mineral and Mining Sector Investment and Business Guide - Strategic Information and Regulations
28.   Central African Republic Mineral and Mining Sector Investment and Business Guide - Strategic Information and Regulations
29.   Chad Mineral and Mining Sector Investment and Business Guide - Strategic Information and Regulations
30.   Chile Mineral and Mining Sector Investment and Business Guide - Strategic Information and Regulations
31.   China Mineral and Mining Sector Investment and Business Guide - Strategic Information and Regulations
32.   Colombia Mineral and Mining Sector Investment and Business Guide - Strategic Information and Regulations
33.   Comoros Mineral and Mining Sector Investment and Business Guide - Strategic Information and Regulations
34.   Congo Mineral and Mining Sector Investment and Business Guide - Strategic Information and Regulations
35.   Congo, Dem. Republic Mineral and Mining Sector Investment and Business Guide - Strategic Information and Regulations
36.   Cook Islands Mineral and Mining Sector Investment and Business Guide - Strategic Information and Regulations
37.   Costa Rica Mineral and Mining Sector Investment and Business Guide - Strategic Information and Regulations
38.   Cote d'Ivoire Mineral and Mining Sector Investment and Business Guide - Strategic Information and Regulations
39.   Croatia Mineral and Mining Sector Investment and Business Guide - Strategic Information and Regulations
40.   Cuba Mineral and Mining Sector Investment and Business Guide - Strategic Information and Regulations
41.   Czech Republic Mineral and Mining Sector Investment and Business Guide - Strategic Information and Regulations
42.   Denmark Mineral and Mining Sector Investment and Business Guide - Strategic Information and Regulations
43.   Djibouti Mineral and Mining Sector Investment and Business Guide - Strategic Information and Regulations
44.   Dominican Republic Mineral and Mining Sector Investment and Business Guide - Strategic Information and Regulations
45.   Dubai Mineral and Mining Sector Investment and Business Guide - Strategic Information and Regulations
46.   Ecuador Mineral and Mining Sector Investment and Business Guide - Strategic Information and Regulations
47.   Egypt Mineral and Mining Sector Investment and Business Guide - Strategic Information and Regulations
48.   El Salvador Mineral and Mining Sector Investment and Business Guide - Strategic Information and Regulations
49.   Equatorial Guinea Mineral and Mining Sector Investment and Business Guide - Strategic Information and Regulations
50.   Eritrea Mineral and Mining Sector Investment and Business Guide - Strategic Information and Regulations
51.   Estonia Mineral and Mining Sector Investment and Business Guide - Strategic Information and Regulations
52.   Ethiopia Mineral and Mining Sector Investment and Business Guide - Strategic Information and Regulations
53.   Fiji Mineral and Mining Sector Investment and Business Guide - Strategic Information and Regulations
54.   Finland Mineral and Mining Sector Investment and Business Guide - Strategic Information and Regulations
55.   France Mineral and Mining Sector Investment and Business Guide - Strategic Information and Regulations
56.   Gabon Mineral and Mining Sector Investment and Business Guide - Strategic Information and Regulations
57.   Gambia Mineral and Mining Sector Investment and Business Guide - Strategic Information and Regulations
58.   Georgia Mineral and Mining Sector Investment and Business Guide - Strategic Information and Regulations
59.   Germany Mineral and Mining Sector Investment and Business Guide - Strategic Information and Regulations
60.   Ghana Mineral and Mining Sector Investment and Business Guide - Strategic Information and Regulations
61.   Greece Mineral and Mining Sector Investment and Business Guide - Strategic Information and Regulations
62.   Greenland Mineral and Mining Sector Investment and Business Guide - Strategic Information and Regulations

63.   Guatemala Mineral and Mining Sector Investment and Business Guide - Strategic Information and Regulations
64.   Guinea Mineral and Mining Sector Investment and Business Guide - Strategic Information and Regulations
65.   Guinea-Bissau Mineral and Mining Sector Investment and Business Guide - Strategic Information and Regulations
66.   Guyana Mineral and Mining Sector Investment and Business Guide - Strategic Information and Regulations
67.   Haiti Mineral and Mining Sector Investment and Business Guide - Strategic Information and Regulations
68.   Honduras Mineral and Mining Sector Investment and Business Guide - Strategic Information and Regulations
69.   Hungary Mineral and Mining Sector Investment and Business Guide - Strategic Information and Regulations
70.   Iceland Mineral and Mining Sector Investment and Business Guide - Strategic Information and Regulations
71.   India Mineral and Mining Sector Investment and Business Guide - Strategic Information and Regulations
72.   Indonesia Mineral and Mining Sector Investment and Business Guide - Strategic Information and Regulations
73.   Iran Mineral and Mining Sector Investment and Business Guide - Strategic Information and Regulations
74.   Iraq Mineral and Mining Sector Investment and Business Guide - Strategic Information and Regulations
75.   Ireland Mineral and Mining Sector Investment and Business Guide - Strategic Information and Regulations
76.   Israel Mineral and Mining Sector Investment and Business Guide - Strategic Information and Regulations
77.   Italy Mineral and Mining Sector Investment and Business Guide - Strategic Information and Regulations
78.   Jamaica Mineral and Mining Sector Investment and Business Guide - Strategic Information and Regulations
79.   Japan Mineral and Mining Sector Investment and Business Guide - Strategic Information and Regulations
80.   Jordan Mineral and Mining Sector Investment and Business Guide - Strategic Information and Regulations
81.   Kazakhstan Mineral and Mining Sector Investment and Business Guide - Strategic Information and Regulations
82.   Kenya Mineral and Mining Sector Investment and Business Guide - Strategic Information and Regulations
83.   Korea, South Mineral and Mining Sector Investment and Business Guide - Strategic Information and Regulations
84.   Kuwait Mineral and Mining Sector Investment and Business Guide - Strategic Information and Regulations
85.   Kyrgyzstan Mineral and Mining Sector Investment and Business Guide - Strategic Information and Regulations
86.   Laos Mineral and Mining Sector Investment and Business Guide - Strategic Information and Regulations
87.   Latvia Mineral and Mining Sector Investment and Business Guide - Strategic Information and Regulations
88.   Lesotho Mineral and Mining Sector Investment and Business Guide - Strategic Information and Regulations
89.   Liberia Mineral and Mining Sector Investment and Business Guide - Strategic Information and Regulations
90.   Libya Mineral and Mining Sector Investment and Business Guide - Strategic Information and Regulations
91.   Lithuania Mineral and Mining Sector Investment and Business Guide - Strategic Information and Regulations
92.   Macedonia Republic Mineral and Mining Sector Investment and Business Guide - Strategic Information and Regulations
93.   Madagascar Mineral and Mining Sector Investment and Business Guide - Strategic Information and Regulations
94.   Malawi Mineral and Mining Sector Investment and Business Guide - Strategic Information and Regulations
95.   Malaysia Mineral and Mining Sector Investment and Business Guide - Strategic Information and Regulations
96.   Mali Mineral and Mining Sector Investment and Business Guide - Strategic Information and Regulations
97.   Mauritania Mineral and Mining Sector Investment and Business Guide - Strategic Information and Regulations
98.   Mauritius Mineral and Mining Sector Investment and Business Guide - Strategic Information and Regulations
99.   Mexico Mineral and Mining Sector Investment and Business Guide - Strategic Information and Regulations

100. Moldova Mineral and Mining Sector Investment and Business Guide - Strategic Information and Regulations
101. Mongolia Mineral and Mining Sector Investment and Business Guide - Strategic Information and Regulations
102. Morocco Mineral and Mining Sector Investment and Business Guide - Strategic Information and Regulations
103. Mozambique Mineral and Mining Sector Investment and Business Guide - Strategic Information and Regulations
104. Myanmar Mineral and Mining Sector Investment and Business Guide - Strategic Information and Regulations
105. Namibia Mineral and Mining Sector Investment and Business Guide - Strategic Information and Regulations
106. Nepal Mineral and Mining Sector Investment and Business Guide - Strategic Information and Regulations
107. Netherlands Mineral and Mining Sector Investment and Business Guide - Strategic Information and Regulations
108. New Zealand Mineral and Mining Sector Investment and Business Guide - Strategic Information and Regulations
109. Nicaragua Mineral and Mining Sector Investment and Business Guide - Strategic Information and Regulations
110. Niger Mineral and Mining Sector Investment and Business Guide - Strategic Information and Regulations
111. Nigeria Mineral and Mining Sector Investment and Business Guide - Strategic Information and Regulations
112. Norway Mineral and Mining Sector Investment and Business Guide - Strategic Information and Regulations
113. Oman Mineral and Mining Sector Investment and Business Guide - Strategic Information and Regulations
114. Pakistan Mineral and Mining Sector Investment and Business Guide - Strategic Information and Regulations
115. Papua New Guinea Mineral and Mining Sector Investment and Business Guide - Strategic Information and Regulations
116. Paraguay Mineral and Mining Sector Investment and Business Guide - Strategic Information and Regulations
117. Peru Mineral and Mining Sector Investment and Business Guide - Strategic Information and Regulations
118. Philippines Mineral and Mining Sector Investment and Business Guide - Strategic Information and Regulations
119. Poland Mineral and Mining Sector Investment and Business Guide - Strategic Information and Regulations
120. Portugal Mineral and Mining Sector Investment and Business Guide - Strategic Information and Regulations
121. Qatar Mineral and Mining Sector Investment and Business Guide - Strategic Information and Regulations
122. Romania Mineral and Mining Sector Investment and Business Guide - Strategic Information and Regulations
123. Russia Mineral and Mining Sector Investment and Business Guide - Strategic Information and Regulations
124. Rwanda Mineral and Mining Sector Investment and Business Guide - Strategic Information and Regulations
125. Sao Tome and Principe Mineral and Mining Sector Investment and Business Guide - Strategic Information and Regulations
126. Saudi Arabia Mineral and Mining Sector Investment and Business Guide - Strategic Information and Regulations
127. Senegal Mineral and Mining Sector Investment and Business Guide - Strategic Information and Regulations
128. Serbia Mineral and Mining Sector Investment and Business Guide - Strategic Information and Regulations
129. Sierra Leone Mineral and Mining Sector Investment and Business Guide - Strategic Information and Regulations
130. Slovakia Mineral and Mining Sector Investment and Business Guide - Strategic Information and Regulations
131. Slovenia Mineral and Mining Sector Investment and Business Guide - Strategic Information and Regulations
132. Somalia Mineral and Mining Sector Investment and Business Guide - Strategic Information and Regulations
133. South Africa Mineral and Mining Sector Investment and Business Guide - Strategic Information and Regulations
134. Spain Mineral and Mining Sector Investment and Business Guide - Strategic Information and Regulations
135. Sri Lanka Mineral and Mining Sector Investment and Business Guide - Strategic Information and Regulations
136. Sudan Mineral and Mining Sector Investment and Business Guide - Strategic Information and Regulations

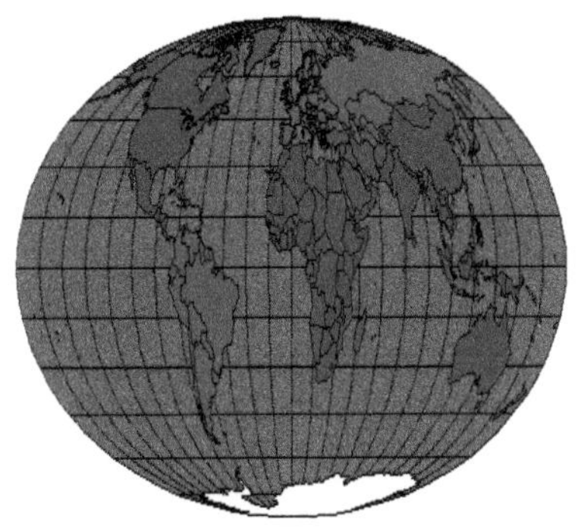

WORLD OIL & GAS SECTOR BUSINESS, INVESTMENT OPPORTUNITIES LIBRARY

Price: $199.95 Each

Title
Global Oil & Gas Sector Business & Investment Opportunities Yearbook
Algeria Oil & Gas Sector Business & Investment Opportunities Yearbook
Angola Oil & Gas Sector Business & Investment Opportunities Yearbook
Australia Oil & Gas Sector Business & Investment Opportunities Yearbook
Azerbaijan Oil & Gas Sector Business & Investment Opportunities Yearbook
Bahrain Oil & Gas Sector Business & Investment Opportunities Yearbook
Bangladesh Oil & Gas Sector Business & Investment Opportunities Yearbook
Benin Oil & Gas Sector Business & Investment Opportunities Yearbook
Brazil Oil & Gas Sector Business & Investment Opportunities Yearbook
Brunei Oil & Gas Sector Business & Investment Opportunities Yearbook
Cameroon Oil & Gas Sector Business & Investment Opportunities Yearbook
Canada Oil & Gas Sector Business & Investment Opportunities Yearbook
China Oil & Gas Sector Business & Investment Opportunities Yearbook
Colombia Oil & Gas Sector Oil & Gas Sector Business & Investment Opportunities Yearbook
Congo Oil & Gas Sector Business & Investment Opportunities Yearbook
Congo, Dem. Republic Oil & Gas Sector Business & Investment Opportunities Yearbook
Cote d'Ivoire Oil & Gas Sector Business & Investment Opportunities Yearbook
Dubai Oil & Gas Sector Business & Investment Opportunities Yearbook
Ecuador Oil & Gas Sector Business & Investment Opportunities Yearbook
Egypt Oil & Gas Sector Business & Investment Opportunities Yearbook
Equatorial Guinea Oil & Gas Sector Business & Investment Opportunities Yearbook
Gabon Oil & Gas Sector Business & Investment Opportunities Yearbook
India Oil & Gas Sector Business & Investment Opportunities Yearbook
Indonesia Oil & Gas Sector Business & Investment Opportunities Yearbook
Iran Oil & Gas Sector Business & Investment Opportunities Yearbook
Iraq Oil & Gas Sector Business & Investment Opportunities Yearbook
Kazakhstan Oil & Gas Sector Business & Investment Opportunities Yearbook

For additional analytical, business and investment opportunities information,
please contact Global Investment & Business Center, USA
at (202) 546-2103. Fax: (202) 546-3275. E-mail: rusric@erols.com

Title
Kuwait Oil & Gas Sector Business & Investment Opportunities Yearbook
Libya Oil & Gas Sector Business & Investment Opportunities Yearbook
Malaysia Oil & Gas Sector Business & Investment Opportunities Yearbook
Mexico Oil & Gas Sector Business & Investment Opportunities Yearbook
Morocco Oil & Gas Sector Business & Investment Opportunities Yearbook
Namibia Oil & Gas Sector Business & Investment Opportunities Yearbook
New Zealand Oil & Gas Sector Business & Investment Opportunities Yearbook
Nigeria Oil & Gas Sector Business & Investment Opportunities Yearbook
Norway Oil & Gas Sector Business & Investment Opportunities Yearbook
Oman Oil & Gas Sector Business & Investment Opportunities Yearbook
Pakistan Oil & Gas Sector Business & Investment Opportunities Yearbook
Papua New Guinea Oil & Gas Sector Business & Investment Opportunities Yearbook
Papua New Guinea Oil & Gas Sector Oil & Gas Sector Business & Investment Opportunities Yearbook
Peru Oil & Gas Sector Business & Investment Opportunities Yearbook
Philippines Oil & Gas Sector Business & Investment Opportunities Yearbook
Qatar Oil & Gas Sector Business & Investment Opportunities Yearbook
Sri Lanka Oil & Gas Sector Business & Investment Opportunities Yearbook
Romania Oil & Gas Sector Business & Investment Opportunities Yearbook
Russia Oil & Gas Sector Business & Investment Opportunities Yearbook
Saudi Arabia Oil & Gas Sector Business & Investment Opportunities Yearbook
Sudan Oil & Gas Sector Business & Investment Opportunities Yearbook
Suriname Oil & Gas Sector Business & Investment Opportunities Yearbook
Syria Oil & Gas Sector Business & Investment Opportunities Yearbook
Trinidad and Tobago Oil & Gas Sector Oil & Gas Sector Business & Investment Opportunities Yearbook
Tunisia Oil & Gas Sector Business & Investment Opportunities Yearbook
Turkey Oil & Gas Sector Business & Investment Opportunities Yearbook
Turkmenistan Oil & Gas Sector Business & Investment Opportunities Yearbook
Ukraine Oil & Gas Sector Oil & Gas Sector Business & Investment Opportunities Yearbook
United Arab Emirates Oil & Gas Sector Business & Investment Opportunities Yearbook
United Kingdom Oil & Gas Sector Business & Investment Opportunities Yearbook
United Kingdom Oil & Gas Sector Oil & Gas Sector Business & Investment Opportunities Yearbook
United States Oil & Gas Sector Business & Investment Opportunities Yearbook
Venezuela Oil & Gas Sector Business & Investment Opportunities Yearbook
Vietnam Investment Pojects and Joint Ventures Hnadbook
Vietnam Oil & Gas Sector Business & Investment Opportunities Yearbook
Yemen Oil & Gas Sector Business & Investment Opportunities Yearbook